CHOPIN

SERIES EDITED BY STANLEY SADIE

The Master Musicians Series

Titles available from Schirmer Books

CHOPIN

Jim Samson

SCHIRMER BOOKS
An Imprint of Simon & Schuster Macmillan
New York

Prentice Hall International
London Mexico City New Delhi Singapore Sydney Toronto

Schirmer Books
An Imprint of Simon & Schuster Macmillan
1633 Broadway
New York, NY 10019

First published in Great Britain
Oxford University Press
Walton Street
Oxford OX2 6DP

Library of Congress Catalog Card Number: Available from the Publisher upon request

ISBN: 0-02-864735-1

PRINTED IN GREAT BRITAIN

Printing number
1 2 3 4 5 6 7 8 9 10

Library of Congress Cataloging-in-Publication Data
Available from the Publisher upon request

Typeset by Hope Services (Abingdon) Ltd.
Printed in Great Britain
on acid-free paper by
Butler & Tanner Ltd.
Frome, Somerset

Preface

When I began planning this volume the challenge seemed clear. What is the relationship between a composer and his music? In other words, how do we draw the process of composition into the centre of biography, where it surely belongs? Or, to put it the other way round, how can a composer's life explain his music? Meeting the challenge proved far from easy. Too little is yet known about the mental processes involved in composition to allow any but the most obvious connections to be made. Primary causes remain stubbornly elusive. I came to the conclusion that speculation about these matters would be better placed in a biography, where it might remain speculation, than in a 'life and works', where it would inevitably programme the entire approach. Since we are not (I suggest) in a position to attempt a thorough integration of 'life' and 'works', we had better accept the hybrid character of this genre. It remains, and it probably should remain, two books in one.

And that is true even when, as here, the two books are interleaved through alternating chapters of biography and musical commentary. This is a familiar tactic of recent volumes in the Master Musicians series. There are sensible, pragmatic reasons for it. But it can be a smokescreen, implying a degree of integration which is scarcely justified by evidence or argument. Built into the structure is an emphasis on periods, and a further suggestion that a period in the life coincides with one in the music. I sit on the fence here. Periodization is first and foremost a strategy of presentation in my book. Yet I believe that the strategy has some explanatory power, at the very least as a working hypothesis, and my divisions are therefore very far from arbitrary. They suggest above all that in biography, as also in stylistic history, there are moments in which gradually accumulating minor changes coalesce into a major qualitative change and a new era begins. This is not to deny continuities. Nor is it to argue that life and works march always in step.

I should make a further point about my approach to writing a 'life and works'. As far as possible my aim has been to give—I am tempted to say to restore—something like due weight to the 'life'. In seeking to present a responsible and balanced biography, I identified two problems in particular. The weakest sections of most existing biographies (at least by non-Polish authors) concern the Warsaw years. Even where Polish sources have been carefully researched, the tendency has been to give inadequate measure to the shaping influence of Warsaw's social and cultural world. I hope I have corrected this imbalance. The second issue can only be described as a certain partiality on the part of Chopin biographers. At its worst this amounts to a kind of Chopin fetishism. But even in the most scholarly accounts there has been a conspicuous lack of balance in considering Chopin's relations with other central players in the drama, most notably George Sand. I have tried to look at these matters afresh. But I have also sought to avoid the excesses of posthumous psycho-analysis. Only a certain amount of factual evidence is available to the biographer. The rest is an imaginative 'fleshing out' of this skeleton, perhaps closer to the methods of narrative fiction than we may like to think.

Chapters on the music presented their own problems. In recent years I have published a good deal on the music of Chopin, and much of this material inevitably found its way into the present study. Indeed in some ways the book might be regarded as a synthesis of many of my findings on Chopin over a decade or so of research, drawing together ideas explored in earlier writings, and at the same time rendering them more easily accessible. Beyond this the musical commentaries confront an issue which has always seemed to me problematic in composer monographs. It is all too easy for important themes to be lost through a kind of dispersal of insights across the entire span of the book. In other words, the obligations of a survey can result in a lack of penetration, and a lack of focus on major themes. My approach here has been to isolate one such theme in each chapter on the music. The chapters are subdivided, then, into an initial survey, followed by a focus on a particular issue germane to the repertory surveyed. These more specialized sections, which are subtitled, also contain the most detailed technical commentaries, and they are the only ones to contain music examples.

The sources for a Chopin biography have not greatly changed over the years, though I remain astonished at the variety of interpretations they are required to support. Where possible I have made use of primary or early secondary sources. Chopin's correspondence is badly in need of re-presentation, not to say re-translation, but the existing Sydow edition served my purpose adequately. My debt to George Lubin's Herculean efforts with the Sand correspondence will be obvious from a glance at the references. I have made extensive use, too, of contemporary newspapers and journals in both Warsaw and Paris, and rather more cautious use of memoirs and articles (some in manuscript) by Chopin's friends from the Warsaw years. Other nineteenth-century accounts (including biographies by Szulc and Hoesick) have also proved invaluable, not least as documents of reception history.

Anyone tackling a book on Chopin's music will quickly realize that two volumes are indispensable. The manuscripts catalogue by Kobylańska and the catalogue by Chomiński and Turło have been constantly by my side. They are not without their lacunae, inaccuracies and problems (chronology remains the single most difficult issue), but both are monumental achievements, and we will long remain in the debt of these indefatigable researchers. For the rest, I have been eclectic in my search for guidance, turning to Polish scholars such as Józef Chomiński and Zofia Chechlińska for fresh thoughts about the texture and substance of Chopin's music, to North American analytical theorists such as Carl Schachter for insight into its voice leading and structure, and to French critics such as Camille Bourniquel for suggestive poetic interpretations.

Two points of a technical nature. Throughout the text I have referred to unpublished works by their number in the Kobylańska Catalogue (thus: KK 889 for the early G minor polonaise). This seemed preferable to using Ekier's numbering in the Polish National Edition, since the edition is as yet far from complete, and the introduction (*Wstęp do wydania narodowego*), which contains the numbering, is by no means widely available. Secondly, I confess to a certain inconsistency as to the spelling of Polish names. I have preserved masculine and feminine forms (Antoni Wodziński; Maria Wodzińska), but have Anglicized the plural (the Wodzińskis) for ease of reading.

I am indebted to the British Academy for a research fellowship which enabled me to spend three months working in the Polish National Library and in the Archive of the Chopin Society, Warsaw. Most of the book was drafted during this period. I was the guest, as so often before, of Dr Zofia Chechlińska of the Polish Academy of Sciences, and to her I owe an incalculable debt. I am also grateful to other Polish friends, and especially to the staff of the Music Department of the National Library and to Dalila Turło and Hanna Wróblewska-Straus of the Chopin Society. I am especially grateful to Mrs Wróblewska-Straus for supplying photographs of the composition-draft of the Polonaise-fantasy and other illustrations. John Rink, of Royal Holloway, University of London, has been a source of inspiration and knowledge since my early days of Chopin research. He read the typescript, and—as on other such occasions—made invaluable suggestions. Julia Kellerman was a meticulous and tolerant copy-editor. I am grateful to her. Sue and Lois also helped, and this time they have promised to read the book.

Jim Samson
Bristol, 1995

Contents

Illustrations

In his homeland

On 14 October 1894, a Chopin monument was unveiled at the composer's birthplace in the tiny village of Żelazowa Wola, some thirty miles due west of Warsaw. The initiative came largely from the Russian composer Mily Balakirev, and at a celebration concert in Warsaw three days later Balakirev himself performed the *Lento con gran espressione* in C sharp minor. The concert, organized by the Warsaw Music Society, ended with an arrangement for chorus and orchestra of the Polonaise in A major, Op. 40 No. 1.

Several very different modes of reception are highlighted by these events. First there is the Chopin cult, of which Żelazowa Wola has since become the principal shrine, though it has several rivals.[1] Before the erection of the monument little had been made of Chopin's birthplace, a modest cottage which formed part of an estate belonging to the Skarbek family. The estate was lost to the Skarbeks in the 1850s following the suicide of its last hereditary owner. It was bought by Adam Towiański, son of the philosopher Andrzej Towiański, and the new owner was at first inclined to commemorate the association with Chopin. His plans for a small Chopin sanctuary came to nothing, however, and in the end he and subsequent owners used the cottage mainly as a storehouse. Later, by a curious twist of fate, it was the only building to survive a major fire which razed the manor house and the other outbuildings to the ground.

Balakirev's initiative, supported by the Warsaw Music Society, signalled the beginning of a much wider public interest in Żelazowa Wola. It was regularly visited by music lovers, and in 1931 a committee (including Ignacy Paderewski) arranged for the public purchase of the Chopin house and for its restoration in period style as a museum and small concert hall. At the same time the adjoining land was developed as an attractive park, somewhat marred these days by the effects of pollution from the nearby river Utrata. As the Mecca for Chopin enthusiasts from

[1] Almost every town which can claim an association—however fleeting—with Chopin has a festival or competition. There are, *inter alia*, the 'Chopin Days' at Antonin, the Chopin Festivals at Duszniki Zdrój, Mariánske Lázně, and Valldemosa and, of course, the International Chopin Competition in Warsaw.

all over the world, Żelazowa Wola has become a potent symbol of Chopin fetishism, of a form of appreciation—often promoted by Chopin societies—which idealizes and romanticizes the composer's life and works. Popular biographers, undeterred by the fact that Chopin spent only the first few months of his life there (though he returned from time to time), even find explanatory value in the surrounding scenery, which is far from distinguished. 'Here in Żelazowa Wola, in the unobtrusive Mazovian countryside, one comprehends better than anywhere else how much the music of Chopin is tied up with Polish landscape'.[2]

The Chopin cult exemplifies the popularity of his music, its accessibility to audiences from very different social and cultural backgrounds, and the web of myths in which it is often enmeshed. As such it stands for one important response to Chopin, one means by which his singular creative achievement has been given a social existence. Yet Balakirev's tribute to Chopin also points to a second, and very different, kind of reception. Balakirev was committed to nationalism and to modernism, and he acknowledged Chopin as a powerful inspiration in both respects. For him Chopin was no salon composer, but a radical, progressive figure, and this view was widely shared by other members of the Balakirev circle and by Slavonic nationalists generally in the late nineteenth century. And not only by them. Brahms, Wagner, and Liszt all registered Chopin's innovations, and he left his mark, too, on a generation of French composers working at the *fin de siècle* and beyond. There is a striking paradox here. The 'Ariel of the piano', the 'pianist of the emotions' of popular perception, was at the same time an influential modernist.

The concert of 1894 focuses another polarity in Chopin reception, embodied in the performances of the Polonaise and the *Lento con gran espressione*, a familiar warhorse vulgarized in transcription and a little-known miniature scrupulously copied by Balakirev from one of several manuscript sources. The choral version of the Polonaise, promoted by the Warsaw Music Society and treated with some disdain by Balakirev,[3] would not have seemed out of place at a time when Chopin transcriptions, especially for voice and violin, were plentiful. It amounted to a wholesale appropriation of Chopin's text, effectively transforming the Polonaise into a quite new composition. Such transcriptions had their own rationale, of course, but they were also symptomatic of the more generally permissive attitude to the composer's intentions evidenced by the performance practice and editions of the time. This approach to performance persisted right through to the early twentieth century, despite the growing tendency of editors and performers alike to fetishize musical texts.

[2] Jarosław Iwaszkiewicz in *Żelazowa Wola* (Warsaw, 1976), p. 12.
[3] See Edward Garden, *Balakirev: A Critical Study of his Life and Music* (London, 1967), p. 140.

In contrast, Balakirev's contribution to the memorial concert points to the emerging 'scholarly' approach of our century, one which sets out to discover and then to recreate as faithfully as possible the composer's intentions. His choice of the *Lento con gran espressione* was significant, and not just because its references to early, Warsaw-period works were appropriate to the occasion (Balakirev's copy was given the title *Reminiscences. Nocturne pour le piano*.[4] The work was virtually unknown when Balakirev played it in Warsaw, and his aim was clearly to introduce a Chopin rarity to Polish audiences. It had remained unpublished during the composer's lifetime, and was first issued in 1875 by M. A. Szulc with the title *Adagio*, along with three early mazurkas.[5] Balakirev had no knowledge of this edition, however, and he made his own copy of the text from a copy by Oskar Kolberg in the possession of Aleksander Poliński.[6] There is a further copy by the composer's sister, made at Chopin's request and corrected by him before he presented it to Maria Wodzińska.[7] And there is also an autograph, significantly different in text from any of the extant copies and clearly not the basis for those copies.[8] Balakirev's performance draws attention, then, to an issue which has dogged Chopin scholars and performers ever since—the complexity of the manuscript tradition and the consequent difficulty in establishing reliable texts, especially for the works published posthumously.

The testimony of one local farmer, then in his nineties, links the Żelazowa Wola of Balakirev's visit with that of Chopin's time.[9] He related to Balakirev and others his memories of the Chopin family during one of their return visits to the Skarbek estate in 1830. It is a colourful account, including descriptions of a piano wheeled out of doors for early evening recitals by the young Fryderyk, and its authenticity is naturally open to question. Yet it may have some basis in reality. Certainly the Chopins maintained friendly relations with the Skarbeks for many years. They often spent their summer vacations at Żelazowa Wola, and we may reasonably assume that Fryderyk accompanied them at least

[4] There are quotations from the F minor Piano Concerto and the song 'Życzenie'.

[5] *Trzy Mazury i Adagio: utwory młodości Fryderyka Chopina* (M. Leitgeber, Poznań, 1875).

[6] The Balakirev copy is currently housed in the museum of the Warsaw Music Society. Shortly after Balakirev's performance in Warsaw (1894) a facsimile of the Kolberg copy was published in *Echo muzyczne, teatralny i artystyczne* and this in turn formed the basis for Natalie Janothy's published edition of the same year (E. Ascherberg, London 1894).

[7] In September 1836, Chopin wrote to his sister Ludwika asking her to make copies of the *Lento*, together with seven songs. He sent these to Maria Wodzińska for her album at a time when he still had high hopes that she would become his wife.

[8] This autograph, once in the possession of Arthur Hedley, is now in the Valldemosa museum in Majorca.

[9] See Krystyna Kobylańska, *Chopin in his Own Land*, tr. Claire Grece-Dąbrowska and Mary Filippi (Warsaw, 1955), p. 98.

until he entered the Warsaw Lyceum, aged fourteen. The visit of 1830 took place just a few months before he left Poland for good.

In the late eighteenth century the Skarbeks were an aristocratic family in decline. In addition to Żelazowa Wola, they had a larger estate at Izbica in Kujawy, and another, recently acquired, at Potrzubyn in Pomerania. The purchase of Potrzubyn, largely on credit, was the final step which led to the financial collapse of Count Eugeniusz Skarbek, who was obliged to flee the country to escape his creditors. His eldest son, Fryderyk, a noted economist, historian, and man of letters in later life, related in his memoirs how his father had always lived well beyond his means.[10] He described, for instance, the magnificent festivities arranged for his mother's name day, at a time when it was already obvious that financial ruin was imminent. Even the sale of Izbica and Potrzubyn was not enough to pay the mounting bills. With the departure of her husband, Countess Ludwika Skarbek had little option but to file for divorce, and she brought up her children at Żelazowa Wola with the help of a distant relative, Tekla Justyna Krzyżanowska, later to become Chopin's mother.

Little is known of this lady. Her baptism certificate, dated 14 September 1782, gives her parents as 'gentle-born' Antonina and Jacub Krzyżanowski and her godparents as Countess Justyna Skarbek of Izbica and Mateusz Ko(r)?nowski of Sarnowo. Count Eugeniusz Skarbek, as yet unmarried, is also named on the certificate. The fortunes of the Krzyżanowski family remain a mystery,[11] but for whatever reason, possibly financial, Justyna was sent to the Skarbeks while still a girl to act as a companion and housekeeper. Quiet and retiring in disposition, and devoutly religious, she was brought up in the manner of most Polish girls of good family, acquiring, it seems, passable ability as a pianist and singer as well as the usual social and domestic skills.

Countess Skarbek also owned houses in Torun in her own name, and was obliged by Prussian law to spend a specified period of each year in that city in order to retain her claim on the property. She usually took the entire family to Torun for the winter months, but in 1802 she decided to leave her son Fryderyk, then aged ten, with a neighbouring family so that he could begin lessons with a new tutor. This was a Frenchman from Lorraine called Mikołaj Chopin, whose duties as tutor to the wealthy Laczyński family, relatives of the Skarbeks, were just then coming to an end. The lessons were a success and from that point Mikołaj Chopin entered the service of Countess Skarbek. French tutors were highly fashionable with the Polish gentry, but Fryderyk Skarbek recounts in his memoirs that Mikołaj Chopin was a cut above the usual,

[10] Fryderyk Skarbek, *Pamiętnikach* (Poznań, 1878).

[11] It is possible that Ignacy Krzyżanowski, who took some lessons from Chopin in 1844–5, may have been a distant relative. See Mieczysław Tomaszewski, *Chopin: A Diary in Images*, tr. Rosemary Hunt (Cracow, 1990), p. 200.

not least because he made no attempt to turn his pupils into honorary Frenchmen. Skarbek also tells us something of his tutor's early life, and the picture has been rounded out by subsequent research in France.[12]

There was a strong Polish connection in Lorraine, dating back to the conferment of the Dukedom of Lorraine and Bar on the deposed Polish King Stanisław Leszczyński by his father-in-law, Louis XV. Among the exiled Polish aristocrats who gravitated to the area was a certain Count Pac, lord of the manor at Marainville, where Mikołaj Chopin was brought up. The son of a wheelwright, Mikołaj was undoubtedly a talented, largely self-taught boy, literate and hard-working, and as such he quickly came to the notice of Count Pac. When the count's steward, another Pole named Adam Weydlich, returned to Warsaw in 1787 to oversee the Polish affairs of his master, the young Mikołaj Chopin, then aged seventeen, accompanied him as a clerk. He was given a job as a bookkeeper at the tobacco factory run by Weydlich, and in that capacity he remained for some five years. A letter to his parents from this period has survived, and it suggests a young man cautious and pragmatic in outlook, keen to better himself and perhaps a little dull. In the letter he explains his decision to remain in Warsaw, referring to the dangers of conscription in post-revolutionary France. And this needs to be borne in mind when we consider his later participation in the uprising (led by Kościuszko) which followed the Second Partition of Poland in 1793. Mikołaj Chopin may well have found Poland congenial. But he was not the stuff of heroes, and it is likely that his enrolment in the Warsaw National Guard was calculated to secure advancement in the aftermath of the uprising.

As it turned out, the uprising was a failure and led directly to the third and last of the partitions in 1795. Mikołaj was left without a job and with no means of support, and it seems that at this point he gave serious consideration to returning to France. Any such plans were thwarted by illness, and in the end he remained in Poland, took Polish nationality and secured employment as a tutor in the Łaczyński household, where he remained for six years before joining the Skarbeks in 1802. When he married Justyna Krzyżanowska four years later, he had lost all contact with his humble origins in France. The couple remained with the Skarbeks for a further four years, spending two fairly extended periods with the family in Warsaw, mainly to avoid the troop movements near Żelazowa Wola in the wake of Napoleon's capture of Prussian-held

[12] See G. Ladaique, 'Les ancêtres paternels de Frédéric Chopin', in *Sur les traces de Frédéric Chopin*, ed. Danielle Pistone (Paris, 1984), pp. 17–28. Here Chopin's French ancestry is traced back to an Antoine Chappen living in the late seventeenth century. His son François, great-great-grandfather of the composer, settled in Xirocourt in the valley of the river Madon and changed his name to Chopin. The family was in the main of well-to-do peasant stock. For a brief account of Mikołaj Chopin's life, see Wincenty Lopaciński, 'Chopin Mikołaj (1771–1844)', in *Polski słownik biograficzny* (Cracow, 1937), vol. 3, pp. 426–7.

Warsaw. It was in Warsaw that their first child, Ludwika (named after Countess Skarbek), was born on 6 April 1807. Following their return to Żelazowa Wola, a second child, Fryderyk Franciszek, was born to the Chopins on 1 March 1810.[13] He was baptised in the parish church at nearby Brochów on 23 April, and his godparents were Anna and Fryderyk Skarbek, though the latter was in Paris at the time and had to be represented by someone else at the ceremony. The boy was named after his godfather and his paternal grandfather.

Biographers have not been slow to find special significance in the composer's Polish–French parentage, and there is a certain neatness in this, given that he divided his life almost equally between the two countries. In later life Chopin was indeed responsive to the claims of two very different, even incompatible, social worlds, both of which were essential to him. This duality, given expression in his circles of friends, in the two major loves of his life, and perhaps indirectly in his music, may be conveniently represented by the contrasted ambiences of Warsaw and Paris. But this is not at all to claim that there was some sort of compound of indigenous national qualities in his make-up, still less to argue that such a compound was inherited from his parents. It goes without saying that his personality was shaped at deep levels by parental influence and background, but it is unhelpful to overinterpret this by invoking the treacherous issue of national character.

The Chopin household was committed to staunch middle-class values, among which a sound education, a well-developed sense of morality and an ethos of self-improvement were prominent. Mikołaj Chopin's letters to his son in later life convey this clearly enough. Written in French and slightly solemn in tone, they are replete with worthy sentiments and sound advice, notably concerning moderation in lifestyle, cultivation of the right people, and the danger of offending those in authority. Without doubt these were the principles which guided Mikołaj himself as he gradually made his way in Polish society. When his son was seven months old, he left the Skarbek household and moved to Warsaw, where he had secured a post at the recently founded Lyceum, housed in the Saski Palace.[14] For more than six years the Chopins lived in the right wing of the palace, and it was there that the two younger children were born, Izabella on 9 July 1811 and Emilia on 20 November 1812. Mikołaj rapidly acquired a reputation as a sound teacher, and on 1 January 1812 he took on additional duties as a lecturer in French at the School of

[13] The date is disputed. According to the register of births Chopin was born on 22 February, but he himself always gave the date as 1 March (notably in the biography he supplied for Fétis's dictionary), and this is the date most widely accepted today. By a curious coincidence the date of his godfather Fryderyk Skarbek is also disputed by a ten-day difference.

[14] The Saski (Saxon) Palace no longer exists. It was on a site facing present-day Victory Square (currently occupied by the Tomb of the Unknown Soldier), and its gardens are still known as the Saski Gardens.

Artillery and Engineering. Shortly after that (1 June 1814) his post at the Lyceum was upgraded to lecturer in French language and literature.

His position within the 'French colony' in Warsaw is by no means easy to determine. For obvious reasons the French were regarded with suspicion by the Russian authorities, and were kept under surveillance. They were also viewed ambivalently by the Polish population. In some quarters there was a rather snobbish cultivation of everything French, strengthened for a time by a short-lived idealization of Napoleon, whose cause was well served by Polish troops. But elsewhere there was resentment, and especially among the older generation who had unhappy memories of waves of French immigrants at the turn of the century. Mikołaj Chopin seems to have kept his distance from the liberal circle, associated in particular with the journal *Constitutionelle*. As Fryderyk Skarbek put it, he was 'not saturated with the principles of republican freedom nor with the bigotry of most French immigrants'. Rather he mixed socially with respected figures such as the eminent physician Dr Girandot and the ambassador Count de Moriolles, from whom he would no doubt have received all the latest news from Paris. He was also careful to maintain friendly relations with the Russian establishment, including the Viceroy of Poland, Grand Duke Constantin Pavlovitch (brother of Csar Alexander), who kept a careful eye on the activities of the Lyceum. Moreover, as Fryderyk Skarbek remarked, he managed to earn the respect of the indigenous Polish community as an honoured and reliable teacher.

He was a well-read man, with a predilection for Voltaire, and he was apparently modestly talented on the flute and violin. But it was almost certainly his wife, Justyna, who had the greater enthusiasm for music. There are accounts by some of their boarders (admittedly written many years later)[15] of frequent music-making in the Chopin home, with Justyna singing to her own accompaniment at the piano, and it is fitting that her favourite song, 'Już miesiąc zeszedł' (The moon has waned), later found its way into Chopin's *Fantasy on Polish Airs*, Op. 13. It is no doubt a testament to the lively cultural ambience of the household that three of the four Chopin children developed literary and musical interests. Such interests would also have been fostered by the private High School for Girls attended by Chopin's sisters, since it included among its teachers Klementyna Tańska Hoffmanova, a leading light of Warsaw artistic circles, with her own salon in her appartment at the Zamoyski's 'Blue Palace'. Klementyna Tańska was idolized by at least one of the Chopin girls. When Fryderyk stayed in the Ojców valley near Cracow in 1829 (on his way to Vienna), his letter to the family included

---

[15] See Eustachy Marylski's *Memoirs* (manuscript copy) in the National Library, Warsaw, and Eugeniusz Skrodzki, 'Kilka wspomnien o Szopeniie z mojej młodosci', in *Bluszcz* (1882), nos. 32–6.

a note to Izabella that he had slept in 'the very same rooms' as Tańska.[16]

Izabella later married Antoni Barciński, a mathematics tutor who became an inspector of schools and eventually a director of steam navigation on the Vistula. She was the only one of the Chopin children to live to a good age, and the only one who seems to have had limited involvement with artistic pursuits, though she was genuinely fond of music and collaborated with her elder sister Ludwika in some early literary exercises. Ludwika herself published (under a pseudonym) a short book based on the family journey to the Silesian health spa Duszniki in 1826, together with several translations and poems. She was also gifted musically, had piano lessons with Chopin's teacher Wojciech Żywny, composed a little, and frequently played duets with her brother. Of all the family it was she who was closest to him. Indeed the bond between them was one of lasting strength, and Chopin always felt able to confide in her, right to the end. In 1844 she visited him in France with her husband Józef Kalasanty Jędrzejewicz, a teacher of Administrative Law at the Institute of Rural Economy at Marymont (near Warsaw), and her warmth of personality and general cultural awareness made a deep impression on Chopin's companion George Sand. For a time (until the separation of Chopin and Sand) the two women corresponded warmly, Sand enclosing notes to Ludwika in Chopin's letters to his family. Later, when the composer was dying in Paris, Ludwika returned to France to be with him, and she took much of the responsibility for distributing his manuscripts and personal effects following his death in 1849. She herself died six years later at the age of forty-eight.

By all accounts the youngest child, Emilia, was the most gifted of the sisters. So at least we might assume from Fryderyk Skarbek's obituary and the accompanying note by Klementyna Tańska, and also from the remarks in Wójcicki's book on the Powazki Cemetary.[17] Wójcicki devoted six pages to her, including a summary of the short play *Omylka, czyli Mniemany filut* (The Mistake, or The Supposed Rogue), written by Emilia and Fryderyk for their father's name-day on 17 April 1824. Emilia's death from tuberculosis at the age of fourteen was naturally a major tragedy for the family, though it is worth remarking that such early deaths were far from unusual at the time. Among Chopin's friends and acquaintances almost everyone lost someone close. Tuberculosis was especially common. As well as Emilia, it may have brought down Chopin's father and possibly also Ludwika, though the matter remains

---

[16] See Kobylańska, *Chopin in his Own Land*, p. 165. For a discussion of the Chopin family, see Janina Siwkowska, *Nokturn czyli rodzina Fryderyka Chopina* (Warsaw, 1988), 2 vols.

[17] Kazimierz Wladysław Wójcicki, *Cmentarz Powazkowski* (Warsaw, 1855–8), 3 vols., vol. 2, pp. 16–21.

uncertain. It also claimed his close friends Jan Białobłocki and Jan Matuszyński, and in due course the composer himself.

Relatively little is known of Chopin's early childhood in Warsaw, though undocumented legends about his musical gifts abound. Later correspondence leaves us in no doubt about the affection he felt for his family, and they for him, and there is no reason to doubt the reports of Skrodzki and Marylski that it was a secure, well-ordered and loving family background, marked by simple pleasures and by a devotion to hard work. Although there is little reference to his mother in Chopin's correspondence, it seems that she was especially close to him ('his only passion', claimed George Sand in her autobiography) and that she had a caring, loving nature. All in all, the household provided exactly the right protective environment for a boy whose health was delicate, as Chopin's undoubtedly was, even at an early age. He was not sent to primary school, nor even to the early preparatory classes at the Lyceum, though this had less to do with health than with the internal structure of the Lyceum. In the first three years pupils followed much the same syllabus as other secondary schools in Warsaw, while the 'real' Lyceum began at the fourth year. This was the point at which Chopin enrolled, and until then he remained at home and was tutored by his father and possibly also by some of his sisters' teachers.

The lifestyle of the Chopins was that of a moderately well-off bourgeois family and they were closest socially to other professional people in the city, doctors and teachers in particular. The salons they attended were not glittering social occasions but had rather the character of literary or scientific gatherings. There are accounts, for instance, of Mikołaj Chopin and Samuel Bogumił Linde, Principal of the Lyceum and himself an eminent scholar, attending meetings of the Society for the Friends of Learning at Fryderyk Skarbek's salon. Contacts with academic circles increased when the University of Warsaw was established in 1817, since at that time the Lyceum moved to new premises alongside the University in the Kazimierzowski Palace, an impressive building on Krakowskie Przedmieście. The Chopins took rooms in the right annex and inevitably they became friendly with University teachers such as Juliusz Kolberg, Kazimierz Brodziński, and Feliks Jarocki, all of whom lived in the residential quarters of the palace. There was a significant German component among the Warsaw intelligentsia at this time, and it is striking that many of the Lyceum and University teachers were either Silesian Germans or German-educated Poles. It was through such contacts that Chopin was able to visit Berlin in 1828.

The Chopin household may have been unequivocally bourgeois in tone, but the composer was no less at home with titled Polish families. His own mother was from a noble, if impoverished, family, and her relatives the Skarbeks were as much friends as employers. Count Fryderyk Skarbek took a close interest in his godson's musical career and on entering the University in 1818 he seems to have taken active steps to promote it. Moreover Mikołaj Chopin ran a boarding-house (both at the Saski and the Kazimierzowski palaces) for some of the Lyceum pupils, and most of these were from the minor landed gentry (*szlachta*). The *szlachta* were admittedly rather more numerous than their approximate counterparts in west European society, and their lifestyles were often fairly modest. Those who still had an estate in the country would typically spend the winter months in the city and return to the country in spring. But many lived an essentially bourgeois existence, boasting a 'name' but no property or means, and these were often obliged to enter the professions, albeit frequently retaining the customs (and even the dress) of their class in 'Old Poland'. Fryderyk Skarbek, who himself became a professor at Warsaw University, tells us that even such an honourable profession was regarded by many *szlachta* as beneath their dignity. When he entered the Lyceum Chopin became close friends with a number of boys from this background, and spent several summer vacations at their country estates.

There was a chasm separating such middle gentry as Chopin's schoolfriends from the small handful of very wealthy, politically influential aristocratic families at the top of the social hierarchy in Poland. Yet although social status counted for a good deal, access to the great families was easier in a relatively small city such as Warsaw than in major west European capitals. As a gifted young musician, Chopin was invited to salons in the very best society—at the Warsaw palaces of the Zamoyskis, Czartoryskis, Sapiehas, and Lubeckis among others. Such salons played an important role in the life of Poland at that time, bringing together creative people from all walks of life, evaluating scientific discoveries and new artistic movements, and often forming a major forum for political debate. Each salon tended to have its own character and its own clientele. It is known, for instance, that the young Chopin played at the salon of General Mokronowski, famed for its patriotic promotion of old Polish customs and manners, and also at that of Teresa Kicka, which encouraged rather the most progressive literary and artistic trends of the day, boasting among its regulars the writers Julian Ursyn Niemcewicz, Juliusz Slowacki, Valerian Krasiński, and Stefan Witwicki. We know (from memoirs by Klementyna Tańska's sister) that Chopin also performed at the Grabowska salon,[18] at the conservative literary evenings of Kalenty Koźmian and at Belvedere Palace, home of the Grand Duke Constantin.

[18] Aleksandra z Tańskich Tarczewska, *Historia mego życia* (Warsaw, 1967; original edn. 1842), p. 243. One of those at Countess Grabowska's described Chopin as 'a child not yet eight years old, who, in the opinion of the connoisseurs of the art, promises to replace Mozart'. See Fredrick Niecks, *Chopin as a Man and Musician* (New York, 1973, original edn. 1888), 2 vols., vol. 1, p. 32. For a general discussion of Polish salons, see Alexander Kraushar, *Salony i zebrania literackie Warszawskie na schyłku w XVIII i w ubiesłym stoleciu* (Warsaw, 1916).

The visits to Belvedere were especially significant. Constantin was notoriously unpopular in Poland, and with good reason. But Mikołaj Chopin was well aware of the honour bestowed on his son when the ducal carriage arrived to take him to Belvedere, where he would improvise to the Grand Duke and then play in the garden with his (illegitimate) son. Nor is this the only indication that the young Chopin was treated almost as a social equal in the palaces of the aristocracy. It is obvious from his later contacts with Prince Antoni Radziwiłł, Governor of the Prussian province, that genuine talent was a passport to social acceptance in the highest circles. And there was never any doubt that Chopin qualified on the score of talent. From his earliest years he was widely recognized by Warsaw society as a musical prodigy—a performer and composer of genius. He continued to move in such circles throughout his Warsaw years, and they provided outlets for his playing and composing which were denied to most young Polish composers at the time.

Aside from salon performances, he made occasional public or semi-public appearances, of which one of the earliest was a performance on 24 February 1818 of an E minor Piano Concerto by Adalbert Gyrowetz. This took place in the Radziwiłł Palace at a Benevolent Society soirée organized by Julian Niemcewicz, who gave a highly coloured account of the preparations for the concert.[19] Later in the same year Chopin played to the Empress Maria Feodorovna, mother of Czar Alexander and the Grand Duke Constantin, and presented her with copies of two recently composed polonaises, no longer extant. And just a year after that he played to the singer Angelica Catalani and received an inscribed gold watch for his efforts. In the last years of his life he remembered that occasion fondly.[20]

As a child Chopin improvised constantly at the keyboard, and it is likely that he would have made relatively little distinction between an improvisation and a composed work. Of the very earliest compositions, two polonaises from 1817 have survived. The one in G minor was lithographed at the time by Canon Izydor Cybulski, director of the School of Organists and until the establishment of the Congress Kingdom (1815) one of the only active music publishers in Warsaw (he had purchased a small printing-house from Józef Elsner). The polonaise was dedicated to Countess Victoria Skarbek, daughter of Ludwika, and the Warsaw press (*Pamiętnik Warszawski*) responded to its publication with a eulogy: 'The composer of this Polish dance, a young lad barely eight years old, is . . . . a true musical genius. Not only does he play the most difficult piano pieces with the greatest ease and the most extraordinary taste, he is

[19] See William Atwood, *Fryderyk Chopin: Pianist from Warsaw* (New York, 1987), pp. 4–5 for an account of this occasion.

[20] See Jeremy Barlow, 'Encounter with Chopin: Fanny Erskine's Paris diary', in *Chopin Studies 2*, ed. John Rink and Jim Samson (Cambridge, 1994), pp. 245–8.

already the composer of several dances and variations, each of which has thoroughly astonished the connoisseurs, especially in view of his tender age.'[21]

Chopin's very early compositions were written out either by his father or by his music teacher Adalbert Żywny. The first surviving autograph, a Polonaise in A flat major, dates from 1821. Currently housed in the library of the Warsaw Music Society, it has hand-drawn staves on wafer-thin paper, is neatly and meticulously written, and reveals as yet none of the idiosyncracies of Chopin's later musical hand.[22] The manuscript is dated 23 April 1821 and has a dedication to Adalbert Żywny 'par son élève Fryderyk Chopin'. The dedication was a name day tribute to the old Czech musician, whose lessons to Chopin were just about to come to an end. They had begun five years earlier when the composer was six and already displayed exceptional gifts at the piano. As an infant he had almost certainly received some guidance, however informal, from his mother, but from 1816 Żywny regularly visited the household, teaching Ludwika and several of the boarders as well as Chopin himself.

It is mainly due to the testimony of the boarders, written in memoirs half a century later, that the image of Żywny as a lovable eccentric, wearing hopelessly outdated clothes and reeking of snuff, was disseminated. It is probably close enough to the mark, and the tone of Chopin's references to 'good old Żywny' in later correspondence rather supports it. But the truth is that there is little reliable information about Chopin's first teacher. One of several Czech musicians living in Warsaw (they included Wilhelm Würfel, with whom Chopin had organ lessons for a time), Żywny worked initially at the court of Prince Kazimierz Sapieha and then as a freelance teacher, apparently much in demand. He was very soon a familiar figure in the Chopin household, joining the family in name day celebrations and, according to Skrodzki and Marylski, often taking his meals there. As to his merits as a teacher, there are conflicting reports. Szulc described him as 'well known and much appreciated as a piano teacher and fanatic of Bach', while Koźmian, who was his pupil for a time, claimed that he was 'perhaps the worst music teacher in Warsaw. But Chopin was his pupil!'.[23]

There was probably something rather defensive in Chopin's own approbation, since later in life he was often at pains to counter suggestions that Warsaw was a musical backwater, and may well have exaggerated Żywny's qualities accordingly. Certainly he would have learnt little about piano technique from his teacher, who was really a violinist

[21] Krystyna Kobylańska, *Chopin in his Own Land*, p. 41.

[22] One of the features separating Chopin's hand from that of his factotum Julian Fontana (who modelled his musical handwriting on Chopin's) is the descending stem, which in Chopin is almost always on the right of the note head.

[23] A. E. Koźmian, *Wspomnienia* (Poznań, 1867), 3 vols. Quoted in Adam Czartkowski and Zofia Jeżewska, *Fryderyk Chopin* (Warsaw, 1970), p. 13.

by training. At the same time he genuinely owed much to the old man's knowledge of Bach and the classical repertory. Ferdinand Hoesick remarked that Żywny, a pupil of Kuchar from the J. S. Bach tradition, gave Chopin nothing but Bach.[24] But if we remember that Bach was little appreciated—indeed scarcely known—in Warsaw at the time, this was undoubtedly a most precious gift, and one which helped to shape the kind of composer Chopin would become. In other respects Żywny knew his limitations, and after five years he decided that his most talented pupil needed to move on.

In a small, close-knit society Chopin's exceptional gifts would certainly have come to the attention of Józef Elsner, the leading figure in Warsaw musical circles. Born in 1769, Elsner was a Silesian German who had been trained in Breslau (Wrocław) and worked in Brno and Lwów before settling in Warsaw around the turn of the century. He was Director of Opera at the National Theatre (where his wife was a singer) and also ran the 'music and singing' classes at the Theatre's School of Drama, founded in 1811. In 1816 the musical component of the School was increased and it became known as the School of Music and Drama. Elsner expended much time and effort in trying to found a separate School of Music and in 1821 he succeeded with the establishment of the Institute of Music and Declamation, better known as the Warsaw Conservatory.

It is likely that Chopin's first contact with Elsner was in 1817 or 1818, around the time of his first published work and first public concert. It is also likely that he had informal advice and even some private lessons with the eminent teacher before entering the High School of Music in 1826, though the extent and nature of this teaching remains undocumented. Indeed for information of this kind we rely essentially on early biographers such as Karasowski and Szulc, whose advantages of proximity to Chopin's family and acquaintances are at times outweighed by their rather permissive approach to documentation. The one certainty is that Elsner introduced the thirteen-year-old Chopin to a harmony textbook by Karol Antoni Simon in 1823, and this may well have been the trigger for sporadic lessons in music theory. Chopin's preference for the polonaise in these formative years would certainly have been fostered by Elsner, since his own Conservatory students were encouraged to cut their teeth on polonaises. But the young composer also turned out mazurkas and waltzes during his Lyceum years, and he tried his hand, too, at rondos and variation sets, the most characteristic genres of bravura concert music. In short, before he began formal composition classes in 1826 he was already a composer of recognized achievement.

Whatever Elsner may have taught Chopin in the way of theory and composition, he would have offered little more than Żywny in keyboard

[24] Ferdynand Hoesick, *Chopin: życie i twórczość* (Cracow, 1962–8; original edn. 1910–11), 3 vols., vol. 1, p. 58.

technique. Chopin started to take organ lessons from Wilhelm Würfel, a distinguished pianist on Elsner's staff at the Conservatory, around 1823, but in most important respects he was a self-taught performer. It has even been plausibly suggested that his singular approach to piano technique and pedagogy may have developed in part because of his unorthodox training. In any event his performing career continued in the pre-Lyceum years, though it was confined mainly to the salons. The one major exception was another appearance at the Benevolent Society on 24 February 1823, this time organized by Józef Jawurek of the Conservatory. Chopin played a concerto by Ferdinand Ries, and the *Kurier dla płci pięknej* (Courier for the Fair Sex) reported it as follows: 'We can claim with certainty that we have never before heard a virtuoso in our capital who could, at such a tender age, overcome remarkable difficulties with ease, and play the most beautiful adagios with both accuracy and feeling.'[25]

Chopin quickly gained the reputation of a 'second Mozart' in Warsaw circles, both as composer and pianist. He was, in short, a 'child prodigy'. It is rather easy to exaggerate the importance of this for his later development, especially as recent research in educational psychology suggests that the notion of the prodigy has been overvalued in the past.[26] It may well be that musical gifts are less specific and inherent than was once thought, and that there is an element of fortuity in the channelling of an undifferentiated aptitude for abstract thought ('prodigies' are especially common in music, mathematics, and chess) into one specialism rather than another. Given a sympathetic context, notably supportive or ambitious parents, a 'snowballing' effect may take place, whereby burgeoning skills and creativity in any one area may well block out other areas, while at the same time enabling a level of attainment inaccessible to most of us. Whatever the truth of this as a general principle, it describes Chopin's development rather well. Once his passion for music had been triggered in childhood, he pursued it single-mindedly and to the near exclusion of other intellectual and artistic interests.

The fact that Chopin was a so-called prodigy had probably only a limited bearing on the kind of composer he would become. But it is worth noting that, in common with other composers gifted with a remarkable facility in childhood, he tended to think in sounds rather more than in concepts, a distinction which, however apparently crude, has some explanatory value in discussions of compositional process. From the start playing and composing were inseparably linked in his mind, and they remained so throughout his life. Even in maturity he was unable to compose without a piano. His first thoughts about a piece invariably took shape at the piano in a manner closely akin to improvisation, and his exploration of new creative possibilities was intimately connected to

[25] *Kurier dla płci pieknej*, 26 February 1823.
[26] See, for example, M. J. E. Howe, *The Origins of Exceptional Abilities* (Oxford, 1990).

14

the physical immediacy of the instrument, its limitations and its potentialities. In this sense, at least, the earliest childhood efforts issued clear signals about the mature composer.

In September 1823 Chopin entered the fourth class at the Lyceum. This was widely regarded as the most prestigious secondary school in Warsaw, drawing its pupils from different social strata (though mainly from the *szlachta*) and from different regions of Poland. The education system in the city was in many ways highly organized and closely integrated, at least from the establishment in 1815 of the Congress Kingdom until the 1830 uprising. There were clearly defined categories of schools with common or related syllabuses, and there was a close relationship between the three 'academic' high schools (four from 1828) and the University.[27] The Lyceum was one of these high schools, and the education Chopin received during his three years there was thorough and broadly-based, including French and German, Greek, mathematics, physics, Polish history and literature, art, and music (mainly singing). The teachers were in several cases noted scholars with impressive publication lists, and pupils from the higher classes were entitled to attend University lectures and to use the University library. It seems that Chopin was a good, but not exceptional, student. He had a special aptitude for drawing, and it is worth noting that the Lyceum art master was the eminent painter Zygmunt Vogel.

Chopin's entry to the Lyceum coincided with a general tightening up of discipline. Not only were masters made responsible for the behaviour of those boys living in their vicinity, but special curators were appointed by the Grand Duke Constantin to oversee and censor the activities of the high schools and the University. Constantin was distinctly nervous of the new 'Romantic' culture emanating from Wilno, fearing (with good cause) that it would fuel the smouldering political unrest associated above all with intellectual circles. Accordingly the reports of these curators, who monitored the behaviour of the boys both within and outside the school, were of considerable importance, especially when it came to the awarding of prizes. This should be borne in mind when we consider Chopin's academic success at the end of his first year, when he received a prize 'moribus et diligentiae'.

Chopin was already familiar with some of the Lyceum pupils through his father's boarding house, but his years of formal study saw the beginnings of several lasting friendships with classmates. He was especially close to four of them, Tytus Woyciechowski, Dominik Dziewanowski, Jan Matuszyński, and Jan Białobłocki. But he also became friends with Eustachy Marylski, whose memoirs are a valuable biographical source, with the brothers Wilhelm and Oskar Kolberg, whose father lectured at the University and who went on to have distinguished careers as an

---

[27] See Tadeusz Frączyk, *Warszawa młodości Chopina* (Cracow, 1961), pp. 135–81.

engineer and ethnographer respectively, with the playwright and novelist Dominik Magnuszewski, and with the three Wodziński brothers, whose sister Maria would later be his first great love. During his adolescent years he poured out his feelings first to Białobłocki and then to Woyciechowski, but in later years he developed a deeper friendship with Matuszyński, who moved to Paris in 1834 and remained there until his early death in 1842. Julian Fontana, with whom Chopin later developed an important professional relationship, was also a Lyceum pupil at this time, but there is no record of any close friendship between the two boys before they became fellow students at the Conservatory, when they frequently played duets. Chopin's affections may have shifted somewhat as the years passed, but he retained some contact with these and other Polish friends throughout his life, even during his most cosmopolitan days in Parisian society. It has often been remarked that he revealed himself most completely in his letters to Poles (indeed he said himself that he could only relax fully in their company), and it is clear that these early friendships were of unusual formative importance.

At the end of his first year at the Lyceum Chopin was invited by Dominik Dziewanowski to spend the summer at his country estate at Szafarnia, not far from Żelazowa Wola. It was usual for the better-off Varsovians to leave for the country at the end of July, and in earlier years Chopin almost certainly accompanied his parents on their annual visits to the Skarbek estate. The invitation to Szafarnia was repeated the following year (1825), and his letters of these two summers indicate that the Dziewanowskis looked after him well, administering the medications prescribed by his French doctor (pills, linden tea, and acorn coffee), presenting him to several of the local gentry, including a branch of the Potocki family, and generally engaging him in outdoor pursuits, including attempts at horse riding. 'I am not reading or writing but I am playing music, drawing, running, making the most of the lovely air', he wrote on 10 August 1824 (one of his first known letters).[28] In the second year there was more extensive sight-seeing, including a visit to Torun, where he saw Copernicus's house and other buildings of historical interest, though he seems to have been more taken with the distinctive spice cake (*piernik*) associated with the city.

During his first summer in Szafarnia several of his letters home took the form of a mock newspaper, the *Kurier Szafarski* (Szafarnia Courier), modelled on the *Kurier Warszawski*. It was filled with amusing tales of petty domestic dramas and the antics of farm animals, and all told by 'M. Pichon' with a lively wit and humour which he retained throughout his life. This is an aspect of his personality which can rather easily be smothered by the more tragic and romantic associations cultivated by the early biographers. Józefina Wodzińska (sister of Maria) recalled it in

[28] *Korespondencja Fryderyka Chopina* (hereafter *KFC*), ed. B. E. Sydow (Warsaw, 1955), 2 vols., vol. 1, p. 37.

these terms: 'The fact that Frycek was already thought to be the finest pianist in Warsaw interested us much less than his love of fun and games. Of all the boys he was the most willing to joke and play . . .'[29] Izabella also commented to Hoesick on his sense of fun and love of practical jokes, and there are similar remarks in Skrodzki's reminiscences. He was a good mimic and caricaturist, as we know from his letters and drawings from Berlin a year or two later, and he greatly enjoyed devising and taking part in amateur theatricals. The comedy which he and Emila wrote and produced for their father's name day in December 1824 would find an echo many years later when he organized similar entertainments at Nohant, the country home of his companion George Sand.

Much has been made of Chopin's contact with folk music during his two youthful visits to Szafarnia. But this issue needs to be handled with care. It is true that he wrote to his family about his encounters with folk-song during his first summer in Szafarnia, describing a melody sung by the village children and then a mazurka from a 'village Catalani'.[30] In the second summer, too, he gave an account of folk melodies sung by 'old peasant women whining through their noses' to the accompaniment of a single, three-string violin (he notated the refrain), and of some Jewish melodies which attracted him. It is also true that in later life he himself made a clear distinction between such folk music in its natural setting and the published arrangements by Kolberg. 'A future genius . . . will one day arrive at the truth, and restore it [Polish folk music] to its full value and beauty. Until then, folk songs will remain hidden under all that paint . . .'[31] But it would be possible to overrate the significance of his first-hand contacts with peasant music during these summers in Szafarnia, and subsequently. Undoubtedly the raw energy of peasant music had an input to his own mazurkas, but so too did the urbanized 'salon dances' which would have been very familiar to Chopin from his earliest years in Warsaw, not least from his regular attendance at so-called *thés dansants*. His contribution to musical nationalism was real and important, but it did not in the end hinge solely or even principally on the recovery of some notionally 'authentic' peasant music.

During his first visit to Szafarnia Chopin played a Kalkbrenner concerto and an early version of his own 'Little Jew' Mazurka (Op. 17 No. 4) at a soirée in the Dziewanowski home. His repertory was already extensive, and his powers of improvisation legendary, and on his return to Warsaw from Szafarnia he continued to perform at salons and semi-public gatherings. The poet A. E. Odyniec recalled one outstanding improvisation at Teresa Kicka's, where it seemed that Chopin entered an almost trance-like state. Again we should treat such reminiscences with care. Did Chopin really claim, as Odyniec goes on to tell us, that not even the greatest of his later triumphs afforded him a deeper

[29] Ferdynand Hoesick, *Slowacki i Chopin* (Warsaw, 1932), p. 49.
[30] *KFC*, vol. 1, p. 44.   [31] Ibid., vol. 1, p. 193.

satisfaction that this improvisation?[32] Public appearances are more reliably documented. In May 1825 he improvised on Józef Długosz's new instrument, the aeolopantaleon, at the Conservatory, and the concert was so successful that a special recital was arranged for Csar Alexander I, who was just then on an official visit to Warsaw to open a session of the Polish Diet. On this occasion Chopin improvised on Karol Brunner's aeolomelodikon at the Evangelical Church, and received a diamond ring from the Czar. In June he again played and improvised on the aeolopantaleon, earning himself a good notice in the *Allgemeine Musikalische Zeitung* of Leipzig, and the following month he performed Moscheles's G minor Concerto at the Conservatory.

He continued to compose, of course, and in June 1825 his Op. 1 appeared, a Rondo in C minor dedicated to the wife of the Lyceum Rector, Samuel Bogumił Linde. It was lithographed by Antoni Brzezina, the principal music retailer and publisher in Warsaw since the establishment of the Congress Kingdom. He also composed variation sets, numerous polonaises, including one on motives from Rossini's *Il Barbiere di Siviglia* and one using a theme from *La Gazza Ladra*, as well as mazurkas, waltzes, and marches. Many of these pieces are no longer extant, and we know about some of them only through a description of the album (now lost) of Izabella Grabowska, wife of the Education Minister and an enthusiastic patron of music. Chopin attended her salon and developed the habit of inscribing pieces in her album.

In the midst of playing and composing, Chopin seems to have found time for an active social life. Cafés were forbidden to the Lyceum pupils, but he and his friends frequented the theatre, and there was a constant run of name day parties, balls and informal dances. On 12 February 1826 he wrote to Jan Białobłocki that he had been out every evening 'from Sunday to Thursday' at one event or another.[33] Perhaps it was all a bit too much, for his health failed badly in the winter of 1826, his final year at the Lyceum. Emilia was also ill that year, and the following summer the children went with their mother to Duszniki, a health spa in lower Silesia. It was a tedious episode for Chopin, the boredom alleviated only by his performances at two charity concerts on a very poor piano, and it was certainly no replacement for Szafarnia. But the visit to Duszniki is clear evidence that Chopin's health was giving serious cause for concern. Marylski remembered him as 'something of a weakling'.[34]

It is probable that he contracted tuberculosis in very early childhood, and he subsequently developed serious neuralgia and also symptoms which we would associate today with various allergies. In later life he had to endure constant coughing fits every morning before he could do anything constructive, and this in turn led to permanent inflammation

---

[32] Antoni Edward Odyniec, *Wspomnienia z przeszłości opowiadane deotymie* (Warsaw, 1884), pp. 325–6.
[33] *KFC*, vol. 1, pp. 62–4.   [34] See note 15.

of his throat. It is not clear at which point Chopin came to accept that he had consumption. He was regarded as consumptive by certain of his associates at an early stage, and was diagnosed as such by the Majorcan doctors in 1838. But ostensibly he and Sand rejected that diagnosis, and they were reassured by French doctors on several occasions in the early 1840s that there was no trace of the disease. Adam Zamoyski suggests, intriguingly, that two schools of medical thought, rather than faulty diagnoses, lay at the root of these divergent opinions; that the French doctors did not regard tuberculosis as contagious and diagnosed it only when damage to the lungs, as opposed to the larynx, had been detected.[35] In any event, the reality was that for most of his adult life he suffered acute discomfort and often much worse, especially during the winter months. This must surely have exerted a profound influence on his whole outlook on life and indeed on his approach to creative work, though it goes without saying that equations such as Field's 'talent of the sickroom' are simplistic in the extreme.

Immediately on his return to Warsaw Chopin enrolled (a few weeks late) for the three-year course at the High School of Music, which is often described as the Warsaw Conservatory. There has been considerable confusion and misunderstanding surrounding this stage of his education, concerning both his reasons for leaving the Lyceum when he did and the exact nature of his studies in the High School. For pupils planning to go on to the University the normal practice was to take the sixth class at the Lyceum for a second time. Chopin's decision to go to the High School rather than the University exempted him from this requirement. He left, in other words, because he did not need to repeat the sixth class, and not because of illness or failure in the examinations. Nor was his attendance at both Conservatory and University classes in any way exceptional. It has been claimed that this represented some sort of compromise between his own wishes and those of his father.[36] The explanation lies rather in the structure of the courses at the High School, which after much argument was granted a formal link with the School of Fine Arts at the University, where Elsner had the status of Professor of Counterpoint and Composition. Third-year students of Theory and Practical Composition accordingly took their classes at the University and were entitled to attend lectures in other disciplines.

The early history of the Conservatory (Institute of Music and Declamation) is far from easy to unravel.[37] When the Institute was founded in 1821 an Italian singing teacher of doubtful competence, Carlo Evasio Soliva, was appointed against Elsner's wishes, and at a higher salary than Elsner himself. Elsner's position as Rector was not

[35] Adam Zamoyski, *Chopin: A Biography* (London, 1979), p. 173. See also below, chapter 9, note 41. [36] Zamoyski, p. 35.
[37] See *150 lat panstwowej wyzszej szkoły muzycznej w Warszawie*, ed. Stefan Sledziński (Cracow, 1960).

threatened, but Soliva was given a special title of 'Director'. There was intense rivalry between the two men, culminating in the establishment of the High School of Music under Elsner, while Soliva remained as Director of the Conservatory, now a branch of the High School. The difficulty is partly that the term 'conservatory' was commonly applied both to the High School itself and to Soliva's department. The politics were labyrinthine, and at one stage resulted in Elsner's temporary dismissal from his post, but it is enough to make it clear that it was the High School which Chopin entered in 1826; and also to point out that High School students took their instrumental lessons and some other subjects (including languages) at the Conservatory and their studies of theory, thoroughbass, and composition at the University.

Although the matter remains uncertain, it seems that Chopin's position in the High School was rather a special one from the start. Since he had already much experience as a performer, and had studied with one of Elsner's staff, Wilhelm Würfel (who left for Vienna just as Chopin enrolled), he was probably given licence to miss many of the practical lessons and concentrate instead on academic studies, which included seeing Elsner for three two-hour periods a week for lessons in counterpoint and composition. He remarked in a letter to Białobłocki that he also went along to some University lectures in literature and history (Kazimierz Brodziński and Feliks Bentkowski) 'whenever there is some connection with music', but it should be said that reasonable doubt has been shed on this claim.[38] Composition was undoubtedly his main study and it is likely that much of his teaching in this was on an individual basis. Not that he was the only student with real talent. Among his colleagues were Ignacy Dobrzyński (a year above Chopin), Tomasz Nidecki (two years above) and Antoni Orlowski (a year lower). Julian Fontana and Józef Stefani (son of Jan Stefani) were also students at the High School while Chopin was there.

The years at the High School of Music were productive for Chopin. During his early studies with Elsner he composed the *Rondo à la mazur*, Op. 5, following a formula established by his teacher, and also the Sonata, Op. 4, dedicated to Elsner. But the major work from this period was the Variations on 'Là ci darem', Op. 2 for piano and orchestra, and at Elsner's suggestion he offered this, together with the Sonata, to the publisher Haslinger in Vienna, his first approach to a publisher outside Poland. He also wrote numerous shorter pieces, and some of these— including waltzes and songs to poems by Witwicki and Mickiewicz— were inscribed in the album of Elsner's talented daughter Emilia, who later married one of the students, Tomasz Nidecki. Throughout his life Chopin continued to inscribe albums in this way with autographs of short pieces or fragments of longer ones. For some works such 'presen-

[38] *KFC*, vol. 1, pp. 72–4. See Tadeusz Frączyk, *Warszawa młodości Chopina*, pp. 182–222.

tation manuscripts' are the only surviving manuscript sources, while for others they result in multiple, and often divergent, autographs of the same piece, creating notorious problems for the modern editor.

Chopin apparently applied himself to his studies at the High School, and this, together with continued ill health, curtailed his social life, at least during the winter months. Indeed his output was prolific enough to suggest that a good deal of his time was spent simply composing, either at the piano or at the desk. It is worth stressing this, since biographies of Chopin are in the habit of treating his composing as though it were something oddly separate from his 'life'. On the contrary it is clear that composing, in all its experiential complexity, with its challenges and frustrations as well as its pleasures and rewards, became an integral part of Chopin's existence at an early age. It increasingly took precedence over social pursuits, at least on the level of a deeper personal fulfilment. The first year at the Conservatory (1826/7) was not in any case a time for socializing. It was a sad year for the family, due to the slowly deteriorating health of Emilia, who eventually died in April in her fifteenth year. And for Chopin this tragedy was compounded by rumours of the death of Jan Białobłocki, with whom he had developed a close relationship, marked by a succession of letters in the summer months. The rumours proved groundless, but a year later his friend did indeed die of consumption.

On the successful completion of his first-year examinations, Chopin again took to the country, staying (according to Oskar Kolberg) with his godmother, Anna Skarbek-Wiesiołowska, in Strzyżew in the Poznań province. She in turn introduced him to the Governor of the Prussian province, Prince Antoni Radziwiłł, who was then staying at his summer hunting lodge, Antonin, and the journey also included a flying visit to Gdańsk. While he was away the Chopins were obliged to move house, since the University was actively expanding and needed to take over the residential quarters of the Kazimierowski Palace. Their new home was on the other side of Krakowskie Przedmeście in the Krasiński Palace, and there Chopin was able to have his own study, in a kind of attic leading off the main rooms. The larger drawing-room of the new appartment also enabled the family to entertain more easily than before, and the Chopin salon was frequented by artists and teachers—not just the regulars from the Lyceum and the University, but up-and-coming writers such as Bohdan Zaleski, Stefan Witwicki and Maurycy Mochnacki. All three were later active in the uprising of 1830, and Mochnacki came to some prominence when he wrote an influential history of the uprising in 1834. During Chopin's Warsaw years Mochnacki had already established a reputation as a poet and music critic, and as a skilled pianist he often played duets with the composer.

At the end of Chopin's second year at the High School (1827/8) Elsner's report read as follows: 'Chopin F., remarkable talent, second year student, has gone away to improve his health.' This time the trip was to Sanniki on the Vistula river, where the family of his schoolfriend Konstanty Pruszak had an estate, and since it was not far from Warsaw he was able to return home at least once during the vacation. The Sanniki visit was a time of rest and recreation (including walks in the park with the Pruszaks' governess), but also of composition—a version for two pianos of the C major Rondo, and some initial work on the Piano Trio, Op. 8. Then, at the end of the summer, an unexpected opportunity to fulfil a longstanding ambition to visit Berlin came Chopin's way. Feliks Jarocki, a professor of zoology at the University and a friend of the Chopins, had studied in Berlin and was invited to a major scientific congress there. He agreed to take the young composer along, and there was some hope that Prince Radziwiłł would also be there to effect useful introductions. Apart from poking fun at the eminent scientists—not least their eating habits—Chopin spent most of his time sightseeing and visiting the theatre and the piano factories. Among the operas he saw in Berlin were Spontini's *Fernandez Cortez*, Onslow's *Le Colporteur*, Cimarosa's *Il Matrimonio Segreto*, Winter's *Das Unterbrochene Opferfest*, and Weber's *Der Freischütz*, which he already knew from Warsaw. But the deepest impression came from a performance of Handel's *Cäcilienfest* at the Singakademie: 'It came close to the ideal of great music which I have created for myself.'

The trip to Berlin was not an unqualified success. He enjoyed the opera, though with reservations, but he showed little interest in the museums and libraries which he visited with Jarocki. Unlike so many composers of his generation, Chopin's interests were almost exclusively musical, and his letters from Berlin spell out rather clearly a lack of intellectual curiosity about other things, and also a certain defensiveness about this. And musically the hoped-for contacts simply did not materialize. He was too shy to present himself to Spontini, Zelter, and Mendelssohn, all of whom were in the capital, and Prince Radziwiłł was not there to arrange introductions. None the less Berlin did offer Chopin a first glimpse of the world beyond Poland, and no doubt sowed the seeds of dissatisfaction with Warsaw's musical life. On the return journey he apparently improvised during a coach stop in Sulechów in Wielkopolska and he also played at receptions in Poznań given by the Archbishop Tomasz Wolicki and by Prince Radziwiłł. The prince was himself a composer of considerable talent (his opera on *Faust* has some surprisingly good things in it, notably the strophic song 'Pieśń żebraka'), and he clearly took to Chopin. He visited the family in their Warsaw appartment the following year (May 1829), and later invited Chopin to stay at Antonin.

In early October (1828) Chopin was back in Warsaw and immersed in his studies for the final year at the High School. There were some performances during the year, but composition took precedence. Besides numerous shorter pieces he completed the Piano Trio and wrote a further two major works for piano and orchestra, the *Rondo à la krakowiak*, Op. 14 and the *Fantasy on Polish Airs*, Op. 13. It was becoming increasingly clear that Chopin's talents could not be developed much further in Poland, and in April his father applied to the Education Minister Stanisław Grabowski for a grant to enable him to study abroad. Grabowski, whose wife knew Chopin well, supported the application, but it was turned down by the Minister of Home Affairs, Tadeusz Mostowski. This was a major blow, and Mikołaj was bitter about it. So too was Józef Elsner. No one was more aware than Elsner that Chopin needed to find a new stimulus for his exceptional creative gifts. His final report for the High School, written in July 1829, was laconic but eloquent: 'Chopin F., third year student, exceptional talent, musical genius.'

Chopin was now increasingly restless in Warsaw. Yet it would be wrong to suggest that he was starved of either social or musical stimulus there. Warsaw was hardly a leading cultural capital, but equally it was not the provincial backwater it has sometimes been labelled. The Congress Kingdom may have been a sham politically but it did lead to something of an economic and cultural revival in the city, following a long period of instability. After 1815 massive building programmes were instigated, with yet more Italian-designed palaces (the building of the Friends of Learning, the Teatr Wielki (Grand Theatre) and the Mostowski Palace), elegant squares and above all parks, whose gardens were laid out 'à la manière anglaise'.[39] It has been remarked that the juxtaposition of dilapidated town houses, aristocratic palaces, and small manor-houses for the *szlachta* (surrounded by their own stables and servants' quarters) gave the city a curiously hybrid appearance.[40] Yet this perfectly reflected the *mélange* which was so characteristic of Warsaw society. It is worth reiterating that Chopin moved easily between very different social groups in the city—from the most elevated families in the land to the middle gentry and professional circles. Yet although he had friends from humble backgrounds, and was perhaps most at ease with professional musicians of whatever class or nationality, he retained a liking for 'the best society' throughout his life, and could even be described as something of a social snob. His view of society (including the role of the artist) was essentially conservative, and it was strikingly at odds with the more general social meliorism characteristic of progressive artistic circles in western Europe at the time.

This social conservatism is exemplified in his relations with one prominent group in Warsaw. Anti-semitism was deep-rooted among Poles, though it should be said that Jews had a relatively safe haven in

[39] Chopin used the phrase in a letter to Jan Białobłocki, 15 May, 1826: *KFC*, vol. 1, p. 63.
[40] Tadeusz Frączyk, *Warszawa młodosci Chopina*, pp. 59–85.

Poland compared with the massacres and pogroms to both the west and the east. They were allowed freedom of worship and had full access to the education system, including the Lyceum, but their rights of employment and residence were limited, and in countless ways, small and large, they were subject to humiliation. The *szlachta* in particular, affecting a disdain for money, often made the Jew suffer for their dependence on his financial services. The very word 'Jew' became synonymous with 'deceiver' in the Polish language, and was indeed so used by Chopin in later letters about publishers. From Szafarnia onwards, unedifying references to Jews (on occasion 'Kartshnor Jews')[41] are frequent in his correspondence, though the language is not in essence different from that of countless other Poles at the time. There is nothing of Wagner's considered theorizing in Chopin's references to the Jews, but rather an unthinking (albeit unfortunate) acceptance of long-established traditional prejudices, and it is hard to endorse the view of Hadden and some others that anti-semitism represented a sustained motivation in his attitude to the cultural world of the time. In the post-holocaust world it is difficult to get these matters into any kind of perspective.

Returning to Warsaw, we might note that, like other aspects of its formal culture, musical life developed encouragingly in the relatively stable political conditions of the Congress Kingdom. The Opera flourished under both Elsner and Karol Kurpiński, with a repertory of French, Italian, and Polish works, and from the start it was of seminal importance in shaping Chopin's tastes. There were also several attempts to establish concert societies in the city, from the *Resursa muzyczna* (Music Club), founded in 1805, to the *Towarzystwo przyjaciół muzyki religinej i narodowej* (Society for the Friends of Religious and National Music), established in 1815. The *Towarzystwo amatorskie muzyczne* (Amateur Musical Association), founded in 1817, gave Wednesday evening symphony concerts under Franciszek Lessel, Józef Jawurek, and others, though these never quite gained the support of a later important series at the *Resursa kupiecka* (Merchant's Club). Concerts at the *Resursa kupiecka* included the first public performance of Chopin's F minor Piano Concerto on 10 December 1829.

Yet such regular concert series were only modestly successful in Warsaw. It seems that audiences took much more easily to the occasional 'benefit' concerts given in the hall of the National Theatre, often by famous virtuosi passing through on their way to St Petersburg. During Chopin's second year at the High School, Hummel gave several such concerts in Warsaw, and Chopin had an opportunity to meet him. And in his final year there was a series of concerts given by Nicolo Paganini and Karol Lipiński, associated with the coronation of Nicholas I as King of Poland. These were much discussed concerts, with

[41] The Kartshnor was a rough country drinking house, often run by Jews in the eighteenth and nineteenth centuries.

extensive debates in the press about the relative merits of the two violinists, and again the impact on Chopin was considerable. Public taste in Warsaw favoured the 'brilliant' style of performance and composition associated with such virtuosi, and it was to this kind of post-classical concert music that Chopin was most frequently exposed, whether in the salons or on the concert platform.

For all its developing vitality, musical life in Warsaw was a long way behind that of the two great European capitals with which Chopin would soon be associated. He paid a short visit to Vienna immediately after his graduation from the High School, travelling in the company of a university teacher and several fellow students. This was poor compensation for the years of study which a state grant would have permitted, but it gave Chopin his first taste of real success in the wider world. On the way they spent a week in Cracow, where they visited the Wieliczka salt mines and explored the Ojców valley, but on arrival in Vienna Chopin was quickly immersed in the musical world of a major capital. Once more opera was the main priority. He saw Boieldieu's *La Dame Blanche*, Rossini's *La Cenerentola*, Meyerbeer's *Il Crociato in Egitto*, and Méhul's *Joseph in Aegypten*. He also visited piano factories, as he had done in Berlin, but this time with much greater satisfaction. Pianos were not, of course, as standardized then as now. Of the two main types—English and Viennese—Chopin's initial preference was for the light-actioned Viennese model, though in later years there was a change of heart. In Vienna he tried both Graf and Stein pianos, and declared his preference for the Graf instruments. It was a Graf which he played at two concerts given in the Kärntnerthor theatre, a prestigious setting for the young Chopin's début outside Poland.

By any standards these concerts were a stroke of good fortune for a nineteen-year-old composer who was unknown outside his native city. They were partly made possible by the presence in Vienna of his old teacher Würfel, who went out of his way to introduce Chopin to other musicians, including the young virtuoso pianist Leopoldine Blahetka, the legendary pianist and teacher Carl Czerny, the impresario Robert Gallenberg, director of the Kärtnerthor theatre, and the publisher Tobias Haslinger. Haslinger had already received the Op. 2 Variations and Op. 4 Sonata, and he agreed to listen to Chopin playing the Variations. It was this above all which led to a concert on 11 August, though Chopin was initially terrified at the prospect. The concert, which included music by Beethoven, was conceived as a prelude to a comic ballet already programmed for that evening, and it should be noted that the financial 'benefit' went to the theatre manager Robert Gallenberg rather than to Chopin. The original intention was to perform the Op. 2 Variations and Op. 14 *Rondo à la krakowiak* with a small orchestra, but there were difficulties with Chopin's orchestral parts for the Rondo and instead he improvised on the folk song 'Chmieł' and on a theme from

La Dame Blanche. The concert was a huge success, and Chopin reported home that 'everyone clapped so loudly after each variation that I had difficulty hearing the orchestral tutti'.[42] The reviews were generous, with one critic remarking that 'on account of the originality of his playing and compositions one might almost attribute to him already some genius, at least insofar as unconventional forms and pronounced originality are concerned'.[43]

A second concert was quickly arranged for 18 August, and this time the newly copied *Rondo à la krakowiak* was included. Undoubtedly the national elements in the two orchestral pieces (the finale of Op. 2 is a variation *à la polacca*) and in the 'Chmieł' improvisation were a major attraction to Viennese audiences, to whom they would have assumed the character of a colourful exoticism. Chopin became something of a talking point. He wrote with understandable pride to his family in Warsaw: 'If I was well-received the first time, then yesterday was even better. . . . Blahetka told me that nothing astonishes them so much as the fact that I learnt this in Warsaw.'[44] Reviews were plentiful, and for the most part they were good, stressing the singularity of his playing and composing. 'He is a young man who goes his own way, and knows how to please in this way, although his style of playing and writing differs greatly from that of other virtuosos.'[45] But there were also criticisms of his smallness of tone, a theme which would recur in press reports throughout his life. Chopin was well aware of the problem, and may already have begun to question his suitability for the role of public pianist.

He left for Poland the day after his second concert, stopping for three days in Prague, where he was shown around the city by Václav Hanka, the librarian of the National Museum. A very minor composition emerged from this. In the visitors' book at the museum his companion Ignacy Maciejewski wrote a few lines of poetry, and Chopin added a musical setting in mazurka rhythm. He had arrived in Prague armed with letters of introduction from Vienna, and visited among others two of the leading pianist-composers of the day, Johann Pixis and August Klengel. Klengel played to Chopin for two hours and presented him with a copy of his fugues in all the keys, a gift which may have sown a few seeds in the young composer's mind. From Prague he moved on to Cieplice (Teplitz), where he visited the Wallenstein castle and improvised on themes from Rossini at a soirée organized by the burgrave Prince Clary-Aldringen, a relative of the Potocki family. He then spent a week sight-seeing in Dresden, before returning to Warsaw at the end of August.

Chopin spent another fourteen months in Warsaw before leaving the city for good, though at the time of his departure he had every intention

[42] *KFC*, vol. 1, p. 92.   [43] *Allgemeine Theaterzeitung*, Vienna, 20 August 1829.
[44] *KFC*, vol. 1, p. 96.   [45] *Allgemeine Theaterzeitung*, Vienna, 1 September 1829.

of returning. It was a restless period, in which three principal discontents were interleaved. One was a basic uncertainty about his future. Everything in his early development pointed towards a career as a pianist-composer in the highly competitive public arena. Chopin already felt himself to be temperamentally unsuited to this, but he was far from clear about the alternatives. A second factor was his growing dissatisfaction with the musical life of Warsaw, which no doubt seemed fairly provincial following his success in Vienna. He knew that it was essential to travel, and was keen to do so, planning an extended trip to Vienna and then on to Italy, Paris, and possibly England, but again there was an underlying cautiousness and insecurity about taking any major steps in this direction. And finally there were emotional problems of a kind by no means unusual among nineteen-year-olds.

Throughout that final year in Warsaw his attitude to both composing and performing changed subtly but irreversibly. He continued to produce occasional 'social' pieces, including songs, waltzes, polonaises, mazurkas, and écossaises, some of them written into Emilia Elsner's album. But he himself was clear about the status of such pieces, describing his Polonaise in C major, Op. 3 for cello and piano, for example, as 'nothing but glitter, for the drawing-room, for the ladies'.[46] He wrote this piece during a visit to Antonin at the end of October 1829, shortly after his return from Vienna, and it was composed specifically for Prince Radziwiłł, a keen amateur cellist as well as a composer. The stay at Antonin was a pleasant interlude, though Mikołaj Chopin's hopes that Prince Radziwiłł might become a wealthy patron to his son were not in the end realized. At the very least Chopin took great pleasure in playing chamber music and in helping the prince's two daughters, the 'two young Eves in this paradise', with their piano lessons.

At the same time he was working on compositions of an altogether different order, though still within the framework of public virtuosity. Immediately on his return from Vienna he resumed work on the F minor Piano Concerto, Op. 21. Like the two earlier works for piano and orchestra this was tailored to the world of the public pianist-composer, at least in broad outline. Yet it easily transcended the limitations of the *concerto brillante*, and it was the first of Chopin's major compositions to secure a place in the canon of regularly performed works. Indeed it marks in many ways the real onset of his maturity as a composer. There were other indications of a new-found assurance, and above all the composition of two of the études which would in due course form part of Op. 10. In a letter to Tytus (20 October 1829) Chopin remarked that he had produced 'an Exercise, *large en forme*, in the only way I know', and later (14 November), 'I have written a few exercises—I would play them well if you were here'.[47] These were almost certainly the first two

---

[46] *KFC*, vol. 1, p. 112. 　　[47] Ibid., p. 113.

études of Op. 10, since there are early manuscripts (copies rather than autographs) of these pieces with the titles 'Exercise 1' and 'Exercise 2', dated 2 November 1830.

It is worth stressing that these works, undoubtedly products of Chopin's maturity as a composer, were written a year before he left Poland. It has sometimes been suggested that the development of his full creative powers was only possible when he moved into the wider world, but the evidence is against this interpretation, and it is strengthened by the composition of the E minor Concerto, Op. 11 the following spring and summer, together with a number of shorter pieces in which the highly personal, idiomatic voice of his maturity is unmistakable. Chopin's final year in Poland was, in short, a crucially important period during which his artistic personality began to assume something like its final shape. And as his creative voice strengthened, his reservations about the career of pianist-composer increased.

During this final year Chopin gave numerous salon and concert performances, including appearances at the salons of the Moriolles, the Lewickis, and the Cichowskis, at Józef Kessler's well-known 'Musical Fridays', and at the *Resursa Kupiecka*. But for the most part these were private or semi-private occasions, and the pressure to give a major public concert in Warsaw built steadily. Following the *Resursa Kupiecka* appearance on 18 December, when he improvised on a song 'Miotelki' (Brooms), Stanisław Koźmian wrote in the *Kurier Warszawski*: 'Though received with enthusiasm abroad, our fellow countryman has not yet been heard in public in his homeland . . . Is Chopin's talent not the property of his homeland? Is Poland unable to appreciate him adequately?'[48] Later the *Gazeta Polska* (12 February 1830) remarked: 'We hear that Chopin is leaving for Italy, but he will surely not undertake this journey without first giving a public concert in the Polish capital.' In the end he succumbed and agreed to give the F minor Concerto at the National Theatre.

Initially, on 7 February, there was a private play-through at the Chopin salon with just a small audience present, though that did not stop the event being written up (favourably) in the press. Then, on 3 March, a larger rehearsal took place, again at the Chopins', and with the score somewhat revised. Karol Kurpiński directed the small orchestra and both Żywny and Elsner were present in the audience. Again the press reports were enthusiastic. The concert itself took place on 17 March to an audience of nine hundred people, and since Chopin was to receive a share of the 'benefit', it was in a sense his début as a public pianist. The programme was characteristic of such occasions in the early nineteenth century in that it included vocal items and sandwiched a lightweight instrumental work between the first movement of the

[48] *Kurier Warszawski*, Warsaw, 23 December 1829.

Concerto and the other two movements. It concluded with a performance of the Op. 13 Fantasy. There was extravagant praise, but one adverse criticism, echoing the reports of his Viennese concerts. Several critics, including Chopin's friend Maurycy Mochnacki, complained of the smallness of tone, suggesting that the young pianist needed to summon up rather more vigour in later performances. Kurpiński noted something similar in his diary.

Mochnacki's criticism, combined with those of the Viennese critics, must have increased Chopin's self doubts. He chose a different piano for a second concert in the National Theatre, given by popular demand five days later. He changed the programme too, retaining the Concerto, but replacing the Fantasy by the *Rondo à la krakowiak* and ending with improvisations on popular Polish songs. Again there was critical acclaim, but again Mochnacki tempered his praise with a note of caution, arguing that Chopin was wasting his talents on the trivial improvisations which his audience craved. Chopin too had misgivings about this, admitting that 'to tell the truth that's not how I felt like doing things, but I knew that's what they wanted more than anything else'.[49] It was another indication that he was simply not in the conventional mould of the public pianist, that he could summon little enthusiasm for the trivial showmanship demanded by popular taste.

The publicity surrounding the two concerts also proved unpalatable. He strongly objected to a mediocre suite of dance pieces by Antoni Orlowski, based on themes from the Concerto, and also to a proposed portrait and poster to be lithographed by Brzezina and widely promoted. 'I don't want to read anything more about myself or listen to any of the gossip that's going on around me.'[50] The 'gossip' referred to here concerned disputes, by no means new in Warsaw's musical life, between the rival supporters of Elsner and Kurpiński. But Chopin found himself caught up in the argument, and the ensuing embarrassment and humiliation strengthened his conviction that the public stage was not for him. He was happy to appear at the 'benefits' of other artists, as on 8 July when he played the Op. 2 Variations, now published and available in Warsaw, at a benefit given by the singer Barbara Meier. He was also at ease in the salons, and wrote with enthusiasm about his part in a later performance (September) of Spohr's Piano Quintet, Op. 52, a work which may well have left traces on his own compositions. But he resisted the clamour for a third public concert, confessing to Tytus Wojciechowski that he went through hell for several days before such concerts. If we are to believe Liszt, Chopin later told him that 'the crowd intimidates me and I feel asphyxiated by its eager breath, paralysed by its inquisitive stare, silenced by its alien faces'.[51]

[49] *KFC*, vol. 1, p. 116.   [50] Ibid., p. 121.
[51] Franz Liszt, *F. Chopin* (Paris, 1852), p. 119.

During the final months in Warsaw there were clear indications that Chopin's disenchantment with the public concert would very soon be translated into a change in compositional aesthetic. But this was not accomplished overnight, and the major works of the period continued to accept the conventions of post-classical concert music. He was principally occupied with another concerto (Op. 11), this time on a much grander scale, and he also began a fourth concert piece for piano and orchestra, the *Grande Polonaise*, Op. 22. Chopin immersed himself totally in the world of the new concerto, struggling through the summer to complete it, and as his departure from Poland grew imminent, he succumbed to the mounting pressure to give the work at another public concert in the National Theatre. As before, he tried it out at several semi-public rehearsals in the family salon, before submitting it to the public on 11 October in a programme which included arias by Soliva and Rossini as well as the Op. 13 Fantasy. It is difficult to account for the silence of the press on this occasion, though political instability may have been a factor. Chopin did, after all, keep company with men who would very soon participate in leading roles in the November uprising. The performance was conceived as a farewell concert, and it was three weeks later that Chopin finally left Poland.

For most of the year he had talked about leaving, though he was characteristically indecisive about setting a date. Plans for a European tour dated right back to the late summer of 1829, shortly after his return from Vienna. On 3 October he wrote to Tytus of his intention to study abroad, travelling to Italy by way of Vienna and then moving on to Paris, 'though all this might change'.[52] He grew increasingly restive as the year dragged on. 'You cannot imagine how much I lack something in Warsaw now', he confided to Tytus. What he lacked mainly was Tytus's company, since his friend had left for his estate at Poturzyn on the completion of his university studies, but the remark also referred to Chopin's growing dissatisfaction with the musical life of the city. He did admittedly have access to a good supply of printed music at Brzezina's shop, which imported the most recent music from Vienna and Leipzig and kept an extensive catalogue. Like many such retailers, Brzezina's was as much salon as shop, and Chopin spent much of his time there browsing through new publications and playing them on one of the several pianos provided by the establishment.

Live music was another matter. Aside from the two brief trips abroad, Chopin's passionate love of opera and singing was nourished almost entirely by the productions at the National Theatre, and these no doubt had their limitations. Concerts, too, were intermittent and of variable quality. Over the years Chopin had the opportunity to hear some fine performers, including Maria Szymanowska, Hummel, and Paganini, but

---

[52] *KFC*, vol. 1, p. 109.

such occasions were few and far between. There were some worthwhile events during the winter of 1829/30, notably performances of chamber works by Hummel and Sophr at Kessler's soirées, and also a Piano Trio by Beethoven ('I haven't heard anything so great for a long time'), but this was not enough to brighten a dreary season. Things improved in May and June, since a number of concerts were organized to celebrate the Tsar's visit for the new session of the Sejm (Parliament). Chopin met all the visiting artists, including the Prussian king's pianist Sigismund Worlitzer, the French pianist Anne Caroline de Belleville and, above all, the singer Henrietta Sontag. Even so, it was increasingly obvious that Warsaw could no longer satisfy his hunger for music, and he felt acutely the need to widen his experience at all costs.

His discontent was fuelled by growing emotional insecurities. Several of Chopin's early letters refer in a youthful way to feminine attractions, but the first hint of anything more earnest comes in a letter of 3 October 1829, where he confessed to Tytus that 'I have my own ideal which I have been faithfully serving for half a year now without talking of it; I dream of it, the adagio of my concerto [Op. 21] was a souvenir of it, and this morning it inspired the little waltz I am sending you [Op. 70 No. 3]'.[53] The reference was to a young singing pupil of Soliva called Konstancja Gładkowska. This 'ideal' did not prevent Chopin writing from Antonin about the attractions of the Radziwiłł sisters, nor commenting on the pretty young lady with whom he danced a mazurka on the return journey to Warsaw. Nor did it hold in check his glowing reports on the beauty as well as the singing of Henrietta Sontag. 'You cannot imagine how much pleasure I have had from a closer acquaintance—in her room, on the sofa—with this "messenger from heaven" as some of the local worthies call her.'[54] Yet the feeling for Konstancja was no doubt sincere enough, and it served as a focus for Chopin's growing restlessness throughout the year. It was apparently undeclared, though it is unlikely that it would have remained unnoticed by its recipient, despite her later disclaimers.

It seems that at this stage, and perhaps also later, Chopin found it easier to communicate emotionally with men than with women. Before his death in 1828, Jan Białobłocki had served as a confidant, but that role was very quickly taken over by Tytus Woyciechowski, who was himself a competent pianist and whose musical judgement was clearly respected by Chopin. While he craved Konstancja from afar, Chopin poured out his heart to Tytus. 'It is dreadful when something weighs on your mind, not to have a soul to unburden yourself to. You know what I mean. I tell my piano the things I used to tell you.'[55] Tytus was altogether a stronger personality than Chopin, much more practical and decisive, and it was easy for the young composer to become dependent on him.

[53] Ibid., p. 107.   [54] Ibid., pp. 126–7.   [55] Ibid., p. 108.

Following his return to Poturzyń, where he managed the family estate with considerable business flair, there was an extensive correspondence, of which only Chopin's letters have survived. In these letters Chopin emerges as emotionally fragile and indecisive, constantly in need of affection and reassurance. His anguished references to Konstancja may be interpreted as the musings of adolescence, but to some extent they also speak of the future. As a twenty-year-old, Chopin already had something of a dual personality, refined and aloof in 'society', vulnerable and insecure with his intimates. It is easy to recognize in these youthful letters the jealousies and paranoia of which George Sand would later complain.

In mid July there was a visit to the Woyciechowski home in Poturzyń. It was a successful holiday and put some heart into a thoroughly depressed Chopin. In the midst of the restful countryside he had at last an opportunity to talk to Tytus in person, and also to hear some Polish and Ukrainian folksongs. A few weeks later he wrote nostalgically: 'I have a kind of longing for your fields—I constantly think of the birch under your windows.'[56] Among other things Tytus strengthened his resolve to take the plunge and travel abroad for a year or two. No doubt the two also spoke of Konstancja. In any case Chopin broke off the holiday to return to Warsaw when he heard about her imminent debut in the title role of Paër's *Agnese* on 24 July. The critics had mixed views, but Chopin was loyal and wrote to Tytus with enthusiasm. 'Gładkowska leaves nothing to be desired.'[57]

From Warsaw he went with his family on their annual holiday to Żelazowa Wola, his last visit to the village of his birth, but his thoughts were now of more ambitious travel ('two months in Vienna, and then to Italy, even if it means spending the winter in Milan'.[58] By late September he had applied for his passport for Austria, but he continued to postpone the date of his departure. It is obvious from the tone of his letters in these final months that he was in emotional turmoil, anxious to explore the new, yet frightened to leave the familiar. He would miss his family and he would miss Gładkowska, who sang at his farewell concert and wrote two quatrains in his album. The second ended with a couplet, in the conventional manner of such farewells, but doubtless imbued by Chopin with great significance: 'Foreigners can better reward and appreciate you,/But they cannot love you more than we.'

There were other obstacles to his departure. Towards the end of the summer news of the fall of the Bourbon monarchy reached Warsaw. There was an atmosphere of expectancy in the city, as rumours spread that Nicholas I would shortly invade France, now regarded again as a symbol of liberty and progress. As Chopin's friend Mochnacki put it: 'In the end all Warsaw spoke only of revolution.'[59] Despite the censorship,

---

[56] *KFC*, vol. 1, p. 130.   [57] Ibid., p. 130.   [58] Ibid., p. 136.
[59] Mochnacki wrote the definitive nineteenth-century study of the rising: *Powstanie narodu polskiego w r. 1830 i 1831* (Paris, 1834).

the wider political situation was fairly well known in Warsaw. In one letter to Tytus, Chopin referred to the growing unrest throughout the German Confederation, including Dresden and Berlin, and went on to say that his father was very uneasy about his travelling at such a time. Chopin was not himself politically minded, but he counted among his friends activists such as Zaleski, Witwicki, and Mochnacki, all of whom frequented the Kapiuszek (Cendrillon) and the Dziurka (Keyhole) cafés. It is unlikely that he would have remained ignorant of the plots that were being hatched in these circles, and his sympathies would have been with them. Indeed it is quite possible that for a time at least he was associated with them in the eyes of the authorities, and some biographers have suggested that for that reason Mikołaj came to feel in the end that a speedy departure would be best. The journey was booked, cancelled and then re-booked. The final impetus came from Tytus, who confirmed that he could meet Chopin at Kalisz, near the Polish–Austrian border, and travel with him to Vienna.

On 1 November there was a small farewell dinner in Chopin's honour, attended by his father, Adalbert Żywny, Dominik Magnuszewski, and Julian Fontana, and the following morning he said his painful farewells to family and friends. But a great pleasure awaited him on the outskirts of Warsaw. Elsner and a group of friends and students stopped the coach and performed a cantata for male voices and guitar specially composed by the old man for the occasion to words by Ludwik Dmuszewski. The text, including the line 'While you are away, may your heart remain ever with us', appeared the following day in the *Kurier Warszawski*. In Kalisz Tytus boarded the coach as arranged and Chopin left Poland for good.

2

'A virtuoso in his own right'

The music Chopin composed during these years in Warsaw ranges from trivial childhood efforts to mature compositions widely regarded today as among the most significant achievements of the Romantic era. In examining this music collectively we need to bear in mind that the genres and styles of early nineteenth-century music were shaped to a marked degree by the characteristic functions associated with specific venues. Three relatively distinct styles might act as a framework for such an examination. First there is post-classical concert music—'brilliant' polonaises, fantasies, variation sets, and independent rondos—composed above all for display and geared either to the salon concert or to the demands of the competitive, commercial world of the public benefit concert. Secondly there is the much simpler style associated with amateur music-making in the bourgeois and aristocratic drawing-room, including easy dance pieces, songs *am volkston*, and short character pieces. And finally there is the so-called 'Viennese' classical style of the sonata and the cyclic chamber work, regarded even at the time as privileged and directed more to like-minded fellow musicians than to the wider public. These are by no means watertight categories, but they serve at the very least as useful reference points.

The surviving works from Chopin's pre-High School, or Conservatory, years (1817–25) are predominantly in the genres associated with virtuoso piano music. They include four polonaises, a variation set, and a rondo. The keyboard polonaise was securely established as an independent genre by the late eighteenth century and it reigned supreme in the salons of early nineteenth-century Warsaw. It is not in the least surprising, then, that the young Chopin should have turned to this genre for his earliest attempts at composition. There is, however, a clear distinction in style and quality between the first two surviving polonaises, written in his eighth year, and the two later pieces. The G minor and B flat major (KK 889 and KK 1182–3) are in the 'galant' manner characteristic of many keyboard polonaises by late eighteenth- and early nineteenth-century Polish composers, notably those of Michał Kleofas Ogiński (1765–1833). We may wonder at their technical assurance, given the composer's tender years, but we are unlikely to make special claims for them in any other respect. They are no doubt similar in idiom to the many other short pieces composed during these childhood years but no longer extant.

The two later polonaises are an altogether different matter. The first of them, in A flat major (KK 1184), can be reliably dated from Chopin's autograph. Composed in April 1821, when he was eleven, it marked a significant advance in technique on the earlier pieces, registering the influence of the so-called 'brilliant style' associated with pianist-composers such as Hummel and Weber.[1] The G sharp minor Polonaise (KK 1185–7) has not been precisely dated, but it was probably composed two or three years later, and its right-hand virtuosity is both more exuberant and more technically assured than that of the other work. Taken together, the two polonaises indicate that in a rather short time the young Chopin managed to assimilate many of the standard ingredients of bravura pianism. Essentially they are essays in virtuoso figuration, complete with hand crossings, wide leaps, trills and double trills, arpeggio-based passagework, various species of *Rollfiguren* and other stock-in-trade fingerprints of the pianist–composer. And in keeping with the style, this virtuoso figuration was expressed above all through techniques of harmonic embellishment and melodic ornamentation.

Like other composers of post-classical concert music, Chopin allowed such techniques to generate considerable foreground complexity. The harmonic progressions and melodic shapes are relatively simple and classically conceived, but they are embellished by a finely-wrought tracery of decorative figuration, often so elaborate that the music can seem top-heavy, overloaded with detail. This separation of structure and ornament—especially clear in the G sharp minor Polonaise—is to some extent a general feature of the brilliant style, and it argues a close link with the widespread contemporary practice of improvisation, where relatively simple structures would support ornamental figures of conventional cut, easily accessed in spontaneous invention.

This is even more explicit in the Variations on a German National Air (*Der Schweizerbub*) KK 925–7), composed in 1824 'in a few quarter hours',[2] and one of the pieces later sent to Haslinger on the recommendation of Elsner (the publisher added performance markings to Chopin's autograph). The similarity between this piece and a set of variations on

---

[1] The term 'brilliant style', originally used to describe a manner of playing, was applied by late-eighteenth-century theorists to a particular component of compositional practice. The term was later used to describe an entire repertory which had a sharply defined and widely recognized individual profile in contemporary perceptions. The concertos and bravura solos of Daniel Steibelt were among the main progenitors of the style, and it was given its finest expression in the 'public' works of Hummel, Weber, and early Chopin.

[2] According to Oskar Kolberg, as reported by M. A. Szulc in *Fryderyk Chopin i utwory jego muzyczne* (Poznań, 1873).

the same theme by J. F. Marcks was pointed out by Hieronim Feicht,[3] but in some ways these parallels are symptomatic of a much more general conformity in the *airs variés* of the brilliant style. The melodic ornamentation of the variations follows models which were conventional within the style, appearing again and again in sets by Field, Kalkbrenner, Pixis, Klengel, and countless other composers of popular concert music. No less characteristic is the use of 'freer' material in the *minore* variation and the waltz-finale, and above all in the introduction, where the link with improvisation is at its most blatant. Indeed with its rapid changes of texture and mood, Chopin's introduction, like many of Hummel's, might almost be regarded as a 'recorded example of his art of improvisation'.[4]

In the bravura figuration of all three pieces one senses the exhilaration of discovery, as a young composer explores the full potential of his chosen medium. That exploration was certainly facilitated by the relatively simple and standardized formal designs associated with both the polonaise and the classical variation set. There is very little evidence here that Chopin regarded the sectional, block-like construction encouraged by these genres as a problem to be overcome or even mitigated. Nor do we find such evidence in the Rondo, Op. 1. This was Chopin's first attempt at another genre closely associated with popular pianism, and one defined as much by character and tempo as by formal design. Chopin's piece is suitably tuneful and lively, alternating a sprightly rondo theme with virtuoso figurations which function not as melodic ornamentation (as in the Variations) but as harmonic elaboration. Characteristically a framework of classical harmonies is overlaid or 'filled in' by intricately designed passagework based on chromatic sequences. Formally Op. 1 is disjunct, a sequence of themes and figurations 'connected' by transitions, whose contrived nature led at least one commentator to conclude that they were composed after the thematic material was already in place.[5]

It may be worth reflecting even at this stage on the relationship between such early pieces and the great works of Chopin's maturity. It goes without saying that the later works easily transcend the limitations of the post-classical brilliant style. Yet in important ways they can still be traced back to that style. These origins are of some importance, moreover, in any attempt to 'place' Chopin's music in relation to contemporaries such as Liszt, Schumann, and Mendelssohn. The virtuoso figuration of the early works, functioning as either harmonic embellishment or melodic ornamentation, remained a central plank of his later musical style, though as that style took shape the gap between structure

[3] Hieronim Feicht, 'Dwa cykle wariacyjne na temat "Der Schweizerbub" F. Chopina i J. F. Marcksa', in *F. F. Chopin*, ed. Zofia Lissa (Warsaw, 1960), pp. 56–78.

[4] R. Davis, 'The Music of Hummel', *Music Review* (1965), vol. 25, p. 171.

[5] Józef Chomiński, *Fryderyk Chopin*, tr. Bolko Schweinitz (Leipzig, 1980), p. 42.

and ornament gradually narrowed in both the harmonic and the melodic spheres. Equally the alternation of relatively discrete contrasted sections, so characteristic of the youthful pieces, remained at the very least a formal starting-point for many later works, still discernible despite Chopin's strategies of concealment and his subordination of formal contrasts to larger, all-embracing tonal spans.

Throughout the Warsaw period Chopin remained faithful to the three bravura genres of the pre-High School years, and it is fitting that he should have turned to them for the major concert pieces for piano and orchestra (Opp. 2, 13, 14, and 22), composed (or, in the case of Op. 22, begun) during his late Warsaw years. We may use these three genres, then, to follow the composer's progress from apprenticeship to the public concert platform. His continued involvement with variation form is the least easy to trace, given the uncertain attribution of the two solo piano works. There are few, if any, tell-tale traces of a unique Chopin signature in the music of either the four-hand *Variations in D major on a Theme of Moore* (KK 1190–2), tentatively dated 1826,[6] or in the *Souvenir de Paganini* (KK 1203), dated 1829 on the basis of Paganini's Warsaw concerts. But much the same could be said of the *Schweizerbub* Variations or indeed of several other Warsaw-period works. The sparkling virtuosity of such pieces actually courts anonymity. It directs attention to the performer and not to the composer.

In the absence of adequate documentation we cannot be sure about the authorship of either the Moore or the Paganini Variations. The former has the greater claim on Chopin, since Ludwika included it in her list of incipits, but the case is not proven.[7] On the other hand, the *Souvenir de Paganini* is musically the more interesting piece, and some authorities (notably Józef Chomiński) have argued for it on stylistic grounds. Again there is no certainty. Happily no such doubts attach to the orchestral *Là ci darem* Variations, Op. 2, nor to its companion the *Fantasy on Polish Airs*, Op. 13. Chopin wrote the Mozart Variations in 1827 at the end of his second year at the High School of Music. It represents a landmark in his development, not only as his first approach to the orchestra (and therefore to the public concert platform), but also as a definable stage in his mastery of compositional *métier* in general, and piano figuration in particular.

The general conception and design of the work is entirely in line with bravura variation sets for piano and orchestra by other pianist-composers of the time, and commentators have had no difficulty in

[6] See Józef Chomiński and Dalila Turło, *Katalog dzieł Fryderyka Chopina* (Cracow, 1990), pp. 232–5.

[7] Ludwika Jędrzejewicz compiled a list of incipits of unpublished compositions at the suggestion of Jane Stirling. It is unlikely that this was made available to Julian Fontana, when he prepared the posthumous edition of Chopin (Opp. 66–74). It is worth noting that Chopin referred to Ferdinand Ries's set of variations on a theme of Moore in a letter to his family from Szafarnia. *Korespondencja Fryderyka Chopina*, vol. 1, pp. 37–8.

pinpointing detailed correspondences between individual variations and specific textures found in Hummel, Field, and Weber in particular. Indeed this conformity is such that the design of the work fits remarkably closely the 'formula' for ornamental variation sets given by Castil-Blaze in his *Dictionnaire de musique moderne* of 1825, right down to the final *tempo di polacca*.[8] Characteristically there is an unobtrusive (even dispensable) orchestral backcloth designed to set off the soloist, who in turn smothers a well-known tune in cascades of virtuosity. It is, in short a *pièce d'occasion*, carefully tailored to the demands of an audience seeking novelty and display.

For all that, there is an assurance about this work which sets it apart from practically all Chopin's earlier music. It is evident in the bravura of the second and fourth variations, in the quirky individuality of the *minore* variation, and even more in the impressive command of the whole gamut of piano figuration evidenced in the introduction and, in a different way, the finale. This command was undoubtedly acquired through constant playing and above all improvising, which for early nineteenth-century pianist-composers was not so far removed from composing. It is easy to see once more in this piece the connection with improvisation, especially in the introduction, with its capricious changes of texture and mood, its sparkling chord-based passagework and its graceful *fioriture*. Such figuration is rooted in conventional practice, of course, but already in this introduction it begins to cut loose from melodic and harmonic anchors, gaining something of an independent form-building character.

For all its improvisatory character, Op. 2 involved Chopin in much more careful thought and craftmanship than any earlier piece. We can see this not only from the meticulous care he took over the engraver's manuscript of the solo part, where performance markings are of the most detailed kind, but also from some evidence of earlier stages in the compositional process. This is the first work of Chopin where manuscript sources permit us a glimpse, albeit a restricted one, behind the finished product into the workshop. The engraver's manuscript reveals that there was an earlier version of the fourth variation, for instance, with an entirely different figuration, and also that there were earlier thoughts about the endings of the introduction and the first three variations (designed to allow an anacrustic opening to the orchestral ritornellos). In addition there is a surviving manuscript fragment of the fifth variation (with different performance markings) and an abandoned autograph of the full orchestral score.[9] This latter is of special interest, since

[8] F.-H.-J. Castil-Blaze, *Dictionnaire de musique moderne* (Paris, 1825), vol. 2, pp. 262–3.

[9] The fragment of Variation 5 is now in a private collection in Vienna (not in Paris, as reported in Krystyna Kobylańska, *Rękopisy utworów Chopina: Katalog* (Cracow, 1977), 2 vols., vol. 1, p. 38. The rejected autograph of the full score is in the Morgan Pierpont

it contains not only the rejected form of the fourth variation but also a quite different version of the opening of the work, together with some intriguing sketches for detailed passagework.

In contrast the so-called 'sketch' for the *Fantasy on Polish Airs*, Op. 13 (currently in a private collection in Geneva) amounts to little more than the orchestral opening in almost its final form.[10] The Fantasy as a whole is really a pot-pourri, and it was so described by Chopin. But criticism of its lack of unity (by Gerald Abraham and others) is hardly to the point.[11] Again this is a *pièce d'occasion*, a parade of three tunes and their variants designed to titillate by dressing familiar garb in fancy frills. And accepted on these modest terms, the work emerges as somewhat underrated in the literature, even if its points of interest lie more in the detail than in the whole. The introduction already comes close to the kind of orchestrally cushioned nocturne idiom we associate with the slow movements of the concertos, for instance, while the treatment of the second theme hints at a sound world soon to become familiar in Russian music. In general the orchestral writing is of greater interest here than in Op. 2. Given that such pieces would often be performed with a string quintet or indeed with no accompaniment at all, it is striking that several sections of Op. 13 allow the soloist to perform an accompanimental function.

Chopin's final essay in variation form (as opposed to variation technique) was a set of *Variations brillantes*, Op. 12 on a theme of Hérold, composed in Paris in 1832. The conception and execution of this piece is very much in line with the Warsaw pieces, underlining that for Chopin the genre was inseparably linked to the virtuoso style. And this was also true of his involvement with the independent rondo. Following Op. 1 he composed the *Rondo à la mazur*, Op. 5 in 1826–7, the Rondo, Op. 73 (later arranged for two pianos) in 1828, and the *Rondo à la krakowiak*, Op. 14 for piano and orchestra in the same year. And again there was one final essay in the genre (Op. 16), composed (almost certainly) in Paris in 1832 and belonging stylistically with the Warsaw-period music.

Of these, Opp. 73 and 16 come closest to a conventional bravura manner. The other two pieces are rather different in tone, a response no doubt to the influence of folk music. Chopin had already composed several independent mazurkas by the time he wrote the *Rondo à la mazur* (and he had certainly improvised many others). The distinctive modal characteristics of the mazurka, mainly the sharpened 'lydian' fourth, influenced both the melodic and the harmonic substance of the work, affecting, as John Rink argued, even the larger harmonic plan and

Library, New York. See Chomiński and Turło, *Katalog dzieł Fryderyka Chopina*, pp. 227–8.

[10] See Chomiński and Turło, *Katalog dzieł Fryderyka Chopina*, p. 94.

[11] Gerald Abraham, *Chopin's Musical Style* (London, 1939), p. 16.

voice-leading.[12] The folk dance model also resulted in a suppression of the more obviously virtuosic elements found in the earlier rondo. But in overall design Op. 5 follows fairly closely the pattern established by its predecessor, albeit relating themes and transitions a little more closely through the elaboration of a handful of short motives. Formally the two works are straightforward successions of relatively self-contained units.

The orchestral *Rondo à la krakowiak*, on the other hand, moves some way towards a more integral relationship between surface details and an underlying harmonic structure which spans the entire work. It is above all through the example of the Austrian theorist Heinrich Schenker that we are able to make analytically explicit such connections between different levels of musical structure. For many sensitive listeners the advance represented by the *Rondo à la krakowiak* (a work with which Chopin himself was particularly pleased) will simply be felt; there will be an intuitive sense of its more unified substance when compared with Opp. 1 and 5. Schenkerian insights allow us to probe these intuitions and ground them in theory. We can see, for instance, that there are parallelisms of harmony and motive between the different structural levels, so that individual formal units are subsumed by, or nested within, larger underlying progressions.[13]

Chopin's progress from 'formal' composition, based primarily on the juxtaposition of themes, to 'structural' composition, based on organically conceived tonal plans, cannot be charted in a simple chronological sequence. Like most composers, his formative development pursued an erratic course. It is not surprising, then, that a piece such as the *Rondo à la krakowiak* achieves a measure of tonal integration which several later works (including the Rondo, Op. 16) cannot match. The 'brilliant' polonaises of the Warsaw period further exemplify this uneven development. As a group they have really very little in common with the later 'heroic' polonaises composed in Paris, the only ones the composer himself chose to publish. In addition to the four youthful pieces, a further five solo polonaises were composed in Warsaw, together with the *Polonaise brillante*, Op. 3 for cello and piano and the *Grande Polonaise*, Op. 22 for piano and orchestra, which occupied him during his final months in Poland, though it was completed only after he left his homeland. The solo polonaises are the B flat minor (KK 1188–9), composed

---

[12] John Rink, 'The Evolution of Chopin's "Structural Style" and its Relation to Improvisation' (Diss., U. of Cambridge, 1989), p. 77.

[13] Schenker's work is founded on the premise that the masterpieces of tonal composition are based on a hierarchy of interdependent structural levels, ranging from the Fundamental Structure and the 'background' level (in which a simple harmonic progression (I–V–I) in the bass accompanies a contrapuntal linear descent in the treble, known as the Fundamental Line) to increasingly complex elaborations and 'prolongations' of this remote structure at 'middleground' and 'foreground' levels. Schenker's analyses are invariably presented as harmonic reductions designed to reveal the essential structural harmonies of a work.

in 1826 as a farewell tribute to Chopin's schoolfriend Wilhelm Kolberg, the three issued posthumously by Julian Fontana as Op. 71 (1827–8) and the G flat major (KK 1197–1200), composed either in 1829 or 1830.

The B flat minor 'Adieu' Polonaise survives in a copy by its dedicatee, Wilhelm Kolberg. It is a bravura piece, elaborately ornamented, but with a more distinctive melodic profile than the earlier polonaises, and also a closer integration of its ornamental foreground and its structural middleground.[14] An intriguing touch is the incorporation of the aria 'Au revoir' from Rossini's *La Gazza Ladra* into the trio, a common enough gesture in post-classical piano music, but one used sparingly by Chopin. The F minor Polonaise (Op. 71 No. 3) offers even clearer foretastes of the more characteristically expressive ornamental melody (where ornament is a natural outgrowth of melody) of Chopin's maturity, as well as subtle motivic connections between different structural layers. This may well have been the most popular of the early polonaises. It was much admired at Antonin during Chopin's 1829 visit, and it survives in several manuscript sources, including a presentation autograph on elegantly embossed paper with the inscription 'Stuttgard 1836' [*sic*].[15] This differs in some minor respects from the earlier autograph and also from a copy by Ludwika, no doubt because it was copied from memory some eight years after its composition. Such discrepancies provide an early instance of the textual confusion which abounds in the Chopin manuscript tradition.[16]

The D minor (Op. 71 No. 1), surviving in a copy by Chopin's father, is by comparison more conventionally virtuosic, reminiscent of the trio of the earlier G sharp minor in its trilled scalic theme, but hinting too at some of Chopin's mature polonaises in specific gestures, notably in the introduction and in the strumming chords which preface the trio (cf. Op. 53 bars 101–3). But it is the B flat major (Op. 71 No. 2) and G flat major (KK 1197–1200) which are the most ambitious of the early solo polonaises. Not only is there remarkable self-confidence in their handling of all the resources of bravura pianism. They also demonstrate considerable structural assurance, binding securely the often eccentric harmonic sequences and registral contrasts. Yet these pieces are still a long way from achieving the highly individual idiom which has become so closely associated with Chopin. It is that very individuality which most clearly marks his kinship with a romantic aesthetic, and by

[14] The terms 'foreground', 'middleground', and 'background' are used from time to time in this book in their Schenkerian sense. See note 13.

[15] Currently in the Archive of The Chopin Society in Warsaw. See Chomiński and Turło, *Dzieł Fryderyka Chopina: Katalog*, p. 173.

[16] Jeffrey Kallberg has argued convincingly that the endless variants in the manuscript and printed sources for Chopin's compositions reflect nothing so much as the essential fluidity of the very concept of the musical work for him and for his listeners. See 'Are Variants a Problem? "Composer's Intentions" in Editing Chopin', *Chopin Studies 3* (Warsaw, 1990), pp. 257–68.

comparison the early polonaises belong fairly and squarely to the world of post-classical concert music. This is no less true of the *Polonaise brillante* for cello and piano, written in Antonin for Prince Radziwiłł to play with his daughter. Chopin later added an introduction to this piece and it was published as Op. 3 and dedicated to the cellist Josef Merk.

The culmination of Chopin's early involvement with the polonaise was his *Grande Polonaise*, Op. 22 for piano and orchestra, begun in Warsaw in 1830 and completed a few months later in Vienna. This was the last of the four concert pieces for piano and orchestra, and it forms the high-water mark of his contribution to the brilliant style, taking over in a sense where the 'polacca' finale of Op. 2 had left off and demonstrating even greater command of the full resources of piano figuration. It forms an exhilarating coda to Chopin's fleeting involvement with the orchestra, and it comes over even today as an astonishing feat of bravura writing, paralleling in a way some of Liszt's more-or-less coeval experiments in virtuoso keyboard figuration.

Far removed from such public virtuosity is a group of simple songs and technically undemanding piano pieces composed by Chopin largely for domestic consumption during the Warsaw period. Of those traditionally attributed to Chopin, several are now considered of doubtful authenticity, including a *Contredanse* in G flat major and an E flat major Waltz. Others, such as the Funeral March in C minor, issued by Fontana as part of Op. 72 No. 2, and the three Écossaises, Op. 72 Nos. 3–5, are conventional contributions to popular genre pieces of the day. Incidentally, the date of composition has not been reliably determined for any of the five pieces gathered by Fontana as Op. 72 (the E minor Nocturne was published as Op. 72 No. 1).

Of more intrinsic interest are the early waltzes and mazurkas. The two genres remain distinct even at this early stage of Chopin's development, though they are rather less clearly differentiated than in later years. Unlike the mazurkas, the Warsaw-period waltzes are notably different in tone from those the composer himself chose to publish. Five can be attributed with certainty to Chopin, all of them composed either in 1829 or 1830. They are the E major (KK 1207–8), A flat major (KK 1209–11), E minor (KK 1213–14), B minor, Op. 69 No. 2 and D flat major, Op. 70 No. 3, the last apparently inspired by Chopin's feelings for Konstancja Gładkowska.[17] Another Waltz in A minor (KK 1238–9), whose autograph bears neither dedication, date nor signature, may well also date from the Polish period.[18] For the most part these pieces are simpler in design than the mature waltzes, and they avoid virtuosic

[17] See his letter to Tytus of 3 October, 1829. *Korespondencja Fryderyka Chopina*, vol. 1, p. 107.

[18] This possibility is raised by Andrzej Koszewski in his edition *Fryderyk Chopin: Dwa zapomniane utwory* (Cracow, 1965), though more recent commentaries favour a much later date. See Jan Ekier, *Wstęp do wydania narodowego* (Cracow, 1974), p. 63; also Chomiński and Turło, *Dzieł Fryderyka Chopina*, p. 223.

embellishment or bravura figuration. Yet the basic distinction between the 'brilliant' and the 'lyric' waltz is already there in embryo, evidenced in the moto perpetuo arcs of the A flat major in contrast to the gently expressive lilt of the B minor. The E minor, composed at the end of the Warsaw period, is the most prophetic of these early pieces. With its introduction, repeated-note motive (compare Op. 34 No. 2) and bravura coda, it already enters the unmistakable terrain of the more familiar mature waltzes.

Of all Chopin genres, the mazurka is the one exhibiting the greatest continuity from early to late works. Statistically the nineteenth century witnessed a gradual decline in the prominence of the polonaise in Polish music, and a corresponding rise of the mazurka, which came to be regarded—largely through Chopin's example—as the most potent musical symbol of Poland. Unlike the polonaise, which was already a recognized Polish dance in the seventeenth century, the mazurka was established as a national dance (absorbing and synthesizing elements of older regional dances such as the *mazur, oberek,* and *kujawiak*) only at the turn of the nineteenth century. Chopin was not, of course, without precedents when he wrote and improvised keyboard mazurkas in his teenage years.[19] But from a very early stage he made the genre his own, and through it he recorded some of his most individual and private musical thoughts.

Among the earliest known mazurkas are two said to have been improvised in 1825 at the home of Dr Samuel Linde, and later committed to paper at the suggestion of Wilhelm Kolberg.[20] Both mazurkas—the B flat major (KK 891–5) and G Major (KK 896–900)—exist in two separate versions, of which the first versions were published in 1826. The authenticity of a third 'improvised' Mazurka in D major, also existing in two versions of which the first was published in 1829, is rather more shaky, though stylistically the case is quite a strong one. Already in these youthful pieces, simple in texture and phraseology, the unmistakable character of the Chopin mazurka is discernible. It is suggested not only by distinctive patterns of rhythm and accentuation but by an unorthodox approach to part movement, as in some of the left-hand chording of the G major 'Kulawy' Mazurka, by characteristic chromatic alterations, as in the B flat major, and by unusual spacings, such as the high tessitura of the trio of the B flat major. In some ways the D major, with its sharpened lydian fourths and the drone accompaniments of its second version, is the most obviously folkoristic of the three.

Even more adventurous than these 'improvised' mazurkas is the A

[19] See Danuta Idaszak, 'Mazurek przed Chopinem', in *F. F. Chopin*, ed. Zofia Lissa (Warsaw, 1960), pp. 236–68.
[20] Reported by Oskar Kolberg. See Krystyna Kobylańska, *Rękopisy utworów Chopina: Katalog*, vol. 1, pp. 357–60 and 480–1. See also the discussion in the Paderewski edition (*Complete Works*, vol. 10, pp. 215–17).

minor, composed in 1827 and issued posthumously by Julian Fontana as Op. 68 No. 2. With its lydian fourth, bourdon fifth pedal (opening section of the trio), and harmonic curiosities (closing section of the trio), the piece is already in the stylistic domain of the mature mazurkas, and this is also true, at least partly, of the C major and F major, issued by Fontana respectively as Op. 68 Nos. 1 and 3. The chronology of these two pieces is by no means certain (most commentators opt for 1830), and there are further confusions of date over early versions, ascribed to the Warsaw period, of two later and better known mazurkas. The less likely of these attributions is a date of 1824 given by Wilhelm Kolberg to an early version of Op. 7 No. 4.[21] An early version of Op. 7 No. 2, copied from Emilia Elsner's album and first published in the 1902 Supplement to the Breitkopf & Härtel collected edition, has been more plausibly dated 1829, though again there is no certainty.

More than almost any composer of stature, Chopin has been associated with a single medium. Apart from the Cello Sonata, his works for forces other than the piano have seldom made significant inroads to the established repertory, and this includes the songs. In general Chopin's songs, like Mendelssohn's, are closer to eighteenth- than to nineteenth-century traditions. Even the best, and latest, of them (with one exception) remained largely untouched by the aesthetic of the Lied. Already in the Warsaw period he was in the habit of improvising and composing songs to the rhythm of national dances, following a tradition of romances and ballads popular in Polish music of the eighteenth and early nineteenth centuries.[22] Much of this earlier repertory deliberately cultivated the concept of a national style, and there was extensive debate—notably by Józef Elsner and Kazimierz Brodziński—not only about the significance of the folk dance rhythms but about appropriate ways of setting the Polish vernacular.[23] Chopin's songs relate rather closely to this indigenous tradition. Of the composed songs, five date from the Warsaw period. They are 'Precz z moich oczu' (Out of my sight), Op. 74 No. 6, whose first version can be dated (1827) from an autograph currently in the Chopin Society, Warsaw;[24] 'Życzenie' (The wish), Op. 74 No. 1, completed in 1829, though there are earlier sketches; 'Gdzie lubi' (What she likes), Op. 74 No. 5, also 1829;

[21] There is no doubt that Kolberg put the date there, but he was almost certainly in error. Stylistic and paper evidence argue against accepting this date.

[22] See Mieczysław Tomaszewski, 'Verbindungen zwischen den Chopinschen Liederwerken und dem polnischen popularen Volks- und Kunstlied', in *The Book of the First Musicological Congress Devoted to the Works of Frederick Chopin*, ed. Zofia Lissa (Warsaw, 1963), pp. 404–9.

[23] See, above all, Józef Elsner, *Rozprawa o metrycznosci i rytmicznosci języka polskiego* (Warsaw, 1818).

[24] This is M/1460 in the Archive of the Society. It is on the thick, blue-green paper characteristic of several Warsaw-period autographs, with the watermark identifying it as paper from Jan Rasch's mill near Płock.

'Hulanka' (Drinking song), Op. 74 No. 4, and 'Czary' (Spells) (KK 1204–6), both of 1830.

These songs rehearse familiar patriotic, supernatural, and romantic themes in settings of poetry by Chopin's friend Stefan Witwicki ('Życzenie', 'Gdzie lubi', 'Hulanka', 'Czary'), and by Adam Mickiewicz ('Precz z moich oczu'). 'Hulanka' and 'Życzenie' are strophic dance songs (*oberek* and *mazur* respectively), complete with bourdon and, in the case of 'Hulanka', lydian fourth. 'Gdzie lubi' is a through-composed ternary setting with a piano postlude, while 'Czary' is a strophic 'dumka' or rustic elegy. The best of them is the Mickiewicz setting 'Precz z moich oczu', where the finer poetry seems to have evoked from Chopin an intensity of expression and a harmonic richness conspicuously lacking in the others. The manuscript history of the early songs is too complex to explore in detail here. In addition to sketch material, there are multiple versions of some of the songs, not least because all five were copied by Ludwika for Maria Wodzińska's album and several were entered by Chopin into Emila Elsner's album. An examination of these sources is revealing, for it suggests, *inter alia*, that Chopin's revisions may well have taken some account of the example and theories of his teacher Józef Elsner, who had decided views on the proper accentuation of the Polish language and who published a major treatise on the subject.[25]

Elsner's influence on Chopin extended well beyond the songs, of course, and it will be considered later in this chapter, but it is worth pointing out here that several major works from the Warsaw period were a direct result of his teaching programmes at the High School of Music, including the *Rondo à la mazur* (a model favoured by Elsner) and his first attempt at a piano sonata. Elsner's usual practice was to start his composition students on polonaises, marches, variations, and rondos, before introducing them to sonatas at the end of the first year of study.[26] Chopin's early development conforms to this pattern, at least to a degree. His first year at the High School saw the composition of at least one variation set, a rondo and several polonaises, and only at the end of the year did he tackle his first sonata, the C minor, Op. 4. The Sonata was dedicated, appropriately enough, to Elsner, whose acceptance of the dedication is on the title page of the engraver's manuscript (where the work is incorrectly cited as Op. 3).

The Sonata was completed in 1828, and it was one of the works sent to Haslinger in 1829, along with the *Schweizerbub* and *Là ci darem* Variations. Clearly Elsner thought highly of it, then, and with some reason. It may lack the sparkle of the 'brilliant' rondos and polonaises, and the individuality of the mazurkas, but it is carefully crafted and leaves

[25] See note 23.
[26] See Igor Belza, 'Szkoła Elsnera i jej rola w kształtowaniu polskiej kultury muzyczny', in *Portrety romantyków* (Warsaw, 1974), pp. 13–34.

us in no doubt of Chopin's capacity to assume at will the earnest manner of the classical composer, with a capacity for rigorous motive working and closely integrated textures. It may at times sound stilted,
betraying its student origins a little too clearly, but at least there can be
no doubt that the student concerned was an exceptionally gifted one. All
the same it is easy to see why this sonata has failed to stand up to sustained critical scrutiny. Chopin's natural leaning towards accompanied
melody is too obviously cramped by the demands of the genre, especially
in the first of the four movements. The attempts to achieve thematic
integration, both on a bar-by-bar level through closely interwoven imitative devices in all four movements, and on a larger scale through the
monothematic organization of the first (similar to that found in several
Elsner works), sound in the end all too self-conscious.[27]

At this stage in his development Chopin had no real understanding of
the principles of tonal contrast and synthesis at the heart of the classical sonata, though later in life he would find ways of adapting the sonata
principle to his own needs. If anything, the inner dynamic of this early
sonata is closer to Bach, whose music was already well known to
Chopin in his student days. That influence is apparent not only in the
imitative surface of the music, but in its allegiance to an essentially unitary conception of musical form, even in the sonata-form first movement. This is apparent in the monothematic substance of the movement,
and also in its unorthodox tonal argument, complete with monotonal
exposition. Indeed the 'fit' between the underlying tonal scheme and the
classical design of the movement is far from comfortable. Only in the
more relaxed third and more conventionally 'brilliant' fourth movements of the sonata do we sense that Chopin is at ease with his musical
materials.

Another work in which Chopin engaged with the traditional four-
movement cycle is the Piano Trio, Op. 8, begun in the summer of 1828
and completed in early 1829. It was dedicated to Prince Radziwiłł and
performed at Antonin with the Prince and his daughter during Chopin's
stay there in October 1829. There have been committed apologists for
this work,[28] and there are indeed fresh and beautiful moments in all four
movements, but a glance at the score is enough to reveal Chopin's lack
of experience with the medium. He had little grasp of that concertante
interplay of forces which makes for good chamber music. Moreover the
string writing is not only inept itself,[29] but somehow contrives to inhibit
Chopin's usual command of piano textures. The autograph manuscript,

[27] For a discussion of monothematicism in Elsner and Chopin see Alina Nowak-
Romanowicz, 'Józef Elsner and Chopin', in *Chopin in Silesia* (Katowice, 1974), pp. 3–5.
[28] Andrzej Chodkowski, 'Kilka uwag o *Trio* fortepianowym Fryderyka Chopina', in
Rocznik Chopinowski, 14 (Warsaw, 1982), pp. 13–20.
[29] Chopin was aware of the problem and considered rescoring the work for viola rather
than violin.

written on the thick blue-green paper characteristic of other autographs from the later Warsaw years, contains several 'first thoughts' (bars 67–8 of the first movement, for instance) where the composer seems to have been anxious to exploit the medium more fully, but they are quickly rejected in favour of safer, more conventional figurations.

Like the Sonata, the Piano Trio has a distinctly unorthodox tonal scheme, at least in its first movement. Again there is a monotonal exposition, and this time the second group in the reprise modulates to the dominant minor in a curious reversal of the usual classical procedure. Again this might be viewed as further evidence that Chopin had yet to arrive at a full understanding of sonata form, and this is undoubtedly part of the story. But it is worth noting that in the first movements of the two major works of the late Warsaw period—the piano concertos—the tonal schemes deviate from conventional procedures in very similar ways, raising the possibility that Chopin was already reaching, however tentatively, towards a personal adaptation of the most powerful of all the classical formal archetypes.

The two piano concertos, completed during Chopin's final year in Warsaw, belong in general style and layout to the genre of the early nineteenth-century 'brilliant' concerto. In other words, they are closer to concertos by Hummel, Kalkbrenner, Field, and Moscheles than to those of Beethoven, Mendelssohn, or Schumann. Chopin was not short of formal and stylistic models when he set about the composition of the F minor Concerto, Op. 21, the first of the two to be written. But it was Hummel above all who paved the way. Like other pianist-composers of his generation, Hummel developed the Mozartian concerto in the direction of greater virtuosity and a more pronounced focus on the soloist. And this was also Chopin's way. His F minor Concerto is in direct succession from Hummel, and it is worth pointing out that he was happy to play it as a solo, in accordance with a common practice of the day.

Historically, the 'brilliant' concerto of the early nineteenth century sharpened the contrast between the lyrical and the figurative elements of the Mozart concerto. As bravura material became more virtuosic, compensatory song passages became more extended and more obviously lyrical in character. Chopin's Concerto is conformant in that a clear duality of melody and figuration in each tonal region underlies its formal organization. In the first solo (following the orchestral prelude), for instance, both principal themes are followed by sections of bravura figuration, defining in succession the tonic region F minor and its relative major A flat. And the same song-figuration sequence underlies the second solo (the 'development' in sonata-form terminology), which follows the second ritornello. In each case the melody is squared off sharply against the passagework, with a good deal of internal repetition and clearly defined formal divisions. The heart of this movement, then, is melody (subject to decoration and variation) and bravura figuration—poetry and

47

display—and, like the first movements of other 'brilliant' concertos, it tends to highlight these qualities at the expense of Mozart's delicate balance between a ritornello-concertante principle and a developmental-symphonic principle.

Yet in other ways—notably in the procession of motives in the opening prelude, carefully balancing contrasted yet related elements within its apparently seamless flow, this first movement actually *recovers* something of an original Mozartian model. Schumann went so far as to claim that 'if a genius such as Mozart were to appear today, he would write Chopin concertos rather than Mozart ones'.[30] The movement mediates in a sense between the classical and the post-classical, between Mozart and the brilliant style. And this is also true of the slow movement, inspired, according to Chopin in a letter to Tytus Woyciechowski, by his adolescent feelings for Konstancja Gładkowska. Here the delicately drawn ornamental melody owes something to Mozart directly, as well as something to Mozart by way of Hummel. The more recent debt is, of course, the more obvious. It is not difficult to trace a stylistic ancestry (Field as well as Hummel) for the melodic style of the outer sections, just as we can identify Moscheles in the impassioned recitative of the middle section. But this is scarcely to the point. As Gerald Abraham observed, this is really Chopin's first 'nocturne',[31] and it is one of the earliest complete movements in his output which is stamped unmistakably with his personality. Here Chopin's ornamental melody reaches full maturity, and it is the more effective for the comparative simplicity of its harmonic and textural settings.

Through its underlying dance rhythm (the third theme in particular is a *mazur*) and its characteristic popular or rustic episode, the rondo-finale falls into step behind a long tradition of concerto finales, from J. C. Bach through to the brilliant concertos of Hummel and Weber. Such associations are strengthened by eccentricities of scoring which relate the movement specifically to moments in the concertos of Chopin's immediate forerunners, the col legno strings suggesting Hummel's A minor and the *cor de signal* the finale of Weber's second Concerto. As in the slow movement, the formal framework and detailed gestures of Chopin's finale are conventional within the style, but the quality of the music reaches beyond that style in a manner not entirely achieved by the independent rondos of the Warsaw period. Already this is the voice of maturity.

The E minor Concerto, Op. 11, despite its conventional numbering, was composed after the F minor. The slow movement and *krakowiak*-finale are similar in design (though larger in dimensions) to the respective movements of the earlier work. But the first movement of the E

---

[30] Robert Schumann, *Gesammelte Schriften über Musik und Musiker* (Wiesbaden, 1985; original ed. 1854), vol. 1, p. 266.
[31] Gerald Abraham, *Chopin's Musical Style*, p. 34.

minor marks it out as a more ambitious work, a 'grand' concerto. This is already clear from the extended orchestral prelude which introduces the broad, self-contained themes of the work with an impressive symphonic sweep, truly *maestoso*. As in the F minor Concerto, the first solo again alternates sustained melody and bravura figuration, but the second solo breathes a fresher air, unique to Chopin in its elaboration of a ruminative, nocturne-like melody. Much of the beauty of this melody is due to its tonal setting of C major. Since the second subject appears in the tonic major both in the prelude and in the first solo, relief from the tonic region is delayed until this point, investing the C major of the second solo with special significance.

It is striking that here again, as in the Sonata and Piano Trio, the entire exposition (in this case double exposition) is monotonal. And once more the tonal practice of the reprise flies in the face of classical orthodoxy in that the second subject appears in the relative major. Tovey described this tonal scheme as 'suicidal', and it is true that it is no more convincing here than in the earlier works. But it is pertinent to ask why Chopin engaged in these tonal experiments. What they all have in common is a tendency to transfer the weight of tonal activity from the early to the later stages of a work, so that the reprise, far from synthesizing earlier contrasts, actually generates new tonal tensions. The experiments were by no means successful, but they already point to an important dimension of Chopin's later appropriation of the sonata-form archetype, his preference for end-weighted structures in which the reprise functions as apotheosis rather than synthesis.

The two piano concertos are the first major works of Chopin to have an established place in the repertory. Nor is this surprising. There is a quantum leap in assurance between earlier 'brilliant' works, such as the *Là ci darem* Variations, and the concertos. The two works have of course been censured on several grounds, most notably the inadequacy of their scoring and the insecurity of their tonal and formal organization. This censure is not entirely misplaced, but there are, at the very least, mitigating factors. Criticism of the scoring often fails to acknowledge the generic distinctiveness of the post-classical brilliant concerto as opposed to the classical or early-romantic concerto. In a context where pianist-composers would commonly perform their concertos with just a string quintet as accompaniment, or even as solos, elaborate scoring was scarcely appropriate.

Criticism of the tonal and formal organization is less easy to answer. The truth is that Chopin was already straining beyond the framework of the conventional brilliant concerto in these works, and his acceptance of at least the main pillars of that framework can seem at times oddly anachronistic. On one level the two concertos are the twin pinnacles of the brilliant style, and the apotheosis of Chopin's achievement as a virtuoso pianist-composer. But on another level they are admirable precisely for those features which are irrelevant to, or even at odds with, the conventions of the genre. We remember the concertos less for their formal properties than for the beauties of their individual moments, for particular felicities of melody, harmony, and texture which we identify retrospectively as Chopinesque, and which would later find much more congenial generic and formal settings. Indeed they were already finding such settings in a handful of miniatures dating from the end of the Warsaw period.

Four of the familiar Chopin genres were essentially in place, and in something like their mature formulation, before he left Warsaw. They are the waltz, mazurka, nocturne, and étude. The E minor Waltz, for instance, is closer in manner to Opp. 18 and 34 than to the earlier Warsaw waltzes. Equally the C major and F major Mazurkas, Op. 68 Nos. 1 and 3 are already close to the characteristic soundworld of the Op. 6 and Op. 7 Mazurkas, the first sets which the composer himself chose to publish. Even more significant are three works, the E minor Nocturne, Op. 72 No. 1, whose date of composition has not been precisely determined, and the first two of the *Douze Études*, Op. 10, composed during the final year in Warsaw. With these three pieces Chopin's music came fully of age, and it is significant that he wrote them while still in Poland.

The E minor Nocturne was given the date 1827 by Julian Fontana, who published it posthumously, but there is no reason to grant Fontana's date any special privilege (he was notoriously unreliable on such matters), and on stylistic grounds a slightly later date, as argued by Jan Ekier, seems more plausible.[32] Either way, it stands at the head of Chopin's long line of nocturnes, both technically and in the particular affective qualities it achieves. Many of the gestures associated with the characteristic Chopin nocturne appear here for the first time. Admittedly they build upon an idiom which was already well established elsewhere, and not only in works by Field. But that idiom was ultimately transformed, as a vocally inspired ornamentation, including characteristic *fioriture*, was drawn increasingly into the orbit of melodic substance, creating a single continuously unfolding line of immense subtlety and sophistication. With the E minor Nocturne the development of Chopin's melodic style reached a determinate stage.

I have already referred to Chopin's letters to Woyciechowski, where he discusses the composition of his 'exercises'.[33] It is often assumed that these were Op. 10 Nos. 8–11, but there is not a shred of evidence to support the 1829 date assigned to these four pieces by Maurice Brown and sanctioned by endless repetition in the literature.[34] On the other hand

[32] Jan Ekier, *Wstęp do wydania narodowego*, p. 62.   [33] See chapter 1, note 47.
[34] M. J. E. Brown, *Chopin: An Index of his Works in Chronological Order* (London and New York, 1972); original edn. 1960), pp. 42–3.

there is a manuscript copy of Op. 10 Nos. 1 and 2, signed and dated 2 November 1830, the very day that Chopin left Warsaw for good.[35] From this copy (distinct from the later engraver's manuscript for Schlesinger), it is clear that Chopin conceived Op. 10 Nos. 1 and 2 as a pair, since they are titled 'Exercise 1' and 'Exercise 2'.

It is most likely, then, that the 'couple of exercises' composed in Warsaw were the first two of the collection later published as Op. 10. And if the E minor Nocturne represents an important step forward in Chopin's refinement of ornamental melody, these two études are a landmark in his elevation of bravura figuration to a new compositional status. Associations between Op. 10 No. 1 and études by Clementi and Cramer have become a commonplace of criticism, as has the association between Op. 10 No. 2 and the third of Moscheles's Op. 70 Études. But there is another, and deeper, influence at work in these pieces. Just as Chopin's mature melodic style looks beyond its immediate ancestry to Mozart, so his figuration, rooted in the brilliant style, owes something directly to his love of Bach. It was above all the inspiration of Bach which enabled Chopin to transcend his more obvious models, both in the harmonic-figurative patterns of the first Étude and the melodic-figurative patterns of the second. And this raises in a very direct way the whole issue of musical influence, its different levels of operation and the emergence through it of a composer's individual voice.

Pedagogy and other influences

Even the casual listener has no difficulty in recognizing, without necessarily being able to describe, let alone analyse, Chopin's musical style. Chopin, in other words, sounds like no one else. Yet this highly distinctive musical idiom did not appear from nowhere, fully formed. Like all composers, Chopin had an apprenticeship, and his music only gradually shook itself free of formative influences, several of which continued to shape it at deep levels even as they were being rejected on the surface. It will be worth isolating this issue in order to trace some of the sources of his musical style and to help place it in relation to other stylistic currents in early nineteenth-century music.

For any composer, musical education forms one of the earliest, and most potentially enduring, layers of influence. Little can be said about Chopin's early piano lessons with Adalbert Żywny, beyond an early introduction to Bach. But his studies with Elsner can be reconstructed more easily. Although Elsner apparently gave Chopin freer rein than most of his students,[36] his teaching programme in the composition class

[35] Housed in the Chopin Society, Warsaw. M/190–7. Hanna Wróblewska-Straus has established that this is a copy and not an autograph.
[36] See the discussion in Tadeusz Frączyk, *Warszawa młodości Chopina*, pp. 182–222.

set at least some of the pattern for the young composer's early works. It has already been remarked that the programme of the first year at the High School partly determined the sequence of Chopin's output during that year—a chain of miniatures culminating in a sonata. It may be added here that the songs and orchestral pieces written during the second year also conformed to Elsner's programme. Even the choice of *Là ci darem* for the Op. 2 Variations may have been influenced by Elsner, since he used it as a model for discussing classical period form. Chopin's difficulties with scoring in these orchestral pieces, incidentally, are apparent not only in the changes he made to the placing of the wind instruments in the autograph of the *Rondo à la krakowiak*, but also in a correction in Elsner's hand to the horn parts on folio 28 of the autograph.[37]

The mutual regard of Elsner and Chopin is well documented, and it is clear that, although Chopin had rather mixed feelings about his teacher's actual music and was on some important matters disinclined to follow his advice,[38] he absorbed both detailed technical features and larger formal and aesthetic principles from his studies at the High School. Among the former we might count not only the models for Op. 5 and Op. 14, but the Haydn-inspired monothematicism of Op. 4 and—most important—the liking for a mirror reprise in sonata-form works. This latter point is intriguing in the light of Chopin's later development. The mirror reprise, beloved of Elsner himself, was a fingerprint of the 'Polish school',[39] found in Dobrzyński and Nowakowski as well as Chopin, and it eventually found consummate expression in some of the Chopin ballades.

More important than such individual techniques, however, was the general tenor of Elsner's teaching, the texts he himself studied and used in his classes. When Chopin was thirteen (several years before he entered the High School) Elsner introduced him to a book on 'harmony' (in Polish and German) by his friend Karol Antoni Simon.[40] This was one of a plethora of harmony tutors to appear in the 1820s, emphatically pedagogical rather than scholarly in orientation. They were textbooks in the modern sense, a response to the widespread institutionalization of music education in the early nineteenth century. The preface spells out that the book was designed 'for amateurs wanting knowledge of the basics in a clear and simple form', so there are no lengthy discussions of string division or the *corps sonore*. The emphasis is strictly on classification and exemplification—of scales, intonations, intervals and their

[37] This is housed with the Czartoryski Collection of the National Museum in Cracow.

[38] Elsner was one of those anxious that Chopin should compose a national opera. See Chopin's letter to his teacher of 14 December 1831, *Korespondencja Fryderyka Chopina*, vol. 1, p. 204.

[39] It is just possible that Elsner may have been influenced here by the formal theories of Reicha, since he could have known these during his stay in Vienna.

[40] *Nauka harmonii* (Poznań, 1823).

inversions, part movement, and chords—with a final section on accompaniment, in the eighteenth- rather than the nineteenth-century sense of that term. It would have given Chopin little beyond basic rudiments, but it should be noted that they were rudiments firmly grounded in eighteenth-century traditions.

More important were the texts Elsner used at the High School itself. The two indispensable theoretical texts were Albrechtsberger, *Anweisung zur Composition*, and Kirnberger, *Die Kunst des reinen Satzes*.[41] The Albrechtsberger manual works its way through the species to free counterpoint, imitation, fugue, and double counterpoint, suggesting that harmonically reinterpreted species counterpoint formed the central core of counterpoint teaching at the High School. That is confirmed by Elsner's avowed practice, common enough among pedagogues, of making his own harmonic adaptations of Fux.[42]

The Kirnberger treatise would have given a rather different slant to counterpoint teaching, one which regarded the four-part chorale texture as a starting point for contrapuntal activation—distinctly Bachian rather than Fuxian counterpoint. We know that Elsner had special admiration for the Kirnberger from correspondence dating back to his days in Lwów.[43] So it was a basic text for Chopin's tuition, as indeed it was for Mendelssohn's. Recent scholarship has helped us to outgrow a once prevalent tendency to treat late eighteenth-century treatises as prehistories of tenaciously held present-day positions.[44] It is enough to remark that whereas Kirnberger has often seemed grist to the Schenkerian mill, his position was in reality rather close to Rameau, at least in many essentials. That said, it is well known that his preservation of certain elements of thoroughbass tradition led to important and highly public disagreements with the Rameau-Marpurg system,[45] not least about dissonance treatment, and about passing chords and passing keys. And it is true that such views resonate in the music of Chopin.

But all this is easy prey to over-interpretation. Theory teaching at Warsaw was probably anything but dogmatic. It would have embraced thoroughbass, modified species counterpoint, and chordal succession by *Grundbass*. The key point is that for Chopin, as for Mendelssohn, technical training was rooted in late eighteenth-century theory and that, for all the polemics, the basic conception of harmonic structure held by late

[41] See Alina Nowak-Romanowicz, *Józef Elsner* (Cracow, 1957). It is important to emphasize that the Albrechstberger was the treatise of 1790 and not the later Seyfried compendium, which prefaces the manual with harmonic theory of rather different orientation. But it may be worth mentioning that rather later—in the mid-1830s—Chopin was one of the subscribers to the French translation of Albrechtsberger–Seyfried.

[42] Ibid., p. 187.   [43] Ibid., p. 187.

[44] The point is well and often made in Joel Lester, *Compositional Theory in the Eighteenth Century* (Cambridge, Mass., and London, 1992).

[45] For a discussion of the Kirnberger-Marpurg disputes, see Lester, *Compositional Theory in the Eighteenth Century*, pp. 231–57.

eighteenth-century theorists was a great deal more unified than we have formerly supposed. The training of Liszt and Berlioz was of a different order altogether, and that may account in considerable measure for later differences of style and aesthetic.

Much is made of the Delacroix diary entry of 1849 in which Chopin is reported to have identified counterpoint, specifically fugue, as 'like pure logic in music'.[46] Elsner said much the same in *Sumariusz*, just a year or two before the events recorded in the diary.[47] But again such statements should be treated with care. The counterpoint to which Chopin refers is not Fux, but harmonically amended Fux, and the source of the remark was more likely to have been Cherubini, whose treatise Chopin examined in 1841, than anything studied in his youth. We may note that Cherubini uses the same language, describing fugue as the 'foundation of composition'. The more interesting part of Delacroix's diary entry is in any case the reference to Chopin's next remark. 'The custom', Chopin apparently said, 'is to learn the harmonies before coming to the counterpoint.' There may have been an implied criticism of contemporary pedagogy here, as Carl Schachter suggests.[48] But this is by no means certain. It is true that Albrechtsberger–Seyfried, to whose French edition Chopin subscribed in 1833, starts with harmony before coming to counterpoint. But then so did Kirnberger.

The question of priority in music was in fact a much debated one, touching aesthetics as much as theory. Elsner's remarks about counterpoint, written in the 1840s, are in direct conflict with an earlier statement made in the preface to his Harmony treatise of 1807.[49] There he identified harmony as primary, and he went on to draw a frequently used analogy with verbal language. That passage—indeed the whole of the extended preface—is in fact closely based on the text that most strongly influenced Elsner's larger view of music, Forkel's *Allgemeine Geschichte der Musik* of 1788. He undoubtedly used this in teaching, since he took the trouble to have parts of it translated into Polish by Kazimierz Brodziński.[50]

Forkel discusses the elements of music in turn, debating their competing claims for priority, and opting for harmony as primary and originating. In the same text he makes very plain his understanding of music as rhetoric, referring extensively to Mattheson, and going on to list affections, genres, and figures. It is worth mentioning that rhetoric was one of the three subheadings of Elsner's Composition course, along with

[46] *The Journal of Eugène Delacroix*, ed. Hubert Wellington, tr. Lucy Norton (New York, 1948), pp. 194–5.

[47] *Sumariusz moich utworów muzycznych*, ed. Alina Nowak-Romanowicz (Cracow, 1957; original German edn. 1855).

[48] In *Chopin Studies 2* (Cambridge, 1994), p. 175.

[49] *Krótko zebrana nauka generalbasu* (Warsaw, 1807).

[50] See Józef Bieliński, *Królewski Uniwersytet Warszawski (1816–30)* (Warsaw, 1907–12), 3 vols., vol. 3, p. 448.

grammar and aesthetics. Forkel would have been a direct influence here. And the orientation is confirmed by the other German text Elsner admired, though we cannot be sure that he used it in teaching. This was Marpurg's *Kritische Briefe über die Tonkunst*, weekly letters on a wide range of subjects, dating from 1759 to 1764.[51] Aside from lengthy discussions of theory, aesthetic issues are exhaustively rehearsed in the *Kritische Briefe*. They include a pre-echo of the Forkel debate about priority, as well as an endorsement of the Matthesonian understanding of music and rhetoric, together with concrete suggestions about how the affections might be taught.

It is clear, then, that Chopin was as firmly rooted in eighteenth-century aesthetics as in eighteenth-century theory. Elsner's own writings, and indeed Chopin's, endorse a commonly held eighteenth-century view of music as a language with its own meaning, expressed not through syntactic elements but through emotional categories. Elsner's formulation of the analogy between music and language was certainly taken directly from Forkel, but it was already present in almost the same formulation in Kirnberger, and the analogy invaded informal as well as formal writings. Thus Elsner, in a letter to Chopin, described music as a 'language of feelings'; and Chopin himself referred to it as 'l'expression de la pensée par les sons', as 'la langue indéfinie (indéterminée) de l'homme'.[52] Just as Chopin's music has its foundation in classical theory, so too it preserves a good deal of the classical currency of figures and tonal types.

There were, however, other texts admired by Elsner which would have directed his students a stage beyond this classical affective aesthetic, though we can only speculate about their role in his teaching. They include two important French texts, of which the first was the famous Dictionary by Rousseau.[53] Chopin could scarcely have escaped Rousseau while in the company of George Sand, but the contact was already there in his Warsaw days, through his father as well as Elsner. It was probably the aesthetic rather than the technical entries in the Dictionary which interested Elsner, as indeed they did his mentor Forkel, in a review of the Rousseau. These include the entries on genius, on expression, and on imitation. In these last two entries in particular Rousseau moved beyond an affective towards an expressive aesthetic, celebrating the elusive, suggestive powers of music. 'Music does not represent things directly but excites in the soul the same movements which one experiences in seeing them.'

The other French text was Grétry's *Mémoires*, a goldmine of

[51] Alina Nowak-Romanowicz, *Józef Elsner*, p. 188.

[52] *Frédéric Chopin: Esquisses pour une méthode de piano*, ed. Jean-Jacques Eigeldinger (Mayenne, 1993), p. 48.

[53] For a detailed discussion of the dictionary, see Thomas Webb Hunt, 'The Dictionnaire de Musique of Jean-Jacques Rousseau' (Diss., North Texas State University, 1967).

information on social history and aesthetics in the late eighteenth century.[54] Elsner's sympathy for the *Mémoires* (he described it as a 'beautiful book') is telling, especially if we are considering him as a teacher. Grétry's admiration for Rousseau leaps from the pages of the *Mémoires*, not least in Book 6, much of which is given over to a lengthy discussion of pedagogy. In a nutshell, Grétry takes us a long way from Forkel and Marpurg in his descriptions of just what it takes to be a composer of the first rank. The language here is already that of romantic idealism—it is sensitivity to poetry and attunement to the inner truths of the emotions that will lead the aspiring composer to greatness.

Such ideas would have chimed well with Polish writings on the new romanticism, notably Brodziński's treatise *On Classicism and Romanticism* of 1816. I have already alluded to Elsner's collaboration with Brodziński, who made the translation of Forkel. Among the sections translated was that dealing with the rhythmic and melodic characteristics of national musics, including Polish. Elsner actually quoted that passage in one of his own treatises on word setting, and there can be little doubt that such sentiments gave a specific musical resonance to modern ideas of romantic nationalism brought to Warsaw from Wilno by, among others, Brodziński himself.

Such thoughts were commonly known in the Warsaw of Chopin's youth, and whether or not the young composer actually attended some of Brodziński's lectures at the University (as he claimed), he would certainly have been familiar with the ideas, especially given the importance attached to them by Elsner. It seems highly likely that it was in part Brodziński's views on nationalist art which influenced Chopin's change of attitude to folk music. The appearance in 1829 of *Melitele*, in which Brodziński discussed at length the national character of Poles and more particularly the deeper meaning of their national dances, seems especially significant in this connection.[55] It is an early formulation of that equation of folk culture and nationalism which would later (following Herder) prove highly influential in the Slavonic lands, and it is quite possible that it played a part in shaping Chopin's understanding of what he himself called 'our national music'.[56]

Pedagogy formed only one of several strands of influence within Chopin's Warsaw milieu. His debts to other Polish composers were minimal, but his musical tastes and early enthusiasms owed a good deal to Polish musical culture. The most popular and prestigious forms of instrumental music in Warsaw were post-classical bravura concert pieces, and these played a very direct role in shaping Chopin's emerging

[54] Grétry, *Mémoires ou Essais sur la musique*, ed. J.-H. Mees (Brussels/Paris, 1829; original ed. 1789).
[55] For a discussion see Tadeusz Frączyk, *Warszawa młodości Chopina*, pp. 182–222.
[56] See his letter to Tytus of 3 October, 1829. *KFC*, vol. 1, p. 210.

musical style in the early years. Other influences, scarcely less important but of necessity mediated, were Italian and French opera, highly fashionable in Warsaw, and folk music, either in its unadulterated state or popularized as salon dances. And arguably most important of all were influences from Bach and the so-called 'Viennese' classical composers. Bach and Mozart were introduced to Chopin at an early age, through the teaching of both Żywny and Elsner, and they remained for him models of excellence, their influence continuing to operate at levels far below the musical surface, right through to his later music. It should be emphasized that as his musical style matured, his attitude to these models—to the 'weight of the past'—changed radically, and in his later music it arguably came close to the kind of remodelling processes that result from 'the anxiety of influence'.[57]

For the present, however, I concentrate on the formative stages of his creative development, when he responded to and restructured the musical world surrounding him in Warsaw. And here the brilliant style undoubtedly played the central role, underestimated in the past due to the vagaries of historiography. Traditional stylistic histories of music have tended in general to reduce the diversity of late eighteenth- and early nineteenth-century music to two competing paradigms, where a notionally unified period style, labelled 'classical', gives way to a plethora of more individual, though related, styles generically described as 'romantic'. Among the several inadequacies of this interpretation is its injustice to the extensive repertory of post-classical concert music, where virtuosic and ornamental devices already common in Mozart and Clementi were elevated to a form-building status, promoting much greater stylistic uniformity than anything we find in so-called 'Viennese' classical music. Chopin's Warsaw-period polonaises, variations, and rondos belong centrally to this repertory, and their gestures are conformant to the point of stereotype. This first level of influence might be characterized as 'direct emulation'.

It is an easy matter to demonstrate that in broad formal terms Chopin modelled his early concert pieces on this post-classical repertory. But its influence also percolated through to details of harmony, melody and, above all, figuration, often lifted from their original context and treated as isolated features of style. This is the kind of modelling process, blatantly derivative, which is characteristic of formative stages in the creative evolution of any composer from any historical period. But it is worth noting in any case that in these pre-1830 years the notion of originality was not yet the 'historical imperative' it would later

---

[57] The term is Harold Bloom's, in *The Anxiety of Influence: a Theory of Poetry* (New Haven, 1973). Bloom's argument that a creative identity could only be forged through the suppression of influence, resulting in simultaneous emulation and rejection, has been applied to music in a theory of intertextuality developed by Kevin Korsyn: 'Towards a New Poetics of Musical Influence', in *Music Analysis*, vol. 10 nos. 1–2 (1991), pp. 3–72.

become.[58] Influence, in other words, was not necessarily a sign of weakness in the early nineteenth century, though it was soon to become so. Indeed there is some irony in the fact that Chopin himself would later provide an important exemplar for a view of stylistic change which assigns value to originality.

It will be helpful to make Chopin's debt to the post-classical repertory rather more concrete, by looking briefly at figuration in the early music. A few correspondences will illustrate Chopin's ready assimilation of the gestures of the brilliant style, and their continued presence in his mature music. Parallel passages such as Ex. 1 could be multiplied and extended across the repertory to include composers such as Weber, Moscheles, Pixis, Kalkbrenner, Herz, and many others, indicating something of the international currency of the brilliant style. Characteristically figurations are extensions of broken chord patterns already present in Mozart and

Ex. 1

(a) Hummel: Variations, Op. 57, var. 4 and Chopin: Éccosaise, Op. 72 No. 3

[58] See Peter Burkholder, 'Museum Pieces: the Historicist Mainstream in Music of the Last Hundred Years', in *Journal of Musicology*, vol. 2 (1983), p. 120.

(b) Hummel: Fantasy, Op. 18 and Chopin: Polonaise, KK 1185–7

taking their major impetus from the light-actioned Viennese pianos of the late eighteenth century. But they can also include rapid chromatic passages, sometimes in parallel thirds or sixths, together with explosions of right-hand virtuosity which elaborate left-hand chord progressions but rapidly lose contact with the underlying harmony. Often, too, the figurations are ornamental in character, motivated less by harmonic elaboration than by melodic variation. And here John Field was especially influential, cultivating an expressive ornamental melody more attuned to the heavier English piano than to its Viennese counterpart. Chopin tapped this source, too (Ex. 2). And linking both harmonic and melodic figurations are those characteristic *fioriture* popular within the style, and found alike in Hummel, Field, and Chopin (Ex. 3).

Ex. 2
(a) Field: Nocturne No. 9 in E minor

(b) Chopin: Nocturne in E minor, Op. 72 No. 1

Ex. 3

(a) Hummel: Sonata No. 6 in D major, Op. 106, Larghetto

(b) Field: Sonata in A major, Op. 1 No. 2, Allegro

(c) Chopin: Polonaise, Op. 71 No. 2

The *Là ci darem* Variations forms one of the summits of post-classical concert music, and it may be used partly to summarize Chopin's indebtedness to the style. Mozart is the true ancestor of the 'brilliant' variation set and his most notable successor was Hummel. Several Mozartian features found their way into Hummel's sets: a general tendency to move from relatively simple to relatively complex figurations, a final 'pairing' of adagio and allegro variations, a preference for cleanly alternating cantabile and florid passages over a steady alberti-derived bass, and numerous characteristic variation 'types'. These include preserving the theme but adding distinctive accompaniment figures, modifying the theme with elaborate ornamentation (usually in slow tempo), replacing the theme with brilliant figurations, and replacing the theme with a melodic 'paraphrase'. All four types can be found in Chopin's Op. 2, which stands in an obvious line of descent from Mozart through Hummel. The introduction in particular makes the link with Hummel explicit. An obvious point of comparison would be the introduction to Hummel's Op. 75 Variations, with which it shares a multi-sectional form, subtle integration of fragments of the theme into the overall texture, an imitative episode (Ex. 4), recitative-like material and a final elaborate ornamental cadenza.

Bravura figuration and ornamental melody, together with a formal process which squares one off against the other, lie at the heart of the post-classical repertory. It is worth reiterating that precisely these features of style formed the foundation of Chopin's mature musical language. Already at the end of the Warsaw period there were clear indications of how they would later be refined and even concealed in his mature music, eventually to the point at which they all but lost sight of their origins. Yet they remained, at the very least, the essential starting-point for Chopin's musical thought, even in his latest and most sophisticated musical structures. The influence of this repertory was both direct and durable.

A second, rather different level of influence is invoked by Italian opera and Polish folk music, both of which were much loved by Chopin during the Warsaw period and beyond. Here the influence was indirect, in that it involved a recontextualization of stylistic features from one

Ex. 4
(a) Hummel: Adagio, Variations, and Rondo, Op. 75

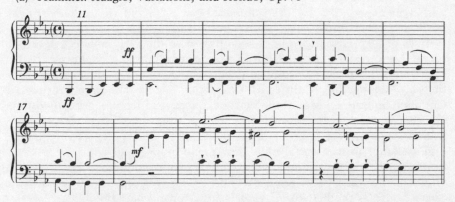

(b) Chopin: Variations on *Là ci darem*, Op. 2

medium to another, and thus an element of interpretation, or, as Meyer puts it, 'deforming of prior meaning'.[59] It is of course difficult to assess with confidence how far the influence was mediated through existing keyboard repertories, since both opera and folksong were standard sources of inspiration for pianist-composers in the early nineteenth century. One certainty is that Chopin was something of a connoisseur of opera singers. He never ceased to debate the merits of leading singers of the day, eulogizing at different times the talents of, among others, Catalani, Sontag, La Malibran, Viardot, Pasta, and Rubini. Already during the Warsaw years he had ample opportunity to listen to visiting Italian singers at the opera, and his journeys to Berlin and Vienna gave him a chance to measure the Warsaw performances against an international yardstick. In common with other pianist-composers, he saw a vital link between vocal bel canto and piano lyricism, pointing to the opera house as the best of all models for aspiring pianists.

It is likely, then, that Italian and French opera played some part in shaping the wide arcs of his melody, together with their characteristic ornamentation. Much of this ornamentation was transparently vocal in origins, stylizing the portamentos, *fioriture* and cadenzas which were part and parcel of the opera singer's art. It is intriguing, for instance, to read Chopin's praise (in a letter to Tytus) for the entirely original and effective use of spontaneous ornamentation made by Henrietta Sontag during her Warsaw appearances.[60] Moreover his subtle 'pointing' of melody notes by means of expressive ornamental detail comes very close to a singer's characteristic tendency to underline the individual words through ornamentation. At times, too, Chopin's tendency to sweeten his melody with parallel thirds and sixths is strongly reminiscent of the vocal duet texture commonly found in early nineteenth-century opera. And there are sections of such strongly characterized *Affekt* (chorales, marches, laments, recitatives) that they inevitably invoke the opera house.

Such vocally inspired gestures came to full fruition in Chopin's mature nocturnes, some of which might almost be compared to an operatic scena. But they were already prominent in the music of the Warsaw period, including, of course, the early E minor Nocturne. It seems likely that his affinity with operative bel canto resulted in a process of stylistic osmosis, where details of style were gradually absorbed into his music and recontextualized. But it is arguable that the influence of opera extended beyond such fingerprints of style to affect Chopin's whole approach to thematic working in his mature music. In its most characteristic form the Chopin melody is of a kind defined by Mersmann in his *Musikästhetik* as 'ornamental'. Like the opera composer, he was less interested in thematic dissection and reintegration on the German model

---

[59] Leonard B. Meyer, *Style and Music: Theory, History, Ideology* (Philadelphia, 1989).
[60] *KFC*, vol. 1, pp. 128–9.

than in the decoration and elaboration of melodic 'arias', often repeated against changing harmonic and textural backcloths. This over-simplifies the position, since Chopin owed something to German *motivische Arbeit*, too, but it may serve at least as a pointer to some of the relevant associations.

In his early mazurkas Chopin turned to yet another musical background, the folk music of the Mazovian plains of central Poland. The rhythmic and modal patterns of the *mazur*, *kujawiak*, and *oberek*, together with characteristic melodic intonations and *duda* drones, are all stylized in these mazurkas. Again, as with operatic influence, it is difficult to say how much was absorbed directly from rural models and how much came indirectly from salon dance pieces. But there are some clues along the way. Shortly after leaving Poland, he wrote to his family from Vienna, 'My piano has heard only mazury', while in his first months in Paris he wrote to Tytus of his attempt 'to express the nature of our national music'.[61] And there are suggestions elsewhere in his correspondence that he had a healthy respect for peasant music in its raw state, though his documented encounters with it are few enough.

The likelihood is that, as with opera, the influence was both direct and indirect, and, again as with opera, parallels are easy to find. Indeed they have been traced by numerous writers, often in an attempt to clinch the case of Chopin's 'Polishness' through concrete associations with folk music.[62] As I shall later argue, this is only part of the truth. Yet the associations are real enough, and they point to Chopin as one of the earliest major composers to absorb detailed melodic, modal, and rhythmic gestures derived from peasant music into the more sophisticated idioms of art music. However obliquely, the early mazurkas evoke the world of the traditional folk ensemble of central Poland, where a melody instrument (violin or *fujarka*, a high-pitched shepherd's pipe) would often be accompanied by a drone (*duda* or *gagda*, a Polish bagpipe) and/or a rhythmic pulse (*basetla* or *basy*, a string bass). Nor is the evocation always so oblique. As Adrian Thomas has indicated, a passage such as the trio from Op. 68 No. 3 'betrays its unadorned oberek origins with an insouciant ease'.[63] There are also deeper influences from folklore. In particular the motivic play characteristic of Mazovian folk models, where it is common to find varied repetitions of one- and two-bar cells, is built into the working of Chopin's mazurkas.

A third level of influence involved the transformation of elements drawn from earlier masters, and especially from the Viennese classical composers and Bach. Here we come close to that 'analytical misreading'

[61] *KFC*, vol. 1, pp. 183 and 210.

[62] See in particular H. Windakiewiczowa, *Wzory ludowej muzyki polskiej w mazurkach Fryderyka Chopina* (Cracow, 1926) and Wieczesław Paschałow, *Chopin a polska muzyka ludowa* (Cracow, 1951).

[63] Adrian Thomas, 'Beyond the Dance', in *The Cambridge Companion to Chopin*, ed. Jim Samson (Cambridge, 1992), p. 155.

identified by Joseph Straus and others as a more subtle form of influence, one which focuses on active choices and decisions made by the composer in the face of 'exemplary works' from the past.[64] Meyer's reference to a composer's originality involving a kind of 'tinkering' with 'archetypes' is also germane to this level of influence. Chopin's response to the Viennese composers and Bach undoubtedly changed as he moved into stylistic maturity, and very much in the direction of creative 'misreading'. Above all he found his own way of reinterpreting the classical sonata-form archetype in the light of a very particular dramatic and expressive purpose, and also a way of rethinking contrapuntal processes in terms peculiarly suited to the piano. But already during the Warsaw period the example of these composers served to enrich his musical thought and helped establish processes which would later contribute to the individuality of his musical style.

The music of the Viennese masters was well known to Chopin during his period of study in Warsaw. Even Beethoven was played and admired, though with reservations, and it is entirely possible that some of Chopin's piano textures represented a response to the later Beethoven, albeit directed to utterly different stylistic ends. But it was above all to Mozart that he was drawn. Temperamentally and in his general aesthetic Chopin remained close to Mozart and, contrary to some later perceptions, he viewed himself as firmly rooted in classical traditions. His tastes and sympathies remained largely untouched by many aspects of the spirit of early romanticism, not least the contemporary enthusiasm for music's links with poetry, nature, and the exotic. Right at the end of his life he compared Mozart and Beethoven in terms which spelt out clearly his commitment to order and balance, his rejection of extravagant rhetoric and theatricality. 'Where [Beethoven] is obscure and seems lacking in unity . . . the reason is that he turns his back on eternal principles; Mozart never.'[65]

I have already suggested that in some of his early concert music Chopin looked beyond Hummel to Mozart, citing in particular formal process in the first movement and melody in the second movement of the F minor Concerto. That link was strengthened in the later E minor Concerto, as even a brief inspection of the slow movement melody will be enough to confirm. Both the texture and the internal construction of the phrase betray their origins in classical (Mozartean) practice, as does incidentally the larger context, where the piano's first thought (Ex. 5) is a new theme, essentially unrelated to the orchestral prelude. At the same time the classical archetype is already reinterpreted to establish the terms of a characteristically romantic idiom. The essential point here is that

---

[64] Joseph Straus, *Remaking the Past: Musical Modernism and the Influence of the Tonal Tradition* (Cambridge, Mass., 1990), p. 21.
[65] See note 46.

Ex. 5   Chopin: Piano Concerto in E minor, Op. 11, second movement

the mature Chopin melody is at least as much a transformation of Mozart as a continuation of Field.

The influence of Bach is a more complex issue to which I will return periodically in this study. It is apparent in the surface contrapuntal working found in some of the early music, notably the first three movements of the Op. 4 Sonata, as Ex. 6 suggests. But already in the first two of the Op. 10 Études, composed during the final months in Warsaw, there are indications that Chopin learnt deeper lessons from Bach. The obvious parallel—often made—is between the C major Étude and the first Prelude of the *Wohltemperiertes Klavier*, but this embodies a larger point. Like Bach, Chopin could construct moto perpetuo figuration which generates a real sense of harmonic flow while allowing linear elements to emerge through the pattern, often in counterpoint with the melodic bass. And this strong 'dissonant counterpoint' was part of a more fundamental debt to Bach, one which enabled the 'eternal principles' of counterpoint to be reformulated in the terms of a very different medium. This will be explored in due course.

Ex. 6 Chopin Sonata in C minor, Op. 4
(a) Allegro maestoso

(b) Minuetto

(c) Trio

It has often been remarked that in the matter of musical form and structure early nineteenth-century composers tended to look back across the so-called 'classical style' to baroque precedents. They favoured, in short, a unitary conception of musical form—a single impulse of departure from and return to tonal stability, involving a process of harmonic intensification and resolution—rather than the dialectic of tonal contrast and synthesis which characterized classical thought. Chopin was the supreme master of such forms, where an apparently simple design might serve as a foil for dynamic, carefully placed intensity curves, purposefully at odds with the 'spatial' formal pattern. And here too the influence of Bach was paramount, already at work in the two études composed in Warsaw. The chromatic line of No. 2, drafted as a series of arcs, achieves an astonishing level of sophistication through its subtly varied interactions with the underlying harmony and phrase structure. The various peaks of the arcs are placed asymmetrically in relation to harmony and phrasing, resulting in a remarkable and exciting plasticity of line. As in Bach, the intensification of the middle section is again achieved through harmony and line. The arcs are reduced to one-bar periods or broken down altogether, while the harmony departs from a prevailing diatonicism to explore chromatic sequential patterns based on fifths cycles with a diminishing period of sequence.

Confronted with the subtlety of these two early études, we are left in no doubt that Chopin was not just on the brink of full stylistic maturity during his final months in Warsaw. He had already arrived there. I will discuss the refinements of this transition from apprenticeship to maturity in a later chapter, but it may be helpful at this stage to summarize some of the formative influences. The foundation layer of his musical style was provided by post-classical concert music, by its figuration, its ornamental melody, and its formal process. The surface features of that style receded from view in later works, but the foundation layer remained securely in place. To this layer were added enriching elements drawn many different musical worlds—influences from contemporary opera and folk music, operating in both cases at different levels of significance, from the *Trivialmusik* of the bourgeois salon, and from the rich inheritance of the Viennese classical masters and Bach. All were transformed by Chopin and absorbed into his own carefully circumscribed world. His unique achievement was to penetrate right to the heart of the piano, and then to draw into its realm the salient characteristics of other musical worlds,'transfer[ring] them', as Liszt put it, 'into a more restricted but more idealised sphere'.[66]

[66] Franz Liszt, *F Chopin*, p. 32.

3

New frontiers

Biographies are histories, and like other histories they adopt strategies for ordering events and interpretations into a coherent narrative. The subdivision of a composer's life into periods is one way of making sense of it, but such periods remain at best impositions, even abstractions, and they carry additional penalties when the 'life' is considered in tandem with the 'works'.[1] The 'Warsaw Period' is an inevitable construction in a Chopin biography, just as the journey from Warsaw to Paris is an inevitable metaphor. But these interpretations are at the very least in search of qualification. There was no abrupt change of attitude and outlook when Chopin left Poland in November 1830. His inloneliness and depression in the months following his departure were in some ways a continuation of the acute emotional stress he had already suffered during his final year in Warsaw, when he came close to what we would describe nowadays as a nervous breakdown. His insecurities during the eight-month stay in Vienna were exacerbated, no doubt, by the absence of family and friends during a period of major political crisis, but they were not the direct result of that absence. With the music, too, there was much greater continuity than a neat periodization will allow. The technical assurance and individuality of some of the works composed at the very end of the Warsaw years give the lie to any suggestion that Chopin found himself as a composer only after he left Poland.

All the same, there is a journey to be traced from adolescent discontents to the self-confident independence of early manhood, and an associated musical journey from early glimmerings of stylistic individuality to the inimitable voice of maturity. An artistic personality was shaped in all its main essentials precisely during these years. Perhaps this does indeed add up to a 'period' but if so, it is one whose boundaries are anything but clearly defined. The departure from Poland has taken on obvious symbolic values, but its effect in reality was to bring to a head the emotional and artistic problems that had been festering for months in Warsaw. Even then it was not until he found himself alone in Vienna

[1] The most sustained attempt to periodize Chopin, embracing and uniting both life and works, is to be found in Mieczysław Tomaszewski's extended entry on the composer in the *Encyklopedia muzyczna*, ed. Elżbieta Dziębowska (Cracow, 1984), vol. 2, pp. 108–92.

following the outbreak of the Polish uprising that these problems came to the fore once again. Chopin had no inkling that he was leaving Poland for good on 2 November, and when Woyciechowski joined him at Kalisz the young men approached their adventure in high spirits.

By 6 November they were in Wrocław, where they spent four days at the inn 'Zur Goldenen Gans'. As usual Chopin made straight for the theatre, attending Raimund's comedy *Der Alpenkönig* and Auber's opera *Le Maçon*, only to complain in letters home about the mediocre singers in the Silesian capital. Chopin had useful connections in Wrocław through his teacher Elsner. He had already met the Kapellmeister Jósef Ignaz Schnabel during an earlier visit, and on his second day he went with Tytus to see the old man and agreed to attend a rehearsal of the orchestra the following morning. According to Chopin, he was invited to try the piano and, when he did so, his accomplishments quite simply frightened off the amateur pianist who was due to play that evening.[2] Whatever the truth of it, Chopin agreed to play at the concert instead and rehearsed the last two movements of the E minor Concerto with the orchestra in the afternoon. The reception of the work by the musicians was lukewarm and in the end Chopin played only the Rondo-finale, together with an improvisation on a theme from Auber's *La Muette de Portici*, 'for the experts', as he put it.[3] In a letter to his family he spoke of one sympathetic listener, who praised the novelty of the form (of the Concerto), and claimed that he had never heard anything like it. 'Perhaps he understood better than any of them.' It is distinctly possible that this was August Kahlhert, who sprang to Chopin's defense a few years later in response to the infamous reviews by the German critic Ludwig Rellstab.[4]

From Wrocław the young men moved on to Dresden. Here Chopin saw *La Muette de Portici* and Rossini's *Tancredi*, visited the famous art gallery ('I seem to hear music when I look at some of the pictures here'), and renewed his acquaintance with the pianist Klengel. He also socialized with some of the wealthy Polish families then living in Dresden (the electors of Saxony ruled as Kings of Poland for much of the eighteenth century), and on one occasion at Salomea Dobrzycka's salon found himself improvising in front of members of the Saxon royal family. It was at this time that he first met Countess Delfina Potocka at the home of her mother Countess Komar. Chopin would later see her regularly in Paris, and counted her a loyal friend, but there is no reliable evidence that the two were ever lovers. Inevitably, this much rehearsed issue will have to be raised at a later stage.

After a brief stop in Prague, Chopin and Tytus arrived in Vienna on

---

[2] See his letter to his family of 9 November, 1830, in *KFC*, vol. 1, pp. 148–9.
[3] Ibid., p. 149.
[4] See Karol Musiol, 'Echoes of Chopin's Wrocław Concert in Musical Criticism and Literature', in *Chopin in Silesia*, pp. 6–8.

23 November. They put up first at the 'Zur Stadt London' in the Fleischmarkt until they found a cheaper hotel, 'Zum Goldenen Lamm', near the Prater. When they had cashed their money drafts they set about finding rented accommodation, eventually settling for a three-room apartment on the third floor of a house in Kohlmarkt street. Naturally Chopin visited the opera, hearing three 'absolutely new' operas during his first week in Vienna—*Fra Diavolo* and *La Muette* by Auber, and Rossini's *Guillaume Tell*—as well as Mozart's *La Clemenza di Tito*. He also practised regularly at Graf's shop, and was promised a Graf instrument for his apartment, free of charge. He was of course planning to give a concert, and with the memory of his earlier triumph in Vienna still fresh in his mind he quickly set about meeting some of the appropriate people. A visit from Hummel augured well, but in other respects things were not promising. Würfel received him, but was now too ill to be of much assistance, Leopoldine Blahetka had left the city, and the previous manager of the Kärntnerthor, Graf Gallenberg, had been replaced by Louis Duport, a less amenable and less generous administrator. Chopin also had a rude awakening when he visited Haslinger, with a view to publishing the two concertos. It transpired that Haslinger had not yet published the Op. 4 Sonata and the *Schweizerbub* Variations sent to him two years earlier, and that he was not prepared to take on either of the concertos unless Chopin would relinquish the copyright. 'From now on, it's "pay up", animal', Chopin wrote in a letter to Warsaw, a recurring theme of his later dealings with the publishing profession.[5]

Despite these disappointments, and a bad dose of cold, Chopin was not unduly discouraged. He looked up Tomasz Nidecki, who had settled in Vienna, visited Czerny and made the acquaintance of the imperial physician Dr Malfatti, who had been a close friend of Beethoven. The Malfattis befriended Chopin and kept an affectionate eye on him throughout the eight months in Vienna. He spent some happy hours with them, eating *bigos* prepared by Dr Malfatti's Polish wife and participating in music-making on several occasions at their country villa just outside Vienna. Dr Malfatti agreed from the start to help him arrange a concert, and on 1 December Chopin wrote to his family: 'I shall be giving a concert, but where, when and how I do not yet know.'[6] He also began making some use of his various letters of introduction, including one from the Grand Duke Constantin himself to the Russian ambassadress in Vienna. All went smoothly until 5 December, when Chopin and Tytus heard news of the uprising which had begun in Warsaw a week earlier, sparked off by an ill-judged attempt to assassinate the Grand Duke. Until this point their intention had been to stay in Vienna for two months at most before moving on to Italy. But the news from

---

[5] *KFC*, vol. 1, p. 158.   [6] Ibid., p. 156.

Poland changed all that. Tytus returned to Warsaw to participate in the uprising, along with just about all Chopin's other Polish friends. He himself wanted to return, but was dissuaded from doing so by Tytus. It seems that there was even a last-minute change of mind, as Chopin made a futile attempt to overtake Tytus and join him after all. Happily for music, it was too late and he returned alone to his Vienna apartment.

There can be no doubt of the anguish Chopin felt at this critical time. Left alone in Vienna, he was shaken into a major review of his life and in particular his attitude to the 'Polish question'. When Chopin was a five-year-old the Congress of Vienna had put paid to realistic Polish hopes for independence. The Congress left the country partitioned as before, but installed a new puppet 'Kingdom of Poland' in the central regions surrounding Warsaw, with Czar Alexander as King and his brother Constantin as army Chief-of-Staff. This was but the final indignity in a long history of oppression which included, of course, the three partitions, each more damaging than its predecessor. No one was fooled by the so-called 'Kingdom', but in its early stages it seemed none the less to offer some glimmer of hope to Poles. Alexander (along with Adam Czartoryski) drew up a Polish constitution and adopted several reforming measures, but it all turned out to be little more than a sham, and in his later years Alexander's policies towards Poland were blatantly repressive. With his death in 1825 and the accession of Nicholas I, repression and censorship were intensified, and Polish dissent grew correspondingly stronger. Increasingly that dissent was channelled into two very different camps, a conservative opposition under the general leadership of Adam Czartoryski (who had kept a low profile in the later stages of Alexander's reign) and a radical opposition associated with student societies and secret revolutionary groups.

Throughout his Warsaw years Chopin lived with the clamour for independence ringing in his ears. In his late teens he became friendly with several of the activists most closely involved in the patriotic and student societies, including Maurycy Mochnacki, Joachim Lelewel, Bohdan Zaleski, and Stefan Witwicki. Such men, frequenting certain well-known coffee houses in the city, looked to any and every opportunity to overthrow the Russian authorities, and Chopin could not have been unaware of their aims. Indeed, it is highly probable that his contacts with such men were monitored and viewed with disfavour by the authorities. At the same time he moved freely in rather different circles, socializing with members of the wealthy aristocracy who actively supported Czartoryski's more measured attempt to secure independence by political means. He even—it has to be said—associated with the Polish–Russian establishment, not least with the Grand Duke Constantin himself. And in this he followed the lead of his father, ever the pragmatist.

In short, Chopin was no revolutionary. But his sympathies were

73

undoubtedly with the Polish cause, and the effect of the uprising was immeasurably to strengthen those sympathies and perhaps even to prod him into questioning the easy political detachment of his Warsaw years. We might conjecture that he began to feel more than a little uncomfortable with his letter of introduction from the Grand Duke. We might conjecture further that in the wake of the uprising Chopin began to take rather more seriously the advice of Elsner, Tytus, Witwicki, and others that he should use his talents to further the Polish cause. He was probably already aware that he would never compose the national opera which alone would have satisfied them ('It is now vital that you should create a Polish opera'),[7] but his attitude to 'Polishness' in music changed, none the less.

It would be possible to overstate this change of attitude. Chopin's enterprise could never be confined by a nationalist aesthetic. But he was not unresponsive to the wider changes which took place following the uprising and the subsequent diaspora. In the absence of any political identity as a nation, Poles came increasingly to depend on a sense of cultural identity to solder the national spirit, and in this they were encouraged by a whole complex of ideas which reached them both from Herder and from the Wilno romantics. Chopin's music was increasingly assigned a role in the development of this cultural nationalism, and to an extent at least he went along with this. His declared attempt to 'express the nature of our national music' amounted to a pioneering approach to the concept of a national style, something qualitatively different from earlier understandings of the notion, and it would later prove highly influential in the development of nineteenth-century romantic nationalism. It is evidenced most clearly in the new note of seriousness with which he approached Polish national dances, picking up on ideas propagated by Brodziński and others in Warsaw on the eve of the uprising.

There were already signs of this in some of the later Warsaw-Period mazurkas, but it was in Vienna that he composed the first nine mazurkas that he himself released for publication, as Opp. 6 and 7, and it was through these that the genre was comprehensively defined. Yet in some ways the truly striking evidence of a major rethinking was less the mazurkas he composed than the polonaises he failed to compose. For several years after the uprising Chopin avoided the polonaise, apart from completing Op. 22. In doing so, he rejected in essence the widespread use of the genre as a conventional means of creating Polish colour, and one presumed to be available to Pole and non-Pole alike. When he returned to the polonaise in the mid 1830s he transformed it utterly. No longer a 'brilliant' concert piece, it became in Chopin's hands a powerful expression, in turn heroic and defiant, of national identity.

[7] Stefan Witwicki in a letter to Chopin, 6 July 1831: *KFC*, vol. 1, p. 179.

Dance pieces apart, there was unmistakably a new 'tone' in Chopin's music from the early 1830s, as it journeyed from a post-classical to a romantic idiom. And if this new tone was already clearly discernible before he left Warsaw, it was undoubtedly consolidated during the Vienna and early Paris years. It would be misleading to attribute it to any single cause. Equally it would be inadequate to explain it (away) in simple terms as the inevitable maturing of an artistic personality, as though other composers of post-classical concert music suffered from some sort of arrested development. The transformation of Chopin's musical style was at least in part a conscious decision. One factor was his growing realization that a concert career was not for him, necessitating a fundamental change in his whole approach to composition. But it seems likely that the new authority in his music from this period was also a response to Poland's tragedy, and to a new-found commitment to express that tragedy through music.

It is customary for biographers to make light of the expressions of grief found in the letters from Vienna. There is affectation, it is true, even allowing for the rather flowery manner which characterized Polish epistolary style at the time. But the underlying sentiment was real enough, and in the anguished pages which he sent to Jan Matuszyński, his confidant of this period, there is clear evidence that Poland was already becoming a symbolic focus for the more melancholy side of Chopin's nature. He was well aware that his friends were in the thick of the fighting and that even his sisters were involved in nursing the wounded. 'If I could, I would sound all the notes that blind, furious, enraged feelings have brought me, in order—in part at least—to work out those songs, sung by Jan's army, whose echoes still wander somewhere along the banks of the Danube.'[8] 'You are going to war, and will return a colonel. May all go well with you. Why can I not even beat a drum!'[9] 'Malfatti tries in vain to convince me that all artists are cosmopolitan. If this is so, then as an artist I am still in the cradle, and as a Pole I have entered my third decade.'[10]

The knowledge of Warsaw's agony was compounded by a more straightforward nostalgia. 'I curse the moment of my departure', he wrote to Matuszyński.[11] Chopin's upbringing had been sheltered, and he was now living away from home for the first time. Moreover he was surrounded by strangers, many of whom were by no means well disposed to Poles in the political climate which followed the uprising. Christmas was, and is, a very special time in Poland, and for Chopin to spend it alone in Vienna was an especially depressing experience: 'I felt my desolation more than ever.'[12] He was missing his family, and he was

[8] Letter to Matuszyński, 25 December 1830: ibid., p. 162.
[9] Letter to Matuszyński, 1 January 1831: ibid., p. 170.
[10] Letter to Elsner, 29 January 1831: ibid., p. 170.
[11] Ibid., p. 162. [12] Ibid., p. 163.

missing Konstancja, in whom he now invested his most ardent feelings, though they were addressed to Matuszyński rather than to the girl herself: 'Konst . . . (I cannot even write her name, my hand is not worthy)'.[13] At times the loneliness and indecision became unbearable. 'Shall I go to Paris? Shall I return home? Shall I stay here? Kill myself? Stop writing? Tell me what to do.'[14]

In response to this situation his lifestyle began to take on a rather characteristic pattern. Among a small circle of initiates, either compatriots or fellow professional musicians, he was fully as ease, unpretentious, lively and entertaining, willing to talk freely and even to speak of his deeper feelings. In Vienna such company included the Malfattis, his fellow student from Warsaw Tomasz Nidecki, the brilliant young Czech violinist Josef Slavik, and the cellist Josef Merk, for whom he added an introduction to the Polonaise for cello and piano (this was published by Mechetti in Vienna as Op. 3). In the later months in Vienna these friends also included the young Polish naturalist Norbert Kumelski. Yet at the same time Chopin was drawn to a more glamorous social world, partly from his natural snobbishness and leaning towards elegant living, and partly as a foil to his very real loneliness. He complained about this socializing in letters home ('I have had enough of the lunches, soirées, and dances; they all bore me'),[15] but in reality he enjoyed it. And despite his failure to make headway professionally, he began to find inroads to 'society'. Already in the early weeks in Vienna he was invited to dinners, receptions, and salons, where he would be perfectly turned out, aloof, charming, reserved, and polished. 'After lunch we take black coffee at the finest café, that's the fashion here . . . Then I pay my calls, return to my place just before dark, curl my hair, change, off to a party. I get back about ten or eleven, never later than twelve. I play, cry, read, stare, laugh, get into bed, blow the candle out and dream about home.'[16]

Music was, of course, the consolation for his moments of very real loneliness. Chopin heard a good deal of it in Vienna, and he did his share of playing in domestic settings. But all in all he was disappointed by the musical life of the city, and by the insular attitudes of the concert-going public. Some of this may have been a projection of his own discontents, but there were genuine grounds for dissatisfaction. Musical life in post-Congress Vienna was no match for its glorious past. Chopin felt that the Opera was on the whole disappointing, and he was unimpressed by the up-and-coming virtuosi of the city, the pianist Sigismond Thalberg and a young violinist-composer called Herz. He also had some caustic words about the waltz craze which was then sweeping the city: 'They call waltzes musical works here! and Strauss and Lanner, who play for them to dance, are called *Kapellmeisters*'.[17] For Chopin the real

[13] Letter to Matuszyński, 25 December 1830: *KFC*, vol. 1, p. 165.   [14] Ibid., p. 164.
[15] Ibid., p. 162.   [16] Ibid., p. 166.
[17] Letter to Elsner, 29 January 1831: ibid., p. 171.

musical life took place neither at the Opera nor at the salon, but in his apartment. Following Woyciechowski's departure he had immediately sub-let their original rooms and moved to cheaper accommodation on the next floor (he shared for a time with an acquaintance from the University in Warsaw, Romuald Hube, who had accompanied him on the first visit to Vienna). It was here that he entered into daily communion with the newly installed Graf piano, improvising and composing in the mornings and again when he returned in the evening. 'On returning home I strike at the piano . . .'[18]

The outcome is well known to us. It was here in Vienna that he composed not only the Op. 6 and Op. 7 Mazurkas, but the first batch of nocturnes which he released for publication, the three of Op. 9 and the second of the Op. 15 set. The *Lento con gran espressione* (KK 1215–22), often labelled a nocturne but not so described by Chopin, was also composed at this time. The precise dates of the Op. 10 Études are not known (apart from the first four), but it is likely that the fifth and sixth, and very possibly others, date from the Vienna months. Other pieces possibly composed in Vienna include several not released for publication— the G major Mazurka, Op. 67, No. 1, the E minor and A minor Waltzes, and a number of songs, including 'Piosnka litewska' (Lithuanian song), 'Wojak' (The warrior), 'Narzeczony' (The betrothed), 'Poseł' (The messenger), 'Smutna rzeka' (Sad river), and another version of 'Precz z moich oczu'. In addition he completed the *Grande Polonaise*, Op. 22 and may well have tried without success to compose a Concerto for Two Pianos. Chopin was now investing all his emotional energies into composing. In a very real sense he was living for and in that activity and the results speak for themselves. There is a strong sense here of music as the only available outlet for the composer's deepest feelings, a sense, too, that the actual process of composition could at times be a harrowing, even agonized, activity.

In every other respect the Vienna months were directionless, marked by a not unfamiliar cycle in which mounting depression breeds growing indolence. 'Even music cannot cheer me up today', he confessed to his album on one occasion.[19] Chopin was acutely aware that he could not continue to live indefinitely on a parental allowance, bolstered by some profits from his Warsaw concerts. But he was conspicuously unsuccessful in arranging a concert. According to some sources, he had a small part in a benefit at the Redoutensaal in April 1831, given for the singer Mme Garcia-Vestris, but when an opportunity to play again at the Kärntnerthor came his way in June, this time at a benefit for the ballet dancer Dominique Mattis, he approached it with little interest or enthusiasm. The hall was empty, the receipts failed to cover expenses, and none of the performers was paid. Even a flattering review of his

---

[18] Letter to Matuszyński, 25 December 1830: ibid., p. 166.   [19] Ibid., p. 167.

performance of the E minor Concerto (in the *Allgemeine Theaterzeitung*) failed to raise Chopin's spirits. He was now more than ever anxious to leave Vienna.

To do so was proving difficult, however. The Russian authorities refused him a passport for Paris and he was obliged to settle for Munich instead. The passport was then lost by the Austrian police and he had to apply for a new one, this time naming London as his destination, in the knowledge that this would take him through Paris. He had the passport signed by the French ambassador in the hope that he might then be allowed to stay in Paris. All this took time, and he was also waiting for a medical certificate (a major cholera epidemic was just then spreading westwards from India and had reached Austria), and for a money order from his father. So Chopin whiled away his time in sight-seeing, finding at the very end of his stay some pleasure in a Vienna just coming into its summer season. In the end he arranged for the money order to be forwarded to Munich, borrowed a sum from a Viennese banker, and set off for Munich with Norbert Kumelski on 20 July.

The journey took them across the Alps from Linz to Salzburg, where they visited the Mozart house. This may have been something of a revelatory journey for Chopin. In a letter to Kumelski from Paris, dated 18 November, he referred to an 'incident' with some Tyrolese singers. He also mentioned a certain Teresa, perhaps one of the singers or someone he had met in Vienna, whose 'legacy' made it impossible for him to taste the 'forbidden fruit' so readily available in Paris. In the same letter he mentioned someone named Benedict, who considered his 'misfortune' a mere trifle.[20] It all seems to add up to Chopin's first sexual encounter either right at the end of his time in Vienna or *en route* to Munich, and to his contraction of a mild dose of venereal disease of some sort.

The stay in Munich was protracted, since the arrival of the money order from Poland had been delayed. Chopin spent a full month there, and took the opportunity to get to know the musical life of the Bavarian capital, including the Opera and its conductor Josef Hartmann Stunz. Stunz invited him to play at one of the Philharmonic's Sunday matinées, and on 28 August Chopin duly gave the E minor Concerto as a solo, together with the *Fantasy on Polish Airs*, Op. 13. The concert was well reviewed in the Munich journal *Flora*, but it was the pianist rather than the composer who was praised. The Concerto was described as 'brilliant and skilfully crafted but without great originality or profundity, apart from the principal theme and the middle section of the rondo'. The Fantasy went down rather better. 'There is something about these Slavonic folksongs that seldom fails to arouse the listener, though it is very difficult to say why. Herr Chopin's Fantasy was applauded from all quarters.'[21]

[20] *KFC*, vol. 1, p. 187.   [21] *Flora*, 30 August 1831.

Shortly after the concert, Chopin's money arrived and he set off alone for Paris, by way of Stuttgart, where he put up at a hotel for some two weeks. It is not entirely clear why he dallied there, since there were regular coach connections to Paris. But a later letter to Woyciechowski suggests that it was a time of agonizing indecision, when he gave serious thought to returning to Warsaw. Without doubt this was one of the darkest moments in Chopin's life, compounding the bad news from home with the general uncertainty of his future. At this point he felt a failure. He was far from the security of home, family, and friends, from the lure of a world where he knew he would be valued, but whose limitations were all too apparent to him. Yet at the same time he had not yet seen any clear evidence that he was capable of establishing a reputation in the international world of music, to which he was no less powerfully drawn.

We can glean something of his dejected state of mind from the Stuttgart entries in the album he had carried with him from Warsaw. He had been given this small traveller's album in 1829, when he was first planning his 'grand tour'. It remained untouched for a year or so, but as his departure for Vienna drew near he began collecting a few inscriptions, including verses by Gładkowska and some lines by Żywny. The first pages of the album had watercolours of Warsaw scenes, Sigismund's column and Krakowskie Przedmieście, and in a letter to Matuszyński Chopin remarked that he often took comfort from these when he felt depressed in Vienna. It was in Vienna that he took to jotting down occasional remarks and observations in the album, and as the months passed it began to assume something of the character of a *journal intime*.

It was to this album that he confessed his morbid thoughts during the Stuttgart days.

No doubt more than one corpse has lain on [the bed]—and for who knows how long? And am I any better than a corpse? Like a corpse I am without news of my father, mother, sisters, or Tytus. Like a corpse I have no lover. Like a corpse I am pale, and my feelings are cold. . . . I have lived enough.[22]

And when the news broke that Warsaw had finally fallen to the Russians on 8 September, Chopin cracked totally. All the insecurities which had haunted him in Vienna were now articulated in a single cry of despair.

Oh God! You are there! You are there and yet you do not take vengeance! Have you not witnessed enough crimes from Russia? . . . Oh father, so this is how you are rewarded in old age! Mother, sweet suffering mother, you saw your daughter die, and now you watch the Russian marching in over her grave to oppress you! . . . Oh Tytus, Tytus! . . . What has become of *her*, where is she now, poor girl? . . .

[22] *KFC*, vol. 1, pp. 183–4.

Perhaps she is already in Russian hands? The Russians may be touching her, stifling her, murdering her! . . . I am helpless, sitting here powerless, suffering through the piano, in despair . . . And what now? God, god, move this earth—let it swallow the people of this century.[23]

Chopin's decision was made for him, and a day or two later he was in Paris. Perhaps there was some sense of the die cast, a feeling that *any* decision was better than the indecision which had plagued him for weeks. At any rate, the earliest letters from Paris (admittedly dating from November, almost exactly two months after his arrival) suggest a young man in distinctly more cheerful mood. Chopin found himself a modest fourth-floor apartment on the Boulevard Poissonière, and he was very quickly intoxicated by the atmosphere of a city quite unlike anything he had known before. His experience of German cities such as Berlin and Munich, and even his eight-month stay in the Hapsburg capital, could not have prepared him for the extremes of squalor and grandeur which he encountered in Paris. As he put it himself, 'You find here the greatest splendour, the greatest filthiness, the greatest virtue and the greatest vice'.[24] He was struck, too, by the permissiveness and inviting anonymity of a great capital. 'Paris is whatever you care to make of it', he wrote to Tytus. 'You can enjoy yourself, get bored, laugh, cry, do anything you like, and no one takes any notice because thousands here are doing exactly the same. Everyone goes his own way.'[25]

The 'July revolution' had enthroned Louis-Philippe a year before Chopin's arrival in the city, and the entrepreneurial spirit encouraged by the new regime very quickly extended to the world of formal culture. The commercialization of art carried its own penalties of course, and in due course it sparked off a *bataille romantique* which enlisted a whole generation of writers and artists, among them Hugo, Lamartine, Balzac, and Delacroix. But musicians were less actively involved in this 'social romanticism' than other artists, and it was to musicians that Chopin was inevitably drawn. He was overwhelmed by the sheer splendour of the productions at the Théâtre-Italien, and even more at Le Péletier, where so-called 'Grand Opera', the collaborative achievement of Véron, Scribe, and Meyerbeer, had already assumed its characteristic form. Chopin wrote eulogies abut Meyerbeer's *Robert le diable*, and the resonance of this work seems to have remained with him for a time. Not only did he collaborate with Auguste Franchomme in composing a *Grand Duo concertant* for cello and piano based on themes from the opera, but he may also have turned to it as one source of inspiration for one of his later masterpieces, the second Ballade.

He attended the opera at every opportunity, and his letters to Warsaw from these early Paris months are replete with commentaries on productions and on individual singers. 'Only here can one learn what

[23] *KFC*, vol. 1, pp. 185–6.   [24] Ibid., p. 187.   [25] Ibid., p. 199.

singing is', he commented. Of Laure Cinti-Damoreau, 'she sings as perfectly as can be imagined . . . and seems to caress the public'; of Giuditta Pasta, 'I have never before seen anything so sublime'; of Maria Felicía Malibran-García, 'miracle! miracle!'; of Luigi Lablache, 'you cannot imagine what it is like'; of Adolphe Nourrit, 'his expression is astonishing'; and of Giovanni Battista Rubini, 'his mezza voce is incomparable'.[26] All this filtered through into the increasingly refined and sophisticated melodic style of his piano music. But it is possible, too, that at the back of his mind he had not yet totally abandoned the idea of composing an opera himself. The decision to do so was spelt out in a letter to Elsner, dated 14 December. 'In 1830 I dared to think that I might come close to your achievement, that if I could not produce a *Lokietek* ['The Elbow-high', an opera by Elsner], then at least some *Laskonogi* ['Skinny Shanks'] might come from my brain. But today, seeing all such hopes dashed, I am forced to think of making my way as a pianist.'[27]

Paris was, of course, a magnet for the great pianists of the day, and at an early stage Chopin was introduced to one of the best of them, Friedrich Kalkbrenner. He had arrived with a letter of introduction from Dr Malfatti to Ferdinand Paër, the court director of music, and through Paër he met several of the city's leading musicians, including Cherubini, director of the Conservatory, as well as Kalkbrenner himself. Kalkbrenner's playing was a revelation to Chopin. 'If Paganini is perfection, then Kalkbrenner is at least his equal, but in a completely different way. It is difficult to describe to you his calm, his enchanting touch—the incredible evenness and mastery in every note he plays. He is a giant stepping on all of us, on Herz, Czerny and the rest of them, and on me too.' Kalkbrenner proposed that Chopin embark on a course of lessons for three years, and Chopin took the proposal seriously. Indeed it was a crucial decision for his future, and he took advice from his family and in particular from his old teacher Elsner. In the end he was persuaded against the idea, mainly by Elsner, who felt—probably rightly—that it would not be appropriate for Chopin at this stage to try to adapt to Kalkbrenner's highly individual piano technique. The point was taken, and in a reply to Elsner, Chopin remarked firmly that he had 'no intention of becoming a copy of Kalk[brenner]'.[28]

The future was still far from clear. Despite his misgivings, Chopin had left Warsaw with the intention of making his way as a public pianist. The experience of Vienna had dented his confidence considerably, but already in the early months in Paris he began to feel again that something of the sort might be possible. At any rate, the alternatives were not obvious, and some resolution was pressing, since he was living well in the French capital and would very soon run out of money. The main

[26] Letter to Tytus, 12 December 1831: ibid., pp. 201–2.
[27] Letter to Elsner, 14 December 1831: ibid., p. 204.   [28] Ibid., p. 205.

priority, then, was to arrange a concert, and he eventually succeeded in doing so, thanks to the contacts he had already established. Those contacts were not exclusively musical. From the start Chopin felt less alienated in Paris, where there had always been close links with Poland and where sympathy for the Polish cause was not just prevalent, but distinctly fashionable. In the very first letter from Paris, he described his lunches with Walenty Radziwiłł and Delfina Potocka, both of whom had been resident in Paris before the uprising. Shortly afterwards he was befriended by Count Ludwik Plater, and later still by Count Wojciech Grzymała, together with Polish sympathizers such as the Marquis de Custine.

Following the defeat of the Polish forces, the number of Poles living in the French capital increased dramatically. They ranged from the group of exiled political leaders gathered around Adam Czartoryski, who held court at the Hôtel Lambert, to radical 'messianic' poet-philosophers such as Adam Mickiewicz, Juliusz Slowacki, and Cyprian Norwid. In due course Chopin would have dealings with both groups. But more immediately, he found himself reunited with several old friends from the Lyceum and High School of Music, as the disbanded revolutionaries gradually made their way to Paris. These included Kazimierz Wodziński, Antoni Orlowski, and Julian Fontana. As he remarked in a letter to Woyciechowski, 'If I am happy at all, at least on the surface, it is above all when I am with my own people, and by that I mean Poles'.[29] The context, in other words, could not have been more different from Vienna. In Paris Chopin was surrounded by Poles and Polish sympathizers, and he was as happy there as he might be anywhere. By securing a residence permit (through the advocacy of Paër), he acquired a welcome measure of stability in the French capital. At the same time, and this is symptomatic of the conflicting claims on his emotions, the permit inevitably alienated the Russian authorities, making it difficult for him—despite later amnesties—to return to his homeland. Chopin went on to quality his remarks to Woyciechowski. Happy on the surface, perhaps, 'but something inside is killing me. . . . I feel sour, bitter, salty, governed by a hideous mixture of feelings'.[30]

The much awaited concert in Paris was originally planned for December at the Salle Pleyel, which had been opened the previous year. Kalkbrenner was a partner in the firm Pleyel & Cie., and through his offices the hall was made available free of charge. He also agreed to perform along with Chopin in his own Grande Polonaise and March for six pianos, described by Chopin as a 'crazy piece'. The series of postponements which followed resulted first from Chopin's difficulties in securing the services of good singers, indispensable to the success of any benefit concert, and then from Kalkbrenner's illness. But in the end the

[29] *KFC*, vol. 1, p. 210.　　　[30] Ibid., p. 210.

Salle Pleyel was booked for 26 February, 1832, and the programme was finalized as Beethoven's String Quintet, Op. 29 (performed by a prestigious ensemble from the Conservatory), vocal arias and duets, an oboe solo, the Kalkbrenner Grande Polonaise and two works by Chopin—the E minor Concerto and the *Là ci darem* Variations. The Variations had recently come in for some major international attention, following the legendary review by Robert Schumann in the *Allgemeine Musikalische Zeitung* ('Hats off, Gentlemen! A Genius'), closely followed by a fanciful account, whose picturesque programmatic references caused Chopin some amusement. Ludwig Rellstab also reviewed the piece in his journal *Iris*, describing it as vandalism to Mozart, a characteristic demonstration of the 'primitive origins of the Slavonic nations'.[31] The polarisation of views embodied in these reviews by Schumann and Rellstab would characterize Chopin reception in Germany for many years.

For various reasons, including high seat prices and a widespread exodus from Paris due to the encroaching cholera epidemic, the hall was only about a third full. Poles were well represented, of course, but there were some prestigious musicians there too, including both Liszt and Mendelssohn and the leading critic François-Joseph Fétis, founder of the *Revue musicale*. Fétis's review of this momentous concert was so farsighted that it will be worth quoting extensively from it.

> Here is a young man who, abandoning himself to his natural impressions and without taking a model, has found, if not a complete renewal of pianoforte music, at least a part of what has been sought in vain for a long time—namely an abundance of original ideas of which the type is to be found nowhere. We do not mean by this that M. Chopin is endowed with a powerful organization like that of a Beethoven, nor that there arise in his music such powerful conceptions as one remarks in that of this great man. Beethoven has composed pianoforte music, but I speak here of pianists' music, and it is by comparison with the latter that I find in M. Chopin's inspirations an indication of a renewal of forms which may exercise in time much influence over this department of the art.[32]

There were some additional criticisms of Chopin's rather soft tone ('he brings little sound out of the instrument'), echoing a point which had been well rehearsed by critics in Warsaw and Vienna, and these remarks would certainly have given Chopin further cause to doubt his prowess as a 'public' pianist. But by and large Fétis was supportive and he correctly foresaw that Chopin's compositional style would inaugurate a quite new direction in what he called 'pianists' music'. The term itself is

[31] Quoted in Ferdynand Hoesick, *Chopin* (Cracow, 1967; original edn., 1903–11), 3 vols., vol. 2, p. 91.

[32] *Revue musicale*, 3 March, 1832.

interesting, for it puts in a nutshell the widely perceived distinction between virtuoso concert music and the so-called Viennese classical style.

'All Paris is stupified', wrote the loyal Orlowski. But the truth is that Chopin had great difficulty in following up the undoubted critical (but by no means financial) success of this first concert in Paris. He tried to gain an invitation to play at the prestigious *concerts du conservatoire* but was unable to do so, despite his useful contacts with Baillot and Cherubini. Nor were there many other openings in a city where cholera continued to rage, with serious implications for the world of formal culture. Once more financial pressures mounted and occasional private lessons to members of the Polish community, supplemented by some money from his mother, were by no means enough to live off. Chopin's next solo appearance, on 20 May, was at a charity concert organized on behalf of cholera victims by the Prince de la Moskova, son of Napoleon's Marshal Ney, so this clearly brought him no financial reward. Indeed it seems to have been rather unsuccessful in other ways too, with the usual criticisms about his tone and projection. By now Chopin was surely aware that he must find an alternative to the career of public pianist.

That alternative began to emerge in the latter half of 1832 and it became ever clearer during the following year. It depended largely on his growing contacts with the wealthy and the great in Paris. Such contacts increased steadily during 1832, partly through his friends among the exiled Polish community, and partly through his association with the artistic 'aristocracy', including of course the most fashionable musicians and composers. In the Polish community he soon became a familiar figure, well known at the soirées given by the Platers and Komars, by Delfina Potocka, and (a little later) by the Czartoryskis. Here he was the ideal guest, perfect in manners, a little aloof, with a natural air of distinction, and with the enviable capacity to cast a magic spell on the company as soon as he sat at the piano.

He was no less popular with artists and musicians. The pianist and composer Ferdinand Hiller was especially close to him, taking over something of the role of confidant from Woyciechowski and Matuszyński. Liszt, too, was attracted to Chopin, and was quick to recognize and appreciate his originality both as pianist and composer. The two men may have been temperamental opposites, but they had great respect for each other's very different talents, at least in the early days. Chopin was also befriended by Berlioz, whose music he simply could not understand, and by Mendelssohn, who appeared in Paris from time to time and whose compositions seemed worthy but mediocre to Chopin. Whatever his views on their music, he enjoyed cordial personal relationships with both men in these early Paris years, though they had receded from his life by the late 1830s. Also part of the circle were the young cellist Auguste Franchomme, who would remain a close friend throughout his life, and the poet Heinrich Heine.

Chopin met with such men either at restaurants or at one or other of their apartments, where there would be heated discussion about music, literature, and ideas. It has to be said that Chopin was deeply interested in only one of the three. At a time when progressive composers turned increasingly to the worlds of literature and painting as direct sources of inspiration, when there was an increasing preoccupation with the expressive and denotative powers of music, Chopin remained cautious of programmes and descriptive titles. Unlike Liszt, Berlioz, and Schumann, who were all men of the new age with a wide general culture, he remained at least as close to an earlier classical aesthetic as to the spirit of romanticism. The respect he commanded in artistic circles was based, then, not on his prowess as a thinker, but on his exceptional musical gifts, allied to the inevitable attractions which attend a personality wrapped in secrecy.

Both these groups—the Polish *émigrés* and the artists—offered an entrée to 'the highest circles' of French society, to the great and the good, the titled and the wealthy. Towards the end of 1832 Chopin found himself in constant demand socially, and it was largely due to this that an alternative career began to open up to him, quite possibly more by default than through any conscious planning on his part. His sources of income from the winter of 1832 onwards were threefold. His performances in private drawing-rooms would often, though by no means always, attract some financial reward, usually discreetly forwarded at a later date. His published music also provided a modest income, and already by the end of the year he had made some progress in this area. But his principal means of earning a living was as a teacher. Other pianist-composers taught, of course, but Chopin was soon in such demand that he could charge an exorbitant rate (twenty francs a lesson) and could actually avoid, rather than deliberately seek, opportunities to give public concerts. His was a special path, and it had major repercussions on his compositional style. Since he avoided the concert hall, he also avoided concert music, apart from one or two works which still lingered in the world of the brilliant style. Instead he felt able to concentrate his creative energies on music whose attention to detail and refinement of nuance were ideally suited to small groups of initiates in society drawing-rooms, and here his reputation was very soon legendary.

There is some suggestion in the literature that this success—social and professional—came quite suddenly at the beginning of the winter season in 1832, the result of a chance meeting with Prince Walenty Radziwiłł followed by a performance at the home of Baron James de Rothschild. The story is unsubstantiated, and almost certainly apocryphal, but it is true that his reported success followed a summer of further doubt and indecision about his future. His letters record his nostalgia for friends and family in Poland (his older sister Ludwika married Kalasanty Jędrzejewicz in September), and his uncertainty about remaining in Paris, and reports from friends such as Orlowski confirm that his mood was black. He considered taking advantage of his passport for London, and there is even a hint that he may have thought of a move to America, prompted by his acquaintance with Pleyel's American representative Paul Emil Johns, to whom he dedicated the Op. 7 Mazurkas. For whatever reason, such uncertainty had vanished by the beginning of 1833, and he was able to write with pride to Dziewanowski that he had 'entered the best society'. 'I sit with ambassadors, princes and ministers; and I don't even know by what miracle this is, for I have never crowed about myself.'[33] And a little later in the same letter: 'The students at the Conservatoire, the pupils of Moscheles, Herz, Kalkbrenner, in a word, accomplished artists, take lessons with me.'

Chopin's teaching was by all accounts (and there are many) exceptional, as indeed was his playing.[34] All are agreed on the originality of his technique, inadequate to the public concert perhaps, but perfectly suited to the *soirée intime*. Descriptions are colourful: 'The marvellous charm, the poetry and originality, the perfect freedom and absolute lucidity of Chopin's playing cannot be described. It is perfection in every sense . . .'[35] 'Every single note was played with the highest degree of taste, in the noblest sense of the word. When he embellished—which he rarely did—it was a positive miracle of refinement.'[36] '[The audience applauds] that enchanting pianist who speaks a seductive language with his fingers and discloses his soul through his playing, which in turn leaves nothing to be desired.'[37] 'It is as though the piano had been transformed in some way and had become a totally different instrument, responding to the fiery touch of a genius, at once gentle and passionate.'[38]

His technique was largely self-acquired, and this may well have had some bearing on its pronounced individuality. Moreover this attempt to communicate it to pupils resulted in a teaching style quite unlike those of other pianist-teachers of the time. The *Projet de méthode* sketched out for the benefit of younger pupils some of the basic principles underlying that technique.[39] It comprises several texts at various stages of completion, but there is enough material to give a good indication of his

[33] Letter to Dominik Dziewanowski, January 1833: *KFC*, vol. 1, p. 223.

[34] The classic text is Jean-Jacques Eigeldinger, *Chopin: Pianist and Teacher*, tr. Naomi Shohet with Krysia Osostowicz and Roy Howat, ed. Roy Howat (Cambridge, 1986; original French edn., 1979).

[35] C. E. and M. Hallé, *Life and Letters of Charles Hallé* (London, 1896), p. 31.

[36] Wilhelm von Lenz, *The Great Piano Virtuosos of Our Time*, ed. Philip Reder (London, 1983; original German edn., 1872), p. 55.

[37] *Revue et Gazette musicale*, Paris, 27 February, 1842. [38] Ibid.

[39] See chapter 2, note 52.

approach. What Chopin called the 'mechanism' of playing is described there in deliberately simple terms, promoting a natural hand shape, with the elbow on a level with the white notes and the hand pointing neither in nor out, and an acceptance, controversial at the time, of the imbalance and functional independence of the fingers rather than an ambition to equalize them. B major is regarded as the paradigmatic scale for a natural hand shape, and it is used to explore different varieties of cantabile legato in an attempt to demonstrate the many possible timbres which can be drawn from the instrument, always to be achieved 'without force'.

Chopin was against the mindless mechanical practice of technical exercises, arguing that the interest and enthusiasm of the pupil must be engaged on a musical level, and that exercises must always be directed to the larger goal of creating music. He did of course devise exercises, but unlike those of Kalkbrenner or Herz, for example, they were designed to encourage flexibility in the wrist so that the hand might function without restriction. 'The goal is not to play everything with an equal sound, [but rather] it seems to me, a well formed technique that can control and vary a beautiful sound quality.'[40] He encouraged his pupils to play them with varying shades of dynamics and articulation, and he paid special attention to the diminished-seventh chord as a means of establishing the smooth movement of the thumb under the other fingers while retaining a 'natural' hand position. In the interests of fluidity of movement and evenness of tone he was quite prepared to sanction highly unorthodox fingerings. Ultimately for Chopin elements of technique could not be separated from elements of musical style. And for that reason it will be worth deferring further discussion of technical issues until we examine the études, where performer and teacher meet at the highest level of creativity.

Such was Chopin's new routine of teaching and gracing the salons that he gave no solo public performance throughout 1833, though he took part in duets and larger ensembles at concerts organized by other artists. There was a clutch of these events at the end of March and beginning of April, starting with a benefit concert given by Hiller on 23 March. The programme was the usual mixture of orchestral music, vocal solos, and duets and chamber works (with a cello solo composed and performed by Franchomme), and at its centre was a performance of Bach's Concerto for Three Harpsichords, given (on pianos of course) by Chopin, Liszt, and Hiller. A week later, on 30 March, Chopin played at a benefit given by a young pianist composer, Jean-Amédée le Froid de Méreaux. He frequently played duets with Méreaux, and at the concert they performed a duet based on Hérold's *Le Pré aux Clercs*, composed by Méreaux (not the Hérold Variations composed by Chopin later in the

---

[40] *Frédéric Chopin: Esquisses pour une méthode de piano*, p. 74.

same year, as sometimes reported). A few days after that, on 2 April, he was on the stage of the Théâtre-Italien, performing the Sonata, Op. 22 for four hands by Liszt at a grand benefit arranged by Berlioz on behalf of Harriet Smithson. And the next day he took part in an eight-hand piano arrangement by Henri Herz of a theme from Meyerbeer's opera *Il Crociato in Egitto* at a concert organized by Herz. Liszt and Herz's brother were the other performers.

There was some disruption in June 1833, when he moved apartments for the second time in Paris. He had moved to the Cité Bergère (No. 4) towards the end of 1832, but as his income increased he felt able to rent something larger and more stylish. He moved, in fact, to an apartment already well known to him, in 5 rue de la Chaussée d'Antin. It was sub-let to him by Dr Hermann Franck, whom he had often visited with Hiller, Liszt, and Franchomme, and who was just then spending a period in London and Berlin. 'I am very comfortable in these rooms where we often used to meet', he wrote to Hiller.[41] And once he had settled in he devoted the summer very largely to composition, as he was to do also in subsequent years. The Variations, Op. 12 on a theme of Hérold (from the opera *Ludovic*, which Chopin heard in May) were composed at this time. And so were the first and third of the Op. 15 Nocturnes, the Bolero, Op. 19, and the E flat major Waltz, Op. 18. In addition he completed the études which would soon be published as Op. 10. Dedications on these and other works of 1832–3 reflect the social world then available to Chopin.

In the autumn Dr Franck decided to give up the apartment, and Chopin stayed on, taking in an old Silesian acquaintance whom he had known in Warsaw, Dr Aleksander Hoffmann. Some fifty years later Hoffmann's widow told Ferdinand Hoesick that at this time Chopin had an affair with Countess Delfina Potocka, and the story gained credence for a while through the publication of a spurious, and now infamous, correspondence between them.[42] It is certainly possible that Chopin was involved with someone during these early years in Paris, since already in November 1832 his old teacher Elsner referred to 'the young lady with whom (according to your sister Ludwika) you are about to be united'.[43] But if Chopin had indeed planned to marry (and there is no hint of this in his own letters), Delfina could certainly not have been his choice. Mme Hoffmann's evidence is in any case demonstrably unreliable on other counts, and there is no reason to suggest that she was right about events which took place long before she had even met her husband.

Elementary psychology suggests otherwise. Chopin may well have

[41] *KFC*, vol. 1, p. 228.

[42] Two major scientific studies of these texts (of which none are original sources) have been made. See *Chopin Studies 1* (Warsaw, 1985), pp. 153–79, and George Marek and Maria Gordon-Smith, *Chopin: A Biography* (New York, 1978), pp. 258–67.

[43] *KFC*, vol. 1, p. 221.

been prepared to tussle with a Tyrolese singer, but with Delfina Potocka he would have preferred unspoken adoration or innocent flirtation to anything remotely like a physical relationship. Indeed he was once greatly amused that he had been suspected of seduction, professing his astonishment that 'anyone could imagine me *capable* of such a thing'.[44] That he admired Delfina and was close to her is beyond question. That he was infatuated with her is likely. Nor can we rule out absolutely the possibility of a liaison during this period. But it is hard to understand how biographers have found it possible to weave the story of Delfina happily into the web of their narrative without a shred of reliable evidence to support it.[45]

One certainty is that the timid young composer who had arrived in Paris quite unknown two years earlier was fast becoming an established figure. His reputation in musical circles continued to grow, and it was enhanced, as was his income, by an increasing body of published music. Apart from the private publication of some early music, he had first gone into print in Warsaw when Brzezina & Co. lithographed the Op. 1 Rondo. Other early pieces were published by Haslinger (Op. 2) and Mechetti of Vienna (Op. 3), but in early 1833 he sold publishing rights to Maurice Schlesinger (after tentative negotiations with Farrenc) and at the end of the year his music began to appear 'simultaneously' in France (Schlesinger), England (Wessel & Co), and Germany (Kistner, and later Brietkopf & Härtel).[46] Simultaneous publication, designed to avoid piracy, was a common enough practice at the time, but Chopin's negotiations with these publishers reveal him as a surprisingly shrewd business-man, well capable of maximizing his advantage financially. The German publisher was especially important in this respect, since Brietkopf had agents and distribution networks throughout the world.

These publishing contracts were all the more crucial for Chopin in that he had effectively abandoned the public concert, with its related promotional apparatus. One English critic remarked later that where other pianists would promote their music by 'announc[ing] a concert or see[ing] company at Erard's or Broadwood's . . . M. Chopin . . . quietly publishes 2 [*sic*] Waltzes'.[47] So the flood of publications in late 1833 and early 1834 inaugurated an important stage in the wider dissemination of his music. The newly published compositions included some major

[44] Letter to Tytus, 12 December 1831: ibid., p. 204.

[45] See, for instance, Ruth Jordan, *Nocturne: A Life of Chopin* (London, 1978). The justification for building the Potocka affair into her biography is given by Jordan in the preface: 'Having given much thought to the arguments for and against the authenticity of the letters and seen the photostat reproductions in Chopin's hand as well as the text in the hand of the copier, my feeling is that the ayes have it', p. 12.

[46] By far the most comprehensive and perceptive account of Chopin's dealings with his publishers is in Jeffrey Kallberg, 'Chopin in the Market-Place', *Notes*, vol. 39, nos. 3 and 4, March and June 1983.

[47] *The Athenaeum*, 22 January 1848.

works from the Warsaw years, notably another edition of the *Là ci darem* Variations, the Piano Trio, the *Fantasy on Polish Airs*, the *Rondo à la krakowiak*, and the E minor Concerto, as well as more recent music from the Vienna and early Paris years. The first three sets of mazurkas to be published (Opp. 6, 7, and 17) came out at this time, as did the Op. 9 Nocturnes, Op. 10 Études, Op. 16 Rondo, and Op. 18 Waltz. And shortly after their publication, critical notices began to appear in France, Germany, and England. This, too, initiated a recurring pattern in Chopin reception. By and large, reviews of the music in later years were more often consequent on publication than on performance.

In France the *Revue et Gazette musicale de Paris* (initially the *Gazette musicale*) was especially supportive. 'From the first moment he appeared on stage he created for himself a new path'[48]; 'Of the four of them [the Op. 17 Mazurkas], our favourite is without doubt the last. . . . It is here that the music reveals itself in all its poetic excellence to a degree to which ordinary speech cannot rise.'[49] The image of Chopin as a composer of deep seriousness suited the purpose of the *Gazette*. This was a journal committed to a sustained war against the 'piano industry' and to the journalistic support of that industry elsewhere in Paris, notably in *La France musicale*, which managed to ignore Chopin almost entirely at this time.[50] In Germany Chopin was well served by the *Allgemeine musikalische Zeitung*, as also of course by Schumann's *Neue Zeitschrift für Musik*, but attacked (at least until 1839) by Rellstab's *Iris*. In England there was a similar division, with *The Musical Standard* and *The Athenaeum* (Henry Chorley) broadly favourable, and *The Musical World* (J. W. Davison) antagonistic.

Critics aside, the music sold, and Chopin was confirmed in the view that he could earn a living, though only a modest one, without recourse to the public concert. His only appearances during the 1833–4 season were at other pianists' concerts (another performance of the Bach Concerto for Three Pianos with Liszt and Hiller in December 1833) or at informal soirées. These latter included many evenings with the friends of Vincento Bellini, who arrived in Paris in the autumn of 1833 and with whom Chopin felt much affinity during the brief period of their acquaintance. Hiller's descriptions of these evenings are in themselves a telling indication of Chopin's new-found contentment at this time. Success was coming his way and agreed with him. He was now fully settled in Paris, and had put well to the back of his mind any plans to leave. Above all he was with friends. Hiller himself was one of these, though his adoration for Chopin was perhaps not reciprocated in full measure. If anything, it was to August Franchomme that Chopin felt closest, and it was

[48] *Gazette musicale*, Paris, 15 May 1834.　　　　　　[49] Ibid., 29 June 1834.
[50] The rivalry between the two journals was fierce, and even resulted in a duel between Schlesinger and one of Herz's pupils. To his intense embarrassment, Chopin was called as a witness at the trial on 29 April 1834.

no doubt a special pleasure to spend a few days in the autumn with Franchomme's family near Tours.

The Polish community continued to play an important part in his life, of course, and in particular three friends from Warsaw days. Following the defeat of the uprising, Julian Fontana joined the exiles in Paris before moving to London in an unsuccessful attempt to establish himself as a pianist-composer. He returned to Paris at the end of 1833, and from that point he played an increasingly important role in Chopin's professional life. For some ten years, before his departure for America in 1844, Fontana was Chopin's principal copyist, and one of the very few who could claim to have influenced even in minor ways the course of Chopin's music.[51] When he returned to Paris in 1853 (after a flying visit to Europe in 1848), he continued his service to Chopin by undertaking the posthumous publication of the unpublished music at the request of the Chopin family. There can be no doubt of Fontana's devotion to the composer. Chopin, on the other hand, was quite prepared to abuse the friendship and made shameless use of Fontana's willingness to undertake no end of chores to make his life more comfortable.

The company of Wojciech Grzymała, a colourful entrepreneur who managed somehow to live off his wits in Paris, was no doubt more con-genial to Chopin, though he was not above using Grzymała, too. In Warsaw he had known the older man only slightly. Grzymała was a man of wide cultural interests who frequently wrote on musical matters in the Warsaw press. His reviews were not always flattering to Chopin, but he did at least recognize the exceptional nature of the young man's gifts and tried as far as possible to promote them. Like many others, he drifted to Paris after the uprising, and he developed there—at least until the late 1840s—an entirely unsuspected capacity to earn a living from financial speculation. His friendship with the composer dated from this period, and it grew closer over the years. Increasingly Grzymała, very much a man of the world, took on an almost paternal role in Chopin's life, especially during the liaison with George Sand.

The arrival of Jan Matuszyński in the spring of 1834 was especially cheering to Chopin. After the uprising Matuszyński completed his med-ical studies in Germany, and he moved straight from there to a teaching post at the École de Médecine in Paris. The two men had not met since Chopin's final year in Warsaw, but they had been close friends there and had kept in touch through correspondence. Nothing could have been more calculated to complete Chopin's general sense of well-being in Paris than Matuszyński's arrival. Since the arrangement with Aleksander Hoffmann had not really worked out, Chopin proposed that Matuszyński move in immediately to Chaussée d'Antin. Only a month or two earlier his father had written of his concern that 'you do not have

---

[51] See, for example, Jim Samson, 'An Unknown Chopin Autograph', *The Musical Times*, July (1986), pp. 376–8.

a real friend living with you. It is miserable to be entirely on one's own, with no one to talk to'.[52] Another problem was solved.

In May 1834, Chopin and Hiller set off for Achen for a musical festival organized by Ferdinand Ries. There they heard Mozart's 'Jupiter' Symphony, Beethoven's Choral Symphony, and Handel's *Deborah* in an orchestration by Hiller. They were joined by Mendelssohn, who was then conductor of the orchestra at Düsseldorf, and the three men spent all their time together, playing each other's music, and, as Mendelssohn put it in a letter to his family, 'learn[ing] one from the other'.[53] Mendelssohn had his reservations, though, and went on to remark that the other two 'suffer somewhat from the Parisian mania for despair and emotional exaggeration, and too often lose sight of tact and calm and purely musical understanding'. Following the festival they went on a trip on the Rhine, and stayed at Düsseldorf, Koblenz, and Cologne. It was a pleasant interlude of the kind Chopin loved most, keeping company with fellow musicians, playing music, and talking about music.

When he returned to Paris for the remainder of the season and a summer of intensive composition, he was returning home. He now had a successful career, a close circle of friends, and a high standing in society. One matter alone remained unresolved for a young man aged twenty-four. Without doubt it preyed on his mind, and very soon steps would be taken to rectify it. Shortly after his return he received a letter from the mother of the three Wodziński boys, who had boarded with the Chopins in Warsaw. It was an invitation to visit the family in Geneva. Maria Wodzińska, whom Chopin had last seen as an eleven-year-old ('I used to chase [her] through the rooms at Pszenny in days gone by'), appended a short composition to the letter, and Chopin was delighted with the gesture, improvising on the theme at a salon in Paris.[54] He refused the invitation to Geneva, and it was more than a year later that he met Maria again in Karlsbad. Nevertheless, the stage was set for a new chapter in his life.

[52] *KFC*, vol. 1, p. 234.
[53] Quoted in Frederick Niecks, *Chopin as a Man and Musician*, vol. 1, p. 273.
[54] Letter to Feliks Wodziński, 18 July 1834: *KFC*, vol. 1, p. 242.

4

'A rebirth of pianistic art'

The chronology of Chopin's early music is anything but well established. The broad outlines are clear, of course, but there remain many imponderables. For numerous works there is no surviving autograph, and even where autographs are extant they do not always yield an accurate date, despite the advantages of recent paper research.[1] Nor is contextual evidence always available. Difficulties are especially acute in the works of the Warsaw period, but they persist even in the music of the Vienna and early Paris years. It will be worth scotching some of the more common misconceptions at the outset. It has already been noted that Brown's attribution of Op. 10, Nos. 8–11 to the Warsaw period is unsupported by reliable evidence. Only the first four of the Études can be dated accurately. Early copies of Nos. 1 and 2 were signed and dated '2 November 1830', just before Chopin left Warsaw for Vienna, while the autograph of No. 4 was signed and dated 'Paris, 6 August, 1832' and No. 3 'Paris, 25 August 1832'. We also know (from a Schlesinger letter to Kistner) that all twelve Études ('ein Meisterwerk') were complete by October at the latest.[2] So it is possible that the third Étude, much favoured by Chopin himself, was the last of the cycle to be composed. Beyond this there is no concrete evidence to help us date the remainder of the Études, and that includes No. 12, the so-called 'Revolutionary Study', traditionally associated with the Stuttgart days, when Chopin learnt of the final defeat of the insurrection.

There are other dubious traditions, notably a report that the first Scherzo and first Ballade were sketched in Vienna in 1830–1. This probably emanated from misleading evidence given by Maurice Schlesinger in a newspaper interview of c. 1860,[3] and it has been repeated in the

[1] Watermark identification is helpful with some of the Warsaw-period music, since early nineteenth-century Polish paper is highly distinctive and can be identified and dated with relative ease. In some cases this has helped in the revision of chronology. Paper is a less useful tool with music of the Paris years, except as a very general and crude guide, i.e. allowing us to infer that similarly formatted paper may suggest a similar period of composition, as with the autographs of Op. 23 and Op. 26.

[2] See Zofia Lissa, 'Chopin w świetle korespondencja współczesnych mu wydawców', in *Muzyka* (1960), no. 1, pp. 3–21.

[3] Ibid.

literature ever since. The date has even been used as a basis for making rather curious interpretative assessments in some recent scholarship.[4] A much later date—certainly no sooner than 1833, and probably 1834–5—is indicated for both works on stylistic grounds and for the Ballade on paper evidence, too.[5] Lengthy gestation periods were not characteristic of Chopin and it is likely that he followed his normal practice with the Scherzo and Ballade, beginning them a year or at most two years before their publication in 1835 and 1836 respectively.

There are uncertainties, too, about the chronology of some of the bravura concert pieces of the Vienna and early Paris years. The completion of the *Grande Polonaise brillante*, Op. 22 was almost certainly a project of the early months in Vienna. But Chopin also worked on a proposed Concerto for Two Pianos at this time.[6] A little later in Paris he may have begun drafting a third Piano Concerto, for as late as 1834 his father asked in a letter if it had been finished. There is no way of knowing how much, if any, of the work was written and when it was finally abandoned, but it is often surmised (without any concrete supporting evidence) that the later *Allegro de concert*, Op. 46, published in 1841, is an arrangement of the first movement of either the proposed Concerto for Two Pianos or the third Piano Concerto.[7] Certainly the stylization of ritornello–concertino contrasts makes this a superficially plausible hypothesis, but such a stylization was far from unprecedented in the solo piano literature. The matter must remain unresolved, but it is worth recalling that the practice of playing concerto movements as solos was well established, and would later be formalized by Alkan in his Concerto for Solo Piano.[8]

During the early stages of his stay in Paris Chopin's interest in bravura concert pieces seems to have revived briefly, as he tried once again to make a name on the concert platform and perhaps to ingratiate himself somewhat with the fashionable musical public. The *Grand Duo concertant* for cello and piano, based on themes from Meyerbeer's *Robert le diable*, was a collaboration with Auguste Franchomme, written shortly after his arrival in Paris in 1831. While in Vienna he had begun collaborating with Josef Slavik on something similar for violin and piano. The Rondo, Op. 16 was probably composed during the winter of 1832–3, while the *Variations brillantes*, Op. 12 on Hérold's 'Je vends des

[4] Wiesław Lisecki argues that the waltz elements in Op. 23 were inspired by Chopin's period in Vienna, and understands the term 'ballade' in its older sense of dance song rather than as a response to literature. See 'Die Ballade von Frederic Chopin—literarische oder musikalische Inspirationen', in *Chopin Studies 3* (Warsaw, 1990), pp. 305–18.

[5] See note 1. The paper type is identical to that of Op. 26, prepared for Schlesinger in 1835.

[6] See his letter to his family, 22 December 1830: *KFC*, vol. 1, p. 160.

[7] It is so stated without ambiguity in *Selected Correspondence of Fryderyk Chopin*, trans. and ed. Arthur Hedley (London, 1962), p. 122. The reference to a third Piano Concerto is in a letter to Chopin from his father, 11 April 1835: *KFC*, vol. 1, p. 256.

[8] Schumann's *Concert sans orchestre* (*Troisième grande sonate*) is rather a different case.

Scapulaires' was written in the summer months of 1833. The Bolero, Op. 19 also dates from 1833. Stylistically all these pieces may be grouped together. They belong to a world which was rapidly fading in Chopin's music as his compositional interests moved away inexorably from the conventional genres of the concert-hall.

It is very likely that Auguste Franchomme's contribution to the composition of the *Grand Duo* amounted to little more than technical assistance with the cello part. As Schumann put it in *Neue Zeitschrift für Musik*, 'I suspect that Chopin must have sketched it throughout, while Franchomme said a gentle "yes" to everything'.[9] The work is in every respect an entirely unremarkable pot-pourri of themes from the Meyerbeer opera, principally the Romanza and Chorus 'Non pietà' from Act I and the Terzetto 'Le mie cure ancor del cielo' from Act V. As in many such pieces, the main interest lies in the elaborate improvisatory piano writing of the slow introduction. But one technical point should be mentioned. The tonal organization of the *Duo* is of a kind later dubbed 'progressive' or 'directional', with the introduction in C sharp minor, the andantino in E major, and the closing allegretto (interrupted by a slower andante cantabile) in A major. There is nothing unusual about such schemes in the popular repertory of post-classical concert music. And it is worth underlining this, in view of the 'directional tonality' and 'two-key schemes' found in major compositions such as the second Ballade and the Fantasy, Op. 49. Commentators seldom invoke this particular background, preferring to understand Chopin's practice as a striking anticipation of some late-nineteenth-century tonal structures.

Certainly the tendency to unveil the main tonality of a piece only by degrees was a marked fingerprint of Chopin's musical style, and we encounter it again in the Bolero. Here the opening section of the fantasia-like introduction elaborates (through figuration) a dominant preparation of C major. The resolution of this is in the 'più lento' second section, but it remains purposefully ambivalent both in harmony and phrase structure as Chopin gradually prepares the A minor of the main bolero theme, finally converting it to A major in a coda derived from the second main theme. The opening C major now assumes something of the character of a harmonic curtain, lifted at the end of the introduction to reveal the main theme and tonality simultaneously. As for the Spanish element: it is difficult to distinguish between Chopin's 'bolero' and his 'polonaise', though it is the lighter, more brilliant polonaise of the Warsaw period which is evoked here rather than the heroic polonaise of later years.

In general style the Bolero is a concert piece designed to appeal to popular Parisian tastes. And this is also true of the Op. 16 Rondo and Op. 12 Variations, Chopin's last contributions to the genres most

[9] Robert Schumann, *Gesammelte Schriften über Musik und Musiker*, vol., 1, p. 304.

favoured by post-classical pianist-composers. These two pieces demonstrate well the power of genre, and indirectly of social function, to determine musical style. Niecks found it unaccountable that Chopin could have written the Variations at this stage in his development, following the poetry of the early nocturnes and études. 'We can only wonder at the strange phenomenon.'[10] There is indeed a regression in quality and individuality. But the real point is that in choosing these genres Chopin consciously signalled a temporary return to the bravura concert piece, with its (relative) stylistic anonymity. Schumann put it in a nutshell in his review of Op. 12 in *Neue Zeitschrift*: 'They belong altogether to the drawing-room or concert-hall, and . . . are far removed from any poetic sphere.'[11] Chopin was writing *à la mode*, and, accepted on these terms, the music of both works is elegant, stylish, and unpretentious.

The future lay elsewhere of course, signalled by the mazurkas written in Vienna, by the early nocturnes, and by the cycle of *Douze Études* published as Op. 10. There was no absolutely clean stylistic break between the later Warsaw mazurkas, published posthumously, and the earliest sets released for publication by Chopin himself. But by presenting the Viennese mazurkas to the publisher in conventional sets of four and five compatible pieces, Chopin consolidated the genre, and in a sense defined it. He even spelt out in a letter that these pieces were 'not for dancing',[12] which speaks volumes not only about earlier stylizations of the mazurka but about Chopin's growing ambitions for the genre. In these sets Chopin invested the conventional salon dance piece with a complexity and sophistication which immediately transcended habitual meanings, and in so doing challenged the listener to create new ones. It may well be that Brodziński's account of the deeper significance of Polish national dances played some part in this transformation.[13] It is likely too that impinging realities—political and personal—in the months following Chopin's departure from Warsaw made their contribution. In any event, the Viennese mazurkas established a new model for the stylization of folk idioms, marrying elements of peasant music with the most 'advanced' techniques of contemporary art music in a cross-fertilization which would set the tone for Slavonic nationalists generally in the later nineteenth century.

The radicalism of these mazurkas becomes apparent when we compare them with the more conventionally folkloristic songs written during the period. Four of them are Witwicki settings, and of these, 'Posel' (The messenger) and 'Narzeczony' (The betrothed) are lively *krakowiaks*, where the generic constraints of the stylized folksong

[10] Frederick Niecks, *Chopin as a Man and Musician*, vol. 2, p. 222.
[11] Robert Schumann, *Gesammelte Schriften über Musik und Musiker*, vol. 2, p. 56.
[12] Letter to his family, 22 December 1830: *KFC*, vol. 1, p. 161.
[13] See chapter 2, note 55.

(including Ruthenian elements in 'Narzeczony')[14] override any consideration of expression. It comes as a shock to realize that these are tales of tragic love. It is perhaps over-interpreting to see in the other two songs a more direct reflection of current concerns. 'Wojak' (The warrior), for instance, bids farewell to father, mother, and sisters, before continuing: 'Let enemies tremble, we shall wage bloody battle . . . I hear my sisters calling'. It is a strophic ballad, whose equestrian motives inevitably recall 'Erlkönig'. 'Smutna rzeka' (Sad river) is an allegory of tragic loss, and its archaisms, irregular phrasing, and harmonic ambiguities suggest some of the more expansive and expressive settings of Chopin's later years. The other song from this period is a through-composed ballad 'Piosnka litewska' (Lithuanian song) on a poem by Ludwik Osiński, a charming dialogue between mother and daughter with an episode in conventional mazurka style as the girl admits to a meeting with her young man.

The mazurkas of Opp. 6 and 7, in contrast, offer a harmonic sophistication which is seldom found in the songs, even the later ones. Partly this results from stylizations of folk practice, as in the acciaccaturas in the trio of Op. 6 No. 1, the harmonic asperities and unorthodox part movement over a bourdon fifth in Op. 6 No. 2 or the exotic modality in the trio of Op. 7 No. 1, once more on a bourdon fifth. (It is in keeping with 'pastoral' traditions that the trios should be closest to folk sources.) But more often it stems from an extension of progressive tendencies in Western art music. The very opening sentence of the F sharp minor Mazurka, Op. 6 No. 1 is typical, carefully offsetting its four bars of stable diatonic harmony with four bars of evasive chromatic harmony, and enriching both phrases with subtleties which would very soon become fingerprints of style in the mazurkas. In the diatonic phrase, for instance, the sequential tandem of tonic and mediant regions is just such a fingerprint (cf. Op. 24 No. 4), and so, too, is the initiating V harmony (cf. Op. 7 No. 1). In the chromatic phrase, a chain of symmetrically sliding seventh harmonies likewise establishes a model (cf. the so-called 'last mazurka', Op. 68 No. 4, which effectively reverses the diatonic–chromatic sequence). It might be noted in passing that in a presentation autograph of this first published mazurka (in Hiller's album, and dated 'Paris 1832') there are significant textual differences, even in these opening phrases.[15]

The last of the Op. 6 Mazurkas, in the unusual key of E flat minor, captures some additional aspects of the folk idiom, notably a preference for the varied repetition of short motivic fragments. This is especially common in the fast *oberek*-style mazurkas, where constant oscillations of one- or two-bar cells stylize the giddy, whirling motions characteristic of the dance. The 'mixed' modality of the harmony here is also of

[14] Ruthenian, or Ukrainian, elements were not uncommon in Polish songs *am Volkston* in the early nineteenth century.
[15] This manuscript is currently in Cologne (State Archive 1051).

folkloristic origin, and it fuses well with subtly concealed strands of counterpoint emerging from the unorthodox part movement. A surviving sketch for this Mazurka, currently in Russia,[16] suggests that Chopin had earlier thoughts about the voicing, with a version of the alto line originally in the tenor. This in turn resulted in a more conventional form of the tenor counter-melody. The published version is more quirky, throwing the 'false relations' in the harmony into relief, and permitting motivic parallels between several layers of the texture. The whole will repay closer study later in this chapter. There is an intricacy in the counterpoint, a boldness of harmony, and a density of information within an apparently simple texture which clearly marks this music off from the youthful works.

By publishing his mazurkas in sets, Chopin was of course following publishing conventions of the day. But it has been well demonstrated by Jeffrey Kallberg that he was also alive to the musical possibilities of the conventional practice, especially in later sets.[17] This is not to argue for integrated cycles, but for occasional connections, tonal or thematic, between the different pieces in a set, and at the very least for mutual compatibility. Such compatibility is less apparent in the first two opuses, composed (at least in large part) in Vienna, than in the next two, Opp. 17 and 24, written in Paris—probably in 1833.[18] In both these later sets the coherence of the opus is confirmed by the expressive and structural weight of the final piece when compared with the other three. The result is a real sense of closure when the sets are performed as wholes.

These final pieces could scarcely be further removed from the conventional salon mazurka of the early nineteenth century. Right from their opening bars, they signal an earnest intent through a tonally ambiguous introduction, a steady (*kujawiak*) tempo and an expressive *Affekt*. Of the two, the A minor, Op. 17 No. 4 has attracted the more extensive critical and analytical comment over the years, partly because the initial ambiguities are built right into the tonal substance of the piece. Like the Prelude in the same key, this Mazurka is in no hurry to establish its tonic, and much of its expressive character derives from chromatic delaying tactics of several kinds, as also from the nocturne-like ornamental variation of the main theme, the calculated tonal/modal ambivalence and the distinctly unconventional part movement.[19] As in

---

[16] Leningrad; Public Library of Saltykowa-Szczedrina.

[17] Jeffrey Kallberg, 'Compatibility in Chopin's Multipartite Publications', in *Journal of Musicology* (1983), vol. 4. It is worth noting that the two independent 'album' mazurkas dating from the Vienna and early Paris years (KK 1223 and 1227–8) are distinctly more conventional in tone.

[18] See chapter 2 note 21 on the dating of the first version of Op. 7 No. 4. The date for Opp. 17 and 24 is given unambiguously as 1833 in Chomiński and Turło (*Katalog dzieł Fryderyka Chopina*, pp. 114–17), but (characteristically) without supporting evidence.

[19] See William Thomson, 'Functional Ambiguity in Musical Structures', in *Music Perception* (1983), vol. 1, no. 1.

most of the expressive *kujawiak* mazurkas, there is a more blatantly folkloristic trio in the major mode, including bourdon fifths and scalar *fujarka*-style melodic patterns.[20] This is also true of the B flat minor Mazurka, Op. 24 No. 4. But here the major-mode trio, coloured by echoes in the minor, is embedded in an altogether more complex, multisectional form, by far the most ambitious yet attempted by Chopin in the mazurkas.[21] It includes a haunting lydian-mode episode in octaves, and above all a lengthy coda which transforms the main theme into an extended epilogue to the set as a whole.

It is intriguing to compare the tempo indications in Opp. 17 and 24 with those of the Opp. 6 and 7 sets. The only terms used in the earlier sets are 'presto', 'vivace', and 'vivo'. In the later sets, on the other hand, there is just a single 'vivo'. 'Lento' appears three times, 'moderato' twice, and 'allegro non troppo' once; in the autograph of Op. 24 No. 1 Chopin gave 'moderato' initially, but later changed it to 'lento'. These tempo indications are difficult to square with the metronome markings supplied by Chopin himself on the autographs. There is evidence elsewhere that his understanding of 'lento' was a much quicker and more fluent tempo than today's,[22] but aside from that, it seems likely that the terms were intended to signal the character of these opuses as much as their tempo. Of the eight pieces, there is not a single quick-tempo, *oberek*-style mazurka. It is rather as though Chopin had been anxious to spell out the weight and significance he attached to the genre, confirming beyond any doubt that the keyboard mazurka had been essentially redefined. And from this point onwards, he carved out for the mazurka a very special corner within his output, with a singular repertory of technical devices and a singular expressive content—one which linked (by implication) his own inner emotional world to the spirit of the nation. It is entirely characteristic that his nationalism should have been expressed through the renovation of a simple, 'salon' dance piece rather than through the more usual channels of opera or programmatic reference.

In much the same way his growing involvement with an expressive aesthetic was filtered into the piano nocturne rather than rendered specific in the art song. When John Field published his first three piano nocturnes in 1812, the 'nocturne style' was far from new, especially in French and English piano schools. Nor was the genre title 'nocturne' in any sense a novelty. But it was really only in the 1820s that style and genre came together in a significant and moderately consistent way, especially in piano nocturnes by composers associated with Field in some

[20] The *fujarka* is a high-pitched shepherd's pipe commonly used in the traditional folk ensemble of central Poland.

[21] The autograph for Breitkopf & Härtel (National Library, Warsaw, Mus. 216) reveals that Chopin originally intended a repeat at bars 19–20. Jeffrey Kallberg has discussed similar planned repetitions in Op. 7 No. 1 in 'The Problem of Repetition and Return in Chopin's Mazurkas', in *Chopin Studies*, ed. Jim Samson (Cambridge, 1988), pp. 1–24.

[22] Jan Ekier, 'Frederick Chopin. How did he play?', in *Chopin Studies 4* (Warsaw, 1994).

way.[23] The idea of vocal imitation, whether of the French romance or the Italian aria, remained essential to the nocturne style, and the idiom was facilitated (indeed enabled) technically by the development of the sustaining pedal. This made possible that widespread accompaniment to a vocally inspired ornamental melody which we recognize today as the archetype of the style. Chopin's early E minor Nocturne, composed in Warsaw, fell in line behind an established tradition, then, and it differed from its predecessors in the greater richness and boldness of its gestures rather than in their essential character.

While in Vienna Chopin wrote the *Lento con gran espressione* in C sharp minor, later labelled a nocturne by Oskar Kolberg. The complex manuscript history of this work has been briefly discussed.[24] The autograph currently in Majorca stands apart textually from the extant copies by Ludwika, Kolberg, and Balakirev, most obviously in the polymetric notation which accompanies the first of the quotations from Op. 21. These copies were based on another autograph, now lost. At any rate, Chopin undoubtedly approved the Ludwika copy, since he read and corrected it (along with copies of eight of the songs) before sending it to Maria Wodzińska for her album in September 1836. The *Lento con gran espressione* made up the first four folios of this attractively presented album (now lost), with the inscription, 'Maria', in gold lettering on the cover. It is one of Chopin's most singular compositions, but it should be stressed that there is no very strong case for including it with the nocturnes, beyond some general affinities with the 'nocturne style'. Indeed the self-quotations in the *Lento* create an explicit autobiographical resonance which is more or less unique in Chopin's output.

The three Op. 9 Nocturnes, on the other hand, served to define and formalize the genre for Chopin, rather as Opp. 6 and 7 did for the mazurka. Right at the outset of No. 1 we are presented with three characteristic features. At the level of the motive, there is the close relationship between the melody and the widespread accompaniment figuration (through the opening six-note patterns of both right and left hands), refining and complicating the basic texture associated with the nocturne. Integrative details of this kind became a feature of his mature music, and they were often established at the opening of works, as in the last of the Op. 28 Preludes. At the level of the phrase, there is the immediate ornamental variation of the opening two-bar shape. There are three such variations, increasingly elaborate, in the Nocturne as a whole, and they are all expressive outgrowths of the melody rather than superimposed decorations. This, too, is characteristic. Finally, at the level of the paragraph, the phrase structure is typically deceptive. Only at bars 15–18, as the second theme approaches, is the innocent ear made aware that the

[23] For a discussion, see David Rowland, 'The Nocturne: Development of a New Style', in *The Cambridge Companion to Chopin*, pp. 32–49.

[24] See chapter 1, notes 5–8.

barring of the opening theme implied an iambic (weak–strong) rather than a trochaic (strong–weak) rhythmic pattern. Again this subtle play on symmetries and asymmetries within an apparently simple phrase structure is as characteristic of Chopin as it is of Mozart.

The 'inspired simplicity' of No. 2 in E flat major has rendered it the most famous of all Chopin's nocturnes. It is also the closest in style to the external features of the John Field prototype, and precise parallels have often been proposed.[25] But the originality of the E flat Nocturne has been dulled a little by this familiarity. Quite apart from its harmonic and formal richness,[26] the piece demonstrates clearly how a standard device of the operatic aria and of related keyboard genres could acquire new expressive and formal meaning. I refer to the practice of subjecting a theme to progressively more complex ornamentation, whether improvised or composed, as the work unfolds. This was a conventional expression of virtuosity in the opera house and concert platform, but in Chopin's hands it became a powerful agent of expression, as well as taking on something of an evolutionary and developmental formal function. In the B major Nocturne, Op. 9 No. 3 such cumulative ornamental variation of the main theme gains added potency as it is set off against a middle section which generates tension in more conventional ways, avoiding ornamental melody. The alternation of an ornamental 'aria' and a sequentially developing 'theme' would become a familiar strategy of the Chopin nocturnes, already found in the next opus. Both the E flat major and the B major Nocturnes, incidentally, close with a cadenza which spells out their generic links with the operatic aria as also with the classical and post-classical slow movement.

The Op. 15 Nocturnes marked a significant departure from the Op. 9 set. In particular, they demonstrated that the title 'nocturne', once its connotative values had been clearly established, could attach itself to music of highly varied formal and generic schemes, and even to pieces which seem blatantly to defy the expectations aroused by their title. Only the second of them, the F sharp major, retains a close contact with the model proposed in Op. 9. Here, as in Op. 9 No. 2, supple arcs of melody are given cumulative ornamental treatment, resulting at times—especially in the reprise—in some of the most delicious *fioriture* yet conceived by Chopin. And as in Op. 9 No. 3, these ornamental variations are offset by a tension-building middle section which relies on sequential treatments rather than melodic variation.

The middle section of this Nocturne, like those of Op. 9 Nos. 1 and 3, does not in any sense interrupt the flow of the music; indeed care is taken that it should emerge imperceptibly and smoothly from the opening paragraph. It is above all an agent of intensification, and this, on the

[25] See especially David Branson, *John Field and Chopin* (London, 1972).
[26] See John Rink, ' "Structural Momentum" and closure in Chopin's Nocturne, Op. 9 No. 2', in *Schenker Studies 2*, ed. H. Siegel and C. Schachter (Cambridge, forthcoming).

whole, is characteristic of the nocturnes. In the F major Nocturne, Op. 15 No. 1, however, there is a 'real' middle section, a contrasted figuration in the tonic minor whose relation to the outer sections is of a kind not entirely characteristic of nocturnes. Indeed the discontinuity is all the greater because of Chopin's treatment of the later stages of the first theme. By introducing a cadential extension of two bars at bar 20, he strengthens our sense of a reprise at bar 22, only to interrupt its progress with the new figuration at bar 25.

It is difficult to avoid cross-referencing this Nocturne with the rather later second Ballade. Here, too, an 'innocent' pastoral melody in the same key alternates with an impassioned figuration in the minor (this time the mediant minor), a confrontation of 'genres' which positively invites programmatic interpretation. Moreover like the second Ballade's siciliano, the opening melody of Op. 15 No. 1 is less innocent than it seems. Beneath the bland surface continuities of its triplet accompaniment there are numerous harmonic and contrapuntal subtleties. What begins as a simple accompanied melody tends increasingly towards a concealed contrapuntal texture in which the four voices gain a greater measure of independence. And as they do so, they generate chromatic harmonies which cast a very special light on the unfailing diatonicism of the melody. Chopin's artistry resides precisely in this kind of refinement, where an apparently simple surface conceals a wealth of sophistication.

Jeffrey Kallberg has written with insight about the G minor Nocturne, Op. 15 No. 3, one of the most unusual pieces in the Chopin *œuvre*. Not only has he demonstrated that the tonal structure of the piece has a synthesizing function in relation to the cycle as a whole. He has further suggested that the curious blend of genres in the piece, a mazurka and a chorale side by side beneath the umbrella of an nocturne, may well have been a political statement by Chopin, fusing the national dance with the messianism characteristic of Polish romantic nationalism.[27] This may be over interpreted, but it does provoke us into considering how early-nineteenth-century listeners might have responded to Chopin, as far as this may be deduced from contemporary accounts. Much more than in our own time, they would have related his music to real or imagined contexts. The work was understood to mediate larger realities—social, cultural or stylistic—and its meaning was therefore dependent and contingent. Genre was one way in which it could point beyond itself, and the characteristic play of genres in Chopin has been one of the major casualties of our modern, holistic view of his music, concerned as it is with integration rather than combination. If the confrontation of pastorale and étude in Op. 15 No. 1 already invites programmatic interpre-

[27] Jeffrey Kallberg, 'The Rhetoric of Genre: Chopin's Nocturne in G minor', in *19th-Century Music* (1988), vol. 11 no. 3, pp. 238–61.

tation, how much more so the confrontation of mazurka and chorale in Op. 15 No. 3?[28]

The major achievement of this creative period was the set of Études, Op. 10, whose composition spanned the Warsaw, Vienna, and early Paris years. Didactic pieces for keyboard, whether described as 'exercises' or 'études', had a lengthy history before Chopin published these Études in 1833. As the piano soared to popularity in the early nineteenth century, such pieces naturally flourished, appearing both as supplements to the many *Méthodes* and as independent sets. Chopin's relationship to these prototypes has been discussed already in connection with the first two Études. Links with figurations in Cramer and Moscheles respectively are certainly detectable here, and are a telling pointer to one layer of influence, but the more profound debt is no less certainly to Bach, and not only in the technical respects mentioned earlier. Both composers achieved a perfect balance between technical and artistic aims, between the classroom and the concert. As Schumann remarked of the Chopin études, 'imagination and technique share dominion side by side'.[29]

Unlike the bigger concert studies of Liszt, Chopin's études retain an obvious didactic function, addressing one principal technical problem in each piece and crystallizing that problem in a single shape or figure. They form an appropriate workshop, then, for further examination of his approach to piano technique. The C major Étude immediately raises a seminal requirement for Chopin playing, and one which he himself emphasized when he worked on the piece with Friederike Streicher.[30] It is the necessity to maintain a flexible wrist and supple hand, so that the wrist and not the arm is in movement, traversing the keyboard in such a way that the hand can remain in its most 'natural' position. In the first Étude the performer is of course greatly helped in this by Chopin's pedalling. He told his pupils repeatedly that 'the correct employment of [the pedals] remains a study for life',[31] and this is borne out by the meticulous and detailed pedal markings on his autographs for many of the Études. In view of this it is intriguing that there are no autograph pedal markings for the slower legato Études, Nos. 3 and 6. It is likely that in such pieces Chopin's use of the pedal would have been sparing, avoiding a 'lazy' legato and allowing contrapuntal strands to emerge and recede from the texture with clarity.

In the C major Étude, on the other hand, the pedal is clearly indispensable to the articulation of the massive, striding arpeggios, and Chopin's markings can be transferred without controversy from the early nineteenth-century (Pleyel) piano, whose sustaining capacity was

---

[28] Kallberg demonstrates from the surviving sketch of the 'chorale' that Chopin may well have originally planned a ternary design, returning to at least part of the opening section: ibid., pp. 248–50.

[29] *Neue Zeitschrift für Musik* (1826), vol. 4, pp. 45–6.

[30] Jean-Jacques Eigeldinger, *Chopin as Pianist and Teacher*, p. 68.   [31] Ibid., p. 57.

limited, to the modern grand. This is by no means always the case. In the E flat major Étude, Op. 10 No. 11, the harmonic rhythm is similar to that of the first Étude, and Chopin's pedal indications are also similar. However, on today's piano, the melody—effectively the 'surface' of a succession of arpeggiated chords possibly inspired by Moscheles's Op. 70, No. 2—will tend to be lost if we follow Chopin's pedalling. There is clearly a strong case here for reinterpreting the composer's instructions to accommodate the modern instrument. And this is just one of several such instances, reminding us that there are grey areas in the matter of a so-called 'definitive text'. It should be added in passing that although Chopin largely excluded the una corda pedal from his text, he apparently made magical use of it in performance.[32]

The autograph of the second Étude is notable for its detailed fingering instructions, requiring the long fingers to pass over one another without the help of the thumb so that the 'sempre legato' may be maintained throughout. The result is an unorthodox fingering, typical of Chopin's willingness to cast convention to the winds if the musical outcome justifies it. A further and more blatant example is his use of the thumb on the black keys, indicated not just in the fifth ('black key') Étude, where we would of course expect it, but in the sixth in E flat minor, where it helps the performer maintain the legato of the countermelody alongside the sustained bass notes. Chopin often spelt out his fingering requirements in detail in this way, and in general the results exploit rather than conceal a hierarchy of finger strengths, cutting against the grain of contemporary practice. At the same time, as the fingered scores of several pupils testify,[33] he was always prepared to be flexible, adjusting fingerings to meet individual needs, including, of course, hand size. What he sought above all was a capacity to control every possible shading of the music, and fingering was designed to promote this. So, too, was his requirement that pupils play the Études with different dynamics, different tempos, and different modes of articulation. Indeed in Op. 10 No. 10 such contrasts in articulation are composed into the piece.

The E major, Op. 10 No. 3, is a study in the control of legato melody and in its appropriate phrasing. Chopin, like many pianist–composers in the early nineteenth century, directed pupils to the opera house to find the most appropriate model for the development of a consistent sound quality, a 'singing' tone and a well phrased line. Carl Mikuli pointed out that for Chopin a piece played with unconvincing phrasing was rather akin to someone declaiming a poem in a language he did not understand.[34] He was aware, of course, that the composer could not legislate in some absolute way for a sensitively phrased performance. But his phrase and dynamic markings for Op. 10 No. 3 are of the most detailed kind, clearly designed to 'point' the sub-phrases within a melody whose

---

[32] Jean-Jacques Eigeldinger, *Chopin as Pianist and Teacher*, p. 58.
[33] Ibid., pp. 39–41. [34] Ibid., p. 42.

rhythmic structure is one of calculated irregularity. It is the more annoying, then, that insensitive editors later saw fit to modify this, along with many other examples of Chopin's original phrasing.

The melody of Op. 10 No. 3 is one of Chopin's most haunting and memorable, and it must be performed as a living, breathing organism. This means not just a respect for Chopin's own phrase and dynamic indications, but some discreet application of rubato. In general the evidence suggests that Chopin's rubato was closer to baroque-classical practice than to the exaggerated tempo fluctuations of some of his contemporaries.[35] In the E major Étude it is clear that melody and accompaniment are closely tied together, and that the one must breathe with the other, and this is also true of the E flat minor Étude, Op. 10 No. 6. But elsewhere, and especially in nocturnes, or passages in nocturne style, some separation of function between the two hands seems to have been intended, where the left hand, in Mikuli's words, 'always played in strict time, while the [right hand], singing the melody, either hesitating as if undecided, or, with increased animation, anticipating with a kind of impatient vehemence as if in passionate utterances, maintained the freedom of musical expression from the fetters of strict regularity'.[36] Liszt (apparently) captured this through an analogy: 'Look at the trees! The wind plays in the leaves, stirs up among them and the trees remain the same. That is the Chopinesque rubato.'[37] It is worth pointing out that in some of his more impassioned gestures, as in parts of Op. 10 Nos. 9 and 12, Chopin actually 'composed in' a rubato of this kind.

Technical issues aside, the *Douze Etudes*, Op. 10 have special significance within Chopin's output as the opus which most clearly signified his transcendence of the 'brilliant style', confronting virtuosity directly, but conquering it on home ground. We cannot be sure at what stage Chopin decided to group the Études into a cycle of twelve. Nos. 1 and 2 were clearly intended as a pair, as the Warsaw manuscript refers to 'Exercise 1' and 'Exercise 2'. So were Nos. 3 and 4, since the autograph of No. 3 has the instruction 'attac[c]a il Presto con fuoco'. In both cases the pairs are tonal relatives, as are 5–6, 9–10, and 11–12. Nos. 3 and 4 were probably the last to be composed, and by then Chopin had almost certainly decided on an order for the set. But the autographs show an intriguing change from the published numbering, with Nos. 7–10 originally numbered 6–9. It is not entirely clear why this was changed, nor indeed how the twelve pieces were eventually assembled into their final order, but in any event that order admirably displays the wide range of their forms, figurations, and moods.

[35] See David Rowland, 'Chopin's Tempo Rubato in Context', in *Chopin Studies 2* (Cambridge, 1994), pp. 199–213.

[36] Carl Mikuli, in the foreword to his edition (Leipzig, 1880); trans. in Schirmer's edition (London, 1949), p. 1.

[37] Jean-Jacques Eigeldinger, *Chopin as Pianist and Teacher*, p. 51.

The two slow Études, Nos. 3 and 6, form the expressive high points of the cycle, achieving a power and intensity without precedent in Chopin's earlier music. The E major is above all a triumph of form, and it points already to an enduring principle of Chopin's tonal architecture, a counterpoint of goal-directed progression and arch-like symmetry. The opening melodic phrase already expresses this counterpoint, its cumulative, bar-by-bar transformations of the opening motive plotted against a 'static' arch design, with a central peak in bar 3 and a transformed reprise in bars 4 and 5. I have illustrated elsewhere how this design is inflated to a larger level with the powerfully climactic middle section, whose main tension points are plotted against carefully measured formal proportions.[38] The warmth and passion which characterises this Étude is replaced in the E flat minor by an intense brooding chromaticism, embodied not only in the larger harmonic movement but in the tortuously circling countermelody in the tenor. The interplay of the four voices here recreates in terms idiomatic to the piano, with its capacity to shade and differentiate voices, something of the spirit of Bachian counterpoint.

Between these two legato pieces are moto perpetuo Études of contrasted character. No. 4 in C sharp minor is a bravura march-like piece of exceptional power and energy. The figuration, tricky for both right and left hands, is conventional in provenance, but Chopin allows it to build a relentless momentum by skilfully varying the pace of his sequential progressions, compressing them in the central section until they culminate in a climax of shattering power, marked both by a new motive and a new texture. No. 5 in G flat major, on the other hand, is frothy and vivacious, a sparkle on the black keys. Chopin complained on one occasion that Clara Wieck had chosen to perform 'just this Étude', describing it as the 'least interesting for those who do not know that it is written for the black keys'.[39] But the brunt of his objection was that she played the piece by itself, suggesting that the 'black key' study was designed to be heard in context. Certainly it lacks those hidden, intricate details and ambiguities which enliven the textures of some of the other études.

No. 7 in C major is a case in point, its figuration apparently conventional but in reality concealing a wealth of information, including several 'voices' within the pattern, fragmentary counter-motives which emerge and recede from the texture, and subtly varied repetitions of the main substance. It is akin to a Bach invention, refusing to release its tonic anchor for more than a few moments, and carefully gauging its points of return through cadential extensions (bar 33, bars 42–3). No. 8 returns to the tempo, metre, and figuration of No. 4, but now in a lighter vein which nicely sets off the plangent, and at times impassioned, tone

[38] Jim Samson, *The Music of Chopin* (London, 1985), pp. 63–5.
[39] In a letter to Fontana, 25 April 1839: *KFC*, vol. 1, p. 347.

of its successor in F minor. The latter is one of the few études to focus its technical demands on the left hand, whose widespread accompaniment figuration, played 'allegro molto agitato', requires careful control of the three middle fingers if it is to be executed smoothly and evenly. The impulsive 'parlando' intensifications of Chopin's restless melody are striking features of this Étude, anticipating similar devices in the most popular, as well as the most powerful of the set, the so-called 'revolutionary' study, No. 12 in C minor.

In this C minor Étude Chopin achieves new heights of dramatic and expressive intensity, taking over but greatly extending some of the classical associations of the key. It is more to the point to invoke Mozart and Beethoven here than to make initially tempting comparisons with the 'demonic' works of Liszt,[40] Chopin's contemporary. The cut of the main theme is in the tradition of earlier C minor works, though Chopin intensifies its individual moments in a successful bid to wring the last drop of *Angst* from well-tried gestures. There is no shortage of drama, rhetoric, and passion in the early nineteenth-century piano repertory. What sets this piece apart is the elemental strength of its structure, such that the 'tornadic passion' of its urgent, impetuous melody strains against the formal framework but is contained. It is hardly surprising that this piece should have generated its Stuttgart associations. As Niecks remarked, 'the composer seems to be fuming with rage'.[41] And the expressive sequence it describes cries out for metaphor. Ashton Jonson answers the call in his description of the reprise of the first theme: 'its force is broken, it stammers in its utterance, the rage dies out of it, only the pathos is left, and it ends with a questioning phrase like a broken sob as modern and human as Siegmund's questioning of Brünnhilde. Then with a dying effort it gathers itself up and rushes with a defiant shout on the guns and bayonets of the enemy.'[42]

Following the publication of Op. 10, Chopin composed two pieces which belong somewhat to the same world as the Études. They were written in 1834 and remained unpublished during the composer's lifetime. One is the *Presto con legerezza* in A flat major, sometimes described (though not by Chopin) as a Prelude. Like several of the Op. 10 Études and for that matter some of the Op. 28 Preludes, this is a Bach-like moto perpetuo movement in which figuration shapes structure.[43] The other, the so-called Fantasy-impromptu, Op. 66 in C sharp minor, is a much more significant work, and Chopin's decision to leave it unpublished remains somewhat puzzling.[44] He himself described the

---

[40] There are also striking parallels with the first Piano Sonata by Weber.

[41] Frederick Niecks, *Chopin as a Man and Musician*, vol. 2, p. 253.

[42] G. C. Ashton Jonson, *A Handbook to Chopin's Works* (London, 1905), p. 41.

[43] See Józef Chomiński, *Preludia* (Cracow, 1950), p. 22.

[44] Arthur Hedley suggested that Chopin was all too aware of its similarity to the E flat Impromptu, Op. 80 by Moscheles; in *Chopin* (London, 1947), p. 156. This seems unlikely, since he was happy enough to publish Op. 10 Nos. 2 and 11, no less close to études from

piece as an 'impromptu', and although his debt to individual impromptus by other composers may have been considerable, the term itself carried very little generic meaning in 1834.[45] On the other hand, when Chopin returned to the title 'impromptu' three years later, he did so partly in order to *define* a genre, at least for his own purposes, and he allowed the unpublished impromptu to serve as his model. As we shall see, the links between this piece and the A flat Impromptu, Op. 29 are explicit and of several kinds.

One other genre was defined during the early Paris years. Already in some of the Warsaw-period waltzes there were signs that the characteristic 'tone' of the Chopin waltz was beginning to crystallize. In August, 1832 he wrote the G flat major Waltz, posthumously published as Op. 70 No. 1, and to a large extent this is already a waltz of maturity. But it was two years later that Chopin composed the first of the waltzes he himself authorized for publication, the E flat major, Op. 18. As with the earliest published mazurkas and nocturnes it was this, the first published waltz, which most obviously clarified his understanding of the genre. Here for the first time he aligned himself with the model proposed by Weber in his influential *Aufforderung zum Tanz*. As in the Weber there is an initial 'announcement', followed by a pot-pourri of contrasted tunes, alternating lyrical and figurative types and closing with an exciting coda incorporating an accelerando or 'stretto' effect. There are no less than seven separate ideas here, and they include features which would soon become fingerprints of the Chopin waltz—moto perpetuo melodic arcs, suave Italianate thirds and sixths, piquant cross-rhythms, and showers of sparkling acciaccaturas.

Here in Op. 18, Chopin effectively redefined the category 'salon music', just at the time that he withdrew from that category genres such as the mazurka. Lenz called them 'not waltzes but enchanting rondos'.[46] The music undoubtedly aims at immediate appeal, at an attractive lightness and airiness of mood; yet it does so with no loss of quality. While the E flat major Waltz is transparently designed for the salon, it is by no means *Trivialmusik*, a mere spin-off from more serious work. In its own way it is no less polished and sophisticated than the more overtly ambitious works. Chopin was indeed writing 'light music', but it was light music in a new spirit, or rather a much older spirit. In this and in subsequent waltzes he designed beautifully finished miniatures which accept the atmosphere of the salon and the conventions of the society dance and elevate both into an art-form of refinement and sophistication.

Moscheles's Op. 70. It should be noted that the source for this work was a presentation manuscript, and that other pieces for which such a manuscript is the only source were also left unpublished.

[45] I have discussed this in 'Chopin's F sharp Impromptu—Notes on Genre, Style and Structure', in *Chopin Studies 3* (Warsaw, 1990), pp. 297–304.

[46] Wilhelm von Lenz, *The Great Piano Virtuosos of our Time*, p. 53.

Chopin's piano writing

I have already indicated that Chopin's music was shaped in most of its essentials by the world of post-classical concert music. Within that world a hierarchy of values subordinated work to genre and genre to performance, so that in a very real sense the primary role of the work was to exemplify. Although Chopin transcended this world, he also remembered it. His innovations arose from, and were implied by, the post-classical repertory and they were conditioned in every particular by its central assumption—that work and performance are inseparably fused. There was even some suggestion, notably from Moscheles, that Chopin the performer held a sort of monopoly on Chopin the composer.[47] At the very least there was a unique sensitivity to the instrument itself, to its limitations and potentialities, and this in turn continues to have a bearing on the performance and reception of the music today. Since it drew its substance so very directly from the nature of the piano, the recreation of that substance makes special demands on the performer and elicits special responses from the listener.

To understand fully Chopin's skilful and imaginative approach to the instrument we need to invoke both historical and analytical perspectives. The piano may have been well established in Chopin's time, but it was by no means uniform in type. Performers tended to seek out their favourite instrument and would be as closely associated with a piano manufacturer as with a publisher. Chopin was no exception. Despite an early liking for Viennese Graf instruments and a later interest in Broadwoods, his enduring love was for French pianos, and especially Pleyels. In his early days in Paris he played mainly on Pleyel fortepianos, with single escapement action, and their transparency and registral differentiation perfectly suited the intricacies of texture in which he revelled, highlighting especially the contrapuntal dimension of his harmonic practice. Later he used larger concert Pleyels, noted for their mellow, rich tone and sensitivity of touch, and he also kept a Pleyel pianino for teaching purposes. Yet although the Pleyel was well matched both to his performance style and his to ideal venues, Chopin was perfectly happy to play from time to time ('when I feel out of sorts') on the more brilliant and uniform Erards favoured by Liszt.

The differences between these early nineteenth-century Pleyels and Erards were real, but of a relatively subtle kind. Both piano makers brought the early piano to a condition of optimum sophistication, drawing upon some of the best features of the much more obviously

---

[47] Moscheles's remarks on Chopin are recorded in *Aus Moscheles' Leben*, a publication in two volumes prepared by his wife, Charlotte, between 1872 and 1877. For a discussion of his views on Chopin see Emil F. Smidak, *Isaak-Ignaz Moscheles: The Life of the Composer and his Encounters with Beethoven, Liszt, Chopin and Mendelssohn* (Vienna, 1988), pp. 120–2.

contrasted Viennese and English pianos of the late eighteenth century. At that time the differences between instruments were not only greater in themselves: they had a more obvious formative influence on the keyboard styles which were just then beginning to emerge. To over-simplify, the light-actioned Viennese instrument, notably the Steins beloved of Mozart, favoured rapid, non-legato figuration and elaborate ornamentation. The deeper-toned English instrument, associated with Clementi, Dussek, and the so-called 'London school' of pianists, promoted heavier chordal writing and cantabile melody. Even when physical differences had been largely ironed out, something of this stylistic difference remained, and against that background Chopin's early études and nocturnes take on a rather special significance. They bring together in a single composer two separate, though increasingly interactive, lines of development within the history of the early piano.

Much of the bravura figuration in the Op. 10 Études derives ultimately from a style of playing and composing associated with the Viennese piano, with Mozart and later with Hummel, Weber, and Moscheles. The sustained melodic lines characteristic of the early nocturnes, on the other hand, take their origins in French and English pianism—in the sonatas of Louis Adam, in some of the music composed by Dussek in London in the 1890s,[48] and, of course, in John Field. It would be easy to paint an over-schematic picture here. By the 1820s these paths had criss-crossed in various ways, as pianist-composers enjoyed an exhilarating voyage of discovery into every aspect of the developing instrument's potential. Nevertheless, at least part of the accomplishment of Chopin's early études and nocturnes involved an element of synthesis, drawing together and restructuring the achievements of existing 'schools' of playing and composing.

There was of course much more to it than this. As Chopin's pianism divested itself of the external characteristics of the brilliant style its distinctive profile began to stand out increasingly clearly not only against that style, but against other styles of piano writing which were beginning to crystallize in the early nineteenth century. These can be associated, though by no means exclusively, with particular pianist-composers and particular centres. They are anything but watertight categories, but are distinguishable as tendencies none the less. One such style was aligned to a Prague–Vienna axis, drawing certain aspects of Dussek's achievement into the orbit of an emerging lyrical 'character piece' associated with Tomášek, Voříšek, and Schubert. Later in the century this manner was echoed by Dvořák and by composers from further afield such as Grieg. Vocal imitation was a determinant of the idiom, but it was the stylized folksong rather than the operatic aria which inspired these lyric pieces, with their melodic priority, uncluttered textures, and

---

[48] It is distinctly possible that some of Dussek's writing for the harp may have influenced the development of his keyboard style, and especially his accompaniment patterns.

regular sentence structures. Chopin remained largely unmoved. Similar textures in his dance pieces have a different origin. Yet there are occasional moments in his music—in the Op. 29 Impromptu, for instance, and in parts of the A flat major Ballade—which seem to glance in this direction.

A more 'symphonic' manner of piano writing can be associated with Beethoven, Schumann, and Brahms, notable for its heavier chordal textures, its massive contrasts of density and dynamics, and its tendency to bind the two hands together, often in rhythmic unison. Here the style is largely harmonically directed. Left-hand patterns are conditioned by the demands of chord progression and widened sonority is achieved primarily through the octave doubling of triadic harmonies. Again Chopin kept his distance from these essentially Austro–German developments (whose ultimate legatee was Schoenberg), turning to the 'symphonic' manner only in his late sonatas and polonaises. Attempts by Zofia Lissa and others to trace closer connections between Beethoven's pianistic style and Chopin's are not without some point, but they are at the very least a prey to over-interpretation.[49]

If we categorize these styles very crudely in terms (respectively) of melodic and harmonic priority, we might identify a third style as proto-impressionist in its tendency to foreground texture and colour. This was in the main an extension of the brilliant style, and it was associated above all with Liszt, and to an extent with lesser figures such as Thalberg. It grew partly from elaborate colouristic embellishments of melodic substance, extended to the point at which figurations—often delicate washes of sound—carry their own structural values. Through the later works of Liszt this idiom left a marked imprint on some of the piano textures of Debussy and Ravel. Chopin's pianistic style remained largely distinct from this tradition, too, but he was much closer to it than to the others, and at times he moved unambiguously into its territory. The delicious sprays of figuration in the trio of the C sharp minor Scherzo are a case in point, as are the *jeu perlé* figures of the Berceuse and the F sharp major Impromptu.

In the end, Chopin's pianism remains triumphantly separate from any such genealogies we might care to construct. In carving out a defined space for himself in the stylistically plural world of early-nineteenth-century piano music, he effectively created his own tradition, unwittingly laying the foundation for a substantial corpus of piano music in the later nineteenth century and beyond. The influence of his unique pianistic style operated on many levels, and it will be discussed in due course, but for now it is enough to point to its most obvious inheritance—the piano

[49] Zofia Lissa, 'Elementy stylu Beethovena w twórczości Fryderyka Chopina', in *Studia nad twórsczościa Fryderyka Chopina* (Cracow, 1969), pp. 176–201. See also Marie Kubień-Uszokowa, 'Stosunek Chopina do Beethovena', in *Chopin a muzyka europejska*, ed. K. Musiol (Katowice, 1977), pp. 25–41.

music of Russian and French composers of the late nineteenth and early twentieth centuries. Balakirev and Fauré were the most immediate of the beneficiaries, but the Chopin piano style left its trace on later composers too, on Lyadov and Skryabin in Russia, Debussy and Ravel in France.

That style encompassed three very broad categories of piano texture, exemplified, though not in any exclusive way, by the principal genres of the Vienna and early Paris years. It will be worth differentiating between them as an initial step towards closer analysis. The mazurkas and waltzes represent the first and most straightforward category, where the basic model of the texture is derived from the functional dance and its music. The nocturnes form a second category, comprising an ornamental cantilena with widespread broken chord accompaniment. The études make up a third category, one whose main component is figuration, albeit of numerous kinds. Within certain constraints Chopin not only introduced many variations on these basic models, but concealed a wealth of subtle detail within their external layers. Needless to say, the categories overlap in several ways. Yet they remain recognizably differentiated, and they can be traced throughout Chopin's *œuvre* as a whole. Hence the 'nocturne' manner is no more confined to the nocturnes than is figuration to the études.

Underlying these categories of texture we may trace a common approach to the medium. Carl Schachter reached to the heart of the matter with his description of 'Chopin's unparalleled mastery of free, idiomatically pianistic counterpoint'.[50] He went on to identify those aspects of the medium which distinguish its idiomatic counterpoint from that of other media, namely its uniformity of sound, its diminuendo on every note, its capacity for dynamic shading, and its sustaining pedal. More than any previous or coeval composer, Chopin knew how to exploit all these qualities in an integral way, so that age-old devices could be conceived afresh in terms insolubly welded to the instrument itself.[51]

In his early published mazurkas Chopin accepted in broad terms the inherited constraints of the genre, a right-hand periodic melody, often of short-breathed repeated motives, with a left-hand accompaniment articulating the dance rhythm, either through a dactyl pattern which separates the bass note from the other chord members, or through repeated chords. But within this framework Chopin introduced countless enriching subtleties of pianistic style. The right-hand layer allows frequent variation both of tessitura, ornamentation, and voicing, while the left hand varies the spacing and internal constitution of chords, hints at concealed motives, and allows fragments of voice leading to emerge and

[50] In his review of my book, *The Music of Chopin*. See *Music Analysis* (1989), vol. 8, nos. 1–2, pp. 187–96.

[51] These points did not go unnoticed in Chopin's time. See especially Johanna Kinkel's remarkable essay on Chopin, 'Friedrich Chopin als Komponist: Geschrieben im Jahre 1855. Aus ihrem Nachlass', in *Deutsche Revue* (1902) vol. 27, pp. 93–106, 209–23, 338–69.

recede. As a result there is much more 'information' in Chopin's textures than in those of his immediate predecessors, and a much more rapid rate of change from one to another.

A few examples will help make these points specific. The third and fourth of the Op. 6 Mazurkas present an immediate and obvious contrast, in that No. 3 exploits abrupt changes of register, spacing and voicing, while No. 4 occupies an unchanging texture-space, confined for the most part within two octaves. It will be worth looking more closely at these mazurkas. Ex. 7 illustrates something of the diversity of texture afforded by No. 3. Within the right-hand layer there is contrast of register and of voicing, as a narrow-compass, single-voice bass phrase gives way to a wide-compass duet phrase in the treble. The bipartite structure

Ex. 7   Mazurka, Op. 6 No. 3

of the treble phrase is matched by the change in the accompaniment pattern from bourdon fifths to full chords. Later sections increase the diversity (Ex. 8), while exploiting the capacity of the piano to allow voice leading to cross the boundaries between full chordal and duet textures (a), to pick out inner pedal points (b), and to change from chordal to unison texture without loss of continuity (c).

Ex. 8   Mazurka, Op. 6 No. 3
(a)

Ex. 8 cont.:
(b)

(c)

Op. 6 No. 4, in contrast, builds a single layer of texture from interactive contrapuntal voices in both hands, launched by a bass tonic which never returns at this register. Although this texture has the appearance of strict obbligato voice leading, its real art is one of suggestion, once more drawing on the specific qualities of the piano to enable hidden voices to emerge fleetingly from the web of counterpoint. Something of this is conveyed by Ex. 9, and it reveals further how subtle variations of voice leading are permitted on repetition.

Ex. 9   Mazurka, Op. 6 No. 4

The dance rhythm of the Mazurka acts as a much less serious constraint on Chopin's left hand than one might initially suspect, even in these early published mazurkas. We need only look at the left-hand layer of Op. 7 No. 3 to see that in a single piece Chopin could move through no less than seven quite distinct patterns, as Ex. 10 indicates. They range from conventional dactyls and repeated chords to fragments of two-part counterpoint and extended tenor melody (which has to act at the same

Ex. 10   Mazurka, Op. 7 No. 3

time as its own bass). It is intriguing to contrast this with the accompaniment of Op. 7 No. 4 (Ex. 11). Here the unorthodox part movement of an unbroken stream of chords invites the performer to exploit the piano's capacity to 'shade' the chords in order to bring out linear motives.

There is a similar kaleidoscope of textures in the Opp. 17 and 24 Mazurkas. The pianistic devices used in these sets are in essence those already established in Opp. 6 and 7, but they are in new juxtapositions and take on fresh meanings as a result. The duet texture of Op. 6 No. 3 reappears both in Op. 17 No. 1 and in Op. 24 No. 1, for example,

Ex. 11 Mazurka, Op. 7 No. 4

(a)

(b)

while its brief *unisono* passage is elaborated into a larger self-contained section in Op. 24 No. 4. Equally the left-hand melody of Op. 7 No. 3 finds its counterpart in Op. 24 No. 2, just as the semitonally inflected chords of Op. 7 No. 4 are echoed in Op. 17 No. 2 (especially from bar 39). There are new devices, too, including the high-tessitura 'piping' of

Op. 17 No. 2 and Op. 24 No. 2, the carefully phrased hemiola patterns in the middle of Op. 24 No. 3, and the intricate two-part counterpoint in the right hand of Op. 24 No. 4. Most surprising of all is the ornamental melody in the outer sections of Op. 17 No. 4, a melodic style so seldom found in the mazurkas that we might be tempted to question the genre. Here we have an early instance in Chopin of generic interpenetration. The natural setting for this melodic style is not in the mazurkas at all, but rather in the nocturnes.

The early nocturnes take their starting-point from an established model of texture, but they elaborate that model in many ways, most obviously by enlarging the texture-space of the accompaniment layer and by diversifying the patterns available within it. The result is a characteristic thinning-out of the texture, where the sustaining pedal binds together wide-ranging figures which can cover as many as three octaves. This, combined with a chromatically flexible, rhythmically pliable ornamental melody, amounts to a highly characteristic 'Chopin sound', instantly recognizable even to the untutored ear. Zofia Chechlińska has pointed out that this sound is already there in all its essentials in the youthful E minor Nocturne, describing the piece as an 'encyclopaedia of textures, which, when subsequently perfected, were to become the basis of later individual nocturnes'.[52] This is even true of the melodic layer taken in isolation, since it is presented with ornamental variations, in octaves, in 'Italianate' thirds and with a countermelody.

Each of these melodic treatments is present in the first of the Op. 9 Nocturnes, too. But the artistic level here is much higher than in the earlier piece, as even a glance at the expressive ornamentation of the opening phrase (Ex. 12) suggests. Throughout this and other such melodic paragraphs a delicate balance is maintained between core elements, vocally inspired and even at times literally singable, and decorative extensions and interpolations which are idiomatically pianistic, even

Ex. 12   Nocturne, Op. 9 No. 1

---

[52] 'The Nocturnes and Studies: Selected Problems of Piano Texture', in *Chopin Studies* (Cambridge, 1988), p. 160.

if they partly stylize vocal practice. It is precisely this blurring of the distinction between 'vocal' substance and 'pianistic' ornament that lies at the heart of some of Chopin's most gloriously effusive melodies. A few parallel extracts from the melodic line of the F sharp major Nocturne, Op. 15 No. 2 will make the point (Ex. 13). Yet the impact of such

Ex. 13   Nocturne, Op. 15 No. 2

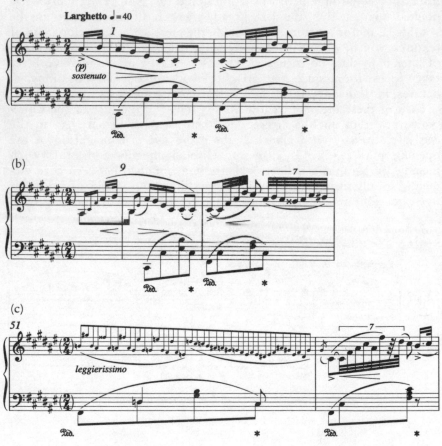

118

melodies remains in the end utterly dependent on the accompaniment layer. It is above all the accompaniment that enables the piano to preserve the illusion of a single 'voice' in the melodic layer.

The integrative role of the accompaniment in Op. 9 No. 1 will be apparent from Ex. 12. But more fundamental to the nocturne style as a whole is the provision of a rhythmically stable, fluid motion which promotes continuity, filling the 'gaps' in the melody and thus helping it to simulate vocal legato, supporting it when it takes off in flights of ornamental fancy (Exx. 12 and 13) and binding together its impulsive contrasts of register and dynamics (Ex. 14). It may be noted, too, that formal contrasts are underlined by texture. In the *sotto voce* section of Op. 15 No. 2 the melody is presented in octaves, the accompaniment pattern is narrowed in compass and the entire musical process is shifted down in register.

Ex. 14   Nocturne, Op. 15 No. 2

The accompaniment figures used in the three Op. 9 Nocturnes (Ex. 15 a–c) illustrate the diversity of patterns employed by Chopin in this, his first published set of nocturnes. There is an obvious concern to break away from schematic patterns in favour of semi-autonomous instrumental figures. The Op. 15 pieces widen the range of accompaniment figures yet further, and they develop the basic texture in other ways too, notably through the closer interaction of these figures with the melodic layer. The accompaniment may 'shadow' the melody within a narrow texture-space; it may flower into countermelody; it may move unobtrusively from a supportive to a directly collaborative role; or it may participate directly in an intricate web of motivic particles. In each case the counterpoint is facilitated, if not enabled, by the capacity of the piano to shade the dynamic levels of individual voices with infinite nuance.

In the middle section of the first Nocturne in F major the range of devices extends further still, reaching well beyond anything conventionally associated with the 'nocturne style'. Here again we seem to cross genres as Chopin offers us figurations of a kind more usually found in the études. There are parallels with Op. 10 No. 7, as Ex. 16 indicates. The two passages are very different in mood, but the similarities in their

Ex. 15 Three Nocturnes, Op. 9
(a) No. 1

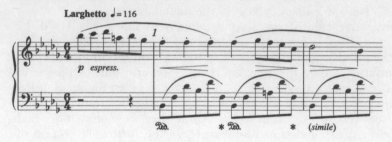

(b) No. 2

(c) No. 3

lay-out draw our attention to a basic aspect of Chopin's pianistic style, obvious enough in itself, but worth emphasizing because of its implications. I have already referred to 'layers' several times in the preceding discussion. Such terminology is justified mainly because Chopin drew his compositional ideas more directly than any of his predecessors from the performance constraints and possibilities of the separate hands, the limitations of compass within each of them, and the absence of any such limitation between them.[53] Naturally these constraints and possibilities face any composer of piano music, but in Chopin's case it was not just a matter of making adaptations. The physical properties of the two hands formed the essential starting-point for his musical thought.

[53] This is discussed by Zofia Chechlińska: ibid., pp. 148–50.

Ex. 16
(a) Nocturne, Op. 15 No. 1

(b) Étude, Op. 10 No. 7

The separation of the two hands is a fundamental component of Chopin's figuration, then, and their various collaborations—of many and subtle kinds—need to be viewed against this background. On occasion they may fuse together into a single layer, proximate in distance, even identical in function, but such fusions mark a departure from the norm of his pianistic style, and will tend to be heard as such. Right from the first two of the Op. 10 Études, composed in Warsaw, this separation into two layers, functioning as 'sonoristic counterweights', is apparent.

The first two Études also set the terms for the main categories of figuration, generated respectively by harmony and melody, and these categories are replicated elsewhere in the Op. 10 collection. There is the harmonic figuration of No. 5, for example, or again of No. 11. The arpeggiated chords in this later Étude may well have been indebted to Moscheles, but Chopin surpasses his model both in technical terms—the 'stretching' in both hands—and in the sophistication of his texture, allowing the melody to shift from one voice to another while tiny fragments of countermelody emerge from the chording. Then there is the melodic figuration of No. 4, similar in outline to that of No. 2, but extending beyond its predecessor to offer a rare instance of textural inversion in Chopin. The pattern comprises three bars of right-hand priority and three of left-hand priority, separated by a bar of collaboration (Ex. 17). It is worth noting, too, that by changing the figure in bar 3, Chopin not only increases the range and intensity of the music; he also allows a hidden repetition of the descending motive in bar 2, once more

Ex. 17 Étude, Op. 10 No. 4

using the piano's capacity to highlight individual strands of the textural web.

Elsewhere in the Études Chopin's textures blur the boundaries between such categories as melody, harmony, and figuration, and even between principal voice and accompaniment. The driving arpeggios in the left hand of No. 12, for example, are as much a motivic counterfoil to the main theme as a harmonic accompaniment in any conventional sense. Conversely the left-hand figuration of No. 9 allows a two-note motive to be drawn into the orbit of the melody, creating a shared element between two layers which in other ways remain separate. Intensification in this F minor Étude is achieved by a gradually widening texture-space, expressed (characteristically) by a scalar descent from

122

the tonic in the bass voice (bars 17–25), and a doubling of the melody into octaves. The widened sonority which results again makes skilful use of the natural resonance of the different registers of the instrument. And in a rather different way this is no less true of the figuration in No. 8, where the three elements of the texture are perfectly gauged in speed and compass to the registral qualities of the piano (Ex. 18). Chopin, incidentally, was happy to let the pedal catch the dissonant notes of the upper voice here, though the effect is very different on today's pianos.

Ex. 18   Étude, Op. 10 No. 8

The interpenetration of functions within Chopin's figurations tends in two opposing directions, towards a differentiated pianistic counterpoint on the one hand, and an undifferentiated sonority on the other. The four voices of the sixth Étude well illustrate the former tendency. Superficially this is a 'melody' and 'accompaniment', but it comprises four elements which balance each other in counterpoint, albeit not the formal counterpoint of Bach (Ex. 19). These elements are not legitimate 'voices', since from time to time they disappear from the texture or transmute into thicker chords, but the resulting variations in density and 'voicing' are perfectly moulded to the resonating timbre of the piano, where independent lines can be added or lost with no threat to the contrapuntal flow nor to the illusion of a homogeneous texture.

Ex. 19   Étude, Op. 10 No. 6

The middle section of the third Étude will serve to illustrate the latter tendency, the leaning towards undifferentiated sonority. Here the figuration is released from conventional tonal constraints, splintering into symmetrically mirrored patterns which move largely in parallel motion (Ex. 20). Such figurations still function essentially as harmonic prolongation, but in their detailed structure they allow chromatic symmetries to override diatonic hierarchies, and it would be difficult and pointless to attempt a conventional 'functional' analysis of their chord progres-

Ex. 20   Étude, Op. 10 No. 3

sions. Much more than in Chopin's earlier music (apart from some of the figurations of the two concertos), we sense in such passages harmony dissolving into 'colour', to use a common metaphor.

It was in these early mazurkas, nocturnes, and études that the Chopin piano acquired its unmistakable sound. The immediate origins of his textures and figurations are not far to seek. It is a straightforward exercise to relate the mazurkas to the likes of Maria Szymanowska, the nocturnes to John Field and the études to Moscheles. But it was above all the transformation of these early nineteenth-century models which led to the most distinctive and influential pianistic style of the nineteenth century. In examining that transformation we are inevitably drawn back to the influence of Bach, discussed already in this study. At the heart of Chopin's imaginative piano writing lies a recreation, in terms entirely idiomatic for the piano, of Bach's ornamental melody, figuration, and counterpoint. All three textural types receded somewhat in the era of the classical sonata, and they were in a sense invented afresh by Chopin during these years of early maturity. The achievement of his individual pianistic style was at once the discovery of something new and the recovery of something lost.

5

The best society

During the winter season of 1834–5 Chopin settled into a stable routine of composing and teaching, together with occasional concert appearances. By this time he was earning reasonable sums from teaching, and a certain amount from the sale of his music. He could afford to live stylishly, but he made no effort to put money aside, and for the rest of his life he proceeded on this rather 'hand to mouth' basis. As a result he was frequently short of funds, and the more so in that he enjoyed the luxuries of life. On such occasions he would hastily prepare a few further manuscripts for publication, or alternatively negotiate an advance on compositions not yet written. By all but withdrawing from the concert platform, he had forfeited the kinds of sums available to Liszt, for example, and he remained uncomfortably dependent for his income on a demanding regime of teaching, and on negotiating, or relying on his faithful Polish friends to negotiate, the best possible terms with publishers, all of whom he regarded as 'Jews'. Despite his high fees as a teacher, it was a precarious living.

Needless to say, he continued to move in exclusive social circles, and as the months passed his social and professional lives became ever more closely intertwined. Adolf Weissmann remarked with only a little exaggeration that 'the music lesson was transformed for him into a fashionable pleasure, a continuation of the salon'.[1] It is true that some of his pupils had their sights set on performing careers, and a few were modestly successful in this, including Princess Marcelina Czartoryska, who came to him in 1844 after studying with Czerny in Vienna. But most were gifted amateurs from wealthy, often aristocratic, families, with no intention to enter the profession. Already in 1834 this pattern was in place. In that year he took on three of the children of Count Thun-Hohenstein, from one of the oldest and wealthiest of the German–Bohemian families. And Chopin was sufficiently esteemed by the Thun-Hohensteins to stay with them the following year (along with his parents) at their castle in Děčin (Tetschen) on the river Elbe. As the

[1] Adolph Weissmann, *Chopin* (Berlin, 1912), p. 48.

years passed, the list of well-born pupils lengthened, a roll-call of some of the social élite of Paris.

In performing, too, Chopin tended to avoid what he would probably have regarded as the more vulgar aspects of the profession. Like his music lessons, his appearances as a pianist formed part of the fabric of his social life. For Chopin, performing was above all a form of intimate communication addressed to select groups of intimates. The salon, with all its connotations of exclusiveness, of small circles of connoisseurs and dilettantes, of a feminine ambience, of a retreat from the 'tasteless' public domain, was his natural setting. It would be possible to idealize this, of course. There is ample contemporary evidence of the shallow tastes of even the grandest Parisian salons of the day. But it is clear, and was made so by Liszt among others, that Chopin was something of a special case, that he dictated his own terms both musically and socially. Several years later George Sand warned Delacroix not to bring strangers along to hear Chopin play, as he was 'terrified of outsiders'.[2] In the best sense of a much abused term, he was widely regarded by 1834–5 as the 'salon composer' *par excellence*.

There were, all the same, some public appearances during that season, mostly at concerts given by friends and acquaintances, where Chopin could assume a fairly modest role in the proceedings. The first was at a benefit for Berlioz, given at the Conservatoire on 14 December. The main work on the programme was *Harold in Italy*, but Chopin played the Romance from the E minor Concerto, and was, as usual, given a solid review in the *Gazette musicale*. On 25 December he collaborated with Liszt in a concert given at a music school run by François Stoepel, an eccentric piano teacher with a highly colourful history. Chopin's music was not performed on this occasion, but he played duets with Liszt, performing the latter's *Grand Duo* and a piano duet by Moscheles. In February he played at a concert given by Hiller at the Salle Erard, just before his friend returned to Germany. Again Chopin was content to take a back seat, playing in a piano duet with Hiller. Then, on 15 March, after a period of bronchitis when he began coughing blood in an ominous way, he took part in a concert at the Salle Pleyel, organized by Kalkbrenner for the début of his pupil Camille Stamaty. The programme is not known in detail, but it seems likely from the list of performers that the *Grande Polonaise* for six pianists by Kalkbrenner was given once again.

There were two much more public events in April. The first was a charity concert organized by Princess Anna Czartoryska at the Théâtre-Italien on 5 April on behalf of Polish exiles in Paris. Despite teething difficulties over the singers, this turned out to be an important event, conducted by François-Antoine Habeneck, whose concert series at the

---

[2] *George Sand Correspondence*, hereafter *GSC*, ed. Georges Lubin (Paris, 1964–76), 12 vols., vol. 4, p. 407.

Conservatoire was just about the most prestigious anywhere in Europe. The singers included the famous tenor Adolphe Nourrit, greatly admired by Chopin, and the other pianists were Liszt and Hiller, who played one of Hiller's piano duets. The centrepiece of the programme, however, was the E minor Concerto by Chopin, deemed by the loyal *Gazette musicale* as 'full of originality and ingenuity', and 'a great success'.[3] Other reviews were not so positive, however, and it may well be that the account given by Fétis comes closer to the mark: 'Chopin counted on a magnificent success: but he only just collected a few bravos from his most devoted friends.'[4]

Much later, in 1874, Wojciech Sowiński discussed this concert, arguing that the coldness of the Paris audience so discouraged Chopin that for a long time he would not perform in public.[5] In fact he had long known that he disliked such occasions, and the reception of the Concerto could have been no more than confirmation of his feelings about them. There was one further public concert that season, and it was to be his last such event for many years. On first arriving in Paris Chopin had sought without success an opportunity to perform at Habeneck's *concerts de conservatoire*. He was finally invited to do so on 26 April 1835, shortly after the charity concert and quite possibly because of Habeneck's direct involvement in that concert. Intriguingly he chose to play not one of the concertos, but the *Grande Polonaise brillante*, preceded by an *Andante spianato* specially composed for the occasion. This time there was real critical acclaim, but Chopin's mind was made up, and for several years he resolutely refused invitations to give a public concert.

His main business of the year was, as always, composing, and here there were important developments. Precise chronology again eludes us, but we do know that by the summer of 1835 several major works were ready for the publisher. They included the two Polonaises, Op. 26, the first Scherzo, Op. 20 and the first Ballade, Op. 23. These works marked new departures in several respects, not least as the first of his extended compositions to turn aside from the familiar classical and post-classical genres, sonatas, variations, rondos, and the like. Having addressed issues in musical materials—harmony, melody, and figuration—in the mazurkas, nocturnes, and études of the Vienna and early Paris years, Chopin now set out to consolidate these achievements within the context of more large-scale works. His solutions were as ever fresh and novel, even to the point of achieving a kind of generic renovation—inventing, or at the very least redefining, the genres which might best suit his musical needs. To the more enlightened critics it was gradually becoming clear that one of the most radical and penetrating musical minds of the post-Beethoven era was at work in the intensely private

---

[3] *Gazette musicale*, Paris, 12 April 1835.   [4] *Revue musicale*, 19 April 1835.
[5] See Mieczysław Tomaszewski, *Chopin: A Diary in Images*, pp. 117–18.

world of Chopin's study, distilling and refining the achievements of public and salon pianism into a singular musical style of compelling vision.

The power of his music in these extended works has left biographers at something of a loss. Many were inclined to make simple equations ('it seems impossible to make a clear distinction between his music and his personality').[6] At various times they invoked Chopin's natural air of distinction, his 'prince-like charm', refinement of manner, and other-worldliness, all of which suggested to them certain qualities in the music. So too did his illness ('through music he discloses his suffering'),[7] his love of the feminine world of the salon, and, of course, his patriotism. The coarser, more spiteful, side to his personality was usually ignored in such commentaries, and so, too, was the narrow conservatism of his outlook on almost all, including social, issues.

Simple associations of this kind are treacherous, and seldom penetrate to those deeper mental reserves which feed the creative process. The truth is that on these more fundamental levels of creativity we know little about the relationship between a composer and his music, and this goes for figures of more conventionally 'heroic' cast, too. Truly exceptional creative talent in music remains more than a touch mysterious, often attaching itself to people who are far from exceptional in other ways. Much of the mythologizing of Chopin's life was due precisely to this paradox, to the need to transpose to the man something of the richness and fascination of the music. And nowhere is this more evident than in discussion of his romantic associations.

The fateful meeting with Maria Wodzińska in September 1835 came after a summer devoted to things Polish, and the effect of the meeting may well have owed a good deal to this larger context of nostalgia. In a letter to his family in 1832, Antoni Orlowski captured the ambivalence, even the conflict, right at the heart of Chopin's life as an exile in Paris. 'He is the latest fashion. We shall doubtless soon be wearing gloves *à la Chopin*. But he is tormented by homesickness.'[8] It was, after all, some five years since he had seen his family. In a letter of April 1834, Izabella had already broached the possibility of a meeting between Chopin and his parents: 'It may happen one day, but when?'[9] Moreover Chopin had debated returning to Warsaw on numerous occasions. But despite the official amnesties he was nervous, and probably with reason, of renewing his Russian passport and putting himself at the mercy of Russian officials in Warsaw, especially given the circumstance in which he had obtained French residency. Equally, and perhaps for similar reasons, his father had misgivings about visiting France. In the end they

[6] Hippolyte Barbedette, *Chopin. Essai de critique musicale* (Paris, 1869), p. 65.
[7] Ibid.
[8] Quoted in Ferdinand Hoesick, *Chopin: życie i twórczość*, vol. 2, p. 67.
[9] *KFC*, vol. 1, p. 238.

hatched a tentative plan to meet on neutral territory at Karlsbad some-time in the summer of 1835, and Chopin waited for further news.

The news came in July while he was staying at Enghien, a fashionable spa just to the north of Paris. He had availed himself of an invitation from his new friend and admirer the Marquis de Custine, whose St Gratien villa was beautifully positioned on the edge of the lake. Custine had been somewhat ostracized by respectable society, following a homo-sexual scandal, but he became a leading light of literary and artistic cir-cles. He was himself a writer, mainly of travel books, a genre in the ascendant in the 1830s, but above all he was a host of legendary gen-erosity, placing his considerable resources at the disposal of those he deemed talented. He was known to be a Polish sympathizer, and this no doubt fostered his friendship towards Chopin in the first instance, though he may well have had other designs on the composer. In any case, Chopin became very much part of his circle and Custine's loyalty to him proved to be enduring. It was while enjoying these weeks at Enghien that Chopin had news of the imminent arrival of his parents at Karlsbad (now Karlovy Vary in the Czech Republic).

His response was immediate. After quickly arranging for a French passport he made the very long trip by mail coach to Karlsbad, reach-ing the spa town late on 15 August, a matter of hours before his par-ents' arrival. The three spent most of a month together. 'Our joy is indescribable', Chopin wrote to Ludwika. 'We never stop telling each other how much we have been thinking of one another.'[10] They were not of course aware of it, but this was to be their last meeting. The time was spent in relaxation, walks, leisurely meals, and musical soirées, where Chopin was joined by the cellist Jozef Dessauer. The Thun-Hohenstein family were also taking the waters at Karlsbad at the time and they insisted that the Chopins stay at their home in Děčin on the way back to Warsaw. Chopin accompanied his parents to Děčin and they stayed a few days at the Thun castle before setting off for Warsaw on 14 September. The Count's daughter Jozefina, Chopin's former pupil, remarked that the composer was utterly dejected on the day following his parents' departure, but that he recovered well enough during the remainder of his stay with the Thuns. He presented Jozefina with the manuscript of his A flat major Waltz, Op. 34 No. 1, composed during the summer, dating the manuscript 'Tetschen 15 September 1835'. And when the Waltz was subsequently revised for publication it was dedi-cated to Jozefina.

On 19 September Chopin left Děčin, accompanying one of the Count's sons to Dresden, and it was on his arrival there that he bumped into Feliks Wodziński. There had been some correspondence between Chopin and the Wodziński family during the previous year, including a

---

[10] *KFC*, vol. 1, p. 260.

further invitation to Geneva in February. But the meeting in September was entirely unexpected, and Chopin was of course invited to call on the family, who were staying in Dresden for the summer. He was undoubtedly greatly taken with Maria, now a mature sixteen-year-old, darkly attractive and gifted in the way of educated young ladies of good family. She was an accomplished pianist and singer, could turn her hand to composing, and was a talented painter, as her watercolour portraits of Chopin testify. For Chopin, then twenty-five, the attraction was probably heightened by their shared background in Warsaw, since Warsaw was much on his mind just then. Quite possibly this was the first time he had encountered someone who would make a suitable match, and from this point on he may well have begun to map out a new future for himself as a family man.

He stayed a further two weeks in Dresden, and the letter sent from Maria to Paris later in the month could only have strengthened his feelings for her. While avoiding explicit reference to any deeper feelings, she made it very clear how much Chopin was missed in Dresden. It is also plain that along with the affection there was a real respect for his genius. By the time Chopin received that letter he was very ill. He had returned to Paris by way of Leipzig, where he spent a day of music-making with Mendelssohn, Schumann, and the fifteen-year-old Clara Wieck, later described by Chopin as the only woman in Germany who could play his works. It was apparently an enjoyable day. Mendelssohn wrote to his sister at the time that Chopin 'has his own perfectly formed manner. And if that manner is very different from mine, I can none the less get on splendidly with it.'[11] From Leipzig he set off for Paris by way of Heidelberg, home of his favourite pupil, Adolf Gutmann, and it was here that he had a major bronchial attack, similar to the one in March of the previous year. This time the attack was so serious that reports of his death were circulated, and were actually published very much later (December) in the Warsaw press. These reports came to the attention of the Wodziński family, and may well have sown the first seeds of doubt about a proposal which they were almost certainly expecting. Significantly the Wodzińskis visited the Chopins on several occasions over these winter months.

Chopin arrived back in Paris in late October for the 1835–6 season and began the usual round of teaching, playing, and composing. Maria's brother Antoni, not the most reliable of characters, had arrived in the city, and this placed an extra burden on Chopin's shoulders, since he had been charged by the family to look after the boy. He did so conscientiously and at some personal expense until Antoni took himself off to fight in the Spanish civil war; Antoni never did pay off a loan Chopin made him at this time. But in other respects the routine of the season

11 Ibid., p. 407.

was much as before, with minor appearances as a pianist at soirées given by Charles Schunke and the Duke Décazes, and unhappily another bout of ill health in March. A pattern was already forming in this regard. This was the third successive year of major illness, and for the rest of his life Chopin was regularly laid up for a period during the winter months as consumption steadily took its toll.

Once more he spent much of the spring and summer alternating between Enghien and Paris, but when the Wodziński family arrived at Marienbad in July he promptly set off to join them, arriving there in poor health towards the end of the month. He spent the whole of August at Marienbad and then followed Mrs Wodzińska and her two daughters to Dresden. It was on 9 September, his last night in Dresden, 'at the twilight hour', that Chopin finally proposed marriage to Maria. The girl apparently consented, but her mother kept him waiting for an answer. She gave him grounds for hope, but said that she must first consult her husband, then in Poland, and that until she had done so, and they had both had ample time to consider the matter, the 'engagement' should remain secret.

As in the previous year, Chopin called in on Schumann at Leipzig on his way from Dresden to Paris, giving him a copy of the G minor Ballade, with the intriguing comment that it was his favourite among his own works, and playing the opening of the second Ballade, not yet complete, and the first two of the Op. 25 Études. Schumann's description of Chopin playing the first Étude is evocative: 'Imagine an aeolian harp', he remarked, with 'a deeper fundamental tone and a softly singing melody . . . a billowing of the chord of A♭, swelled here and there by the pedal' and 'through the harmonies . . . in sustained notes a wonderful melody . . .'[12] For his part, Chopin kept a certain distance from the Leipzig circle and remained healthily sceptical of just this kind of poetic imagery. There is some irony in this as he was already commonly described in journals as the 'poet of the piano'.

On his return to Paris in October 1836 he and Matuszyński moved into a new, rather chic apartment, a stone's throw from the old one, at 38 rue de la Chaussée d'Antin, and characteristically they furnished it in the most elegant and expensive manner. In the meantime he waited anxiously for his answer. It was at this time that he asked Ludwika to copy some of the songs and the *Lento con gran espressione* for Maria's album, and he also sent autographs to the Wodzińskis and undertook various other chores for them in direct response to their numerous requests. There were, of course, letters to and from the Wodziński home at Służewo, near Torun, with Maria's contributions in the form of brief, surprisingly formal, postscripts to her mother's letters. Initially the tone was moderately encouraging but, as the weeks and months passed, the

[12] Quoted in Frederick Niecks, *Chopin as a Man and Musician*, vol. 1, p. 310.

communications from Poland became less frequent and less warm. Although he did not abandon hope, Chopin must have realized that the Wodzińskis were losing enthusiasm for the whole affair.

The constant references in Teresa Wodzińska's letters to Chopin's health were not simply a kind of maternal solicitude (she had earlier described Chopin as her 'fourth son'). She had herself seen evidence of his frailty, quite apart from the reports widely circulated in Poland, and both she and her husband would naturally have been gravely concerned about linking Maria with someone who might well not reach his fiftieth birthday ('Look after your health since everything depends on that').[13] There is also the matter of social standing. Adam Zamoyski, who ought to know, has argued that this would have played little part in the decision, since the Wodzińskis, for all their wealth, were by no means of the high aristocracy.[14] But Chopin later sent the *Allegro de concert* to Aleksander Hoffman with the words 'to the Silesian craftsman from the street musician', apparently a direct reference to Wincenty Wodziński's disparagement of his profession.[15] Social class may not have been at issue, then, but Chopin's capacity to keep his daughter in the accustomed style clearly was.

During the period of waiting, Chopin existed in a state of private depression and public gaiety. This condition was by no means new to him, but the polarity was perhaps greater than usual during this year. The public gaiety is the easier to record. In the early part of the season his social life became entwined a little with that of Liszt. In October Liszt and Marie d'Agoult installed themselves at the Hôtel de France, following a period in Switzerland. Shortly afterwards George Sand and her two children took a room in the hotel, and Sand became a regular at the Liszt salon, where the artistic élite of Paris frequently gathered. Chopin had grown apart from Liszt over the years, and he found the general atmosphere of the salon pretentious and oppressive. Nevertheless, he did spend several evenings there in November and he in turn invited the Liszt circle, including George Sand, to the Chaussée d'Antin. These evenings took place between October and December 1836, and they culminated in a soirée at Chopin's apartment on 13 December, attended by Heine, Sand, Marie d'Agoult, Liszt, Custine, Eugène Sue, Nourrit, Pixis, Grzymała, Matuszyński, and Delacroix, whom Chopin had first met at Liszt's the previous May. Shortly after that soirée Sand returned to her country home, Nohant, for the winter.

There are accounts of these early meetings by Sand herself, by Liszt, and by the composer Józef Brzowski, a fellow student of Chopin's who

[13] *KFC*, vol. 1, p. 287.   [14] Adam Zamoyski, *Chopin: A Biography*, p. 137.
[15] See Franciszek German, 'Chopin Relics in Upper Silesia', in *Chopin in Silesia*, pp. 16–18.

arrived in Paris in 1836 and became part of his circle for a time,[16] and there are passing references in Chopin's correspondence. The one certainty is that there was little of promise here for a future relationship. Chopin's first impressions were far from favourable. 'I have met a great celebrity, Mme Dudevant, known as George Sand', he wrote to his family. 'Her appearance is not to my liking. Indeed there is something about her which positively repels me.'[17] 'What an unattractive person La Sand is', he apparently commented to Hiller. 'Is she really a woman?'[18]

For the rest, his social life centred around meetings with Polish emigrés, notably with the conservative aristocratic group centred at the Hôtel Lambert. Chopin involved himself in the fund-raising activities of the Czartoryskis, attended many of their soirées, and played occasionally at the benefits they arranged for Poles in exile. He also had social contacts with literary figures of a more radical political persuasion, including Julian Niemcewicz, Juliusz Slowacki, and Adam Mickiewicz. Although their paths crossed on several occasions during this season, not least at the Christmas supper, Chopin and Mickiewicz were never particularly close. Indeed Chopin's relations with Mickiewicz's Polish Literary Society, to which he had been elected an associate member in 1833, remained somewhat ambivalent, and he was clearly something of a disappointment to the Society. Chopin was, in his own words, 'no revolutionary', and he refused to use his talent in any directly political way. Other engagements involved the Polish musicians who arrived in trickles in Paris, and inevitably gravitated towards Chopin. Józef Brzowski was a case in point, and during the same season Karol Lipiński also turned up. Chopin found himself organizing soirées and concerts for such musicians, and all this took time. Most important of all there was of course his own intimate circle, including Grzymała, Fontana, and Matuszyński, whose wedding he attended as a witness on 21 December 1836.

The Marquis de Custine was a sort of honorary member of these Polish circles, and Chopin continued to pay frequent visits to Enghien. We learn of one such occasion from an account by Józek Brzowski, who in early June 1837 described a visit to St Gratien right at the end of the previous year. By this time Chopin had been waiting for some eight months for a definitive answer from the Wodzińskis, and privately he was in a state of some anguish. Yet there is no hint of this in Brzowski's account.[19] The outing involved a donkey ride from the nearby village of Montmorency into the adjoining countryside as far as Rousseau's Hermitage. On the return journey to Montmorency Chopin and Brzowski were soaked through in a downpour. They then took their

---

[16] See the extracts from Brzowski's Diary, quoted in Czartkowski and Jeżewska, *Fryderyk Chopin*, pp. 206–31.
[17] Mieczysław Karasowski, *Fryderyk Chopin* (Warsaw, 1882), 3 vols., vol. 2, p. 75.
[18] Quoted in Frederick Niecks, *Chopin as a Man and Musician*, vol. 2, p. 8.
[19] Czartkowski and Jeżewska, *Fryderyk Chopin*, pp. 223–33.

hired cabriolet to Enghien where they had arranged to meet one of Custine's friends, Count Ignacy Gurowski, with whom they enjoyed a very liquid dinner before returning to St Gratien for a musical evening which continued until well after midnight. Brzowski and Chopin then returned to Paris. It was hardly the kind of lifestyle Teresa Wodzińska had in mind when she cautioned Chopin to look after his health, and it is symptomatic of what seems to have been a hectic social life during the entire 1836–7 season.

As the summer approached, and Paris society evacuated to the country or abroad, Chopin turned down several invitations for the summer months, including one from Nohant. He was, of course, anxiously awaiting news of the Wodzińskis. In particular he was hoping to join them for the summer months, and was reluctant to leave Paris for any length of time until he knew of their plans. For this reason an invitation from Camille Pleyel to spend two weeks in London in late July seemed an acceptable compromise. Stanisław Koźmian, who was then living in London and was detailed by Fontana to act as guide, gives some indication of Chopin's 'dreadful state of mind' at this time.[20] He had been banking on the summer months to meet Maria again and to extract a definite answer from her parents, yet it was becoming more and more doubtful that he would have any opportunity to see them. Accordingly his mood was sour, and he was certainly in no frame of mind to appreciate London. The climate disagreed with him, and he made no attempt to contact London's musical circles, sight-seeing extensively, attending concerts, and visiting the opera entirely incognito. Later Mendelssohn and Moscheles learnt to their surprise that Chopin had been in the English capital without calling on them. Only on one occasion was his identity revealed. He and Pleyel attended a dinner given by James Broadwood, and he was unable to resist trying the piano after the meal. 'Mr Fritz', as he had been introduced to the assembled company, was soon unmasked.

During this interlude a letter from Teresa Wodzińska was forwarded to London. It has not survived, but judging from Chopin's reply it may have put paid to any meeting that summer, and probably also to any future hopes for Maria's hand. When he returned to Paris Chopin made a bundle of all the Wodzińska letters along with a flower which Maria had given him in Dresden. The bundle was found among his possessions after his death, and on one of the envelopes he had written 'My Sorrow', a gesture powerfully suggestive of his private depression in the wake of the Wodzińska affair. Four years later Maria, by a curious coincidence, married the son of Fryderyk Skarbek, Chopin's godfather, only to divorce him shortly afterwards. She later remarried and died in 1896 at the age of seventy-seven.

[20] Quoted in Ferdinand Hoesick, *Chopin: życie i twórczość*, vol. 2, p. 145.

It is hard to know what Chopin's real feelings for Maria were. After all, they were based on precious little time spent in each other's company. In total there were only two such periods, one of two weeks and the other of just over a month. It is difficult to resist the impression that there was a good deal of idealization in the relationship, especially given Maria's tender years. Yet the shattering of a dream is painful in itself, and with his hopes of marriage dashed, Chopin found himself alone and depressed in Paris for the rest of the summer. It was the more dispiriting in that the city was for the most part empty of his usual circle of friends. And to make matters worse, he was short of money, following an unusually extravagant year. It had also been an unproductive year, and in the autumn Chopin, free of distractions and anxious to make up for lost time, threw himself into teaching and composing once again. To earn some money as quickly as possible he began preparing some of his existing works for publication, including the Op. 25 Études and the Op. 29 Impromptu. But he also worked on new compositions such as the second Scherzo, the Nocturnes, Op. 32, both published in December, and on the *Marche funèbre* which would later be incorporated into the B flat minor Sonata. Those inclined to relate Chopin's works directly to incidents in his life will have no difficulty at all with the *Marche funèbre*.

There is little documentation of his life during the winter months, beyond an appearance in late February at one of the regular concerts given at the Tuileries for Louis-Philippe and the royal family, and two appearances at benefit concerts the following month. The first of these, on 3 March, was a concert given by the young pianist Alkan, whom Chopin already knew well and who would later become his neighbour on the Square d'Orléans. It was an alarming occasion, in which Chopin collaborated with Alkan himself, his teacher Pierre Joseph Zimmerman, and Chopin's pupil Adolphe Gutmann in Alkan's eight-handed arrangement of Beethoven's Seventh Symphony. When asked to repeat the performance a few years later, Chopin shrewdly pleaded insufficient stamina. Later in the same month he travelled to Rouen to participate in a concert by Antoni Orlowski, who had settled there as director of the Philharmonic at the Théâtre des Arts and was anxious to make an impact. Schlesinger sent Ernest Legouvé to cover the concert for the *Revue et Gazette musicale*, and Legouvé concluded his review with an allusion to the famous 'contest' which had taken place the previous year in Paris. 'In future when the question is asked, "Who is the greatest pianist in Europe, Liszt or Thalberg?", let the world reply "It is Chopin!" '[21]

A matter of weeks after the Rouen concert, in late April Chopin met George Sand once again, this time at the salon of Countess Charlotte Marliani, wife of the Spanish consul in Paris and a friend of Mme Sand. Chopin regularly attended the salon, along with members of the Liszt

[21] *Revue et Gazette musicale*, Paris, 25 March 1838.

circle, Grzymała, and the Czartoryskis. Indeed the personnel was largely that of the Hôtel de France a year earlier. And when Sand visited Paris in April 1838 she stayed with the Marlianis, where she inevitably met Chopin on several occasions. They saw each other at Grzymała's, too, and on 8 May at Custine's Parisian apartment. By then it was clear to the intimate circle that Sand and Chopin were drawing together, a development viewed by Marie d'Agoult as 'quite delicious'. On one occasion he received a scribbled note from Sand with the words 'on vous adore', to which her friend the actress Marie Dorval had added 'et moi aussi'.[22] Chopin stuck the note into his album.

When they had last met some fifteen months previously there had been no sign of any attraction between Chopin and Sand, certainly not on his part. Yet in the Spring of 1838 their love was kindled almost instantly. Such matters are of course imponderable, but it is perhaps not so surprising that each should have seen the other in a very different light on the later occasion, since both had come through a difficult period involving a sense of loss, in Chopin's case concerning Maria and in Sand's her estranged mother. Both were in a reflective frame of mind, less inclined than usual to pose and accordingly more receptive to the special qualities of the other. Although it would not have been viewed by either of them in this light at the time, it was quite possibly Sand's very strong maternal instinct which drew her to Chopin right from the start. Just then he certainly needed mothering. But posthumous psychoanalysis carries its penalties, and I repeat, such matters are imponderable.

When she returned to Nohant in mid May, the relationship had not yet developed much beyond whispered intimacies.[23] Sand, no slouch in these matters, was disturbed by the tardy pace, though she was all too well aware of a practical obstacle in the form of her current lover, Félicien Mallefille, a dramatist friend of Marie d'Agoult who was just then acting as a tutor to her son, Maurice. Back in Nohant, she was in an agony of indecision, articulated in an astonishing letter, running to more than five thousand words, sent to Grzymała at the end of May. From certain remarks it is clear that it was in reply to a letter from Grzymała in which he apparently warned Sand not to play with Chopin's emotions and told her also about Maria Wodzińska. Grzymała's letter almost certainly followed discussions with Chopin, who had sent him a note urgently seeking advice.[24] It has been an easy matter for biographers to point to the inconsistencies in Sand's reply, as indeed in her other writings, and in her behaviour generally. But it was Gastone Belotti who came closest to a real understanding of such inconsistencies when he remarked with great insight that she 'lived her truths

[22] *GSC*, vol. 4, p. 395.
[23] See her letter to Grzymała, May 1838: ibid., pp. 428–39.
[24] *KFC*, vol. 1, p. 325.

one at a time, each cancelling the last'.[25] The marathon letter to Grzymała was in a way a speeded up form of this process. It is perhaps not appropriate to dismiss it for a lack of integrity.

In it she expressed her concern, among other things, at the reasons for Chopin's abstinence. It seems that he had muttered something about 'certain actions' spoiling the memory as he left Grzymała's house one evening. For Sand this was lamentable. 'It is just this manner of separating the spirit from the flesh that makes convents and brothels necessary', she wrote. She considered that 'he had the wrong reasons for abstaining. Until then I thought it good that he refrained from respect for me, from shyness or from loyalty to another.' Yet the likelihood is that it was indeed simple shyness that held Chopin back. He was an inveterate flirt with young ladies of all social backgrounds, but his actual sexual experience was probably extremely limited, and he cannot have been unaware of Mme Sand's history. His remarks at Grzymała's were probably no more than a cover story.

Sand's letter rehearsed all the various options with regard to Maria Wodzińska and Mallefille, for all the world as though she were thinking aloud. In the end she arrived at four alternatives, which in effect reduce to three: that Chopin would be happy with Maria alone, with Sand alone, or with both women, albeit in two quite different ways, in which case she (Sand) could follow suit and share her love between Chopin and Mallefille. Earlier in the letter she had made a little more specific the terms of this third option, using a rather strained geographical metaphor. She argued that if the bonds holding Chopin were a Russia, she must strive to release him from these bonds, but that if they were a Poland, she must be his Italy, 'which we visit and enjoy on spring days, but where we cannot reside permanently, since there is more sun than beds and tables, and the necessary comforts of life are elsewhere'.

Having exorcised the problem in self-analysis, she promptly yielded to instinct. The marathon letter was immediately followed by another. 'I will be in Paris on Thursday on business. Come and see me and do not tell the boy [Chopin]. We will surprise him . . .'[26] She arrived on 6 June. As it happened Chopin was not surprised, since he had been fore-warned of her visit by the Marlianis, with whom she planned to stay. Clearly in a state of the greatest agitation, he dashed off a note to Grzymała, who was already assuming the role of father-figure in his life, with the suggestion that they have dinner together. 'We'll go from there to the Marlianis''. Events were clearly moving rapidly towards the inevitable denouement, and within days Chopin and Sand were lovers.

From the start it seemed an unlikely pairing, given their contrasted backgrounds and personalities. No partner could have been further

[25] See 'Three Unpublished Letters by George Sand and their Contribution to Chopin Scholarship', in *The Musical Quarterly* (1966), vol. 52, no. 3, pp. 283–303.
[26] *GSC*, vol. 4, p. 445.

removed from Chopin's conservative, devoutly Catholic roots, from his refined, rather aloof manner, and from his fastidious respect for all proprieties. Although she was still only thirty-four when the affair began in June 1838, Sand had lived a full life, to say the very least, and little of it had been concerned with proprieties. Shunted between an austere grandmother and an indifferent mother, she was brought up mainly by the former at Nohant in Berry, and from childhood she developed a deep attachment to the old eighteenth-century manor house which she would later inherit. With her grandmother's death in 1821 she moved to her widowed mother in Paris, but promptly escaped her difficult ways by marrying Casimir Dudevant, with whom she settled in Nohant. It was an unhappy marriage, but there was consolation in her son, Maurice, and in her daughter, Solange, commonly thought to be the product of an early affair with Stéphane Ajasson, the first of a long line of lovers. It was her relationship with the young writer Jules Sandeau, however, which led directly to her separation from Dudevant, and for some time she lived with Sandeau in Paris, making periodic visits to her children in Nohant, and earning a living by writing.

Until she arrived in Paris, Sand's writing was only one of several accomplishments, of a kind and at a level not so unusual among young ladies of a certain class. She was also trained in music, for example. All this changed in the early 1830s. Her professional career was launched in 1832 by the novel *Indiana*, the first to be written under the *nom de plume* George Sand. Its plea for women's rights in extra-marital affairs had a fairly explicit autobiographical resonance. And she followed this immediately by the no less successful and no less autobiographical novel *Lélia*, which depicts marriage as an unnatural state destined to kill passion and, ultimately, love. The relationship with Sandeau did not survive her entry into the sophisticated world of Paris literary circles, where her unorthodox lifestyle, including her habit of dressing as a man and her close and, easily misinterpreted association with the actress Marie Dorval, very soon became notorious. So, too, did her succession of affairs.

These included a brief and notorious encounter with Prosper Merimée, closely followed by a stormy relationship with Alfred de Musset and a more placid but ultimately suffocating liaison with Pietro Pagello, the Italian doctor who had cured Musset during their visit to Venice. Both she and Musset came to agree in later years that it was a mother's love she had felt for him, and it is hard not to see in this a kind of premonition of her later feelings for Chopin. Next in line was Michel de Bourges, the leading republican lawyer who was enlisted to help her obtain a legal separation from Dudevant. This was eventually achieved, with Dudevant gaining much of Sand's income from her Paris *pied-à-terre* (she effectively lost the use of this), but with Sand regaining Nohant, as well as custody of Solange and, in due course, of Maurice also. She had most of what she wanted, but financial pressures were considerable and she was obliged to write constantly to maintain her income.

We approach the time of her first meeting with Chopin. In August 1836 Sand went on a carefree vacation in Switzerland with her friends Liszt and Marie d'Agoult, and in October followed them to the Hôtel de France. At this time she was having a brief affair with the Swiss poet Charles Didier, who was awaiting her in the Hôtel de France following that soirée at Chopin's on 13 December 1836. 'There was tolerably pleasant intimacy between us', Didier wrote in his journal the following day. 'But something seemed to be eating away at her from within. As dawn approached she became terribly depressed.'[27] She was also at this time increasingly engaged by movements which might be loosely subsumed under the term 'social romanticism', involving that lyrical blend of utopian socialism, illuminism, and republicanism which proved so highly palatable in French literary circles of the pre-1848 years. In the 1840s Sand would herself become active politically, but in the late 1830s it was a more woolly, less defined notion which attracted her, a form of utopianism preached by the Abbé Lamennais and Pierre Leroux, with the far from modest aim of bringing about a new, regenerate mankind. It need hardly be said that such ideas would not have endeared Sand to Chopin during those early meetings in 1836. Indeed throughout their time together he shared few of her intellectual enthusiasms.

None of this seemed a problem in the spring of 1838, when the two were caught up in the first blush of romance. Sand took an attic room near the Marlianis, allowing them some privacy, while Chopin continued teaching at the rue de la Chaussée d'Antin. They spent most evenings at the Marlianis', and it was only those members of the small circle of intimates at the Marlianis' who were aware of the relationship. That circle included Eugène Delacroix, whose famous double portrait of Sand and Chopin, where Chopin is seated at the piano, while Sand stands 'curiously attentive and subdued' behind him, dated from that time. The painting was later cut in two, with Chopin currently housed in the Louvre and Sand in Copenhagen. Delacroix would grow closer to both of them over the years, but already he was something of a confidant for Sand. 'You imagine that this happiness cannot survive?', she wrote to him. 'If I trust my memory and my reason, then it certainly cannot. But if I trust my heart and feelings, it seems to me that it can last for ever.'[28]

The one fly in the ointment was Sand's current 'official' lover, Félicien Mallefille, of whom Chopin was becoming increasingly jealous, though Mallefille himself suspected nothing. When he visited Paris on one occasion he was introduced to Chopin and actually wrote a poem inspired by his playing. He sent this to Chopin along with a letter, in

---

[27] Quoted in William G. Atwood, *The Lioness and the Little One: the Liaison of George Sand and Frederic Chopin* (New York, 1980), p. 8.

[28] *GSC*, vol. 4, pp. 482–3.

which incidentally he referred to the '*Ballade Polonaise* of which we are so fond', an intriguing and suggestive title for the (second?) Ballade, and one which begs a number of questions. He was even encouraged to write an appreciation for the *Gazette musicale*. It was hardly fair play. In August Sand sent the unfortunate man on a fortnight's trip to Normandy with Maurice to allow more space for herself and Chopin. It was at this point that Mallefille apparently realized what was happening, and on his return to Paris he brought the unfolding drama to something of a climax, albeit one in which tragedy borders on farce. The details are not entirely clear, but it seems that he placed himself strategically across the street from Chopin's apartment, and when Sand appeared lunged forward, pistol in hand, his revenge thwarted only by the timely arrival of a large wagon. Mallefille was of course dismissed, and took the whole thing very badly indeed. But for Sand and Chopin the episode served above all as a spur to leave Paris.

George Sand had in any case been giving some thought to spending the winter months in Italy. As so often in her life, she was driven by the needs and desires of her son, Maurice, who was already suffering from a kind of rheumatism. But a trip to the south seemed a good idea for Chopin, too, since he was habitually ill in winter. They discussed the plan at length at the Marlianis, and it was here that Majorca was proposed as an alternative. As the Spanish consul in Paris, Manoel Marliani frequently played host to Spaniards, and it was probably two of them, the diplomat Don Juan Mendizabal and the musician Francisco Frontera (usually known simply as Valldemosa from the village of his birth), who proposed the Balearic Islands as ideal for their purposes. Chopin was predictably cautious about the whole plan, and several of his friends, notably Grzymała and Custine, viewed it with the gravest misgivings. Both of them were seriously worried about his health. 'Consumption has taken possession of his face', wrote Custine. And later: 'He is following her to Spain . . . He will never leave that country.'[29] But Sand's mind was made up, and preparations were shortly under way for a truly extraordinary episode in both their lives.

They made the long journey to Perpignan separately. Sand, the children, and their maid from Paris took a leisurely carriage trip, with various detours to visit friends, and arrived on 30 October after twelve days' travelling. Chopin reached Perpignan the following day after a four-day journey by mail coach. Then it was on board *Le Phénecien* for Barcelona, where they stayed at the hotel 'Quatro Naciones' for five days, mainly sightseeing in the city but venturing out on one occasion to make a depressing and rather hazardous trip into its environs, where they saw some evidence of the civil war then raging in Spain. In the afternoon of 7 November they boarded the small steamer *El Mallorquin*

[29] Quoted in *Correspondance de Frédéric Chopin*, ed. B. E. Sydow, D. Chainaye and S. Chainaye (Paris, 1953), 3 vols., vol. 2, p. 279.

bound for Palma, and arrived there in bright sunshine just before noon the following day.

At the Marlianis' Chopin and Sand had been assured that Majorca was well prepared for travellers, and they had no doubt expected to put up immediately at a suitable inn. Instead Sand tramped the streets of Palma in an increasingly desperate search for accommodation of any kind, eventually settling for two small rooms in a rather seedy area of the town. Already in these first few hours the culture shock must have been considerable. The next day, feeling the worse for the rough, oily peasant food of southern Europe, and the ubiquitous mosquitos, they resumed their search, making use of letters of introduction to the French consul Flury and the French banker Canut. Eventually a house, ominously and all too aptly called 'So'n Vent' (house of the wind), was secured by Flury, and they moved there after six days. It was situated just outside the town and was sparsely furnished and without window panes, which tenants were supposed to supply, but the setting was picturesque and the weather was still spring-like. 'I am in Palma', Chopin wrote to Fontana, 'among the palms, cedars, cacti, olive trees, orange and lemon trees, aloes, figs, pomegranates . . . the sky is turquoise, the sea lapis lazuli, the mountains emerald, the air heavenly . . . I am really coming alive. I am close to all that is beautiful. I feel a better man.'[30]

They both settled down to work, Sand working through the nights on her new novel *Spiridion*, while Chopin tried to complete his cycle of Preludes, Op. 28, a remarkably innovatory conception quite unlike anything he had written before. Pleyel had been detailed to ship a cottage piano to Majorca, but it had not yet arrived, and Chopin found it almost impossible to compose without a good piano. The one he rented locally was of limited help. At least he was working and in moderately good health, but this, alas, was not to last. The Majorcan winter did eventually make itself felt, and 'So'n Vent' was soon damp, cold, and filled with acrid smoke from the charcoal burner, which had no chimney attachment. Chopin was quite unable to withstand such conditions for long and in a short time he was ill again and coughing blood. He saw no fewer than three local doctors and word quickly spread that the mysterious newcomer had a contagious disease. As a result they were obliged to leave the house and to pay to have it fumigated (a requirement of Spanish law in cases of consumption).

Happily George Sand had also heard about three rooms with a small garden in an old Carthusian monastery, recently dissolved, at Valldemosa, a few hours' journey from Palma. It was used as a state guest house during the summer but virtually deserted in winter. Since the rent was so little she had taken this on along with 'So'n Vent', and the family decided to move there following their eviction. For a few days

[30] *KFC*, vol. 1, p. 327.

they stayed with the French consul, but they finally unpacked in Valldemosa on 15 December, furnishing their three-room 'cell' with some primitive beds, tables, and chairs they had purchased locally. Here they settled for the next two months, sharing the monastery with only three bizarre fellow 'guests', one of whom put up Sand's maid. Chopin viewed it all with distinctly mixed feelings. In a letter to Fontana at the end of December he described their accommodation in graphic detail, concluding rumly that 'in short, I am writing to you from a queer place'.[31] Yet in the same letter he followed a description of his difficulties with publishers and with the non-appearance of Pleyel's piano by claiming that 'all this is as a grain of sand compared with the poetry of everything here, the colours of a natural setting as yet unspoiled by man. There are few indeed who have disturbed the eagles which fly overhead every day.'

The matter of Pleyel's piano was in any case shortly resolved, though not without some *Angst*. It arrived at Palma in late December, but sat at the customs for some three weeks while Sand tried to negotiate with the customs officials, who were demanding a sum not far short of the price of the instrument. It finally arrived at Valldemosa in mid January, when Chopin had all but completed the Preludes. Still, he was able to write to Pleyel on the twenty-second, 'I am sending you my *Préludes*. I finished them on your little piano which arrived in the best possible condition in spite of the sea, the bad weather and the Palma customs.'[32] In the same letter he indicated further that he would soon have finished the second Ballade, the second of the Op. 40 Polonaises and the third Scherzo. He also composed the so-called 'Palma Mazurka', Op. 41 No. 2 in Majorca and probably worked on the Op. 37 Nocturnes and the B flat minor Sonata while at Valldemosa.

Sand, meanwhile, revealed her true resourcefulness during this period. She was obliged to nurse Chopin, whose health and spirits deteriorated rapidly in January, to the point at which he seldom ventured out of doors. Sand recorded that during their whole stay they went on only one long walk, to the Ermita of the Holy Trinity high in the mountains, a journey later put to good use in *Spiridion*. At the same time she undertook most of the cooking, shopping, and other domestic chores, and this proved no easy task. During the stay at Valldemosa she had virtually no contact with the nearby villagers, who clearly regarded the group with the utmost suspicion and were reluctant even to sell them basic provisions at a realistic price, so that she often had to depend on the French consul in Palma.

Later she wrote of the Majorcans, and the Spanish generally, with the greatest bitterness, both in her autobiography and in *Un hiver à Majorque*. But there is little evidence to suggest that she made even the

---

[31] Ibid., p. 332.   [32] *Correspondence de Frédéric Chopin*, vol. 2, p. 291.

slightest effort to understand this peasant culture, preferring simply to dismiss it as one utterly alien to her own. Which of course it was. As Bartoleme Ferrà pointed out, there could be few meeting points between the conservative, Catholic, *ancien régime* of the Majorcan populace and the modern writer of liberal social, and political views, who penned contributions to *La Revue indépendante*, *La Réforme*, and *L'Éclaireur* from the cells of a monastery which was still revered by the locals after the forceable expulsion of its monks.[33] For them the very presence of the French party in the monastery was a profanity. Two years later, Sand wrote (in *Un hiver à Majorque*) that 'almost to the end of our stay we were unaware of how profoundly our way of life shocked them', an unwitting testimony to her indifference to the community in which she found herself—through her own choice. When the plan had first materialized the previous October, Sand had taken Majorca on trust, without really investigating the conditions into which she was bringing the ailing Chopin, not to mention her two children, for such a long period.

That said, she coped with the adversities heroically, even purchasing a goat and sheep to provide basic sustenance. At the same time she spent several hours a day on her children's education, and most of the night on her own work. Both she and Chopin were under considerable pressure to come up with manuscripts for which they had either been paid advances or made loans, and Sand's most pressing commitment was to finish *Spiridion*, much of which was inspired by the Majorcan setting, and to revise *Lélia* for a new edition. It has been well observed that the nature of the revisions to *Lélia* is telling.[34] Almost all Sand's novels are rooted firmly in her own experience, and none more so than *Lélia*. One important difference in the revision is that chastity becomes elevated to an ideal plane, and one by no means incompatible with love. This almost certainly reflected current realities. It seems likely that there was real physical passion between Chopin and Sand in the early days of their relationship. She had after all written to Delacroix of 'the delicious exhaustion of a fulfilled love'.[35] But this probably lasted for a short time only, and may well have evaporated totally by the time the party were settled in Valldemosa. In the face of Chopin's developing illness, Sand's powerful maternal instinct was no doubt taking precedence over any other feeling.

The illness had reached an appalling state by late January, and Sand had good cause to fear for his life. She was by then anxious to leave the island, but she was unsure about the effect of such a journey on the ailing Chopin. Eventually it became clear that nothing could harm him

---

[33] Bartolome Ferrà, *Chopin and George Sand in Majorca*, tr. James Webb (Palma de Mallorca, 1936), pp. 55–63.

[34] William G. Atwood, *The Lioness and the Little One*, pp. 115–16.

[35] *GSC*, vol. 4, p. 480.

more than prolonging the stay, and on 12 February the group made their way back to Palma, complete with Pleyel's piano, which Sand eventually managed to sell to Canut. As they approached Barcelona in *El Mallorquin* Chopin was in a dreadful state, haemorrhaging badly. Sand sent a note by dinghy to the French naval commander, who sent a boat to fetch the party to his own ship. They remained on board the French ship for a further day, while the ship's doctor gradually stopped Chopin's haemorrhaging, and then put ashore and booked themselves into the 'Quatro Naciones' once again. Here they stayed for eight days, apart from a day or two at the nearby seaside town Arenys de Mar. Then, on 22 February, they boarded *Le Phénecien* for Marseilles.

There followed a long period of convalescence. They stayed for two days with Dr Cauvière, a friend of the Marlianis who had been detailed to look after Chopin, and then moved into the hotel 'Darse', owned by Manoel Marliani's brother. This was fairly close to Dr Cauvière's home, and Chopin was regularly visited by the doctor. According to Sand, he was given a very thorough examination and no major illness was found. It is difficult to know how much self-deception was involved in such avowals, both from Sand and from Chopin himself. References to his consumption can be found in the correspondence of their friends before the Majorcan excursion, and the Palma doctors, much ridiculed by Chopin, diagnosed it specifically. Yet Chopin's letters from Majorca continue to refer only to bronchial attacks (he chastised Matuszyński for not adequately preparing him for these), and Sand was only too happy to accept Dr Cauvière's assurance that there was nothing wrong that a good rest could not cure. In a letter from Marseilles, 7 March, Chopin wrote to Fontana quite specifically, 'they no longer consider me consumptive'.[36] However faulty the diagnosis, the prescription was certainly the right one. Chopin's weak constitution had been ravaged by the inclement conditions of the island and even more by the travel, and for the next three months he remained at Marseilles rebuilding his strength.

This suited George Sand well enough, since the 'holiday' had taken its toll on her own health (she was rheumatic, and suffered acutely during this period), and she was happy to spend her days writing, looking after her 'little Chop' and keeping at bay the various callers who had quickly learnt of the two celebrities on their doorstep. Chopin, meanwhile, recovered sufficiently to read a bit (he received a copy of Mickiewicz's *Dziady* from Fontana), and to begin composing again, working mainly on the C sharp minor Scherzo. He also tried to sort out his finances in the wake of Majorca, and this far from easy task is fully documented in the correspondence.

His contribution to the expenses of the trip had been based on an

[36] *KFC*, vol. 1, p. 337.

advance from Pleyel for the Preludes and on two separate loans. One of these loans was to be paid out of the balance due from Pleyel on receipt of the Preludes, and the other from the sale of the German rights. It seems that Pleyel refused to pay the balance until he had been paid (by Canut) for the piano. Chopin then suggested to Fontana, whose industry and patience in these matters was extraordinary, that he try to sell the French and English rights of the second Ballade to Pleyel, together with universal rights to the Op. 40 Polonaises. He set up an elaborate back-up scheme, should all this fail, displaying a hard-headed potential for maximizing his advantage and a general deviousness in dealing with these 'Jews', as he insisted on describing them, which is a far cry from popular images of an 'Ariel of the piano'. 'If Pleyel makes any difficulties, go to Schlesinger and tell him I'll give him the Ballade for France and England for 800, and the Polonaises for France, England and Germany for 1500 (if that frightens him, suggest 1400, 1300 or even 1200). If he mentions the Preludes (he'll have heard about them from Probst [the Breitkopf & Härtel agent]), tell him they were promised to Pleyel a long time ago.'[37] There is plenty more of the same, in letters to the long-suffering Fontana and Grzymała. One result of it all was that Schlesinger was replaced by Troupenas as Chopin's French publisher for several major works of this period, including the B flat minor Sonata, F sharp Impromptu, Op. 37 Nocturnes, second Ballade, third Scherzo, and Op. 40 Polonaises. Another was that Chopin had to borrow money from Grzymała and to re-let his apartment on the Chaussée d'Antin. By mid March he had already decided to spend the summer months at Nohant.

For Chopin the time in Marseilles was uneventful, and even rather tedious. On 27 March he wrote to Grzymała that it was an ugly place 'and bores us somewhat'. On 1 April they moved from the 'Darse' to the 'Beauvais', and a few days later George Sand began secretly arranging for Pleyel to have a piano sent to Nohant. One major cloud darkened Chopin's horizon at the time. His friend Adolphe Nourrit, the tenor, who had lost ground at the Paris opera and had moved to Naples, committed suicide there by throwing himself from a window. Chopin was deeply shocked by this, and when Nourrit's widow and family arrived in Marseilles with the body on their way to Paris, he agreed to play the organ at a memorial service in the cathedral.

By then Chopin was feeling very much healthier, and was actually commiserating with Fontana and Grzymała, both of whom had come down with something. More ominously, there are references in his letters which indicate that Matuszyński was coughing blood at this time, an early intimation that he too was consumptive. At the beginning of May Dr Cauvière deemed Chopin well enough to embark on a trip by *Le Pharamond* to Genoa. He badly needed a break from Marseilles and

[37] Letter to Fontana, 12 March 1839: ibid., pp. 339–40.

the party spent a fortnight of pleasant sight-seeing in Genoa. Then, on 22 May, they set off for Nohant, taking a ferry to Arles, and proceeding from there by carriage. On 1 June Chopin caught his first glimpse of the old manor house, Nohant, which would play such a prominent role in his life for the next eight years.

6

'A new world for myself'

When Chopin composed his Two Polonaises, Op. 26 he effectively created a new genre. In the early nineteenth century the polonaise, like the mazurka, already carried a nationalist charge in dramatic works by Polish composers (Stefani's *Cud mniemany* was the exemplary work), but that charge was very much less potent in keyboard stylizations. There its energy was largely diffused by the general conformity of the post-classical keyboard style, and also, paradoxically, by the underlying cosmopolitanism of national dance pieces. Chopin himself, after all, composed three écossaises, a bolero, and a tarantella without, one assumes, any intention to promote nationalist causes in Scotland, Spain, or Italy. His Warsaw-period polonaises accepted for the most part the conventions of the 'brilliant' concert or salon dance piece, and in general style they are heavily indebted to polonaises by non-Polish composers, above all Hummel and Weber.

I have already suggested that by abandoning the polonaise when he left Warsaw Chopin signalled his rejection of the cosmopolitanism of the genre. Significantly he released none of the solo polonaises of the Warsaw period for publication. And when he returned to the genre some five years later he redefined it in such a way that any lingering associations with the conventional dance piece would be dispelled. Instead, the polonaise became a powerful symbol of Poland, a proud evocation of past splendour transparently designed to draw attention to present oppression. It became, in short, an agent of cultural nationalism. Right from its aggressive opening bars the C sharp minor Polonaise, Op. 26 No. 1 announced that this would be a very different kind of dance piece. For one thing, the piano writing departs significantly from the textures already established in the mazurkas, nocturnes, and études of the Vienna and early Paris years. Chopin clearly wanted to maximize the strength and volume of the instrument, and he achieved this at the beginning of the piece by juxtaposing powerful octaves with full chordal writing in rhythmic unison. The effect is more orchestral than almost anything in his earlier music.

A 'massive' sonority is generally characteristic of the mature polonaises, though it is achieved by a variety of textural means. In the second

of the Op. 26 pieces, in E flat minor, there are again full chordal textures in the middle register, but there are also passages where the power
is generated from the brittle quality of registral extremes, with the middle ground filled in largely through the offices of the sustaining pedal.
This produces a weight and density of sound which is in sharp contrast
both to the thinly spread arpeggiations of the nocturnes and to the finely
chiselled figurations of the études. The pedal is obviously important in
maintaining the volume and density of sound here, but so too is the
ornamentation.

This is not, of course, the ornamentation of the nocturne style. Where
the Chopin nocturne sets out ideally to fuse ornament and substance, the
Chopin polonaise tends rather to prise them apart. Indeed an essential
part of its distinctive character lies in just this separation of an elemental background—often made up of conventional cadence formulae and
archetypal scalar or triadic themes—and forcefully articulated, strongly
characterized foreground gestures. In both Polonaises of Op. 26 the
dynamic, upward-leaping ornamental figures (scalar and chordal) are
clearly directed towards energy and power than than display or expression. Characteristically they are marked 'con forza' in the second
Polonaise, where they are also inverted and combined with trills so that
Chopin can maintain maximum volume. Such figures are commonly
found in the late polonaises.

Much of the heroic tone of the polonaises results, then, from a rather
specific kind of rhetoric, where individual moments are invested with
such power and significance that they stand out in sharp relief against
less differentiated backgrounds. This is already clear in the opening
'announcements' of the two Op. 26 Polonaises—in the juxtaposition of
a terse, almost violent rhythmic figure and a conventional chordal phrase
in No. 1, and in the rapid alternation of two standard polonaise formulae, deliberately dislocated, in No. 2. In both introductions the gestural
character of the music is heightened by a dramatic and substantive use
of dynamic levels, a contrast of *fff* and *p* (for the polonaise theme) in
the C sharp minor, and a gradual crescendo from *pp* to *fff* in the E flat
minor. Stylized introductions of this kind are characteristic of the late
polonaises, a legacy of the functional dance here elevated into a powerful, rousing, tension-building anacrusis.

If we compare the main polonaise themes of the two pieces, or at least
their opening sentences, we find that the cumulative, anacrustic quality
of the introductions spills over into thematic substance. Both sentences
have something of the quality of a 'preparation' for their own cadences.
And this, too, is a general characteristic of the mature polonaises, where
'introduction' and 'preparation' assume unusually important structural
functions. Melodic contour contributes to the sense of delayed closure
in both themes, but it is harmony above all which generates their extraordinary sense of energy and momentum, maintained right through to

the final bar, where they collapse abruptly onto the standard cadential formula of the genre. In the C sharp minor the tonic resolution is postponed by a secondary emphasis on the subdominant, while in the E flat minor it is delayed still further by a disruption of the phrase structure.

Formally the two polonaises preserve the traditional large-scale ternary design of the stylized dance piece, together with its high degree of internal repetition.[1] But in spite of the literal repetitions, the larger sweep of the music is compelling, the result not only of underlying harmonic schemes which convincingly subsume formal divisions within larger structures but of motivic parallelisms between the sections. In No. 1, for instance, the first note of the introduction initiates an ascending scalar pattern which carries on through the main theme and is then inverted in the brief subsidiary theme in E major (bar 34). This inversion in turn generates the main theme of the trio in D flat major. There is nothing arcane about such associations. They can easily be heard, even by the untutored listener. But they are symptomatic of Chopin's developing formal mastery, his capacity to enrich and, in the best sense, to obfuscate familiar schemata.

Relative to Chopin's deliberately restricted musical world, the Op. 26 Polonaises have something of an epic quality. This is partly due to their nationalist ambition, their perceived status as a kind of pianistic expression of Polish history. But it is more than this. It seems likely that in 1834–5, following the composition of the Op. 10 Études and the early nocturnes, Chopin was much preoccupied with the need to find congenial vehicles for his larger thoughts. Significantly the sets of two polonaises (Opp. 26 and 40), were eventually replaced by single works (Opp. 44 and 53). Along with Op. 26 he composed two other (relatively) large-scale works in the mid 1830s, the first Scherzo, Op. 20 and the first Ballade, Op. 23. Even more than the polonaises, these works harness the achievements of the early Paris years—in melody, figuration, and harmony—to the needs of extended forms, and it is significant that in both cases Chopin turned aside from the conventional classical and post-classical genres. More than that, he deliberately used genre titles which had little or no connection with the existing solo piano repertory.

The term 'scherzo' customarily designated a movement of a cyclic or multi-movement work. Contemporary lexographers described it in terms of its literal meaning (jest), its triple metre and its lively tempo, and of these characteristics Chopin preserved the last two in Op. 20, together with the basic tripartite design. But in other respects he expanded immeasurably both the scale of the 'scherzo' and its expressive range,

---

[1] The autograph manuscript of Op. 26 No. 1 raises ambiguities about its intended repetition structure. See the discussion in Jim Samson, *The Music of Chopin*, p. 225 (chapter 6, note 11).

quite apart from transforming it into an independent piece.[2] Certainly little is left of the 'jest' in this work, which is characterized rather by an almost demonic power and energy, surely destined to disconcert contemporary audiences. As Schumann famously remarked, 'How is gravity to clothe itself if humour wears such dark veils?'[3] Yet for all the novelty, it is not difficult to relate the first Scherzo to the characteristic materials and formal methods of the brilliant style, even if these have now been given a quite new expressive meaning. Essentially the work encloses a popular melody (almost certainly based on the opening phrase of a Polish carol) within a bravura figuration, exactly in the manner of post-classical models.

The difference lies in the treatment of these formal components. The even rhythm and unchanging texture of the B major trio (the Polish carol) is made possible here by a surrounding figuration of unprecedented drive and energy, establishing immediately the ambition of the genre in Chopin's hands. That figuration is also skilfully differentiated. In the first section melodic and harmonic information is minimal, and the main weight of the argument is carried by rhythmically propelled arpeggiated figures. In the second section (bar 69), in contrast, the phrase structure is 'stretched' in such a way that the figuration loses its urgency and insistence. And this in turn allows voice leading to emerge, and to play a more prominent role in carrying the music towards its major climaxes.[4] The shift in emphasis here is handled with great subtlety, and it is characteristic of the 'shading' of function, commonly found in Chopin, between texture or sonority (determined by values independent of precise pitch content) and more conventional motivic or harmonic argument.

If the first Scherzo maintained an obvious formal link with postclassical traditions, the first Ballade took a step beyond those traditions. By using the title 'ballade' for a piano piece Chopin invoked a wide range of reference in both musical and literary contexts. Contemporary dictionaries tell us that the musical connotations of the term were exclusively vocal until the 1840s.[5] Chopin's use of it would inevitably have suggested analogies with ballad settings by, among others, Schubert and Loewe, as well as with contemporary (especially French) opera, where the term was frequently used to describe a simple narrative song, usually strophic. It is significant that early advertisements for Op. 23

[2] There were, however, other independent scherzos before Chopin, noted, for instance, in Whistling's *Handbuch der musikalischen Literatur* (Leipzig, 1817).

[3] Robert Schumann, *Gesammelte Schriften über Musik und Musiker*, vol. 1, pp. 284–5.

[4] This is discussed in detail in Jim Samson, *The Music of Chopin*, pp. 159–63.

[5] The earlier dictionaries, such as Koch's *Musikalisches Lexikon* (1802) and Gollmick's *Kritische Terminologie für Musiker und Musikfreunde* (1833), tend to describe the Ballade as a dance song, derived from the Italian Ballata. Slightly later dictionaries, such as Schilling's *Universal-Lexicon der Tonkunst* (1835), refer to the 'modern' use of the term as a category of art song based on the poetic ballad.

included the phrase *ohne Worte*, and that the piece is in the compound duple metre appropriated by vocal ballads from earlier pastoral traditions.

At the same time the title had rather obvious literary associations in the early nineteenth century, when the medieval and, more particularly, folk genre was effectively reinvented for romantic literature, with blatant nationalist connotations. Chopin's use of the term 'ballade' established his closest point of contact with the literary preoccupations of his contemporaries, though he avoided the kind of explicit programmatic reference commonly found in Liszt or Schumann. It is entirely characteristic of Chopin that literary inspiration should have been channelled in this way into a piano piece with a generalized rather than a programmatic literary title. I have already observed (chapter 4) that in a similar way his expressive aesthetic was filtered into the piano nocturne rather than made specific in the art song, and his nationalist commitment was expressed through a renovation of the salon dance piece rather than through opera or programmatic reference. In all three cases he drew upon the non-musical world discreetly, and without challenging the essential condition of absolute music.

Unlike the Scherzo, the Ballade draws heavily on the sonata-form archetype, couching its materials in a through-composed, harmonically directional structure where variation and transformation are seminal functions, integration and synthesis essential goals. In a way it represents a reinterpretation of classical sonata form, and one which was influenced in several ways by the more popular concert music of the early nineteenth century. To begin with, the structure is heavily end-weighted. Its rising intensity curve leads first to a reprise, which is more apotheosis than synthesis, and then to a bravura closing section, marked off from the work, as in post-classical traditions, by a change of metre as well as by its non-thematic substance. Even the basic character of the themes spells out the work's continuing links with the world of popular pianism. This is especially obvious in the pivotal episode in E flat major at bar 138, which has all the characteristic phraseology of a quick waltz. But this explicit association also sheds light on the two main themes of the Ballade, which draw upon the generic features of a slow waltz and a barcarolle respectively. The presentation of themes related to popular genres within a sonata-form framework is perfectly symptomatic of the larger tendency of Chopin's music to elevate popular traditions to a high level of creativity, where they need lose nothing in sophistication to the more prestigious sonata-symphonic genres.

More than any earlier work by Chopin, the G minor Ballade is a triumph of architecture, and from the start it achieves its effects through calculated ambiguities. The opening recitative initially implies C minor (a comparison with Mozart K. 491 makes the point), before its Neapolitan quality is revealed and it dovetails, through a subtle motivic link,[6] with the G minor theme. The opening motive of this theme in turn embodies on a small scale the central ambiguity of the work's larger structure, a 'counterpoint' between formal symmetries and goal-directed development. The mirror reprise (tonal and thematic) encourages a symmetrical interpretation of the formal process, where the E flat waltz episode would form the peak of an extended arch. And this interpretation is strengthened by the parallel figurations either side of this central peak.[7] Yet running counter to this reading is the strongly directional, sonata-like momentum of the music, its inexorable progression through tension-release patterns towards the structural dominant at bar 207. As in all the ballades, this follows rather than precedes the restatement of the two main themes, and it unleashes a powerfully climactic closing section in the tonic.[8] Such formal ambivalence is an enriching aspect of the Ballade, a measure of its quality.

With the Two Polonaises, Op. 26, the first Scherzo and the first Ballade, all composed around the same time (1834–5), Chopin established models for his future engagements with larger forms. For each of the three genres there were to be three further opuses, and it is intriguing that the cycles ended (as they may well have begun) in the same year. The A flat major Polonaise, E major Scherzo, and F minor Ballade, Chopin's last essays in these genres, were all composed during 1842–3. In other words the complete corpus of mature polonaises, scherzos, and ballades was composed between 1834–5 and 1843. By the time he arrived at Nohant in June 1839 Chopin was about half-way through, having completed the Op. 40 Polonaises, the second and third Scherzos and the second Ballade.

He had already completed the A major Polonaise, Op. 40 No. 1 when he left for Majorca ('you already know the [polonaise] in A major', he remarked to Pleyel in a letter from Majorca),[9] and it is clear from the title page of the rejected engraver's manuscript that it was to have been dedicated to Tytus Woyciechowski. In Majorca he wrote its companion piece in C minor, writing to Fontana that 'you will find an answer to your sincere and genuine letter in the second Polonaise'.[10] We now know from a recently discovered autograph that the middle section of the C minor was substantially revised, much to its advantage, the following summer at Nohant. This was done to please Fontana ('I will keep changing the second half of the polonaise for you as long as I live. Perhaps you won't like yesterday's version either, although I racked my brains

---

[6] Jim Samson, *The Music of Chopin*, pp. 176–7.

[7] The pitch symmetries in these passages, whole-tone and octatonic respectively, are discussed in Jim Samson, *Chopin: The Four Ballades* (Cambridge, 1992), p. 47.

[8] The term 'coda' is an inadequate, and strictly inaccurate, term for the closing sections of the first, second, and fourth Ballades.

[9] 22 January 1839: *KFC*, vol. 1, p. 335.   [10] 7 March 1839: ibid., p. 337.

over it for a full 80 seconds'), and following that revision the entire opus was dedicated to him.[11]

As in Op. 26, Chopin seems to have set out with the intention of composing two complementary and contrasted pieces. The A major has become the most popular of all Chopin's polonaises, and it is not difficult to see why. In some ways it is the most straightforward of the mature polonaises, and at the same time the most ideologically explicit. Little is left of the stately dance in this music. If anything, it is a martial summons whose gestures positively insist on metaphor, notably in the D major middle section with its trumpet fanfares and rumbling cannons in the bass. It is perhaps not too fanciful to see here both an image of the old Poland, warlike and chivalrous, and at the same time a call to arms for the new Poland, and it is perhaps the one piece of Chopin which might justify Schumann's reference to 'concealed guns'. Significantly it is one of the only polonaises positively to eschew dynamic contrast; the music never drops below *forte*.

The second Polonaise is by no means so one-dimensional. If we are to indulge further in such fantasies, it is Poland's present tragedy rather than her past splendour which is portrayed, in music of a dignified, melancholy aspect. The texture is distinctive. As in the Prelude, Op. 28 No. 22, the left hand plays the tune in octaves, acting as its own bass, while the right-hand chords flower occasionally into wisps of countermelody. In the trio, too, Chopin is generous to the left hand, first allowing it to shadow (in octaves) the melody of the main A flat major section, itself a monument to enharmony, and then supplying it with an elaborate semiquaver tracery in the central F minor section, where it generates in the process lively points of dissonance with the right hand. This semiquaver tracery was one of the gains of Chopin's revision in Nohant, incidentally, along with a more strategic approach to the harmonic goal at bar 79.[12] Chopin's '80 seconds' were well spent.

The second and third Scherzos were composed in 1837 and 1839 respectively, with No. 3 completed during Chopin's period of convalescence in Marseilles. Both take their origins in a 'scherzo and trio', but much more than the first Scherzo they reach beyond the simple ternary design towards a more integrated, organicist approach to their materials, leaning in effect towards the sonata principle. This is partly a matter of thematic integration, in that both works make use of a kind of 'parent cell' from which much of their thematic and even their harmonic substance may be derived, but it is also a matter of formal succession. In both works there are unexpected 'openings' in the form, and these take us off into powerfully developmental sequences.

---

[11] *KFC*, vol. 1, p. 365.
[12] See Jim Samson, 'An Unknown Chopin Autograph', in *The Musical Times* (July 1986), pp. 376–8.

In the second, in D flat major,[13] the relationship between part and whole is especially close, in that the initial motive is inflated both to the level of harmonic organization in the opening paragraph and to the level of tonal organization in the work as a whole.[14] Moreover the trio is also drawn into this web of relationships, paralleling the main scherzo material through its third-related tonal scheme (and also through its sequence of unstable–stable material). This closely woven fabric of motivic and tonal relationships, together with a solid framework of symmetrical periods based on the eight-bar sentence, creates an essential foil to the explosive contrasts generated on the surface of the music. Right from the start it is the regular measurement of eight-bar sentences which 'contains' the powerful surface oppositions of texture, rhythm, and dynamics.

Formally the D flat Scherzo is the most ambitious of the four, embodying all the drives and conflicts of a sonata movement and synthesizing them through development. Symptomatic of this is the tendency of the material to open out into entirely unpredictable directions. The expected reprise of the scherzo material is replaced by just such an opening of the form at bar 476, for example, resulting in what can only be described as a powerful development section. And when the reprise finally creeps in on the ebb of a single extended rhythmic impulse, it has all the structural weight of a sonata-form recapitulation. Within the reprise Chopin opens the form on a further two occasions—at bar 692, where earlier material (bar 109) is extended, and at bar 716, where the cadential figure is unexpectedly interrupted by the return of the B section of the Scherzo. In sonata-form terms we have, then, a developmental coda as well as a development section.

The surface gestures of the C sharp minor Scherzo are as close to Liszt as Chopin ever comes, both in the bravura octave passages of the outer flanks and in the delicate washes of colour which decorate the trio, a 'hymn' in the tonic major which recalls in some ways the trio of the B minor Scherzo. In this work, too, there is an unexpected opening of the form, transforming the 'scherzo and trio' schema into a much more ambitious and sophisticated design. Following the second trio in E major/minor, where we expect a heightening of tension in preparation for the scherzo reprise, Chopin instead interpolates a quite new sequence. He slows the harmonic rhythm to a near standstill before unfolding a sustained, expansive melody which grows in passion and intensity until the powerful octaves at bar 567 signal a non-thematic bravura coda. In context the entire sequence is remarkable, a fitting conclusion to one of Chopin's most unusual and original works.

The earliest reference to the second Ballade is in a letter from Chopin to Fontana, sent from Majorca on 14 December 1838: 'I expect to send

[13] See Heinrich Schenker, *Free Composition*, tr. and ed. Ernst Oster (New York and London, 1979; original German edn. 1935), vol. 2, fig. 153.
[14] I have discussed this in *The Music of Chopin*, pp. 163–7.

you my Preludes and Ballade shortly.'[15] The autograph prepared for the first French edition was probably completed in February 1839, and it is one of the most heavily corrected of Chopin's surviving fair copies; the several layers of creative process were revealed by Saint-Saens in a penetrating and pioneering source study of creative process.[16] Programmatic references have frequently been cited for all four Ballades, following Schumann's remarks about Mickiewicz,[17] but particularly for No. 2. Aside from Schumann's reporting, there is a reference in the correspondence of Henryk Probst to the 'pilgrim's ballade', a possible link with Mickiewicz, and Mallefille also referred to the 'Polish ballade'.[18] Tradition has it that the work was inspired by Mickiewicz's ballad *Switeź*, which recounts how the maidens of a Polish village were beseiged by Russian soldiers. They pray that they might be swallowed by the earth, and when their wish is granted they are transformed into beautiful flowers which adorn the site of the village.

It would be rather easy to map this plot on to the musical processes of the Ballade if Chopin had legitimized such an exercise through a title or programme. The main formal design of the work hinges on the confrontation, mediation, and transformation of two sharply contrasted materials, a siciliano melody in F major, carrying a wealth of pastoral connotations (cf. the G major Nocturne, Op. 37 No. 2, composed shortly after the Ballade), and a brutal étude-like figuration in A minor (cf. the so-called 'Winter Wind' Étude, Op. 25 No. 11). Such generic allusions, together with intertextual associations of various kinds (notably with Meyerbeer's *Robert le diable*) encourage us to read the Ballade as a 'narrative' of innocence under threat.[19] Even the two-key scheme of the work (F major/A minor) supports such an interpretation.

Narratives and programmes aside, we can again relate the juxtaposition of popular melody and bravura figuration to the brilliant style, and of all the ballades this one is closest to the formal methods characteristic of that style. Yet the sonata-form plot is also invoked by several features. At bar 83 the siciliano theme returns in the manner of a repeated exposition, only to allow a deceptive cadence at bar 96 to inaugurate an impassioned modulatory development section where the theme is transformed to a point at which it can lead naturally into the contrasted figuration. As in the G minor Ballade the reprise at bar 140 is marked by the return not of the first theme but of the second (the figuration) and

[15] *KFC*, vol. 1, p. 332.

[16] Camille Saint-Saens, 'A Chopin M.S.: The F major Ballade in the Making', in *Outspoken Essays on Music*, tr. Fred Rothwell (London, 1922, repr. 1970).

[17] Robert Schumann, *Gesammelte Schriften über Musik und Musiker*, vol. 4, p. 57.

[18] For a discussion, see Jeffrey Kallberg, 'The Chopin Sources: Variants and Versions in Later Manuscripts' (Diss., U. of Chicago, 1982).

[19] For the Meyebeer connection, see Anselm Gerhard, 'Ballade und Drama: Frederic Chopins Ballade opus 38 und die französische Oper um 1830', in *Archiv für Musikwissenschaft* (1991), vol. 48, no. 2, pp. 110–25.

again in its original tonal setting, suggesting a mirror reprise which is not in the end completed either tonally or thematically. Once more, as in the first Ballade, there is a bravura closing section with a contrasted rhythmic character. Taken together with the compound duple metre, these links between Op. 23 and Op. 38 are already enough to suggest that Chopin had a clear view of the ballade as a genre.

The polonaises, scherzos, and ballades of these years reveal Chopin's growing preoccupation with large forms, culminating in the composition of the B flat minor Sonata during his first summer at Nohant (the slow movement was written two years earlier). Yet his interest in the epic during this period was matched by an interest in the epigrammatic. Whether we regard them as a single cyclic work or a collection of miniatures, the twenty-four Preludes, op. 28 count among Chopin's most radical conceptions, not least because of their sheer brevity. They are more condensed in scale than anything in the earlier nocturnes or études, though there are some comparable 'aphorisms' among the early mazurkas. And once again their title is provocative. 'I must admit that I do not wholly understand the title that Chopin chose to give these short pieces', wrote André Gide.[20] The truth is that the Op. 28 Preludes gave a quite new meaning to a genre title mainly associated in the early nineteenth century with the contemporary practice of 'preluding' in extempore performance. Indeed they might almost have been devised to banish such associations once and for all.

The preludes of Clementi, Hummel, Kalkbrenner, and Moscheles all retain close links with the traditional inductive functions of an improvisatory prelude—testing the instrument (especially its tuning), giving practice in the key and mood of the piece to follow, preparing the audience for a performance, and so forth. At the very least Chopin's pieces transcend such associations. They demand to be regarded as *works* of substance and weight, not composed-out improvisations. If we seek a helpful context, it is to be found rather in the *Wohltemperiertes Klavier*, and it is no doubt significant that Chopin brought the Bach with him to Majorca, where he put the finishing touches to his own preludes. Like each volume of the '48', Chopin's pieces form a complete cycle of the major and minor keys, though the pairing is through tonal relatives (C major/A minor) rather than Bach's monotonality (C major/C minor). But the affinities reach far beyond the cyclic tonal scheme, which was in any case fairly common in the early nineteenth century.[21]

Much of the figuration, for instance, has origins in Bach. We might think of the moto perpetuo patterns of the E flat minor (No. 14), the E

[20] André Gide, *Notes on Chopin*, tr. Bernard Frechtman (New York, 1949: original ed. 1948), pp. 32–3.

[21] For an interesting theory of the influence on tuning and temperament on Op. 28, see Jean-Jacques Eigeldinger, 'Twenty-four Preludes Op. 28: Genre, Structure, Significance', in *Chopin Studies* (Cambridge, 1988), pp. 167–94.

flat major (No. 19), and the B major (No. 11), a kind of three-part invention. There are parallels here with Bach's fifth Prelude from Book 1, or the twenty-first from Book 2. Like Bach, moreover, Chopin constructed figurations which allow linear elements to emerge through the pattern, as in the 'trill' motives of the C major (No. 1) and D major (No. 5), similar to No. 12 from Bach's Book 1. This, of course, is part of a much larger debt to Bach the contrapuntist, evident in the polarity of melody and 'singing' bass in the E major (No. 9) and in the dual function of the bass as harmonic support and polyphonic (melodic) line in the B minor (No. 6).[22] And especially characteristic are contrapuntal figures made up of a subtle compound of discrete though interactive particles, as in the C major (No. 1) and F sharp minor (No. 8). Formally, too, the Preludes evoke baroque practice, crystallizing a single *Affekt* in a single pattern and unfolding either within a ternary design (Nos. 15 and 17) or as a simple statement with conflated response (Nos. 3 and 12). Also from Bach comes the fundamental pattern of scale followed by cadence, which underlies most of these pieces. The external patterns are straightforward, then, but lengthy tomes could be written about the subtle and varied means by which Chopin integrates sections across formal divisions, or about the dynamic, carefully paced intensity curves with which he overlays his simple formal designs.

Gide's query is not fully answered by the Bach connection, powerful though it is. 'Preludes to what?', he went on to ask. Chopin's are indeed the first preludes to be presented as a cycle of self-contained pieces. He sought and achieved in them something close to perfection of form within the framework of the miniature, expertly gauging the relationship of substance to scale, so that each piece can stand alone—issuing a challenge, as Jeffrey Kallberg puts it, to 'the conservative notion that small forms were artistically suspect or negligible'.[23] Each Prelude is itself a whole, with its own *Affekt* (the widest range of moods is encompassed), its own melodic, harmonic, and rhythmic profile, and even its own generic character (at various times Chopin evokes the nocturne (No. 13), the étude (No. 16), the mazurka (No. 7), the funeral march (No. 2), and the elegy (No. 4).

At the same time, the individual Preludes contribute to a single overriding whole, a 'cycle' enriched by the complementary characters of its components and integrated by the special logic of their ordering. From a purely formal viewpoint, that ordering is determined by the tonal scheme, tracing as it does a circular path through the rich and varied landscape of the individual pieces. But arguments have been ventured for

[22] See Charles Burkhart, 'The Polyphonic Melodic line of Chopin's B minor Prelude', in *Frederic Chopin: Preludes Op. 28*, a 'Norton Critical Score', ed. Thomas Higgins (New York, 1973), pp. 80–8.
[23] Jeffrey Kallberg, 'Small "Forms": In Defense of the Prelude', in *The Cambridge Companion to Chopin*, pp. 124–44.

a deeper unity based on motivic links between the Preludes, extensive enough to justify describing the work in its entirety as an extended, organically conceived cycle.[24] Whatever the truth of that, Op. 28 remains an utterly unique achievement, albeit one with a legacy. Later composers were happy to follow Chopin's lead in broadening the generic meaning of the 'prelude'. It is enough to refer to Skryabin's Op. 11 collection, which follows Chopin's tonal scheme, to the sets by Fauré and Rachmaninov, and to the Nine Preludes, op. 1 by Chopin's later compatriot Karol Szymanowski. We might mention also the two books of Preludes by Debussy, the composer who, more than any other, translated Chopin's idiomatic achievement into the language of twentieth-century pianism. None of these sets would have taken the form they did without the example of Chopin.

During this pre-Nohant period Chopin consolidated some of the genres established during the Vienna and early Paris years. There were four songs, 'Pierscień' (The ring), 'Leca liście' (Leaves are falling), 'Moja pieszczotka' (My darling), and 'Wiosna' (Spring), all eventually to be gathered by Fontana into the collection posthumously published as Op. 74. There was the A flat major Impromptu, Op. 29, the second impromptu composed by Chopin but the first to be released for publication (1837). There were five Nocturnes, the two of Op. 27 (1835), the two of Op. 32 (1837), and the first of the Op. 37 set (1838). There were the three Waltzes of Op. 34, of which No. 1 was written in 1835 and Nos. 2 and 3 in 1838, and a further A flat major Waltz, posthumously published as Op. 69 No. 1. There were two cycles of Mazurkas (Opp. 30 and 33), along with the first and third of the posthumously published Op. 67 set, and one of the Op. 41 set. And, finally, there was a further cycle of *Douze Études*, Op. 25, composed, it would seem, over several years and published in 1837.

The composition of 'preludes', 'études' or 'exercises' was a basic activity for early nineteenth-century pianist-composers, and in this respect at least Chopin conformed to type. Moreover, there was some continuity in his production of these pieces. The first two of the Op. 10 Études (originally called 'exercises') were composed in Warsaw in 1830 and the last two in Paris in 1832. He began the Op. 25 Études shortly after (the precise date is unknown) and completed the set in 1837. The Preludes then occupied him during 1838–9, and the *Trois nouvelles études* (designed for inclusion in Moscheles's and Fétis's *Méthode des méthodes*) were composed in 1840. The Prelude, Op. 45 completed the series in 1841. In other words, for some eleven years he chiselled away fairly consistently at pieces described variously as études (exercises) and preludes.

The figurations of Op. 10 are extended in several ways in the Op. 25 collection. The striding right-hand arpeggios of Op. 10 No. 1, for

---

[24] See Józef Chomiński, *Preludia* (Cracow, 1950), p. 101 ff. Also Eigeldinger, 'Twenty-four Preludes Op. 28: Genre, Structure, Significance' in *Chopin Studies* (Cambridge, 1988).

instance, are given to both hands in Op. 25 No. 12, so that the tolling chorale-like melody emerges through the figuration with awesome power. (Chopin changed 'con fuoco' to 'molto con fuoco' on Gutmann's copy prepared for Breitkopf & Härtel.) Equally the arpeggiated accompaniments to a top-voice melody in Op. 10 No. 11 are redefined in Op. 25 No. 1, where the sustaining pedal is used to create delicate, impressionistic waves of sound. And in both cases the strength of the music rests partly in the unobtrusive originality of the harmony, where chromatic adventures are concealed by fluid rhythms and evenly flowing figurations. The melodic figuration of Op. 10 No. 2 is similarly recreated in the right hand of Op. 25 No. 2, though here it combines with the composed-out harmonies of the left-hand to create a two-part texture of remarkable fluidity and contrapuntal 'edge', bringing together cross-rhythms and syncopations. The melodic figuration of Op. 10 No. 2 is extended in other ways too in the later set, notably in the double notes of Op. 25 Nos. 6 and 8 (thirds and sixths respectively), where the flowing, mainly conjunct lines in the right hand generate spicy harmonic asperities with the left-hand accompaniment layer.

The true parallel to the 'revolutionary' Étude of Op. 10 is the so-called 'Winter Wind' Étude, Op. 25 No. 11, though the function of the hands is neatly inverted here. In the 'Winter Wind' it is the left hand which takes the stirring march-like theme, its dotted rhythms reminiscent of Op. 10 No. 12, while it is the right hand which sweeps across the keyboard to effect a dramatic counterpoint to the theme, a chromatic figuration which, again like that in Op. 10, No. 12, is anything but a mere accompaniment. When Op. 25 is played as a whole, this piece joins with Nos. 10 and 12 to form a powerfully expressive climactic conclusion to the cycle. The collective effect of these three adjacent minor-key pieces, each more impassioned and expansive than its predecessor, is overwhelming, and all the more so in that the earlier études maintain for the most part a much lower emotional temperature.

The one exception is the 'mournful and melancholy' seventh,[25] which functions as a kind of 'slow movement' for the cycle, not unlike the sixth of the Op. 10 set. Like the B minor Prelude, it cultivates an expressive left-hand 'cello' melody which suggests rather fully supplies its bass, breaking the melodic flow surreptitiously from time to time in order to sound a functional bass note, or using the occasional grace note along with the sustaining pedal to hint at one. Much more than in the B minor Prelude, however, the left-hand melody acts in concert with a melodic upper voice, a 'Duet between a He and a She', as Niecks quaintly puts it.[26] The interplay between the two melodies is endlessly inventive, and it is worth pointing out in this connection that Chopin's revisions on the Breitkopf & Härtel manuscript were mainly aimed at an enhancement

[25] Stephen Heller, quoted in F. Niecks, *Chopin as a Man and Musician*, vol. 2, p. 254.
[26] Ibid., p. 254.

of the right-hand countermelody.[27] For the most part the right hand responds to the main cello tune, often beginning the phrase with a literal imitation before taking its own path, but at times it takes the greater melodic initiative, while the left hand assumes a tension-building ornamental role. There is little else in Chopin quite like these sweeping rhapsodic left-hand ornaments, sometimes anacrustic to the phrase, sometimes cadential, as in the remarkable *fioritura* of bar 27.

Elsewhere in Op. 25 Chopin explored the kind of intricate figurations which would shortly come to fruition in some of the preludes. It is useful, for instance, to compare the basic figure of Op. 25 No. 3 with those of Op. 28 Nos. 1, 5, and 8. In all four cases the figure is sculpted out of several interactive particles, forming a kind of fused counterpoint which reveals its subtlety only to the microscope. In such pieces the value and significance of texture or sonority as a compositional element in its own right becomes abundantly clear. Quite simply the musical figures contain much more information, and are in that sense much denser, than anything we might find in comparable essays by earlier composers. Moreover, as Simon Finlow has observed, the larger structure of Op. 25 No. 3 matches its detailed working in subtlety and sophistication.[28] Here Chopin allows the key of B major to assume an apparent stability within the F major context, a goal which turns out to be illusory in that the 'key' is really a prolongation on a deeper structural level. The point would not be worth making, were it not that such tonal deceptions are so highly characteristic of Chopin, reaching their fullest expression in masterpieces such as the Op. 49 Fantasy and the fourth Ballade.

From Op. 27 onwards, Chopin published his nocturnes in contrasted pairs rather than in groups of three. As with the polonaises, this was in itself an indication that individual pieces within an opus had greater weight (though not necessarily length) in the later years. The two of Op. 27 are perfectly complementary, the darkly brooding C sharp minor of the first transformed enharmonically into the consolatory D flat major of the second. Both accompaniment figures have a wider span than in Chopin's earlier broken-chord patterns and they make room for hidden voices, especially at the reprise of the D flat major where the figure is subtly but significantly changed to make this possible. In both cases the melody which unfolds after the scene-setting introduction is one of calculated unpredictability. We need only consider the play on E major and C sharp minor at bars 6 and 7 of No. 1, together with the interruption of the voice leading at bars 10, its eventual resumption at bar 11, and the disruption of phrase structure which results.

Even at this foreground level of melodic design it is the constant play

---

[27] This manuscript, housed in the National Library, Warsaw, is in the hand of an unknown copyist, but with autograph revisions.

[28] Simon Finlow, 'The Twenty-seven Études and their Antecedents', in *The Cambridge Companion to Chopin*, pp. 50–77.

on a network of probable outcomes which creates the richness of the music. And much the same is true of the larger formal design, where the two nocturnes work rather differently. The C sharp minor depends on contrast, enclosing within its outer flanks a faster, more dramatic middle section which culminates unexpectedly in a brief waltz-like episode in D flat major (there are echoes, too, of the polonaise), a gesture strongly reminiscent of the first Ballade and second Scherzo. The D flat major rather conceals its structural methods within an apparently seamless melodic flow. On closer inspection, however, we note the alternation of two distinct melodic shapes, one through-composed and non-repetitive, the other a stanzaic melody with symmetrical periods and internal repetitions. The first is aria-like, elaborated with ever more expressive ornamentation, while the second is developmental, allowing its ornamentation to build the music in a dynamic and evolutionary way towards its major tension points. The difference in formal methods between these two nocturnes resonates powerfully in Chopin's music as a whole, and it is significant that in both cases the argument is deemed to require an extended synthetic coda.

A close study of the nocturnes will quickly disabuse anyone inclined to disparage Chopin as a master of form. No two of them are alike in this respect, yet in each case the deceptively simple external design conceals an ingenious solution to the problem of integration. Like those of Op. 27, the two Nocturnes of Op. 32 adopt very different formal schemes. The startling B minor instrumental recitative which interrupts the flow of the B major Nocturne in one of Chopin's most unusual codas has often, and rightly, attracted comment. But the originality of the gesture has distracted us from other subtleties. Not only is the idea of interruption built into the recurring cadential figure of the piece (bars 6–7); it is also implicit in the formal sequence. The flow of the music is such that we can easily fail to notice that the opening melody never returns, but that certain phrases from it are incorporated into new contexts almost in mosaic fashion. In contrast the A flat major Nocturne is concerned precisely with the transformation of meaning when the opening melody does return, now 'enlarged' by the experience of a powerfully climactic middle section.

Of the remaining works composed during these years the most significant are the Op. 34 Waltzes and the two sets of Mazurkas, Opp. 30 and 33. The minutely detailed corrections on the engraver's manuscript[29] of Op. 34 No. 1, especially to the left-hand layer and to the final bars, give some indication of the care Chopin lavished on the waltzes. They may be 'light music', but that in no sense argues a loss of sophistication. Indeed the second of the set, in A minor, has a deeply expressive lyricism which leans towards the slower *kujawiak* mazurkas, with which it

[29] Housed in the library of the Warsaw Music Society.

has clear generic links. The first and third, on the other hand, recapture the atmosphere of the Op. 18 Waltz, and repeat many of its characteristic gestures—the rhythmic pattern of the announcement (No. 1), the swaying thirds and sixths (No. 1), the moto perpetuo arcs of figuration (Nos. 1 and 3), the chains of acciaccaturas (No. 3), and so forth. The underlying pot-pourri form of Op. 18 is also the background against which these pieces unfold, though their formal organization is anything but primitive. The A flat major in particular blends an arch-like symmetry with the pot-pourri scheme by allowing the reprise of the first theme (the closure of the arch) to open out into a new moto perpetuo theme and coda.

In the Opp. 30 and 33 Mazurkas Chopin took a step in the direction of greater structural tautness and homogeneity, and also of greater abstraction. The folk models here are more distant than in previous sets, a background against which refined and often arcane harmonic and motivic working is projected. The major exception is the *oberek*-style D major, Op. 33 No. 2. Here the whirling repetitions and vamping diatonic harmonies only barely stylize the foot-stamping or heel-clicking energy of the dance in one of the most exhilarating mazurkas of the entire series. For the rest it is mainly through call and response models, melodic ostinatos, folk ornaments, and repetition structures that the regional dances make their presence felt. The general mood is often remote from the raw vitality of the peasant dance. The opening pieces of both sets are poignant and nostalgic in tone, for instance, with characteristic chromatic enrichment in the 'con anima' central episode of Op. 30 No. 1. The final pieces are also reflective in character; indeed Op. 33 No. 4 is actually marked 'mesto' by the composer (as was Op. 33 No. 1 on the engraver's manuscript[30] before Chopin cancelled it in favour of 'Lento').

As in the previous two cycles, Chopin clearly conceived these fourth pieces as true finales, with greater structural weight than their predecessors, and he is at pains to conclude them in novel and interesting ways. In both cases the technique is essentially one of studied understatement. In Op. 30 No. 4 the coda dissipates all the passion of the work in a characteristic falling chromatic sequence. In Op. 33 No. 4 the ending is even more elliptical, playing on the Neapolitan character of the second limb of the main theme to suspend activity through an oscillating falling fifth before cadencing in a deliberately insouciant, almost offhand, manner.

Issues in musical style

The identification of a musical style depends on the recognition of repetition units. Past repetitions are codified by a style just as future

---

[30] Housed in the National Library, Warsaw.

repetitions are invited by it. In other words, compositional norms are created, and these in turn are confirmed by their temporary falsification, by deviations from the norms. One way of understanding a style, then, is as an integrated complex of norms and deviations. Yet a style also implies an element of negation, since decisions are made in response to an existing stock of handed-down, 'pre-formed' materials, the inherited norms and schemata of larger style systems. As Leonard B. Meyer observed, it is precisely the selection (within certain constraints) from these pre-formed materials and the particular transformation of their schemata which constitutes a style.[31] The process involves (simultaneously) an element of suppression and an element of dependency.

It may be helpful, then, to understand style in music in relation to a dialectic between universal and particular, collective and unique, schema and deviation, and to view the process as almost endlessly recursive. Thus the 'classical style' is a particular category in relation to the general characteristics of Western tonal music of a specific historical period, but a general (universal) category in relation to such derivatives as the so-called 'brilliant style'. On the other hand, the brilliant style may itself be regarded as a general category against which the particularity of individual composers' styles (Hummel, Weber, early Chopin) might be registered. And so on down to stylistic periods within a composer's output, to individual works within a period and to sections within a work. In each case the particular selection from a group (or deviation from a schema) on one level generates a new group (or schema) on another level. Moreover the interaction of universal and particular operates within as well as between levels, since the deviations are indispensable to the function and value of the schema in the first place. The stylistic analysis of an individual work, for instance, will be truly revealing only if it addresses what Adorno described as the 'complex relationship of *deviation* to *schema*, rather than just the one or the other alone'.[32]

Early nineteenth-century piano repertories present us with an unusually complex and interesting working of this model. In these repertories new modes of expression sought to break free of the old, partly owing to social change—the demands of specific taste publics in the benefit concert and middle-class salon—and partly in response to an emergent expressive aesthetic, clearly signalled by influences from vocal music and from literature. There was a characteristic interpenetration of the familiar and the novel in these repertories, as composers projected new thoughts against the backcloth of a classical heritage, and at the same time sought ways to escape that heritage. Thus the bravura pieces of the brilliant style and the lyric or 'character' pieces of early romanticism represented in their different ways an accumulating challenge to the clas-

---

[31] Leonard B. Meyer, *Style and Music: Theory, History, Ideology* (Philadelphia, 1989).

[32] T. W. Adorno, 'On the Problem of Music Analysis', tr. Max Paddison, in *Music Analysis*, vol. 1, no. 2, p. 173.

sical sonata. Yet the shadow of the sonata continued to fall across such pieces, adapted and transformed in as many ways as there were composers.

The emergence of Chopin's distinctive musical voice around 1830 needs to be viewed against this background. It was shaped by his particular selection from the pre-formed materials first of the brilliant style and then of the classical style. This involved significant deviation from, and transformation of, the characteristic schemata of those general styles. At the same time the schemata themselves form a vital, living part of the music, an aspect of its material with which, and against which, the composer worked. In very general terms Chopin transformed the nature and role both of bravura figuration and of ornamental melody. At the same time, and on a deeper level, he absorbed the formal juxtapositions of the brilliant style into tonally regulated wholes which could provide new contexts for the classical sonata-form archetype, as well as for time-honoured principles of voice leading and counterpoint.

These transformations of existing devices crystallized into an integrated musical style with its own compositional norms in the works of the early 1830s, which remain distinct in certain essentials from those of the Warsaw period. As a general style this remained stable at least until the early 1840s, when a further change took place—not a radical departure, but enough of a shift to invite separate discussion and to justify periodization. Within the general category 'Chopin's musical style', then, there are particular stylistic categories defined loosely by periods. And within those periods there are further stylistic categories, defined, as I shall show in chapter 8, principally by genre. For the present I shall look only at the generality of the 'middle-period' style, focusing on the works of the late 1830s. At root this style involved a synthesis of elements drawn from post-classical popular concert music and aspects of the so-called 'Viennese' classical traditions. Both will be invoked constantly in the descriptions of particularities which follow.

The second of the Op. 25 Études raises a central issue about musical materials in Chopin, concerning the nature, and in particular the density, of his figurations. The matter was discussed in chapter 4, but some reiteration will be appropriate here, in the context of a larger examination of musical style. In spite of the diversity of figurations in Chopin's music, they are often reducible at base to two types of 'pre-formed' material, derived from standard melodic and harmonic figurations of both classical and post-classical traditions. Yet even the most apparently simple of them are dense with information. Although the right-hand layer of this piece is a melodic figuration and the left-hand layer a harmonic figuration, for instance, the message is confused by a characteristic blurring of function between melody and figure in the right hand and between broken chord and contrapuntal line in the left hand (Ex. 21). It is easy enough to see the origins of such a passage in earlier keyboard

Ex. 21 Étude, Op. 25 No. 2

writing, but Chopin makes a much greater investment in the texture, enriching it with calculated ambiguities.

Three strands are discernible—independent yet interdependent. In the right hand the arcs of figuration are shaped and paced with as much thought to melodic design as to figurative pattern. They lie somewhere between the two. Nor is this unique to Op. 25 No. 2, as a glance at the B major, E flat minor and B flat minor Preludes will immediately indicate. The melodic-figurative arcs of Ex. 21 have their own internal coherence, and they are presented in a phrase rhythm frequently adopted by Chopin—compare the opening right-hand figurations of the eighth of these Études, for instance, or those of both the Fantasy-impromptu, Op. 66 and the A flat major Impromptu, Op. 29. The left-hand layer provides a further independent line, rising above a purely harmonic role to generate an ascending linear progression through the bass notes on the bar line. And finally the interaction of the two layers in dissonant counterpoint creates an additional strand to the fabric.

Although the formulation varies enormously, Chopin commonly devised figurations which are rich and complex in this manner. and whose functions shade subtly into those of melody and harmony. The sixth of the Op. 25 Études has many similarities with the second in this respect—again a melodic figuration supported by a motivically enriched harmonic figuration in dissonant counterpoint. But whereas No. 2 builds intensity through classical techniques of sequence and a change in the harmonic rhythm (bar 36 ff.), No. 6 does so by altering the character of both layers and eventually allowing them to dissolve into a composite figuration of chromatic symmetries, losing touch with both melodic and harmonic functions (Ex. 22). In larger works this shading of functions can assume even greater structural importance. The first Scherzo begins by juxtaposing harmony and figuration, before allowing a gradual and subtle mediation between the figuration-dominated first paragraph and the theme-dominated second. And in the first Ballade the progression from the first to the second theme is marked by a similar shading of function, an arch-like symmetry as follows: theme–motive–figuration–motive–theme.

Ex. 22　Étude, Op. 25 No. 6

The interplay of functions within a single figuration can be illustrated in closer detail by the fifth of the Op. 28 Preludes. Here the basic figure is drafted with great subtlety so that a motivic shape can emerge in rhythmic counterpoint to the 3/8 metre within a static preparatory dominant harmony (Ex. 23). With the tonic resolution the underlying metre is clarified, but the figuration and the harmony it outlines become correspondingly more complex, as do the fleeting motivic (voice-leading)

Ex. 23   Prelude, Op. 28 No. 5

connections which emerge through the pattern. Foreground connections of this kind are certainly perceptible even at Chopin's 'molto allegro', but the overall texture is of such intricacy that we may trace them in different ways, finding several alternative motivic pathways through the figuration. And this is compounded by the variations in pattern between parallel passages in the two halves of the Prelude, almost identical but not quite.

The effect is like a kaleidoscope of shifting patterns held in a single frame by an underlying harmonic succession which remains fundamentally clear and simple, in spite of a flurry of surface activity. By liberally 'applying' dominants to his foreground harmonies, Chopin allows the tonal direction to move rapidly around the fifths cycle until it stabilizes briefly on the mediant region. The repeated cycle (with interesting chromatic variations *en route*) then veers back to the tonic rather than progressing to the mediant, thus: I–III: I–I. This potent pairing of intricate, variegated figurations and a strong underlying harmonic structure is absolutely characteristic of Chopin. It amounts to a basic ingredient of his musical style.

No less fundamental is the texture of accompanied melody in all its many varieties. The Chopin melody has given rise to some of the most eloquent literary descriptions of music. Yet even the unequalled account by Proust fails to take account of one simple technical point, already made and illustrated in chapter 4.[33] The beauty of the melody is in most

[33] Marcel Proust, *Remembrance of Things Past*, tr. C. K. Scott Moncrief and Terence Kilmartin, 3 vols. (Harmondsworth 1983), vol. 3, p. 361.

cases inseparable from the accompaniment layer, whose characteristic role is interactive rather than supportive. A glance at the opening phrase of the G minor Nocturne, Op. 37 No. 1 will be enough to confirm this (Ex. 24). Here the discontinuities of the melodic layer in phrase *a* are countered by a smooth conjunct motion in the left hand. The more continuous phrase *b*, on the other hand, has a disjunct accompaniment (bar 3), while the cadential phrase is enriched by motivic parallelism between the two hands. It is worth stressing, then, that 'the Chopin melody' is first and foremost a characteristic texture and not just a line.

That said, the line itself tends to fall into one of two general categories. By far the most common is the stanzaic melody, modelled closely on a well established archetype or 'pre-formed' component, the eight-bar classical period. The internal repetitions in the opening period (bars 1–8) of Op. 37 No. 1 (abac) are characteristic, and they are replicated in countless Chopin melodies. We might compare Op. 37 No. 1 with its immediate predecessor among the nocturnes, Op. 32 No. 2, for example. Moreover, in both cases the continuation of the eight-bar period again follows classical models—a new consequent phrase followed by a repetition of the opening period, though there are differences between the two nocturnes in the detailed working here. Hardly less characteristic is the eight-bar sentence, as in the second theme of Op. 27 No. 2 (bars 10–17), with its two-bar phrase, varied repetition and four-bar liquidation. Again the music is firmly anchored in classical principles of construction.

Ex. 24   Nocturne, Op. 37 No. 1

In addition to such stanzaic melodies, broadly comparable to operatic arias, and much influenced by them in broad stylistic terms, Chopin devised on occasion freer, non-repetitive melodies which unfold continuously in the manner of operatic arioso or even recitative, though eight-bar groupings usually remain the norm. The left-hand melody of Op. 25 No. 7 is characteristic, its rhapsodic character dependent both on interactions with the right-hand layer and on an increasingly exuberant ornamental elaboration. Rather different in character but also non-repetitive is the opening of the D flat major Nocturne, Op. 27 No. 2 (Ex. 25). Here again the eight-bar melody avoids internal repetitions, but it reveals its classical origins in other ways. In particular it builds its expressive character from an unpredictable placing and weighting of the kinds of appoggiaturas which were common currency in the Mozart melody. Familiarity dulls our perception a little in such cases, but two examples of such calculated unpredictability will serve. The A of bar 5 is prolonged for half a bar beyond its expected resolution, extending the phrase to four and a half bars. And the G of bar 9 moves only fleetingly to its predicted goal of A♭, before moving to a less predictable F.

The extension of the phrase structure at bar 5 draws attention to another feature of the Chopin melody, and again one which relates him to Mozart more than anyone. Although the eight-bar period or sentence remains the norm of construction, its underlying regularity is often mitigated by internal asymmetries, as in the two unequal phrases here. There is, as it were, a continuous conquest of symmetry in the phrase structure of his music. A few further examples from the Preludes will reinforce the point. In No. 12 in G sharp minor, the four-bar phrases, clearly established by the opening paragraph, are offset at bar 21 by the

Ex. 25   Nocturne, Op. 27 No. 2

3 + 4 + 1 grouping of the consequent eight-bar phrase. In No. 15 in D flat major the larger phrase structure is itself asymmetrical. Characteristically the opening melody presents a classical eight-bar modified period (a b a b), but this acts as a foil for an irregular consequent period (Ex. 26). Here both melodic parallelism and harmony suggest a modification—by the addition of one bar—to a classical pattern of two four-bar phrases with a two-bar extension (such a pattern is exemplified by No. 8 in F sharp minor at bars 9–18). But Chopin's phrasing leaves open other possibilities, too, as the slurring in Ex. 26 indicates. Such asymmetries are commonly found in the morphology of his music, and they work together with other aspects in infinitely subtle ways. Carl Schachter has discussed this in some detail in relation to the third Prelude in G major, illustrating among other things how the 'extra' bar (bar 11) plays a motivic as well as a larger rhythmic role in the piece.[34]

Ex. 26   Prelude, Op. 28 No. 15

[34] Carl Schachter, 'Rhythm and Linear Analysis: Durational Reduction', in *Music Forum* (New York, 1980), vol. 5, pp. 197–232.

And William Rothstein devoted much of an impressive study to similar features.[35]

If there is any single general principle at work in the development (as opposed to the structure) of Chopin's melody, it is one of cumulative variation and transformation, where the melody is gradually enriched by ornamentation, textural amplification, contrapuntal intensification or elaboration of its accompaniment layer. These processes have both an expressive and a formal function, and they serve to highlight one of the ways in which the characteristic formal 'plot' of a Chopin work deviates from its classical antecedents. There is very often a leaning towards end-weighted structures (especially in extended works), and this will typically involve the enlargement, even the apotheosis, to use Edward T. Cone's term, of the basic materials.[36] There is, it is true, a good deal of literal repetition in Chopin—especially in the dance pieces—but the general tendency is for ideas to return in varied form, even if the changes affect only very minor details of construction. The expressive means vary from delicate ornamental traceries, as in restatements of the main theme of the D flat major Nocturne, to climactic re-scorings, as in the second theme of the G minor Ballade; from evolutionary, goal-directed melodic extensions, as in the C sharp minor Étude, to simple rhythmic alterations and folk ornaments, as in the B minor Mazurka, Op. 30 No. 2. But in every case a form of variation technique is seminal.

And for the most part variation and transformation are more common in Chopin's music of this period than *motivische Arbeit*, though that is found too. Several of the mazurkas involve a rather specific form of motive working which derives ultimately from the regional dance and is characterized by short-breathed, oscillating phrases of one or two bars, usually presented in literal or varied repetitions. But in the scherzos and ballades we find the kind of segmentation and recomposition of themes characteristic of the classical style, albeit directed to rather different, and usually more localized, ends. Only in some later works does Chopin employ motivic dissection as a major agent of temporal progression, in the manner of the archetypal classical development section. More commonly it is associated with particular episodes in a work, creating local intensification, as in the segmentation of the first theme of the G minor Ballade, or an effect of transition, as in the reprise of the D flat major Scherzo. And such episodes tend to remain subordinate to the larger formal processes in a work.

A rather different aspect of thematic process concerns the integration of material through certain unifying 'basic shapes'.[37] On a foreground

[35] William Rothstein, 'Phrase Rhythm in Chopin's Nocturnes and Mazurkas', in *Chopin Studies* (Cambridge, 1988), pp. 115–43.

[36] Edward T. Cone, *Musical Form and Musical Performance* (New York, 1968), p. 84.

[37] The German term *Grundgestalt* was used by Schoenberg to convey his strongly organicist approach to thematic substance. This solidified into an analytical approach in the work of such later commentators as Rudolph Réti, Hans Keller, and David Epstein.

level this is most obvious in the motivic relationship between the melody and the accompaniment layer. This is often established right at the outset of a piece, as in the D minor Prelude, Op. 28 No. 24, where the accompaniment prepares the opening of the theme, or again in the G major Prelude, Op. 28 No. 3 (Ex. 27). But in some works, especially

Ex. 27   Prelude, Op. 28 No. 3

extended ones, Chopin seems to have attempted a more obviously organicist approach to the thematic substance of the whole. In the G minor Ballade, for instance, it is clear that the falling major second of the opening theme (Ex. 28(a)), carefully isolated by Chopin's autograph phrasing and by its placing after the cadential close on a tonic harmony, acts as a unifying shape throughout. Ex. 28(b–d) illustrates some of the ways in which this motive permeates later (formally contrasted) sections of the work, including the bravura 'coda', to use an entirely inadequate term.

The C sharp minor Scherzo is similarly closely integrated in thematic substance, drawing much of its material from an all-pervasive falling semitone motive (A–G#). This is already implicit in the introduction to

Ex. 28   Ballade No. 1 Op. 23
(a)

173

(b)

(c)

(d)

the work, but it is spelled out clearly in the main scherzo theme and is used to effect a subtle link to the trio. In all these cases the motivic links are explicit, but there is a substantial body of analytical work which makes larger claims for 'basic shapes' in Chopin, finding unifying threads well below the surface of the music.[38] Analytical observations in this area need to be made with care, and their value remains properly controversial, but there are convincing insights by Anatole Leikin and David Witten in particular. It is even possible to locate motivic cross-references between the different pieces within a genre, as Józef Chomiński and Jean-Jacques Eigeldinger have done for the Twenty-four Preludes.[39] And we shall note in chapter 8 that there are similar, to my mind more convincing, links between the four impromptus, and between the two late fantasies. Some commentators have gone further, identifying basic shapes underlying a much larger corpus of Chopin's music. Ex. 29 (a–f) gives some indication of the approach.[40]

Ex. 29

(a) Fantasy-Impromptu, Op. 66

(b) Trois Nouvelles Études No. 3

(c) Waltz, Op. 70 No. 3

[38] See Alan Walker, 'Chopin and Musical Structure: an Analytical Approach', in *Frédéric Chopin: Profiles of the Man and the Musician* (London, 1966), pp. 227–57. Also parts of David Witten, *The Chopin 'Ballades': an Analytical Study* (Diss., U. of Boston, 1979) and Antole Leikin, 'The Sonatas', in *The Cambridge Companion to Chopin*, pp. 160–88.

[39] See note 24.

[40] Ernst-Jurgen Dreyer, 'Melodisches Formelgut bei Chopin', *The Book of the First International Musicological Congress Devoted to the Works of Frederick Chopin*, pp. 132–44.

Ex. 29

(d) Polonaise, Op. 26 No. 1

(e) Scherzo No. 2, Op. 31

(f) Nocturne, Op. 27 No. 2

From the start Chopin's harmonic practice was acknowledged as innovatory, even iconoclastic. There were references to his 'peculiar system of harmony',[41] to 'peculiar harmonies which render his works, on first acquaintance, so crude and ungracious',[42] to his 'needlessly crude and hazardous modulation[s]'.[43] Yet much of this novelty is little more than foreground chromatic elaboration of uncomplicated and familiar underlying progressions. The detailed formulations of such chromatic elaboration are pianistic to the core, and they depend for their effectiveness, as Moscheles implied,[44] on the performer's sensitivity to harmonic priority. Often they result from liberal sprinklings of what text-books like to call 'inessential notes', motivated by the integrity of the figure, by the 'law' of chromatic succession, or by both. As Ex. 30 from Op. 25 No. 6 indicates, Chopin's approach to dissonance in such passages is not unlike Bach's or, for that matter, Stravinsky's.

Elsewhere he engages in transformations of the chromatic symmetries commonly found in classical development sections, but with the rate of chord progression often significantly speeded up so that individual impacts are blurred. Two examples from the polonaises will illustrate the point. In Ex. 31 from Op. 40 No. 2 a sense of progression within a single harmony is achieved through a combination of semitonal linear movement and the local attraction of the dominant seventh harmony. The use of a chromatic bass to support chains of foreground V–I progressions was by no means unknown to classical harmony, but Chopin

41 *The Musical Examiner*, London, 31 December 1842.
42 *The Athenaeum*, London, 1 January 1842.
43 Ibid., 26 February 1842.   44 See chapter 4, note 47.

Ex. 30 Étude, Op. 25 No. 6

Ex. 31 Polonaise, Op. 40 No. 2

Ex. 32 Polonaise, Op. 26 No. 1

elevated it to an organic principle of chord connection. Indeed the fifth relationship is so common on the foreground of his harmony that it usually carries no implications whatever for the underlying tonal structure. Ex. 32 from Op. 26 No. 1 is a case in point. Again the semitonal movement poses no serious threat to the security of a stable harmonic anchor point. Such progressions are controlled by a form of 'organic' chromaticism, in which the seventh chord functions as a fundamental harmonic unit (often reinterpreted as an augmented sixth). They are virtually ubiquitous in Chopin, and in slower pieces they can generate a powerfully expressive affective quality. The fourth of the Preludes, a kind of elegy, is characteristic (Ex. 33). Once more the entire sequence elaborates a simple diatonic progression (I–V–I) in the depths.

Ex. 33 Prelude, Op. 28, No. 4

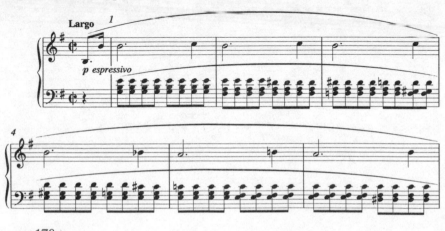

On occasion chromatic symmetries take on a more formal character, suggesting underlying whole-tone or octatonic formations.[45] The figurations which flank the pivotal 'waltz' in the G minor Ballade are representative. These devices proved especially influential in Russia, and so too did the modalities, bourdon pedals, and deliberate archaisms found in the mazurkas, as well as their tendency to reharmonize unchanging melodies, as in Op. 30 No. 2 (Ex. 34). In general Chopin reserved for the mazurkas some of his boldest and most enterprising harmonic adventures, though again they are usually confined to the foreground level of the music. But it would be quite wrong to view the harmonic eccentricities here as derived exclusively from folkloristic idioms. Clearly some of them are, but many result from highly individual extensions of established harmonic

Ex. 34 Mazurka, Op. 30 No. 2

[45] See Roy Howat, 'Chopin's Influence on the *Fin de siècle* and Beyond', in *The Cambridge Companion to Chopin*, pp. 275–8.

179

practice, albeit of an order apparently reserved by Chopin specifically for this genre. In Ex. 35 from Op. 30 No. 4, for instance, the chromatically sliding sevenths are presented in their boldest form yet, with no deference to conventional laws of part movement. Such parallelism is entirely worthy of Debussy.

Ex. 35   Mazurka, Op. 30 No. 4

Although there is almost always a firm diatonic middleground underlying Chopin's chromatic elaboration, it frequently departs from the norms of classical practice. Much of this hinges on his attitude to the fifth relationship. I have already remarked that this is everywhere on the foreground to the harmony, where it is largely without tonal significance. Intriguingly it is employed sparingly at deeper levels of harmonic structure. If we consider, for example, the tonal schemes of the extended works of this period, we will be struck by the avoidance of V as a means of articulating larger formal divisions. In the first and third Scherzos, both in a minor key, the trio (in each case a kind of 'hymn' or 'chorale') is in the tonic major, enharmonically respelt in No. 3. The second Scherzo reverses this sequence in that the D flat major becomes C sharp minor for the trio. I should mention in passing that the 'tandem' of B flat minor and D flat major with which this latter work opens is another important feature of style in Chopin, though Charles Rosen goes too far in noting that 'for Chopin . . . they are more or less the same key'.[46] It is worth remarking on the number of short minor-key pieces whose opening gambit associates tonal relatives in this way, either through a sequential restatement in the relative major, or through a move, real or implied, in that direction (Op. 28 No. 8).

[46] Charles Rosen, *Sonata Forms* (New York and London, 1980), pp. 295–6.

1. Fryderyk Chopin. Portrait in oils by A. Miroszewski, 1829.

2. Chopin's mother, Justyna née Krzyzanowska. Portrait in oils by A. Miroszewski, 1829.

3. Chopin's father, Mikołaj. Portrait in oils by A. Miroszewski, 1829.

4. Krakowskie Przedmieście (Cracow Precinct) from Castle Square. Painting in oils by B. Bellotto. In the foreground Zygmunt's Column, and behind that (on the left) the Warsaw Conservatory.

5. Chopin playing in the Salon of Prince Antoni Radziwiłł, 1829. Heliogravure (1888) by R. H. Schuster after a painting in oils by H. Siemiradzki (1887). Prince Radziwiłł seated right of centre, with Princess Eliza standing by him and Princess Wanda behind her.

6. Salle Pleyel. Unsigned engraving. Chopin gave most of his Paris concerts here.

7. Maria Wodzińska. Self-portrait in pencil, *c.*1835.

8. Fryderyk Chopin. Water-colour by Maria Wodzińska, Marianské Lazné, August 1836, on page 23 of Maria Wodzińska's album.

9. George Sand. The separated left side of an originally combined portrait in oils (with Chopin), by E. Delacroix, 1838.

10. Fryderyk Chopin and George Sand. Pencil sketch by Delacroix for his combined portrait in oils, c.1838. In this original sketch Chopin is playing the piano while Sand is seated with folded arms. In the later portrait she stands behind him.

11. Frydryk Chopin. The separated right side of an originally combined portrait in oils (with Sand), by E. Delacroix, 1838.

12. Rejected Manuscript (autograph) of Impromptu, Op.36, bars 70–85.

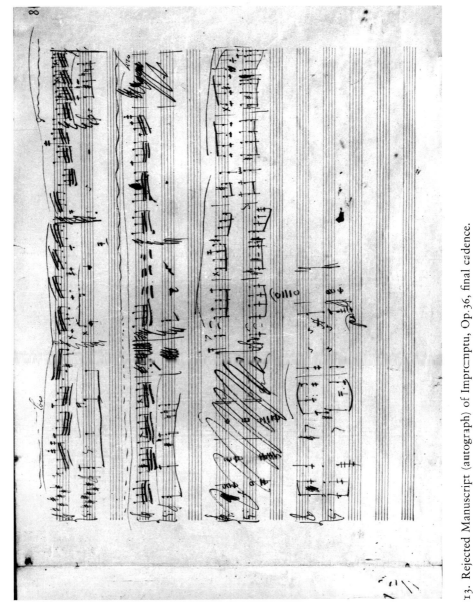

13. Rejected Manuscript (autograph) of Impromptu, Op.36, final cadence.

14. George Sand and friends at Nohant. Painted fan by A. Charpentier. Left to right: the painter Calamatta (serpent), Maurice Sand (on all fours), Charles Didier, Emmanuel Arago (triton), Wojciech Grzymała, the actor Bocage (faune), Liszt (kneeling), Delacroix, Sand holding a bird with the head of Chopin, Félicien Mallefille, Enrico, Solange Dudevant-Sand (lion), Michel de Bourges, G. de Bonne Chose, the painter A. Charpentier.

15. Château de Nohant, George Sand's home in Berry. Pencil drawing by Maurice Sand.

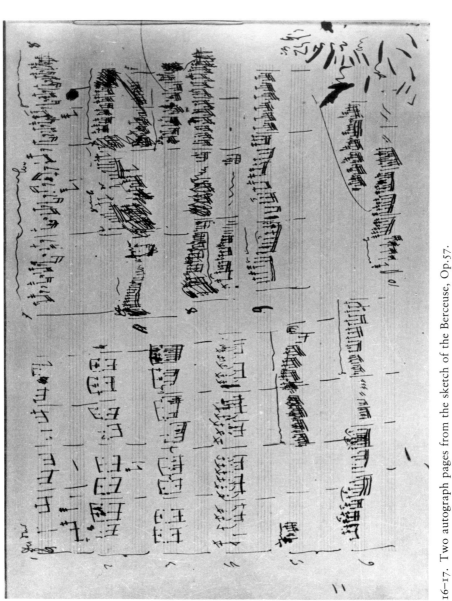

16–17. Two autograph pages from the sketch of the Berceuse, Op.57.

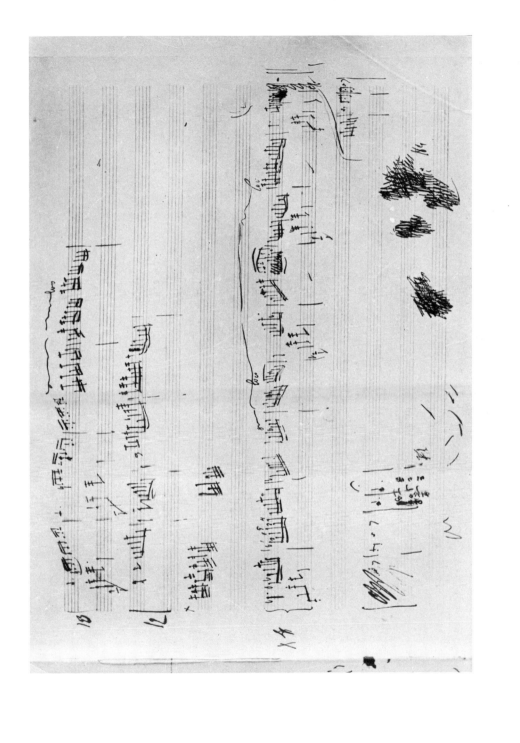

18. Autograph page from the sketch of the Polonaise-fantasy, Op.61.

19. Jane Stirling with her niece, Fanny Elgin. Lithograph by J.-J.-M.-A. Devéria, c.1842.

20. Fryderyk Chopin. Photograph by L. A. Bisson, Paris 1849.

21. The last Moments of Fryderyk Chopin. Painting in oils by T. Kwiatkowski. Standing by the bed is Princess Marcelina Czartkoryska, in the armchair the composer's sister Ludwika, seated on the right Wojciech Grzymała, with Teofil Kwiatkowski standing behind him.

In the four Polonaises of Opp. 26 and 40 there is a similar avoidance of V. The C sharp minor, Op. 26 No. 1, again turns to the tonic minor for its trio, while its companion in E flat minor prefers the sub-mediant region, as does the C minor, Op. 40 No. 2. The A major, Op. 40 No. 1 moves rather to the sub-dominant. Likewise with the first two ballades, where third-related regions dominate the tonal organization, G minor/E flat major in No. 1, F major/A minor in No. 2. If we consider these tonal schemes alongside those of the Warsaw-period extended works, we begin to see an emerging pattern in Chopin's approach to large-scale tonal organization. Essentially his strategy was to reserve the fifth relationship for the latest possible stage of the tonal argument, where it might function as a powerful structural dominant at the background level. Rather than set up a tonal dialectic of tonic and dominant in the classical manner, he engaged in a kind of waiting game, where the approach to the delayed structural V of a work might represent its single most important formal impulse, a powerful background structure underpinning its sectional design.

This accounts, moreover, for numerous tonal strategies in the middleground. Quite apart from the secondary regions (often third-related) which articulate the form, Chopin engages frequently in deceptive tonicizations, prolonging and briefly stabilizing a member of the (mainly diatonic) middleground. Such passages, which are often integrated with their surroundings through enharmony, were called by Gerald Abraham 'tonal parentheses', and they tend to lie somewhere between chromatic embellishments and the modulations of conventional theory.[47] There is nothing new about them, but they are so common in Chopin that they represent a major feature of style. Ex. 36, from the last of the Op. 33 Mazurkas, is characteristic.

The opening of this same Mazurka draws attention to another common feature of Chopin's harmony. The piece opens with chord IV rather than Chord I, creating an impression, highly typical of Chopin, that the music has begun in mid-thought, as it were. Of the four Mazurkas in this opus, only No. 2 begins with a straightforward tonic harmony, while of the Op. 30 set only No. 3 does so. The most characteristic opening is a V–I progression, as in Op. 30 Nos. 1 and 4, and again in Op. 33 Nos. 1 and 3; as Carl Schachter noted, this non-coincidence of the tonal arrival point and the first downbeat neatly avoids square phrase rhythms in the mazurkas.[48] In Op. 30 No. 2 the tendency to begin a piece elliptically is taken further, in that the overall tonal scheme is 'emergent' or 'directional', beginning in B minor and closing in F sharp minor. Each tonal region has its own material and the duality is fundamental on both tonal and thematic levels. The A minor Prelude similarly allows its tonal destination to become clear only gradually, and several of the large-scale

[47] Gerald Abraham, *Chopin's Musical Style*, pp. 91–5.   [48] See note 34.

Ex. 36 Mazurka, Op. 33 No. 4

works of this period likewise begin outside their tonic, including the second and third Scherzos, and the two Ballades.

Most of these pieces are best described as monotonal (in a single key) with a non-tonic opening. The technique is really an inflation and refinement of the tonally inductive prelude or recitative. But it is not always quite so simple. In the second Scherzo the initial B flat minor establishes a structural tension with the main tonality of D flat major, and this tension is later built into the tonal argument of the work. It is scarcely enough to describe the opening (as Schenker does) as a tonal anacrusis.[49] Yet while the B flat–D flat relation is seminal to the work, there is not much doubt which region has priority. Contrary to the popular nomenclature, this is indeed a Scherzo in D flat major. The second Ballade takes the process a stage further. As in Op. 30 No. 2, the alternation of two tonal regions in this work refuses to permit a monotonal analysis. Moreover the F major and A minor are rather more distant than the tonal 'relatives' of Op. 31. The tonal structure of the Ballade can *only* be explained as a two-key scheme, and as such it represents a significant departure from norms of structure in the early nineteenth century.[50]

[49] Heinrich Schenker, *Free Composition*, vol. 2, fig. 13.

[50] For a discussion, see Harald Krebs, 'Alternatives to Monotonality in Early Nineteenth-Century Music', in *Journal of Music Theory* (1981), vol. 25 no. 1, pp. 1–16.

However we understand Chopin's directional tonal schemes theoretically, they are clearly motivated by the same thinking as his delayed structural dominants. Just as the moment of resolution is often postponed until the latest possible stage of a work, so the strategies of postponement are often instigated right at the outset through tonally inductive, ambiguous opening gestures. In this connection it is worth considering for a moment two A minor pieces of very different scale, the second Prelude and the second Ballade. In both pieces the goal is a tradition 6/4–5/3 cadence—a structural V on the background level of harmony—and this powerfully affirmative definition of the tonality is the more cathartic for the ambiguities which precede it. In Op. 28 No. 2 the music opens in a region that can be identified only retrospectively as the dominant minor, and the point of tonal arrival is delayed to the final bars (the 6/4 comes at bar 15). In Op. 38 the scale is of course much larger. In relation to the tonal destination the music opens in the submediant, and, as in the first Ballade, the structural V is reached just before the closing section of the work.

Examination of these tonal strategies on middleground and background levels inevitably brings us centrally to the question of form. Essentially there are two contrasted formal tendencies in Chopin's music, the one towards a continuous, strongly directional form, the other towards a sectionalized ternary design, an expansion of the classical three-part song form. These tendencies make for useful reference points in a discussion of Chopin's forms, but they need to be invoked with caution. Not only is there substantial interpenetration of the two formal principles (witness the second Ballade and second Scherzo). There has also been frequent misidentification, and especially of ternary designs. Many of the pieces commonly described as ternary are in reality much closer to the first tendency than to the second in that their middle section offers an intensification of the material rather than any formal discontinuity. Such pieces are best understood in terms of a single impulse of departure and return. Elsewhere, and especially in the Preludes, the tendency to continuous forms is expressed through a simple bipartite design, a statement with conflated response.

If we look more closely at these so-called 'continuous' forms, we will note that their subtlety resides as often as not in Chopin's control of the 'intensity curve' of the piece, which may well be counterpointed against its formal design—a counterpoint of dynamic shape and static or 'spatial' pattern.[51] What appear to be the simplest of pieces can often reveal unexpected sophistications if viewed from this perspective. I have demonstrated elsewhere that many of the Preludes, for instance, make their point precisely by exploiting this non-congruence of an irregular, unpredictable tension–release structure and regular, predictable phrase

[51] The analysis of music as dynamic 'intensity curve' owes much to the work of Ernst Kurth. But see also Wallace Berry, *Structural Functions in Music* (New Jersey, 1976).

and repetition structures.[52] No. 12 in G sharp minor is characteristic, the 'dislocation' of its tension points almost suggesting that the principle of rubato (rhythmic freedom over a strictly measured pulse) has been inflated to the level of overall form.

This dislocation has the further purpose of heightening our sense of cadential closure. In the second half of the piece Chopin brings the climax forward to a placing in advance of the mid-point rather than after it (as in the first half), and this enables him to strengthen the ending, allowing a longer period for resolution. Strategies of closure, and especially those adopted to postpone closure, are naturally critical to the operation of these continuous forms, since closure must in some sense bridge the gap between shape and pattern, drawing both into congruence.[53] There are no hard and fast rules here. Unlike the G sharp minor, the A minor Prelude sets out to postpone tonal closure until the latest possible moment, and this indeed (as I noted earlier) is the more usual strategy in Chopin. No less characteristic is the conventional nature of its articulation when it does finally arrive. Chopin here relies on the simplest of archetypes, appropriating from the generic convention a descending bass motion followed by a perfect cadence.

Similar principles are at work in some of the more extended continuous forms, and especially in the ballades. Here too, as in the G sharp minor Prelude, there is often a calculated non-congruence between strongly directional impulses and a static, spatialized (and usually symmetrical) formal design; Op. 23 is a case in point. Here too, as in the A minor Prelude, there is a journey towards clarification and denouement, with tonality the principal agent of the narrative; Op. 38 is representative. And here, too, tonal closure is often delayed until the latest possible moment and then realized through a conventional 6/4–5/3 cadential progression, invariably the first appearance of the structural dominant on the background level of the music; any of the ballades would serve. It is this end-weighted 'plot archetype' which accounts for the formal compression (described by Abraham as 'perspective foreshortening')[54] in the closing stages of so many Chopin works, and also for those bravura 'codas' or closing sections, in which all earlier tensions are resolved in a 'whirlwind of musical reckoning'.[55]

The other tendency in Chopin's forms—towards sectionalized ternary designs—might be exemplified by the E minor Étude, Op. 25 No. 5, where a lyrical melody in the tonic major is enclosed within flanking vivace sections. Yet here again the surface is deceptively simple. Chopin

[52] Jim Samson, *The Music of Chopin*, pp. 76–80.

[53] For a detailed discussion of strategies of closure, see Kofi Agawu, 'Concepts of Closure and Chopin's Opus 28', *Music Theory Spectrum* 9 (1987), pp. 1–17.

[54] Gerald Abraham, *Chopin's Musical Style*, p. 46.

[55] See James Parakilas, *Ballades Without Words: Chopin and the Tradition of the Instrumental Ballade* (Oregon, 1992).

takes pains to ensure not just the compatibility of the contrasted sections but an interrelation between them, founded in a common motivic substance. And this is entirely characteristic. Formal divisions are not in doubt in such pieces, any more than they are in doubt in the post-classical repertories to which they relate, but voice-leading connections and motivic parallelisms ensure that continuity is there across the divide. Charles Burkhart draws attention to the role of just such a motivic parallelism in the F sharp major Impromptu, for example, where it mitigates an otherwise uncomfortable tonal disjunction between F major and F sharp major.[56] Examples could be multiplied.

Although such connections help ensure continuity and integration, they do not of course influence the basic distinction between directional forms like the A minor Prelude and sectionalized forms like the E minor Étude. These latter depend crucially on the composer achieving a sense of balance between the contrasted elements, and in Chopin's case this often amounts to the generation of large-scale rhythmic impulses. Dance pieces, not surprisingly, tend to be sectional in design, but their dance-like character often extends beyond local rhythmic patterns to penetrate the larger structure, where eight-bar periods (often with a clear repetition structure) and even at times whole sections seem to create a larger pulse, 'lifting' the music onwards from one moment to the next.

This is true even of extended ternary designs, the scherzos as much as the bigger polonaises. But here Chopin often seeks to soften the contrast between formal divisions by constructing links and transitions, usually of great subtlety. The term 'transition' is overworked in analysis, but the formal function is real enough, and it can clearly be of vital importance to a composer who often works with relatively self-contained contrasted sections. The approach to the central 'hymn' of the third Scherzo well illustrates how two such contrasted sections are mediated in this way. The rhythmic shape of the hymn is already embedded in the consequent of the scherzo theme, and Chopin allows it to emerge gradually by altering its metrical position until it is conformant with that of the hymn. Even the delicate 'afterthoughts' of the hymn (the sprays of figuration) are subtly prepared as the trio approaches.[57]

Discussion of these separate dimensions of style has involved the artificial extraction of particular elements from the rich, complex, fused whole of Chopin's musical idiom. That idiom in the end exceeds the bounds of any attempt to dissect it. It refuses to yield its meanings to any single analytical approach, since all such approaches are transparently limited by the kinds of questions they do and can ask. Our

[56] The term 'motivic parallelism' is here used in its Schenkerian sense. Burkhart's essay is 'Schenker's Theory of Levels and Musical Performance', in *Aspects of Schenkerian Theory*, ed. David Beach (New Haven and London, 1983), pp. 95–112.

[57] I have discussed the mechanics of this in greater detail in *The Music of Chopin*, p. 169.

knowledge of Chopin's musical style will remain incomplete, then, but it may be worth suggesting (rather than presenting) one means by which analysis might help locate it historically, and by 'historically' I mean as a point of intersection between Chopin's time and ours.[58] My suggestion is that light might be shed on the music by approaching it from two polarized perspectives. The organicist analyses of our century (especially those based on Schenker) tell us much about what the Chopin work means to us today, and for that reason alone they are valuable and important, however far removed they may be from the assumptions and presuppositions of Chopin's contemporaries. They can usefully be complemented, however, by approaches which draw support from the late eighteenth-century theory in which Chopin himself was trained. Such approaches would encourage us to hear the work in sequential rather than structural terms, as a succession of styles (even of genres), as combination rather than integration. If we probe no further than the harmonic dimensions, we can see how this pincer movement—homing in on Chopin from eighteenth- and twentieth-century perspectives—might reveal that a unified tonal structure may also form a succession of tonal types, together with their associated generic 'topics',[59] and, above all, their associated figures. The work is neither one thing nor the other, but both.

[58] See the chapter 'The significance of art: historical or aesthetic?' in Carl Dahlhaus, *Foundations of Music History*, tr. J. B. Robinson (Cambridge, 1983; original edn. 1967), pp. 19–32.

[59] Leonard Ratner's term. See his *Classic Music: Expression, Form and Style* (New York and London, 1980).

7

Years of refuge

George Sand has been much maligned by Chopin biographers, as indeed she was by some of his friends. 'The poor man cannot see that this woman has the love of a vampire', was Custine's verdict, and not his alone.[1] Just after the composer's death Grzymała remarked that had Chopin not had 'the misfortune to meet G. S. who has poisoned his whole life, he might have lived to Cherubini's age'.[2] We should be careful of such pronouncements. In part at least they were motivated by jealousy. Wittingly or not, Chopin somehow brought out the worst in his friends, most of whom were confident that they alone knew what was best for him. Protectiveness all too easily bred possessiveness. Grzymała's remark in particular rings false from one who had been a friend to both of them, and one who to all appearances had patronized the relationship. Admittedly Sand herself made an easy target for criticism, and not only in relation to Chopin. With her incessant torrents of prose, vivid and colourful but often lacking discipline, her astonishing capacity for self-deception and self-justification, and her apparent inability to see that her view of things was not necessarily shared by other parties, she positively invited censure.

There was indeed a case to answer in many respects, but there was another side, too. The Chopin biographies seldom convey just what a remarkable phenomenon Sand really was, deservedly one of the most famous women in the Europe of her time, friend and respected correspondent of some of the truly great figures in nineteenth-century letters. Her energy was boundless. An account of her daily routine makes for exhausting reading; and when she finally sat down to write through the night she turned out novels, plays, historical treatises, political tracts, disquisitions on innumerable social and cultural issues, to say nothing of more than thirteen thousand extant letters. That she lacked self-criticism is without question. Unlike Chopin, an inveterate reviser, she rarely tampered with her work. But we can at least salute her exuberance, her disdain for convention, her determination to grapple, however

---

[1] *Correspondance de Frédéric Chopin*, vol. 2, p. 279.   [2] *KFC*, vol. 2, p. 324.

insecurely, with all the issues of the day, and her genuine, if utopian, desire to remedy social injustice.

The long list of lovers was in some ways a further projection of Sand's general inclination to 'live her truths one at a time, each cancelling the last'. And it is indeed a remarkable testament to the strength of her bond with Chopin that her relationship with him lasted as long as it did, a full nine years. Towards the end of that period she wrote to Grzymała, with only a very minor deviation from the truth, 'For the last seven years I have lived like a virgin with him as well as with all others'.[3] Theirs was no conventional love affair, but the Majorcan experience and its aftermath by no means weakened their mutual feeling and dependency. 'We cling to each other with growing affection and trust in happiness', she wrote to Charlotte Marliani from the island. And again, 'He is an angel of patience, gentleness and kindness'.[4] That it lacked the passion of earlier escapades may well have made this relationship all the more important to Sand and the more capable of enduring. Back in Nohant, on 19 June 1839, she carved that date on the window of her room, a gesture which may well have marked the first anniversary of the consummation of their love, though other, very different interpretations have been proposed.[5] In any event, to reach the first anniversary of a love affair was a novelty for Sand, something worth recording.

Most important of all, the relationship left space for each of them to work creatively. They worked together in Majorca, and they continued to do so in Nohant. Whatever may be said against Sand, she offered Chopin a stable home life—the first since his Warsaw days—and it was in the security of a new family that he composed some of his greatest works. It might be added that the upkeep of Nohant was entirely met by Sand, whose astonishing industry as a writer was in large part a financial imperative. Her 'house guest', on the other hand, was without major financial responsibilities or worries during the summers spent there. He was free to compose. During that first summer at Nohant he completed the first, second, and fourth movements of the B flat minor Sonata, Op. 35 (the *Marche funèbre* had been composed two years earlier), three of the four Op. 41 Mazurkas, the second of the Op. 37 Nocturnes, and the F sharp major Impromptu, Op. 36. It was a productive period, even if several of these pieces may have been in progress before the couple arrived at Nohant. 'He has already composed some exquisite things since he has been here', Sand wrote in late June.[6] And Chopin himself was pleased. 'They seem pretty to me', he wrote to Fontana of the mazurkas, 'just as the youngest children appear beautiful to ageing parents.'[7]

[3] *GSC*, vol. 7, pp. 700–1. [4] Ibid., vol. 4, pp. 534 and 569.
[5] See Adam Zamoyski, *Chopin: A Biography*, pp. 174–5.
[6] *GSC*, vol. 4, p. 688. [7] *KFC*, vol. 1, p. 353.

Chopin was initially content at Nohant, a large three-storey manor described by Matthew Arnold as 'a plain house by the roadside with a walled garden'.[8] It was (and is) part of a tiny hamlet on the road from Châteauroux to La Châtre, with an old church and a few farms gathered around the manor house. When Chopin arrived there in June 1839, he was badly in need of a period of rest and convalescence, and he was well aware that the quiet routine of life at Nohant fitted the bill perfectly. He was no doubt attracted, too, by the novelty of such very different surroundings. But he had no real feeling for country life. He had been brought up in one city and had spent most of his adult life in another. He enjoyed the endless diversity and energy of city life, its frivolous amusements, its varied cultural offerings, its lively social round. For him the country was a place to visit occasionally on vacation, as he had often done as a boy, but no more than that. As a result he quickly tired of life at Nohant and became easily bored. He found little joy in the walks, picnics, and excursions arranged by Sand, herself a country woman through and through. She later described how on outings together he would idly pick a few flowers, wander around for a bit and then wait anxiously for them to set off again for home.

His life there was comfortable. He was given a large room on the first floor, separated from Sand's by a shared sitting room, rose late, breakfasted in his room, and spent most of the day composing, interrupted by an occasional piano lesson for Sand's daughter, Solange, or a little tinkering with editorial details in the Paris edition of Bach's '48'. His health improved in this environment, and in August 1839 Sand's local doctor Gustav Papet, like the Marseilles doctor and unlike the Majorcans, ruled out consumption, though, as I noted earlier, this may have been attributable to divergent schools of medical opinion, rather than to faulty diagnoses.[9] What is certain is that he was well looked after. In addition to nursing an often difficult patient, moreover, Sand spent her days tutoring the children, seeing to the needs of the Nohant tenants, keeping a careful eye on her wayward half brother, Hippolyte, and looking after her business affairs. The only semblance of routine at Nohant was that all would assemble at six o'clock for dinner, often served out of doors, followed by music, conversation or entertainments of one sort or another, including theatricals and pantomimes in which Chopin's gift of mimickry was exploited to the full. And only when all guests and family had retired would Sand at last take up her pen, working through much of that first summer on her new play, *Cosima*, destined to begin rehearsals at the Théâtre Français in the autumn.

She was of course well aware of Chopin's restlessness in the country, and did everything she could to keep him entertained. She invited several of his friends to visit them, including Stefan Witwicki, who was

[8] Matthew Arnold, *Mixed Essays* (London, 1879), p. 318.   [9] See chapter 1, note 35.

holidaying nearby and spent a few days at Nohant. Then, at the end of August, Grzymała was persuaded to make the journey and stayed for a fortnight, along with Sand's close friend the lawyer Emmanuel Arago. This was the sort of diversion Chopin craved and needed at Nohant. And by the time Grzymała left in mid-September Chopin and Sand were already beginning to make preparations for their return to Paris, detailing Fontana and Grzymała to find appropriate accommodation, by which they meant two separate apartments, their settings, interior design and furnishings specified by Chopin in the most meticulous detail. His presumption in this regard, especially where Fontana was concerned, beggars belief. 'I quite forgot to ask you to order a hat from M. Dupont in your street. Tell him to make it in the latest fashion . . . and when you pass Dautremont's, my tailor on the boulevard, ask him to make me some grey trousers immediately . . . also a black velvet waistcoat with a discrete pattern . . .'[10] Fontana did the necessary, finding not only a wardrobe but a flat for Chopin at 5 rue Tronchet and two twin-storey summer-houses for Sand in a small courtyard just off the rue Pigalle.

On 11 October the party arrived in Paris. Chopin and Maurice stayed at rue Tronchet, Sand and Solange with the Marlianis until the summer-houses at 16 rue Pigalle were made ready a few days later. For the next eighteen months Chopin based himself in Paris, returning to Nohant only in June 1841. And in Paris, as in Nohant, a routine was quickly established. Chopin would spend his day at rue Tronchet, teaching until around four, and would then make his way to rue Pigalle where he spent the evening, and frequently the night. For the most part he simply resumed the old life of teaching, socializing, and occasional playing. There were some new pupils, including one of his very best, Friederike Müller (later Streicher), who worked with him intensively during this eighteen-month period and was the dedicatee of the *Allegro de concert*, Op. 46. She reputedly played the *Allegro* well, and there are further accounts of her playing the B flat minor Sonata and the first movement of the F minor Concerto (with Chopin on the second piano) at a soirée in December 1840.

There were also some new contacts with professional musicians during this period, and above all with Moscheles. Moscheles visited Paris from his base in England in September 1839, around the time that he withdrew from giving public concerts and just a few weeks before Chopin arrived from Nohant. They met at the home of Moscheles's relative Auguste Léo, the music-loving banker who had advanced Chopin some money to finance the trip to Majorca. Moscheles gave an evocative account of his early impressions of Chopin's playing. 'His harsh modulations . . . no longer shock me, after seeing his slim fingers gliding over the keyboard to execute them with such skill.'[11] In the same

---

[10] *KFC*, vol. 1, p. 363.
[11] See chapter 4, note 47, for documentation of Moscheles's views on Chopin.

letter he remarked, 'Moreover, he professes to admire my compositions, and even if this is not true, he knows them through and through.' There is good reason to believe that it was true, given the stylistic parallels between early Chopin and Moscheles. In any case the, two of them performed at numerous society soirées during October, especially the E major Sonata for piano duet by Moscheles, and at the end of the month they were invited to play at one of the regular court concerts at St Cloud, for which they received attractive gifts from Louis-Philippe. Chopin composed his *Trois Nouvelles Études* at this time for inclusion in the *Méthode des méthodes* by Moscheles and Fétis. Moreover the contact was maintained indirectly right to the final year of his life, when he gave some lessons to Moscheles's highly talented daughter.

There was some change in the pattern of Chopin's social life in the capital now that he and Sand were there together, albeit with their separate establishments. They had been brought together in the first place by the social circle associated with Liszt and Marie d'Agoult, and in the early days of their relationship had moved within that circle. This began to change during the year 1839–40. While they remained close to the Marlianis and also to Delacroix, their relations with Liszt and d'Agoult themselves became distinctly frosty, due mainly to the latter's endless gossiping about Sand, reported faithfully, and no doubt with some relish, by Charlotte Marliani, and apparently condoned by Liszt. At that time the relationship between Liszt and d'Agoult was in any case beginning to founder, and this may have been another factor in the growing animosity between Sand and d'Agoult, especially as Sand had passed on to Balzac some details about Liszt and d'Agoult which found their way into his novel *Béatrix*. The source of this unmistakable caricature was soon discovered or deduced, and Balzac professed himself much amused to have set two such formidable ladies at each other's throats.

With this common element in their social lives removed, Chopin and Sand found themselves moving a little uneasily in each other's circles of friends. Sand had little patience with the salons which were so congenial to Chopin; in particular she found the ambience of the Hôtel Lambert, with its distinct air of élitism, unpalatable. She tolerated the company of Chopin's 'society' friends up to a point, but often refused to accompany him to the fashionable salons. Nor had she much time for some of his closer Polish friends, Grzymała apart, accusing Fontana in particular of bombarding Chopin with gossip, and causing him unnecessary worry, and taking issue with Matuszyński, who was by now convinced (rightly, of course) that Chopin had consumption, as indeed he had himself. Ironically she was attracted rather to the group of Poles associated with the Polish Literary Society, with whom Chopin felt rather uncomfortable. Mickiewicz's messianic view of Poland's destiny appealed to the romantic liberal in Sand, and for a time she involved herself closely with the Polish cause, wielding her pen (as usual) in vigorous support. At the

191

turn of the year (1840–1) she and Chopin attended some of Mickiewicz's lectures on slavonic literature at the Collège de France, following his appointment as Professor of Slavonic Studies.

Chopin, for his part, had little sympathy with Sand's artistic milieu, and was ill at ease in the company of the socialist intellectuals and bohemian artists who frequented the rue Pigalle. Delacroix was an exception. He quickly gained Chopin's admiration and respect, and came to play an increasingly important role in the lives of both Sand and Chopin. Although Chopin's taste in painting really lay elsewhere, he engaged in lengthy debates with Delacroix, listened to him seriously and may even have been influenced by him marginally as he found himself changing direction as a composer in the early 1840s. He also liked the young singer Pauline García, daughter of the noted Spanish singing teacher Manuel García and sister of the famous singer La Malibran. She was the most recent of Sand's protégées and Chopin considered her a musician of rare intelligence and refinement. During her early acquaintance with Sand and Chopin she was courted by none other than Alfred de Musset, but Sand furthered the cause of the new director of the Théâtre-Italian, Louis Viardot, and, following their marriage, the couple were soon very much a part of the Sand–Chopin intimate circle.

Of all her associates, Chopin had least time for the actor Bocage, whose flirtatious manner with Sand appalled him (Bocage, incidentally, thought that Chopin was wasted on music, and should have been a comic actor!). When he learned that there had been an affair between them in 1837, he channelled all his jealousies and insecurities towards Bocage, and eventually extracted a promise from Sand to restrict her contacts with the famous actor. Unreasonable demands of this sort were not infrequent, and it is surprising in a way that she was so acquiescent. There can be no doubt of her solicitude, her determination to protect Chopin from any source of anxiety. She concealed from him anything that might be misconstrued, even her meetings with Grzymała in later years: 'It would cause such a row'.[12] And to Bocage, 'Everything upsets him and gives him pain and I will make unheard of sacrifices for his peace.'[13] There is something here of that 'secret tyranny' of the weak over the strong.

That there were tensions in the relationship is without question. Their different temperaments, reflected in their different circles of friends, made this inevitable. Moreover the absence of physical relations and the reputation of Sand combined to increase his growing sense of inadequacy, his tendencies to jealousy and suspicion. There were already signs of this in 1839–40, and the problem would increase greatly in later years. Nevertheless the emotional bond between Sand and Chopin was no less powerful because it had taken on an essentially platonic character. And

[12] *GSC*, vol. 6, p. 797.   [13] Ibid., vol. 6, p. 803.

it survived right through to the closing stages of their relationship. It is evident particularly in the correspondence, which forms a much more reliable guide to the true state of things than later self-justifying accounts such as Sand's autobiography.

A few examples, well spaced over the years, speak volumes. When Sand and Pauline Viardot went on a brief concert tour to Cambrai in August 1840 (she badly needed to have a break from Paris following the total failure of her play *Cosima*), her son wrote to her, 'You cannot imagine how sad the house is since you left. Chopinet and I stare at each other in candlelight and he opens his large mouth from time to time to say, "My God, I miss someone", to which I reply, "My God, we both miss someone!" '[14] Three years later Sand wrote to Maurice, 'I cannot live without you and my weakling. Tell me truthfully how is he?'[15] And two years later, in 1845, she wrote to Chopin from Nohant, 'I am desolate to think that you are in the coach facing a difficult night . . . Love me, dear angel, my dear happiness, as I love you.'[16] This is scarcely the language of detachment.

The picture we have of this love is, however, notoriously incomplete. Sand destroyed much of the correspondence, some of it in extraordinary circumstances. Following Chopin's death, his sister Ludwika returned to Warsaw from Paris with her daughter and Chopin's last nurse, Stefania Matuszewska. She carried with her the composer's heart (which arrived safely in Warsaw in January 1850), together with a packet of some two hundred letters from Sand to Chopin. Fearing the Russian border guards, she left the letters with friends of Chopin at Mysłowice, where they were discovered, and copied, the following year by Alexandre Dumas *fils*. At the end of October 1851 the originals and copies were returned to Sand in Nohant.

It goes without saying that her destruction of these letters by fire (it is not certain, but highly probable, that the copies were also destroyed) placed a major obstacle in the path of any later objective analysis of one of the most remarkable liaisons of the century. Moreover the motivation for the destruction of the letters remains unclear. Did Sand feel that they prejudiced her later attempts to play down the significance of the relationship? Did she fear condemnation for her part in the breakdown of the affair? Or was it 'an act of absolution' motivated rather by her daughter Solange's vindictive behaviour?[17] Dumas's testimony should not be discounted. 'They were more gracious than the proverbial letters of Mme de Sevigné!'[18]

Although the full story of the relationship will never be known, it seems clear that it was a maternal response, a need to protect, that

[14] Ibid., vol. 5, p. 98.   [15] Ibid., vol. 6, p. 284.   [16] Ibid., vol. 7, p. 97.
[17] Ewa K. Kossak, 'The Correspondence of George Sand Edited by Georges Lubin', in *Chopin Studies 1* (Warsaw, 1985), vol. 1, p. 22.
[18] *KFC*, vol. 1, p. 13.

dominated Sand's feeling for Chopin, as indeed it had her feeling for other close friends and protegés, and of both sexes. 'I look after him like a child, and he loves me like his mother.'[19] In letters to Grzymała, she frequently referred to him (Grzymała) as 'husband' and Chopin as their 'little one'. When she wrote to Paris from the Cambrai concert tour with Pauline Viardot, it was to her three beloved children. What is by no means so certain is that Chopin shared this view of the relationship. With the years, his resentment of Sand's past and his jealousies about her present associations, however innocent (and with one exception they were all innocent), grew more and more obsessive.

There is some irony in Sand's maternal disposition, since her relationship with her real children was far from easy. They had been brought up erratically, spending periods with each parent in turn, often separated from both, educated partly by Sand herself, partly by tutors, and partly at boarding schools. As they grew older, they became increasingly difficult, but in quite opposite ways. Maurice was delicate in health, artistic in temperament (his very real talent was fostered by Delacroix, whose studio he visited regularly), and desperately clinging in his relationship to his mother. Their relationship was indeed exceptionally close, and in some ways it remained the central one in Sand's life, later developing a professional as well as an emotional dimension. Although initially Maurice got on well enough with Chopin, he came to resent him increasingly as the years passed, and he was more than pleased when Chopin and Sand eventually parted.

Solange, in contrast, was petulant and rebellious, impossible to tame, and inclined to exploit Chopin's obvious fondness for her, even as a young girl. As a result, Chopin frequently found himself acting as a mediator between Sand and her headstrong daughter, and he does seem to have been rather blind to Solange's defects, all too plain to everyone else. None of these problems was acute in the early years of their life together as a family, but the tensions were no doubt there, just below the surface. And it was the ambiguous position of Chopin in the family which would eventually lead to the breakdown of his relationship with Sand.

For the biographer this eighteen-month period in Paris is frustrating in its sameness, its paucity of those external events which might be neatly linked to form a lively narrative. Theirs was a quiet, stable domestic life; it even included at one stage an adopted puppy, much to Chopin's delight. For Chopin, the days were given over to teaching (he badly needed to recoup some of the money lost through the Majorcan adventure), and the evenings to conversation, ideally with a few intimates such as Grzymała, Arago, Delacroix, or Pauline Viardot. Occasionally he visited the theatre, followed by supper in a restaurant

[19] *GSC*, vol. 4, p. 570.

or with friends such as the Marlianis and the Viardots. There were a few outings, including one by railway to the village of St Germain and a visit to Custine, recently returned from travels in Russia, at St Gratien.

Little ruffled the surface of his life at this time, apart from a bout of illness in April 1840. The depths were another matter. This was not a productive period for Chopin. In the whole of 1840 he appears to have completed only the *Trois Nouvelles Études*, the song 'Dumka', and the Op. 42 Waltz, though it is difficult to be sure about the exact chronology of the composition (as opposed to the completion and publication) of his music at this time. There may have been good reasons for his low productivity. It seems likely that he was already engaged in what would amount to a major re-examination of his artistic aims during this period. At the very least he was storing up new reserves of creative energy which would give rise to some of the masterpieces of the early 1840s.

The reclusive nature of his life in Paris extended even to concert life. Apart from the Mozart Requiem on 12 December 1840 and Pauline Viardot's début at the Conservatoire on 7 February 1841, Chopin seems to have avoided almost all concerts. It was the more surprising, then, when he emerged from his 'retirement' in April to announce a grand concert at Pleyel's. This may or may not have been motivated by Liszt's triumphant reappearance in Paris with a much praised 'recital' in March (like Moscheles he was beginning to experiment with concerts which lacked the usual supporting artists— real recitals, in our modern understanding of the term). If so, it was certainly Chopin's friends rather than the composer himself who would have been stung into action. Chopin, as usual, was terrified at the prospect, and tried to extricate himself from the concert. In the event it was an unqualified success, both critically and financially. After such a long period of silence, a public recital by Chopin was something to be witnessed. Liszt was there, and he reviewed the concert for the *Revue et Gazette musicale*.

It is hard to see why this review has been taken to be a subtle insult to Chopin, 'seemingly complimentary', concealing sarcasm 'under a veil of flattery'.[20] It is a matter of record that it annoyed the hyper-sensitive Chopin. But to read it today is to be struck by its insights, as perceptive now as when they were made. 'Without seeking spurious originality, the composer is unmistakably himself both in the style and the conception of his works. To new ideas he has given new forms . . . he had no need to shock or to show off . . . he sought to evoke delicate sentiments rather than powerful emotions.' And of the Preludes, 'They are splendidly varied, and require the most careful examination of the craft and thought which has gone into them before they can be adequately appreciated. Yet they sound like impromptu improvisations produced without the slightest effort. They have the freedom and charm of works of genius.'[21]

[20] William G. Atwood, *Fryderyk Chopin: Pianist from Warsaw*, p. 133.
[21] *Revue et Gazette musicale*, Paris, 2 May 1841.

Liszt's was not the only eulogy in the press. The concert was well reviewed generally, and it re-awakened interest in a composer who had apparently disappeared from public view three years earlier. His critical standing was now higher than ever before, as the reviews of the publications which came out in 1840 and 1841 demonstrate. Even Rellstab had a change of heart, proclaiming that either times had changed, or he had changed, or Chopin's music had changed, for now he found it all quite beautiful. A little later (in 1843) Chopin's arch enemy in the English press, J. W. Davison, likewise came round to Chopin, though there may well have been a sub-text here.[22] The one obstacle to complete critical acceptance—especially in Germany—was the self-imposed limitation of medium and the related associations with the salon. This was pointed up even by Chopin's most ardent supporters, including Schumann, and the tag 'salon composer', with all its pejorative connotations, remained obstinately attached to him for most of the century, and in some quarters even beyond.

Shortly after the concert Chopin and Sand returned to Nohant, arriving there in mid-June. Sand had become increasingly restive in Paris, and as the summer approached she was inclined to respond to her half-brother's endless requests that she return to see to affairs at La Châtre. Chopin, too, was ready for a period of sustained composition and had earned enough money from his concert to justify a quiet summer. 'He has placed himself in a position to loaf away the whole summer', Sand quipped.[23] From this summer onwards there was to be a regular rhythm to their lives: summer at Nohant, winter in Paris. Maurice had travelled separately to Nohant with his uncle, while Solange remained for most of the summer at the boarding-school where Sand had sent her in a fruitless attempt to instil some discipline. She joined the rest of the family in August, a week or so after the departure of the Viardots, whose stay at Nohant during the first half of August was the brightest moment of a rather dreary summer.

Much later, in her autobiography, Sand wrote that Chopin always wanted to go to Nohant and then could never tolerate it. No doubt this was close to the mark. At least his creative life blossomed during these quiet periods in the country, and within days of their arrival in June 1841 he was able to send off to Fontana the manuscript of his Tarantella, Op. 43. At the same time he missed the city almost as soon as he arrived, as a whole stream of fussy, rather tiresome letters to Fontana attest. Already before the end of June he had sent his long suffering factotum a hundred francs requesting him to buy no end of trivia, including special soap, Swedish gloves, scent, and ivory head-scratchers, together with the most detailed instructions about where to buy them.

[22] See Charles Reid, *The Music Monster* (London, Melbourne, and New York, 1984), pp. 26–30.
[23] *GSC*, vol. 5, p. 290.

Chopin's dandyism, matched only by that of his friend Delacroix, is plain in letters of this kind.

Yet in the same letter he requested something of rather greater significance. 'You can also include Kastner [*Theorie abregée de Contrepoint et de la Fugue*]' and 'don't fail to send Cherubini's *Traité*'.[24] The reference here was to Cherubini's treatise on counterpoint, a standard textbook at the Paris Conservatoire. Chopin's request is of great interest, since it reveals his growing preoccupation with counterpoint in the later years. The compositional fruits of this preoccupation would be gathered in due course. But in the meantime Chopin lost no time in settling down to a sustained period of work, helped by the long-awaited arrival in August of a new Pleyel piano. During the summer he completed the Prelude, Op. 45, the Op. 48 Nocturnes, and two major works, the third Ballade, Op. 47 and the Fantasy, Op. 49.

Throughout the summer Sand and Chopin somehow succeeded in irritating each other over numerous petty issues, not least petty the difficulties caused by his Polish servant with the domestic staff at Nohant. There was also a rather more serious bone of contention. Chopin had recommended one of his ex-pupils, Marie de Rozières, as a teacher for Solange, and was annoyed to find her gaining more and more of Sand's confidence, especially since at the time she was conducting an affair with Antoni Wodziński. Undoubtedly the heart of the problem lay in Marie de Rozières's access to details of Chopin's unhappy and humiliating relationship with Maria Wodzińska, recently married in Poland, especially as Marie was becoming increasingly intimate with George Sand. He became positively paranoid about what she might be telling Sand, and when the latter postponed a proposed visit to Nohant by Wodziński and de Rozières, he interpreted this as further evidence of the gossip taking place behind his back. His pride wounded, Chopin behaved abominably, alternating between temper tantrums and adolescent sulks. 'The day before yesterday he went a whole day without speaking to anyone.'[25] At root the issue boiled down to authority. As Sand wrote to Marie de Rozières, 'I don't want him to imagine he is the master of the house. He would be all the more difficult in future, and even if he got his way over this he would be no less angry, since he really has no idea what he wants and what he doesn't want.'[26]

Despite the disagreements, Chopin and Sand concluded (after much characteristic indecision on Chopin's part) that on their return to Paris he should give up the apartment at rue Tronchet and move into the smaller of the two summer-houses on the rue Pigalle. He even returned to Paris for a few days at the end of September to supervise the preparation the house for his purposes. They all arrived in Paris on 2 November (complete with two dogs) and Chopin settled in to his new

[24] *KFC*, vol. 2, p. 21.   [25] *GSC*, vol. 5, p. 362.   [26] Ibid., vol. 5, p. 363.

accommodation. There was something of a 'reaction' on the part of some of his well-born pupils, who were reluctant to travel from their elegant districts to the rue Pigalle, and some loss of income as a result. But there were compensations, including the arrival in Paris of the eleven-year-old Karl Filtsch, by all accounts the most talented of Chopin's pupils until his premature and wasteful death from consumption a very few years later.

During the winter season Chopin made several appearances as a pianist, including a second court performance in December, when he played the newly composed third Ballade, and another highly acclaimed concert at Pleyel's on 21 February. On this occasion he was supported by Pauline Viardot (who had sung at the Conservatoire the previous evening with Chopin and Sand in attendance) and Auguste Franchomme, and he again performed the third Ballade along with a selection of nocturnes, études, and preludes. There are also accounts of salon performances, including improvisations, at the Hôtel Lambert and at George Sand's. For the most part, though, it was a quiet time socially. Aside from these few soirées, the record includes only some private dinners with Delacroix and a social evening at Sand's with Mickiewicz and his friend the Swiss poet Caroline Olivier.

This is not surprising, since by late February Chopin was ill again, as was his childhood friend Jan Matuszyński. It is often reported that Matuszyński moved into the rue Pigalle summer-houses in these, his dying, months. In fact he died not in the rue Pigalle but in his own apartment at 20 rue de Verneuil, where he had moved following his marriage. Both Sand and Chopin were present at his death on 20 April, and the blow to Chopin was all but paralysing, the more so as he had just received news of the death of his first teacher, Żywny. It is hard to resist the conclusion that he would have seen in Matuszyński's steady deterioration during these final stages of consumption an image of his own future. Certainly Sand was clear that the best thing to do after the funeral was to return to Nohant at the earliest possible moment.

They arrived at Nohant at midnight on 6 May, and Chopin was soon well enough to get down to serious composition, completing the Op. 50 Mazurkas. Sand remarked in a letter to Delacroix that 'Chopin has written two wonderful mazurkas which are worth more than forty novels and are more eloquent than the entire century's literature'.[27] He was also labouring on some of the great works of his later years, including the A flat major Polonaise, the F minor Ballade, and the E major Scherzo. In early June Delacroix himself arrived at Nohant for a month, the first of several such visits. Before arriving he had warned Sand not to take any trouble, remarking that 'the entertainment I like involves wandering along garden paths talking about music and spending every evening on

---

[27] *GSC*, vol. 5, p. 682.

a sofa listening to music when God takes over [Chopin's] divine fingers.'[28] And in a letter to Jean-Baptiste Pierret: 'From time to time you hear through the window opening onto the garden strains of Chopin's music, blending with the nightingales and the scent of the roses.'[29] Delacroix was clearly drawing closer to Chopin, and was genuinely fascinated by their talks about music. 'He is a man of great distinction, the most genuine artist I have ever met.'[30] Their discussions ranged widely, not excluding the relations between colour and music, though Chopin's ideal 'note bleue' remains an elusive concept.

There was other company that summer, including Marie de Rozières, who arrived in late July and looked after Solange while Chopin and Sand returned to Paris for a week to inspect their new apartments. The Viardots and Witwicki also visited, as did Bocage (briefly), though not Balzac, who was unable to make the journey as promised. The weeks passed in Nohant in much the usual way, with both Chopin and Sand immersed in creative work. Sand in particular was working furiously on her novel *Consuelo*, whose central character was modelled on Pauline García and whose descriptions of the intrigues and rivalries leading up to Consuelo's marriage were based directly on the Pauline–de Musset–Viardot triangle. As she wrote to Bocage, 'the hundred thousand debts I have to pay through exhausting work have put paid to entertainment or idleness'.[31] Despite this, Chopin instigated the idea of a small theatre in Nohant, and played his part in the preparations for it. It would later become something of an institution there, with elaborate improvised pantomimes produced by Maurice on a specially built stage.

As the summer drew to a close, Chopin and Sand became increasingly preoccupied with the need to find alternative accommodation in Paris. Fontana was not prevailed upon to undertake the initial search this time. He was to leave for America two years later in 1844, in circumstances which suggest that there had been a distinct cooling in his relations with Chopin in the early 1840s. In a letter to his sister, Fontana remarked that he had relied upon a particular friend to advance his career, but that he had been rewarded in the end by dishonesty and falsehood.[32] Certainly Chopin's relations with Fontana remain somewhat mysterious. Although the correspondence is extensive, it seems that Fontana was never really part of the Sand–Chopin circle, as Grzymała was, and that Chopin was prepared to use his services while offering little in return (it is not clear if any financial arrangement existed).

It may be worth recording briefly that Fontana returned to Paris in 1852, but that his subsequent years were far from happy. His career as a pianist-composer never really got off the ground, despite numerous

---

[28] *Correspondance générale d'Eugène Delacroix*, ed. André Joubin (Paris, 1936), 5 vols., vol. 2, pp. 104–5.
[29] Ibid., vol. 2, p. 108. [30] Ibid., vol. 2, p. 112. [31] *GSC*, vol. 6, p. 126.
[32] See Adam Zamoyski, *Chopin: A Biography*, p. 206.

attempts, and his lack of professional success was compounded by personal tragedy. His Cuban wife, Camille Dalcour, died in childbirth in 1855, just when he was preparing the posthumous edition of Chopin's piano works (Opp. 66–73) at the request of the Chopin family. The collection of songs, Op. 74, followed in 1859. After his wife's death he returned to America for a further extended period, and then to Paris again, where he engaged in a number of musical and literary pursuits. Fontana was friendly with Mickiewicz during this period, and the poet agreed to act as godfather to his son. In his final years he suffered from a debilitating and painful disease, and took his own life (having arranged for his son to go to his wife's family in New Orleans) in 1869.

Returning to 1842, it was left to the Marlianis to find suitable accommodation in Paris. Sand and Chopin made the journey from Nohant in late July to inspect their new apartments in the Square d'Orléans, part of an attractive urban 'mansion' gathered around a central courtyard. Sand took a suite of rooms on the second floor, while Chopin had a salon and bedroom on the ground floor. The Marlianis also had apartments in the same building, as did Kalkbrenner and Alkan. When they settled in the Square d'Orléans at the end of August, they quickly fell into a rather communal existence with the Marlianis, joining them for dinner most evenings. Sand made her domestic help available to Charlotte Marliani, and Chopin made a financial contribution. His usual practice was to stroll across to Sand's apartment in the early evening, and to return to his own about ten or eleven, just as Sand was settling down to work.

George Sand was not sorry to be relieved of domestic concerns during that winter, as she was working relentlessly on *Consuelo*, whose reflections on music, and especially on the limited value of ostentation and virtuosity, were clearly inspired by Chopin and directed against Liszt. Throughout Sand's writings of this period there are fascinating discussions of music, arguably affording us vicarious insights into Chopin's views in a way that his own letters seldom do. Sand was also engaged during those winter months on a publishing venture shared with Louis Viardot and her socialist mentor Pierre Leroux. This was the *Revue indépendante*, an ambitiously utopian enterprise which, among other things, aimed to publish writings by working-class poets and aspiring novelists. She threw herself into this with typical energy and commitment, cultivating many of the writers personally, and engaging in extensive correspondence with them. In the end the journal failed to make ends meet, and again it was entirely characteristic of Sand's indomitable spirit that a year after the failure of that journal she was engaged in founding another.

Chopin, meanwhile, found in the Square d'Orléans salon a highly congenial setting for his teaching. New pupils arrived, including the Russian Princess Elizabeth Sheremetieff, and this, combined with the income from his Pleyel concerts, gave him more financial security than usual. In November he performed, along with his star pupil Karl Filtsch, at a *grande soirée musicale* at the Rothschilds', and there were some other performances—at the Hôtel Lambert, for example, and possibly at an undistinguished matinée given by Fontana in March just before his departure for America. Composing was done in fits and starts. It had now become a painfully slow activity, as he became more and more self-critical, 'dominated and tormented' by an 'imperious craving for perfection'.[33] At any rate, it must have been during this winter in Paris that he put the finishing touches to three of the masterpieces of nineteenth-century piano music, his final contributions to three genres he had made very much his own, the polonaise, ballade, and scherzo. With these works Chopin reached a very particular stage in his creative development, both an end and a beginning. Following them he found composing more difficult than ever, and for the next two years his output slowed down to a trickle.

In general 1843 seems to have been a low point in Chopin's *vie intérieure*, despite the apparently satisfactory domestic arrangements of the Square d'Orléans. For much of the summer Sand and Chopin were at Nohant by themselves, apart from Pauline Viardot's baby daughter, whom they were looking after and to whom Chopin quickly became devoted. This particular summer in Nohant was to all appearances a melancholy one. Only when they were joined by Delacroix and the Viardots did the atmosphere lighten. It is hard to be sure of the inner dynamic of their relationship at this time, but it is clear at least that Chopin had little interest in Sand's literary and political projects, and seldom discussed them with her, and that he was increasingly paranoid about her friendships with like-minded thinkers. Their divergent interests, and the absence of physical relations between them, do indeed seem to argue for incompatibility on certain fundamental levels, and some of Sand's letters from the period are telling. 'I no longer want anything for myself . . . life seems neither exhilarating nor depressing . . . It is a good three years since I died . . .'[34] And in a later letter to her fellow editor of the *Revue indépendante*, 'Chopin's friendship towards me is in reality a possessive and jealous obsession'.[35] As usual she was pouring her current thinking into her fiction. *Consuelo* speaks of mutual responsibilities—of caring and comfort—as passion wanes, and it was on this level that Sand's devotion to Chopin functioned.

Yet somehow it did function, even though this period. While they were in Paris she was always concerned about her 'little Chopin'. If he remained in his rooms in the evening, she would ask the servants anxiously to report on what he was doing and what sort of mood he was

---

[33] Arthur Hedley's words, in 'Chopin: the Man', in *Frédéric Chopin: Profiles of the Man and the Musician*, ed. Alan Walker, p. 9.

[34] *GSC*, vol. 6, p. 219.

[35] Ibid., vol. 6, p. 915.

in. And when she stayed on in Nohant and he returned to Paris in October 1843 she asked Charlotte Marliani to look after him: 'Here he comes, my little Chopin. I entrust you take care of him despite himself.'[36] At the same time she asked Marie de Rozières (to whom Chopin became reconciled to the point of treating her as something as a confidante in later years) to find some excuse or other to keep an eye on him, and she gave exactly the same instructions to Grzymała and to Maurice. She was also concerned about his finances, asking Grzymała to find out if he had enough for everyday expenses, 'as he often doesn't realize that he has no money'.[37] He in turn wrote to her with nothing but solicitude: 'illness is a long way off, and the future is only happiness'.[38]

There is no need to have a monolithic view of these matters. Sand undoubtedly gave Chopin security, and her devotion to him remained, right to the end. But her primary instinct was to look after him, and it is far from certain that he was content with this. Grzymała's assessment has been quoted already in this chapter. Undoubtedly the idea that Sand 'poisoned his whole life' is a gross overstatement, and presents one side only of a complex question. But there may well have been some grounds for Grzymała's implication that at least in its later stages the inadequacies of the relationship acted as a kind of slow torture to Chopin.

No doubt this state of affairs contributed in large part to his low spirits during the winter of 1843–4. But it was not the only factor. His inability to recapture his earlier fluency in composition, to harness effectively on paper the ideas which still flowed readily enough at the piano, must also have played a role. Then there was his failing health. Sand had stayed behind in Nohant that October partly to deal with business affairs and partly to start up a new journal, *L'Éclair de l'Indre*, with Pierre Leroux and associates in La Châtre. When she returned to Paris at the end of November she was genuinely shocked at Chopin's appearance. Winter illness had become part of the annual cycle, but this particular winter took a more than usually cruel toll of his health. In February he was so poorly that a new doctor, Jean-Jacques Molin, was called in on several occasions, and Chopin took to using homeopathic remedies under his guidance. It is obvious that his deteriorating health must have left its mark on his general mental state, too. A permanent cough coupled with an allergic condition and serious breathing difficulties are hardly conducive to good temper.

There is some intriguing documentary insight into Chopin's state of mind during this critical winter, and indeed into his personality generally, though it needs to be interpreted with care. One of his new pupils in the 1843 season was Zofia Rosengardt, who had travelled from Warsaw specially to study with him. Her diary has been preserved, and in it she portrays a man of violently contrasted moods, cold and distant

---

[36] *GSC*, vol. 6, p. 253.   [37] Ibid., vol. 6, p. 251.   [38] *KFC*, vol. 2, p. 87.

on one day, raving 'like a spoilt child' on the next. 'There is a strange mixture in his character, vain and proud, loving luxury and yet disinterested and incapable of sacrificing the smallest part of his own will or caprice for all the luxury in the world. He is polite to excess and yet there is so much irony, so much spite inside it.'[39] Jean-Jacques Eigeldinger interprets this as a personality clash between Chopin and his highly-strung pupil, with her 'rather manic and disordered attitude'.[40] No doubt this accounted for much of it, especially since there is no suggestion of such behaviour with his other new pupils of the season, Camille O'Meara Dubois and Jane Stirling. Yet Adam Zamoyski adduces further evidence of his petulance, and goes on to suggest, astutely, that Chopin behaved in this way only with professional musicians and never with his society pupils, who remember him uniformly as charming and considerate.[41]

While he undoubtedly developed a capacity to conceal his feelings under a mask of civility and *politesse*, or to translate them into remarks of cutting sarcasm, Chopin's underlying bitterness could scarcely remain unnoticed by those in almost daily contact with him. Personality clash there may have been, but there is a ring of authenticity to Rosengardt's portrait of Chopin, the more so as the intolerance and anger, the sheer frustration, which emerge strongly from it accord well with some of the more exasperated comments in Sand's letters and autobiography. These traits were by no means confined to the winter of 1843, but they seemed to grow more pronounced at this time. It does seem likely that this was another period of questioning, when the apparent security of his new life was thrown again into doubt. And there was one other factor in all this. Since the return from Majorca, Chopin had been far from diligent in corresponding with his family back in Warsaw. It is almost as though the relationship with Sand had slowly drawn him away from his Polish roots, leading to a kind of suppression of one essential part of him. Whatever the truth of that, Warsaw forced itself upon him in the least happy of circumstances just as the winter drew to a close. News of his father's death at the age of seventy-five reached him on 12 May 1844, as he returned from the theatre with Sand. He had died a week earlier, on 3 May.

Throughout their association George Sand clearly regarded it as imperative to protect Chopin as far as possible from disturbing news. She wrote on numerous occasions of the ill effects produced by even relatively minor reports of adversity. The impact of his father's death, then, was predictable. Friends such as Franchomme and the Marlianis rallied round, but a week or so later he was still emotionally and physically shattered, and Sand decided, as always, that the solution was to make

[39] Zofia Rosengardt's diary and letters, Jagiellonian Library, Cracow, MSS. 9261–2.
[40] Jean-Jacques Eigeldinger, *Chopin: Pianist and Teacher*, p. 188.
[41] Adam Zamoyski, *Chopin: A Biography*, p. 214.

for Nohant at the earliest convenient time. Even in the quiet of Nohant, however, Chopin was in a sorry state, suffering from acute neuralgia on top of everything else, and generally uncommunicative. Following the death of his father he found himself reflecting more and more on childhood and on his early life in Warsaw. He even began to think again about his childhood faith, a development which, needless to say, Sand deplored. And it was while turning his mind towards these things that he received the brightest news from Poland, utterly transforming his morbid state of mind. His sister Ludwika and her husband announced their intention to visit France that summer.

Chopin had resisted telling his family in any detail of his relations with George Sand. In their letters to him they broach the subject only occasionally and usually obliquely, as though aware that it was somehow out of bounds. When Miłołaj Chopin died, Sand herself wrote to his widow, a characteristically warm letter of condolence and one which was a great comfort to Chopin's mother. She in turn wrote to Sand, expressing her gratitude to her for taking care of Chopin. With perhaps greater accuracy than she intended, she concluded her letter: 'Fryderyk's mother thanks you warmly and entrusts her dear son to your maternal care. I beg you to act as his guardian angel as you have been my own consoling angel.'[42] When they received news of Ludwika's plan, Sand wrote again to Warsaw, inviting the couple to use her apartment in Paris and insisting that they visit Nohant, and at the same time gently warning Ludwika that she would find Chopin much failed.

On 15 July Chopin met his sister and her husband in Paris, and for ten days he showed them the sights, entertained them, and introduced them to his friends. He returned to Nohant on 25 July and Ludwika and her husband travelled down some two weeks later. This was one of the happiest periods of Chopin's life; 'we are mad with happiness', was his own verdict, in a letter to Marie de Rozières.[43] Contrary to her expectations, George Sand was greatly drawn to Ludwika, whose intelligence and sensitivity were immediately apparent to her. The two women genuinely enjoyed each other's company. For his part Chopin was content to spend hours simply chatting to his sister, while her husband went walking and sketching with Maurice, and Sand worked at her books. The evenings were given over to music, readings, and conversation. At the end of the month Chopin accompanied the couple to Paris and remained with them until 3 September, when he again made the journey back to Nohant. In a letter to Ludwika at the end of September, Sand observed—and it was no less than the truth—that 'you are the best doctor he ever had'.[44]

Chopin made a further brief visit to Paris in late September to deal with publishers—in Fontana's absence he had to resort to this—and

[42] *KFC*, vol. 2, p. 93.   [43] Ibid., vol. 2, p. 104.   [44] Ibid., vol. 2, p. 110.

while there he spent some time with Delacroix ('We chatted for two and a half hours about music, painting and above all yourself', he wrote to Sand).[45] But other than that he remained at Nohant until the end of November, when he began the usual teaching round. It was in this season that he began teaching three of his most talented pupils, the Norwegian pianist and composer Thomas Tellefsen, whose G minor Piano Concerto is a close but rather impressive copy of Chopin; the pianist and composer Karl Mikuli, whose collected edition of Chopin still commands respect today; and Princess Marcelina Czartoryska, who reputedly preserved the Chopin performance style more authentically than any other pupil. Princess Czartoryska was to become an especially close friend in his later years, seeing something of Chopin during his seven months in Britain in 1848 and in his final year in Paris. He also saw a good deal of Franchomme during 1844, and the more so as George Sand had again stayed on at Nohant for the autumn. It was an unusually wintry December, but Chopin's spirits seem to have remained high, and he prepared for Sand's return in the middle of the month with enthusiasm, even down to buying material for a new black levantine for her and explaining carefully to the dressmaker how it should be made.

This was not to last. February 1845 brought further strains in the relationship between Sand and Chopin. His jealousies, never far from the surface, were apparently greater than ever during the spring, and he may have sensed, though he had no way of knowing, that for once they had some foundation. Sand had begun to associate with the young social activist Louis Blanc, and for a brief period they became lovers. The affair was fleeting and seems to have left little mark on her emotionally; certainly Sand's later collaborations with Louis Blanc remained on a more idealistic and seemingly more congenial plane. Nor was it ever revealed to Chopin, who liked Blanc and admired him. All the same, the encounter with Blanc may well have marked some kind of turning point for Sand. Physical love was clearly important to her. Yet she had been quite prepared to live without it for several years of her relationship with Chopin, provided she felt that they were attuned in other ways. As far as we know, the affair with Blanc was her first (and only) act of infidelity during her life with Chopin. That it was possible at all suggests that for Sand the relationship with Chopin was threatened fundamentally, that the spiritual bond between them was breaking.

This is not to claim that the breakdown of the relationship was in some sense inevitable. There is every indication that, although she regarded their union as unsatisfactory in many ways, and a burden to herself, she was committed to Chopin as a long-term partner. Her letters strongly suggest that she was not anxious for any change. On the surface, at least, all was as before, and Sand was content to settle into

---

[45] Ibid., vol. 2, p. 111.

a fairly stable middle age with Chopin. Later she would write to Grzymała that she would never lack the courage and perseverance to stay with him without complaining, and there is no real reason to doubt this. The separation was caused in the end by the larger dynamics of their relationship as a family. It was the intervention of the children, and Solange in particular, which destroyed it, rather than tensions between Chopin and Sand themselves. When they set off for Nohant in June 1845 tensions within the family circle were beginning to come to a head.

8

'The perfection of art . . .'

During his first summer in Nohant (1839), Chopin composed three of the Op. 41 Mazurkas, the second of the Two Nocturnes, Op. 37, and the F sharp major Impromptu, Op. 36. More ambitiously, he completed the B flat minor Sonata, Op. 35. In the tranquillity of George Sand's country home he brought to fruition a phase of creativity which had been initiated in Majorca with the second Ballade, the C minor Polonaise, Op. 40 No. 2, and the twenty-four Preludes, and had continued in Marseilles with the C sharp minor Scherzo. Nohant offered Chopin ideal working conditions, and it is telling that he composed, or at any rate completed, very little during the ensuing eighteen months in Paris. It is likely that other works were at various stages of gestation during this creative 'interregnum', but it was only on his return to Nohant the following summer (1841) that he felt able to embark on a further period of sustained composition. Among the major pieces completed during that second summer in Nohant are the F sharp minor Polonaise, Op. 44, the third Ballade, and the Fantasy, Op. 49.

'You know that I have four new mazurkas', Chopin wrote to Fontana in August 1839, 'one from Palma in E minor, three from here [Nohant].'[1] There are confusions over the ordering of this Op. 41 set. The first French edition (Troupenas) gave them in the sequence E minor, B major, A flat major, and C sharp minor, and this is the numbering followed in most recent editions. The first German edition, however, proposed C sharp minor, E minor, B major, and A flat major, following an engraver's manuscript by an unknown copyist but with corrections in Chopin's hand. This alternative numbering was also widely adopted by later editors. The former is the better option, framing the cycle with its two most interesting mazurkas (the B major and A flat major are relatively conventional in tone) and allowing the weighty and substantial C sharp minor to supply a suitably climactic finale.

While there are no clean dividing lines, it is not unrealistic to view Op. 41 as the last of the middle-period sets, more akin in general style and character to Opp. 30 and 33 than to Op. 50, which marked some-

---

[1] *KFC*, vol. 1, p. 353.

thing of a new departure. Like most of the Op. 30 and Op. 33 Mazurkas, Op. 41 No. 1—the so-called 'Palma Mazurka'—begins evasively with a harmony other than its E minor tonic. The antecedent of the opening eight-bar period reaches its tonic sequentially, approaching first IV and then I by way of their respective dominants. But it is the consequent (bars 5–8) which signals something new, beginning conventionally as a varied repetition of the antecedent, but replacing the diatonic cadence with a phrygian one. There is a self-consciously exploratory quality to this, since the final Mazurka in C sharp minor also adopts the phrygian, rather than the more usual lydian, mode. Here the sequence is reversed in that the opening eight-bar period is phrygian (the consequent is a har- monization of the unaccompanied antecedent) while the second period is diatonic, characteristically a sequential repetition in the relative major.

This final Mazurka is by far the most ambitious of the set, building to a powerful climax through the sequential working which precedes the final statement of its main theme at bar 119. It is also the most reward- ing in harmonic and rhythmic detail. I will single out the passage from bar 65, where a dominant preparation for the return of the opening theme in the tonic is deflected to the submediant major, in itself noth- ing unusual, but striking in context because of a delicious and deceptive play on the metric structure of the theme. And when the anticipated reprise of the theme in the tonic does finally arrive at bar 73 Chopin changes the modal setting yet again, this time sharpening the third degree of the scale to create an 'exotic' augmented second with the phry- gian second degree. Such modal reinterpretations of an unchanging theme would in due course become part of the currency of Russian com- posers and, later still, of Debussy.

One other feature of Op. 41 No. 4 is worth noting in the present con- text, though again it is far from uncommon in the mazurkas. The two main themes have contrasted generic characters, a *kujawiak* and a waltz respectively (compare the two themes of Op. 68 No. 4, the so-called 'last mazurka'). Moreover the waltz-like elements of the second theme, notably its moto perpetuo character, invite us to draw parallels with some of the actual waltzes, especially where such parallels are supported by tonal associations. This interpenetration of genres, and the intertex- tuality it promotes, is highly characteristic of Chopin and it is a promi- nent feature of the two other short pieces composed in Nohant in the summer of 1839.

The G major Nocturne, Op. 37 No. 2, for instance, is more barcarolle than nocturne. Or rather the distance between our expectation of the genre title and the reality of the piece is purposefully wide. It has rather explicit links with the later Barcarolle, Op. 60, not only through the familiar rocking accompaniment pattern established by the left hand but through the swaying 'Venetian' thirds and sixths which run though much of the melodic layer. But more pertinent are its associations with the second Ballade, composed a few months earlier in Majorca. Not only is the second theme (bar 28) closely related in character to the pastoral theme of the Ballade, but the treatment of the two themes in the closing bars is strikingly similar. It is important to see that such cross-references are not simply a matter of incidental affinity. They have a clear generic basis, and they draw attention to the fundamental expressive significance of those popular genres which infuse so much of Chopin's music. The point is strengthened when we consider the other Nocturne of Op. 37, the G minor, already complete when Chopin arrived at Nohant. Here funeral march and chorale stand side by side, rather as mazurka and chorale had done in that earlier G minor Nocturne, Op. 15 No. 3.

The F sharp major Impromptu, Op. 36 likewise draws on popular genres and establishes explicit intertextual links with other Chopin works. It is without doubt one of the most intriguing of all Chopin's works, generically somewhat distant from the other three Impromptus and an important harbinger of the stylistic changes of the 1840s. The opening section is an informal ostinato-variations on a six-bar ground, a technique which was rather novel to Chopin in 1839,[2] but which would play a role in the late style, notably in the Berceuse and the Barcarolle. The middle section is quite different in character from the lyrical melodies at the heart of the other three impromptus. Instead we have a march in the deliberately strident manner of contemporary French opera. There are parallels with march elements in some of the preludes, études, and nocturnes. But the most potent association is with a work yet to come, the Fantasy, Op. 49, whose extended introduction is a tempo di marcia (note especially bars 21 ff.) evoking the same referential code. In both cases the marches introduce a discreet counterpoint of styles such as must have characterized many improvisations of the day, and of course the world of contemporary opera was an important source of styles and materials for the improviser.

The reprise of Op. 36, beginning (oddly) in F major rather than F sharp major,[3] takes the form of a cumulative variation sequence comprising a model and two variations. This, too, is prophetic. There is an association with the fourth Ballade, where again the reprise gives way to a variation sequence and again the thematic and tonal returns are not synchronized. And the parallel extends further in that the second variation in both works grows out of an innocent *fioritura* planted in the theme itself. Even more striking, however, is the parallel with the first of the Op. 55 Nocturnes, also in F minor. Here, too, there is a circular melody, endlessly repeated, and again the reprise begins with an unadorned statement of the theme before Chopin introduces a triplet variation which is then transformed into the non-thematic figuration with which the piece ends. In all these ways the Impromptu seems to be

[2] Unless we include the early *Souvenir de Paganini* of questionable authenticity.
[3] See chapter 6, note 57.

testing out the ground for later techniques. The result is a piece whose novelty is arguably greater than its coherence. Chopin himself had doubts about it,[4] and, as I shall show in chapter 10, he had the greatest difficulty with its construction.

The major achievement of that summer was the B flat minor Sonata, Op. 35, the *sonate funèbre*, to use a programmatic title of which Chopin, for once, approved. Early essays apart, this was his first major approach to the four-movement sonata cycle, whose historical archetype was firmly welded to an Austro–German tradition. Indeed it has been plausibly suggested that he may have modelled the overall shape of the work (i.e. its sequence of movements, with the funeral march following rather than preceding the Scherzo) on Beethoven's Op. 26, a sonata which he frequently taught and played.[5] The *sonata funèbre* was a response to classical precedent, then. Yet that precedent also placed exceptional pressures on the work, generating expectations of its formal process and of its 'unity' (to use a much abused word in music criticism and analysis) which were bound to remain unfulfilled, since the composer was really trying to create something quite different—effectively a new kind of sonata, albeit based on the old. Essentially Chopin used the sonata design as a framework within which the achievements of his earlier music—the figurative patterns of the études and preludes, the cantilenas of the nocturnes, and even the periodicity of the dance pieces—might be drawn together. In the process he retained the basic formal design of the classical sonata, and especially the first movement's differentiation of exposition, development, and reprise, while allowing the respective functions of these sections to be reinterpreted and recontextualized.

In the exposition of the first movement we are presented with three principal ideas following the introductory 'motto' theme—a motivic-figurative first subject of restless urgency, a cantabile second subject of nocturne-like simplicity, and a motivic-chordal codetta of driving energy. What follows is in the nature of an extended response to these ideas—a development section which responds to the introduction and first subject and a reprise which responds to the second subject and codetta. It has been noted that a peculiarity of Elsner's 'Polish school' was an inverted reprise, where the second subject is recapitulated before the first. Something of this practice lingers not only in the Chopin ballades but here in the *sonate funèbre*, where there is no reprise of the first subject. This enables Chopin to conflate development and reprise and to preserve in their combined response to the exposition something of the essential functions of the two themes, where the second resolves the tensions generated by the first.

I have suggested already that a generic approach to this sonata is

---

[4] 'It is perhaps a stupid piece. I can't tell yet, as I have only just finished it.' Letter to Fontana, 8 October 1839. *KFC*, vol. 1, p. 365.

[5] See, *inter alia*, Wilhelm von Lenz, *The Great Piano Virtuosos of our Time*, pp. 47–8.

instructive. Just as a nocturne is embedded in the first movement, so another nocturne (or perhaps a berceuse?) is enclosed within the fiery, aggressive scherzo movement and yet another haunts the middle section of the funeral march. In neither of these later movements does the central song feel like an outgrowth of the flanking sections. It remains remote from them, strengthening our impression of a series of contrasted, relatively self-contained musical worlds juxtaposed rather than smoothly joined. A reductive view would go further and interpret the entire work in such terms, with the finale assuming the character of a baroque-like étude or prelude (compare Nos. 14 and 19 from Op. 28). This is no way diminishes the powerful affective quality of the sequence—a ritualistic funeral march followed by a disintegrative, harmonically elusive, and purposefully insubstantial finale. Indeed an acceptance of the separation involved here and elsewhere in the work (Schumann's 'unruly children under the same roof') helps us to an awareness of the real significance of the thematic associations which bind it together.

It is unnecessary to spell out these associations. They have been the subject of many studies, from Leichtentritt onwards,[6] and their closely integrative aspect will be apparent even to the most hardened sceptic of this approach to analysis, among whom I usually count myself.[7] But given that the insights are persuasive, it is worth reflecting for a moment on the order of composition of the four movements from this viewpoint. Chopin literally built his movements around an already composed funeral march, so that he allowed the undulating minor thirds of that movement to dictate the basic shapes which infuse the other movements, their motives, and, importantly, their figurations. In the finished work, of course, it is the introductory motto which crystallizes the intervallic content, expanding outwards in different but always related ways into the four sharply contrasted movements which follow.

The *sonate funèbre* was the culmination of a creative phase which had begun in the early 1830s. In the Paris 'interregnum' which followed its composition Chopin wrote only the Op. 42 Waltz, the song 'Dumka', a setting of Józef Żeleski, and the *Trois Nouvelles Etudes*, commissioned by Moscheles for the second volume of his (and Fétis's) *Méthode des méthodes*. The Waltz could easily sustain an extended commentary, but for now I will draw attention only to the cross-rhythm of its main theme, since this is also the technical problem addressed in the first and second of the Études, albeit in different, explicitly polyrhythmic, form. The first of these Études, in F minor, extends the kind of arc-shaped melodic figuration found in Op. 10 No. 2 and again in Op. 25 No. 2.

[6] Hugo Leichtentritt, *Analyse der Chopin'schen Klavierwerke*, 2 vols. (Berlin 1921–2), vol. 2, pp. 211–45.
[7] David Epstein observes that subsequent analysts distorted, by greatly simplifying, Schoenberg's notion of *Grundgestalt*. See *Beyond Orpheus: Studies in Musical Structure* (Cambridge, Mass., and London, 1979).

Indeed the parallels with the latter, also in F minor, are explicit, with the polyrhythms giving additional 'edge' to the two-part counterpoint of melodic and harmonic figurations—right and left hands respectively. The second Étude, in A flat major, enhances its polyrhythmic texture with harmonic progressions which are at times almost Lisztian in their mediant relations and augmented triads. And so to the D flat major, whose technically demanding accompanied duet texture, combining staccato and legato in the right hand, is achieved with no loss of elegance. There is a lightness of touch, a delicacy, which is quintessential Chopin.

Simon Finlow has remarked on the incongruity of the *Trois Nouvelles Études* when we consider them in their rightful context, volume 2 of the *Méthode des méthodes*, where they rub shoulders with elaborate and showy concert studies by Liszt, Thalberg, and Henselt.[8] Despite their discreet novelty, Chopin's Études are set apart from such contemporary trends, and their placing in this volume might almost be taken as emblematic of his larger, very specific standing in nineteenth-century piano music, his rootedness in the artistic canon of the past, his dislike of so much of the contemporary musical world and his powerful significance for the future. Or to put it another way, his debt to Bach, his indifference to Liszt, and his decisive influence on Debussy and other composers of the *fin de siècle*.[9]

The point is reinforced when we consider the last of his long line of études and preludes, the Prelude in C sharp minor, Op. 45, one of the fruits of that second summer in Nohant in 1841, and originally designed for inclusion in an album (*Keepsake des Pianistes*) to be published by Schlesinger. 'I have composed a Prelude in C sharp minor for Schlesinger; short, as he requested'.[10] Jean-Jacques Eigeldinger has stressed Chopin's debt to tradition by relating this haunting, evocative piece to a rather specific genre of modulating prelude, tracing antecedents in Bach, Reicha, Beethoven, Clementi, and Field.[11] Certainly it has little or no connection with the Preludes of Op. 28, though it does confirm some of the title's connotations with improvisation through the harmonic 'wandering' of its single motive and through its closing cadenza. In other ways the piece remains somewhat singular in Chopin's output, even (*pace* Eigeldinger) *sui generis*, and certainly unrelated to contemporary virtuosity. In a curious way its individual moments resonate constantly with a wider repertory, recalling Chopin's own *Lento con gran espressione*, hinting at the Beethoven of Op. 27 No. 2, and even

[8] Simon Finlow, 'The Twenty-seven Études and their Antecedents', in *The Cambridge Companion to Chopin*, pp. 50–77.

[9] For an elaboration of this point, see Jean-Jacques Eigeldinger, 'Chopin's Aesthetic Perspective', in *Chopin Studies 2* (Cambridge, 1994), pp. 102–39.

[10] *KFC*, vol. 2, p. 37.

[11] Jean-Jacques Eigeldinger, 'Twenty-four Preludes op. 28: Genre, Structure, Significance', in *Chopin Studies* (Cambridge, 1988), pp. 167–94.

affording intriguing and unmistakable pre-echoes of Mahler (the famous Adagietto of the Fifth Symphony) in its long-held appoggiaturas and in some of its harmonic progressions.

Op. 45 stands in sharp contrast to two bravura pieces also composed in the early summer of 1841, the Tarantella, Op. 43 and the *Allegro de concert*, Op. 46. It seems likely that the Tarentella was inspired by Rossini, since, in a letter to Fontana, Chopin asked his factotum to visit Schlesinger or Troupenas and look out a Tarantella by Rossini (in A) so that he could conform to Rossini's time signature (6/8 or 12/8). The piece remains one of Chopin's least inspired, and it is a little difficult to believe that Schumann was thinking of the same Tarantella when he wrote of the 'wildness of [Chopin's] imagination', of 'the madly whirling dancers before us, until our own senses seem to reel'.[12] The *Allegro de concert*, on the other hand, remains a fascinating and teasing work in the Chopin canon, not least because of the perfectly reasonable, but entirely undocumented, speculation by commentators that it may have its origins in either a Concerto for Two Pianos or a third Piano Concerto dating from the Vienna and early Paris years.

That it is designed as a concerto movement for solo piano, and one whose virtuosity exceeds almost anything else in Chopin, is beyond doubt. Chopin himself referred to it as 'my concerto',[13] and there is an obvious stylization of ritornello–concertino contrasts. But to move from this to the assumption that it is an arrangement of an earlier concerto is perhaps a step too far.[14] Given his practice, shared with other pianist-composers, of playing concerto movements as solos, it is entirely plausible that he would have composed such a movement. There were distinguished precedents, and there would be distinguished successors. Not the least puzzling aspect of the piece is the very special regard in which Chopin apparently held it, and the suggestion that he may have associated it in some way with the Polish cause. In a letter to Aleksander Hoffman in Silesia, in which he enclosed Op. 46, he remarked that it was the work he would choose to play first in an independent Poland.[15]

A more appropriate choice, we might feel, would have been the F sharp minor Polonaise, Op. 44, since it draws together the two most famous Polish national dances, enclosing a mazurka within a polonaise. And here, along with the third Ballade and Op. 49 Fantasy, all completed in Nohant in the summer of 1841, we enter the more exploratory world of Chopin's later music. 'It is a sort of Fantasy in the form of a Polonaise and I shall call it a Polonaise.'[16] With this remark Chopin

[12] Robert Schumann, *Gesammelte Schriften über Musik und Musiker*, vol. 4, p. 270.

[13] Letter to Fontana, 9 October, 1841. *KFC*, vol. 2, p. 42.

[14] John Rink is currently investigating Op. 46 in connection with a forthcoming book on the Chopin concertos, and may well throw light on these matters.

[15] See Franciszek German, 'Chopin Relics in Upper Silesia', in *Chopin in Silesia*, pp. 16–18.

[16] Letter to Pietro Mechetti, 23 August, 1841. *KFC*, vol. 2, p. 32.

indicated a generic expansion which the piece itself arguably justifies only in terms of its length and the 'programmatic' incorporation of a mazurka in the trio. There is little here of the remarkable formal complexity of the later Polonaise-fantasy, which does indeed merit the description 'Fantasy in the form of a Polonaise'. All the same, the epic scale of the piece and its synthesis of the two national dances separate it decisively from the Op. 26 and Op. 40 Polonaises, giving it something of the quality of a dance poem. At the very least Chopin's remark can be taken as a signal of things to come.

In this work, as in the later A flat major Polonaise, Chopin achieved an epic quality by a kind of essentialism, an elemental reduction of the musical materials to dance archetypes, rhythmic and harmonic, which are given a hard-edged, aggressive presentation clearly designed to draw the maximum power and sonority from the instrument. Huneker referred, dramatically enough, to 'booming cannons and reverberating overtones'.[17] The opening Lisztian octaves announce the urgency of the matter, and the insistent varied repetitions which follow—alternations of two separate themes—reinforce the message, especially when the left-hand takes over the main theme in its deepest register. When we reach the 'trio' in the relative major Chopin strips away yet more 'inessentials' to reveal the bare skeleton of an endlessly repeated rhythmic motive followed by V–I affirmations explicitly related to the main theme. The calculated rigidity of this material is overwhelmingly powerful in effect and it adds special poignancy to the gentle, dream-like mazurka which follows, *doppio movimento*. The clash of genres here rather invites the sort of programmatic interpretation enjoyed by Huneker. 'It is profoundly ironical—what else means the introduction of that lovely Mazurka, "a flower between two abysses"? . . . No "sabre dance" this, but a confession from the dark depths of a self-tortured soul'.[18] Liszt, too, picked up on the irony, remarking that the mazurka, 'far from effacing the memory of the deep grief which has gone before, serves by the bitter irony of contrast to augment our painful emotions'.[19]

The Polonaise was part of a major trilogy of extended works composed in 1841. On 18 October Chopin wrote to Fontana from Nohant that he would receive the Ballade (Op. 47) and the Fantasia (Op. 49) towards the end of the week: 'I cannot give them enough polish.'[20] Both works raise the issue of compositional norms, deviating in intriguing ways from the conventions of sonata form, yet at the same time transparently dependent on those conventions for much of their essential meaning. In the third Ballade there is a conventional opposition of primary and secondary themes and of primary and secondary keys,

[17] James Huneker, *Chopin: the Man and his Music* (New York, 1966; original edn. 1900), p. 187.
[18] Ibid., p. 187.   [19] Franz Liszt, *F. Chopin*, p. 55.
[20] *KFC*, vol. 2, p. 42.

presented moreover in a formal context which preserves the functions of exposition, development, and reprise. Yet the inner dynamic which motivates the succession of events is far from orthodox. In relation to the tonal scheme of a sonata-form archetype the first theme closes on I rather than V, the second theme settles in VI rather than V, and the middle section opens with an extended section in I rather than a modulating section. Formally, too, functions are recontextualized. The end of the exposition gives way to a stable episode rather than a development, the 'real' development (in which the opening phrases of the two main themes are fused into a single melodic shape) appears in the course of, rather than before, the reprise, and the work ends with an entirely unexpected return of the waltz-like third theme.[21]

It is easy to argue that such departures from a sonata-form schema are so radical that it is no longer helpful to invoke the schema. Yet this is to ignore the true value of compositional norms as one pole of a vital creative dialectic between the collective and the unique, the schema and the deviation. Sonata form represents the 'ideal type' against which the unique statements of the third Ballade have been counterpointed. This was no less true of the first two Ballades, and I shall show later (pp. 236–40) that the very particular deviations from classical sonata form in these pieces, and in the fourth Ballade, amount to the tentative establishment of a new generic norm. The nature of the themes in Op. 47 supports such a interpretation by establishing clear associations with the earlier Ballades; the barcarolle-like main themes are reminiscent of the first theme of Op. 38, while the pivotal quick waltz reminds us of the very similar gesture of the mid-point of Op. 23. Even the all-important two-note motive at the end of the first phrase of the work (bar 2) echoes the same motive—and at the same point in the phrase—in the G minor Ballade (bars 9–10). There are indeed the clearest formal parallels between these two works, not least in the sequence and transformation of themes in the reprise.

Such links with the past were forged without prejudice to the more forward-looking aspects of the third Ballade. The deceptively innocent tone of the first theme, almost Schubertian in its gentle lyricism, conceals contrapuntal intricacies which, although far from new in Chopin, were about to grow in importance in his music. Through the resources of invertible counterpoint the theme is 'distributed' so that bass and treble interchange roles in a question-and-answer sequence, supported by elegantly shaped countermelodic strands. Such intricacies are there, too, in the second theme, which is related to the first not only through intervallic inversion and a common iambic rhythm, but also through its similar internal organization as a closed paragraph, 'contained' by its clearly defined tonal and thematic frame. In this second theme Chopin gives the

---

[21] I have examined this in closer detail in *Chopin: The Four Ballades*, pp. 56–62.

iambic rhythm a distinctive profile by harmonizing the weak rather than the strong beat, but behind the facile lilt of the melody the part movement is discreetly unorthodox, permitting chords built of no less than five adjacent scale notes. The hidden complexities of these two themes hint at things to come. Above all, they make possible and justify the remarkable textural expansion of both themes in the later stages of the work, when Chopin achieved an intensity of expression with few precedents in his earlier music.

The transformation of themes through textural amplification is by no means unique to the third Ballade. Indeed the 'fully scored' restatement of the first theme is echoed rather clearly in the reprise of the first of the Two Nocturnes, Op. 48, composed around the same time in Nohant. Widely regarded by commentators as among the most imposing and dramatic of the series,[22] and certainly one of the most expansive, this C minor Nocturne allows its reprise to enlarge to powerfully climactic effect one of Chopin's most expressive and poetic ornamental melodies, reducing some of its ornamental filigree in the process. This melody stands as a perfect example of the careful balance between surface asymmetries and background symmetries which characterizes Chopin's music at its best. The background structure is a classical three-part song form, where the eight-bar phrases have an ABA pattern, respectively a period (4-bar antecedent; 4-bar consequent), a sentence (2-bar motive; 2-bar varied repetition; 4-bar liquidation) and a free extension of the opening period.

Against this classically constructed background, strongly reinforced by harmony, the melody twists and turns with an inspired flexibility of rhythm and contour, stabilizing from time to time to allow an illusion of repose, only to indulge once again in flights of ornamental fancy. The momentum is maintained above all by a careful avoidance of congruence in harmonic, melodic, and rhythmic closures.[23] Only at the very end of the entire masterly paragraph are we allowed a completion of all tendencies, signalling the approach of the contrasted middle section. And at that point we encounter again the collision of genres so characteristic of Chopin, and especially the Chopin of this period. The delicately expressive bel canto of the opening section gives way to a heroic march in the tonic major, an unmistakable procession which builds steadily in dynamic level and textural complexity until it yields to the triumphant reprise of the opening theme. Once more the use of a popular genre effectively creates a programmatic dimension, albeit one without specific extra-musical designates.

[22] Karasowski described it as 'most imposing', and Huneker as 'the noblest nocturne of them all'. See Moritz Karasowski, *Frederic Chopin: His Life and Letters*, tr. Emily Hill (London, 1938; original German edn. 1877), p. 404, and Huneker, *Chopin: the Man and his Music*, p. 147.

[23] See Jim Samson, *The Music of Chopin*, pp. 89–92 for a more detailed exposition of this point.

The Op. 49 Fantasy, one of the great works of Chopin's full maturity, carries this further, responding to the connotations of the genre title with a wide range of contrasted materials of a kind beloved of the improviser—slow (funeral) march, operative (grand) march, prelude or recitative, *motivische Arbeit*, and chorale—and binding them together with a strongly directional tonal structure and a clear reference to conventional formal archetypes. In this sense Chopin's use of the genre title has more in common with eighteenth-century classical models than with the fantasies of the post-classical brilliant style. If the spirit of improvisation underlies this work, it is an improvisation in which apparent freedoms and irregularities are couched within a firm, coherent structure. As in the third Ballade, the formal reference point is undoubtedly sonata form, and again Chopin's dialogue with that background is rather free.

Characteristically a 'fantasy' would begin with a slow, improvisatory introduction, and Chopin adopts this convention in Op. 49, as also in his later Polonaise-fantasy. Two extended sections, with clear generic associations, are presented. The opening march is itself bipartite, an opening F minor paragraph suggestive of a funeral march and a later F major paragraph akin rather to the choruses of French Grand Opera. The second section functions as a transition to the first subject, and it is couched in the preluding arpeggiations typical of contemporary improvisation. Through this extended introduction, Chopin establishes the credentials of the piece as a 'fantasy'.

Following it he launches into a sonata-form exposition, with the first subject in F minor/A flat major, the second subject in C minor/E flat major and a new, march-like codetta theme affirming E flat major. While the sonata-form background is unambiguous, the proportions of this exposition—a lengthy introduction, a brief presentation of the main tonal and thematic groups, and a new and again lengthy codetta theme—underline that the work is a 'fantasy' rather than a 'sonata'. The reprise (bar 235) is in the subdominant, allowing Chopin to bring the second subject into the tonic while preserving the tonal relationships of the exposition, thus:

Exposition   Reprise
f – A♭ – c – E♭   b♭ – D♭ – f – A♭

Since the development section highlights G flat major, it will be clear that the surface tonal organization is a chain of ascending thirds, to which the B major of the chorale-like 'slow movement' (a characteristic feature of many early nineteenth-century fantasies, and found again in the Polonaise-fantasy) forms an inspired parenthesis, thus:

f – A♭ – c – E♭ – G♭ – [B] – b♭ – D♭ – f – A♭

It has indeed been plausibly suggested that this tonal scheme is already present in microcosm in the introduction to the work, not just in the

F minor/A flat major of the march but even more in the cycle of thirds underlying the subsequent prelude (bar 43).[24]

The logical, even schematic, organization of surface tonal events outlined here is complemented by a much more compelling background progression to A flat major which has been charted by Carl Schachter in an impressive Schenkerian analysis of the Fantasy.[25] Here the underlying tonal structure is identified as a progression from F minor (the opening march and prelude) through E flat major (the goal of the exposition, or 'first cycle', as Schachter calls it, and also the controlling tonality for the development section or 'second cycle', including the 'slow movement') to A flat major (the goal of the reprise or 'third cycle', affirmed by the coda). This interpretation goes far beyond the identification of these regions as primary. It demonstrates through voice leading not only that a wealth of surface harmonic detail has been accommodated to the larger progression, but also that the final A flat major is not simply the resolution of a single section (the reprise) but of the entire work.

All these pieces (Opp. 43–9) were completed during the summer months of 1841. In general Chopin composed more slowly during these later years, especially while in Paris, but the following summer in Nohant, part of it spent in the company of Delacroix, was again productive. He worked mainly on Opp. 50–5, though some of these pieces were not given a final polish until the winter months of 1842–3. Sandwiched between the Three Mazurkas, Op. 50 (Sand's 'wonderful mazurkas . . . worth more than forty novels') and the Two Nocturnes, Op. 55 lie Chopin's last contributions to three genres he made very much his own, the ballade, polonaise, and scherzo, together with the last of his four Impromptus. His new-found interest in counterpoint is conspicuous in several of these pieces. In rather different ways it enriches the textures of the mazurkas and the nocturnes, genres which seem on the face of it a long way from the spirit of Fux. Strict imitative writing invades the third, and most innovatory of the Op. 50 Mazurkas, in C sharp minor, for instance. Its principal theme is an imitative point, and this alternates with more obviously folk-based materials in an impressively extended structure, really a kind of dance poem or rhapsody. The Mazurka proceeds initially as an extended ternary design, but Chopin frustrates our expectation of the reprise by building the opening motive into an impassioned development section, marked by almost Wagnerian sequences within an enharmonic continuum (compare the last of the Op. 41 cycle), before the entire texture fragments again into the imitative strands of the opening bars.

[24] See Lew Mazel, 'Fantazja F-Moll Chopina', in *Studia Chopinowskie* (Cracow, 1965), pp. 17–218.
[25] Carl Schachter, 'Chopin's Fantasy op. 49: the Two-key Scheme', in *Chopin Studies* (Cambridge, 1988), pp. 221–53.

Counterpoint of a different kind invades the second of the Op. 55 Nocturnes in E flat major. Here Chopin avoids the strict imitation of Op. 50 No. 3, promoting instead a remarkable independence of part movement, and allowing an unorthodox level of dissonance in the interests of linear values. Chopin achieves maximum differentiation of melody and accompaniment in this nocturne, carefully placing the non-chordal notes to sustain harmonic tension and in the process lending to the accompaniment layer a distinctive melodic quality. Much of the piece employs an accompanied duet texture, proceeding in a kind of 'dissonant counterpoint' in which the three lines intertwine and overlap with remarkable ingenuity, their differentiation resulting in an unusual degree of rhythmic complexity. It is worth pausing for a moment to reflect on these two pieces, to consider just how far they have travelled in complexity and profundity not only from generic origins in the functional dance and the vocal transcription respectively, but from pre-Chopin mazurkas and nocturnes and, for that matter, from his own early essays in the genres.

The major extended works of 1842—Ballade, Polonaise, and Scherzo—are seminal, culminating works in Chopin's development, triumphantly confirming the essential elements of these genres, as he understood and (re)defined them. The fourth Ballade is by common consent one of Chopin's masterpieces, and one of the masterpieces of nineteenth-century piano music in general. Few of his extended compositions can match it in formal sophistication and in the powerful goal-directed sweep of its musical ideas. Here Chopin brought to summation the narrative techniques associated above all with the ballades, involving an interplay of strongly characterized generic themes, a transformation of conventional formal successions and a powerful drama of large-scale tonal relationships.[26] The compelling strength of the music will not be explained by any straightforward formal synopsis, but some observations may at least point us in the right direction.

Much of the richness and complexity of the work derives from its unique blend of sonata form and variations. Already there are hints of this in the first theme, a multi-sectional paragraph whose tonal and thematic repetitions signal the 'static' design of a variation set. This implication is more fully realized in the reprise, where the theme is presented as a pair of variations, canonic-fugal and cantabile-decorative respectively. It is a powerfully expressive juxtaposition—on one level a synthesis of the contrasted worlds of Bach and Italian bel canto, yet on another an entirely characteristic succession of contemporary improvisation; 'a stylized improvisation' was Cortot's description of the work. In this sense Chopin's interest in counterpoint in these later years takes on yet another dimension: not only a return to ancient principles of

[26] See the section 'Narratives' in Jim Samson, *Chopin: The Four Ballades*, pp. 81–7.

construction, but a development and transcendence of a standard technique of contemporary improvisation.

The canonic variation in the reprise is not an isolated event in the fourth Ballade. It fulfils earlier contrapuntal tendencies in the exposition, notably the episode at bar 37 and the variation at bar 58, and in the middle section (by no means a conventional development section), especially that subtle interweaving of two strands of the first theme which immediately precedes the return of the introduction. This entire passage is a masterly transition, in the true sense of a much abused term. The introduction creeps in unobtrusively on the remote harmony of A major, preparing the D minor of the reprise, and this in turn reverts to the tonic by exploiting the minor third sequence built into the first theme. Only some way into the process of transition are we made aware that the introduction has insinuated itself into the foreground of the musical argument, a gesture greatly facilitated by the repeated notes it shares with the first theme.

As in the first Ballade, the first theme of the fourth has the generic character of a slow waltz, and the second that of a barcarolle (blended in Op. 52 with a chorale). And again as in Op. 23, the second theme is transformed in the reprise into a powerfully expansive, 'enlarged' restatement. Tonality plays the major role in this climactic transformation of the second theme. In the exposition it had appeared in the subdominant major (B flat). Here in the reprise it is given in the submediant (D flat), though the stability of this region is deliberately in question. But the true goal, as in all the ballades, is the structural dominant which is tactically delayed until the approach to the final bravura closing section, itself a white heat of virtuosity. The arrival of this structural dominant, and its prolongation through a series of *pianissimo* chords, closely recalls the similar stage of Hummel's Op. 18 Fantasy.[27] It is a tempting and useful parallel, but in the end it serves only to underline just what an architectural marvel the fourth Ballade really is. It represents the summation of that unique transformation of sonata form which we find in all four ballades. The main point is that sonata-based formal and tonal functions are here reinterpreted in the light of a particular dramatic and expressive aim, a 'plot archetype',[28] where a gradually rising intensity curve culminates in an end-weighted reprise and 'coda', apotheosis rather than synthesis.

Nineteenth- and early twentieth-century critics had difficulties with the fourth Ballade, widely regarding it as inaccessible.[29] Yet today it is

[27] See the section 'Narratives' in Jim Samson, *Chopin: The Four Ballades*, p. 18.
[28] The term is Anthony Newcomb's. See 'Once More Between Absolute Music and Programme Music', in *19th-Century Music* (1984), vol. 7, pp. 233–50 and 'Schumann and Late Eighteenth-Century Narrative Strategies', in *19th-Century Music* (1987), vol. 11, pp. 164–74.
[29] See Karasowski, *Frederic Chopin: His Life and Letters*, p. 402.

recognized as the mightiest of the four, bringing the narrative manner of the genre to its culmination. In a similar way the Polonaise in A flat major, Op. 53 and the fourth Scherzo represent culminating statements for their respective genres. In the case of the Polonaise Chopin seems to have followed, but greatly to have enlarged and intensified, the formal and expressive model established by its predecessor in F sharp minor. Again there is a tension-building 'announcement', sixteen rather than eight bars in length. And nowhere in Chopin is the preparatory tension so great, the propulsion so electric, as in this introduction. The music is driven by harmony and rhythm, and by a subtle disturbance of its sequence of two-bar units, until the anticipative energy is resolved to monumental effect by the main polonaise theme in the tonic. The theme itself underlines that essentialism which played such a prominent part in Op. 44 and which Chopin clearly viewed as central to the heroic *Affekt* of the genre. It is a series of variants on a standard 6/4–5/3 formula, supported by V–I progressions in the bass, all presented in the fullest 'orchestral' sonority and supported by the most forceful of ornamental devices.

The formal sequence which follows this main theme once more replicates many of the gestures of Op. 44. Again the theme yields briefly to a sostenuto subsidiary theme. And again the 'trio' presents a two-part sequence in which a ruthlessly reductive ostinato phrase (repeated no less than forty-two times) gives way to a more wistful, gentler episode, a brief respite from the surrounding aggression. Finally, in the closing bars of the work the ostinato from the trio is briefly recalled, just as it was (elliptically) in Op. 44. The two pieces, then, are closely related, and taken together they represent one of the strongest statements of nineteenth-century musical nationalism. They epitomize one aspect of Chopin's commitment to his homeland, a kind of historical evocation of Grand Poland which is at the same time suggestive of a *rappel à la guerre*. Such interpretations are not fanciful. The resonance of the genre title, coupled with the rather explicit referential codes established by the music, inevitably suggested as much to Chopin's listeners. There is scarcely a nineteenth-century account of these works which eschews the imagery of patriotism, nationalism, and the call to arms.

The fourth Scherzo, one of Chopin's most remarkable and underrated compositions, is as calm, benign, and untroubled as the Polonaise is fierce and heroic. And in this respect, at least, it departs from the tradition of the first three Scherzos, if anything recapturing some of the original connotations of the genre title. Karasowski refers to its 'kindlier face'.[30] Yet in other, more fundamental ways the E major Scherzo does indeed build upon that earlier Chopin tradition, and triumphantly so. In particular it is concerned with balance and proportion, extending to an

[30] Ibid., p. 403.

221

almost Schubertian timescale a classical juxtaposition of stable eight-bar periods and sentences, and achieving in the process something akin to an 'architecture' of pulses, an inflation to the larger formal process of the joyful springing measures, and at the same time the poise and balance, of a dance. There is little here of the powerful goal-directed momentum of the fourth Ballade, though the central sections of the two outer flanks introduce in a limited way some tension-building, developmental material. Rather, Chopin lays out spacious, relatively self-contained paragraphs, maintaining interest over this lengthy time span (the work has more than twice the dimensions of the first Scherzo) through a delicate juxtaposition of contrasts.

In this latter point he again took up the thread of his earlier Scherzos, all of which in their different ways built the central formal contrast of the traditional scherzo right into their detailed substance, and employed the resources of texture and 'colour' to do so. Here in the E major, Chopin relied on textural contrast to a degree that almost looked to the so-called 'impressionist' composers of the early twentieth century. The main theme, for instance, is really a chain of contrasted elements separated by silence or sustained chords, where the contrasts—in a context of uniform dynamics—are largely textural in character, determined by voicing, register, contour, and articulation as much as by harmony and melody. The effect of such differentiation is the more striking in that it has little to do with drama and opposition, and everything to do with the weighting and placing of essential formal components.

Following these great works, synthetic in the best sense, Chopin's productivity markedly declined. The next three years brought just three significant opuses, a set of Mazurkas (Op. 56) and two utterly contrasted pieces, the Berceuse, Op. 57, and the B minor Sonata, Op. 58. All are works of the highest importance, chiselled slowly and painstakingly from a rich but increasingly recalcitrant vein of inspiration. The Mazurkas are among the most reflective, private and (at times) arcane of the series, teasing the simple dance rhythms with intricate harmonic and contrapuntal puzzles, yet at the same time maintaining contact with the earlier mazurkas through a background conformity of gesture. The alternating sections of No. 1 in B major are characteristic. The opening eight-bar phrase is of a construction commonly found in the mazurkas, and seldom elsewhere—a sentence-like sequential repetition of a two-bar motive which continues beyond its expected four bars and is pulled back, 'lifted', only at the end of the phrase. The gesture is familiar, but the tonality is evasive, as yet avoiding the tonic, and the subsequent interaction of phrase structure, motive, and harmony (bars 9–22) is both subtle and unusual. Likewise the waltz-like moto perpetuo arcs of melody in the second section, common to many of the mazurkas, are given a distinctive ambience by their symmetrical tonal placing a third above (bar 24) and a third below (bar 82) the tonic.

The later stages of the piece are in a similar way both conformant and innovatory. It is in the elaboration of the first theme and in the coda (from bar 143 onwards) that Chopin's most individual harmonic and contrapuntal writing occurs, accentuating tendencies of the earlier mazurkas, but at the same time providing a sophisticated solution to the formal problem of achieving satisfactory closure in a repetitive, essentially stanzaic structure. The piece as a whole is entirely symptomatic of Chopin's capacity to write to certain self-created formulae without ever repeating himself. And its two companions reinforce the point. The second is an *oberek*, its characteristic bourdons and lydian fourths giving way to a singular middle section whose left-hand melody, disturbing the general vivacity of mood, is allowed briefly to blossom into discreet canonic treatments. The third is the most complex, in the irregular phrasing of some of its episodes, in its almost Wagnerian enharmony, and in the contrapuntal intricacies of its coda. In these pieces the genre associations serve only to point up the introspective quality of the music, its meditative, melancholy aspect, which somehow links the composer's private thoughts with the nation's tragedy. Simply by investing the modest dance piece with such weight and sophistication Chopin again spoke of nationalism, albeit in an intimate tone remote from the heroic perorations of the later polonaises.

Chopin's original title for the Berceuse was 'Variantes' and this describes well its final form, a set of sixteen short variations on an ostinato ground. Here the tentative steps taken in the F sharp Impromptu come to glorious fruition.[31] The Berceuse is indeed a work of rarest originality in which ornamental filigree takes on a quite new significance within Chopin's music, precisely because its curve of complexity remains essentially divorced from harmonic progression (a repeating cycle) and dynamic shape (a stable level). It is even divorced from melody, since the identity of Chopin's little four-bar phrase quickly succumbs to the hypnotic influence of the finely wrought passage-work. In this sense Chopin's *variantes* are far from orthodox. They are constructed as a single impulse of departure and return, but one generated almost entirely by ornamental figuration. The underlying harmony remains after all a uniform oscillation of tonic and dominant until the subdominant at bar 55 enables a final tonicization. In a quite literal sense, then, this music is shaped by texture and sonority.

The other major work of 1844 was the B minor Sonata. Indeed it was completed a very few months after the Berceuse, and in the reprise of the main theme of the slow movement there are unmistakable echoes of the familiar rocking accompaniment figure. This significantly changes the character of a theme whose earlier presentation had something of the measured stately tread, the classical poise, of a late Beethoven or late

[31] There are hints of this ostinato variation technique in some of the early works, notably in Op. 13, and (if it is authentic) the *Souvenir de Paganini*.

223

Schubert adagio. And this raises a larger point. In very general stylistic terms this sonata takes a step closer to the German tradition than its predecessor, the *sonate funèbre*, frequently suggesting reference points in German early-romantic, and even on occasion late-romantic, music. Brahms is foreshadowed in the warm, sonorous harmonies of the middle section of the Scherzo, for instance, though the deceptively simple textures here conceal contrapuntal felicities of a kind we come to expect of the later works.

The sequence of these inner movements, with the Scherzo preceding the slow movement, follows that of the B flat minor Sonata. And so, too, does the formal process of the first movement, where the principal group is again omitted from the reprise. But in other respects the B minor is a very different order of sonata. The outer movements point up the contrast. There could be nothing further from the elliptical, understated Finale of Op. 35 than the grandiloquent sonata rondo, with which the B minor races, or rather gallops, to its bravura coda. Particularities aside, this is at least a more conventional way to end a sonata. And the first movement, too, is closer to classical prototypes in one important respect. Here Chopin seems to have found a way to accommodate the close knit motivic argument which all but stifled his natural lyricism in that first attempt at a piano sonata in Warsaw. It is unnecessary to argue for clumsy links between the first and second thematic groups.[32] Rather we might note the process of continuous development and transformation of motives which informs this movement (as close as Chopin comes to Schoenberg's 'developing variation'), together with its close integration of melody and accompaniment and its intricate contrapuntal working. Here, in the first movement of Op. 58, Chopin tackled the historical archetype of the most celebrated and prestigious of the classical forms on its own terms, so to speak, and emerged victorious.

Chopin's genres

The discussion of these major works of Chopin's maturity has persistently highlighted their allusion to popular genres. The role of such generic referents in classical and post-classical music has been undervalued in the past, despite several major studies which bring it into prominence.[33] Leonard Ratner refers to 'topics' to identify styles whose distinctiveness was well recognized by late eighteenth- and early nineteenth-century theorists, and Kofi Agawu further draws upon these designates in his semiological study of dichotomies between expression and

[32] See Alan Walker, 'Chopin and Musical Structure', in *Frédéric Chopin: Profiles of the Man and the Musician*, p. 252.

[33] Much of the following material is based on my article 'Chopin and Genre', *Music Analysis* (1989), vol. 8, no. 3, pp. 213–31.

structure in classical music.[34] In many cases Ratner's topics are syn-
onomous with popular genres, and it is clear from nineteenth-century
criticism that such generic allusions struck listeners much more forcefully then than today. Chopin, as we have seen, made much of this
aspect of classical, and especially post-classical, traditions. His music
drew commonly upon vocal genres, especially from opera, and upon
such popular genres as march, funeral march, waltz, mazurka, barcarolle, and chorale. The most common referents are the waltz and the
mazurka, which constantly slide in and out of more ambitious contexts.
But we might also note some rather specific associations between 'host'
and 'guest' genres: chorale elements in the nocturnes, for example, and
barcarolle elements in the ballades.

It will be clear from this that certain genres play a dual role in Chopin,
and especially those genres which he himself elevated to a new status.
The waltz is a case in point. We might examine all the waltzes as struc-
tured wholes with their own generic identity. At the same time we might
examine all the waltz *elements* as constituents of a referential code
which cuts across generic boundaries, prising open the closed meanings
of the controlling genres to forge links with other moments in Chopin
and beyond. We need only consider the E flat major waltz of the first
Ballade alongside the E major waltz of the second Scherzo (Ex. 37) to
note the parallels not just of musical materials but of placing and

Ex. 37
(a) Ballade No. 1, Op. 23

(b) Scherzo No. 2, Op. 31

[34] Leonard Ratner, *Classic Music: Expression, Form and Style*; Kofi Agawu, *Playing with Signs: A Semiotic Interpretation of Classic Music* (Princeton, 1991).

function, serving in both cases to highlight a 'counterpoint of genres'. There is a similar dual role for the mazurka, the nocturne and even the prelude. Thus the A minor Mazurka, Op. 17 No. 4, plays host to the nocturne, while the G minor Nocturne, Op. 15 No. 3, plays host to the mazurka. Perhaps it is not far-fetched to claim that in this sense the first of the Twenty-four Preludes, Op. 28, plays host to the prelude. It was of course partly through such generic referents that nineteenth-century critics arrived at the descriptive and programmatic interpretations which we tend to dismiss today. A comparison between the central march of the F sharp major Impromptu and contemporary operatic choruses, for instance, would provide some rationale for Niecks's 'procession' and even for Huneker's 'cavalcade'.[35]

Much of the richness of Chopin's music derives from the intersection of such pluralist tendencies and the integrative tendencies which issue, at least in part, from a controlling genre. I will illustrate this briefly by returning to the Fantasy, Op. 49, and specifically to its opening section (bars 1–67), examining the passage within ever widening frames of reference. One frame of reference for the analysis of this opening section would be the work itself as a unique and unified statement. Here the integrative role of the passage would be demonstrated in both tonal and motivic terms, as Carl Schachter has done in his powerful analytical study.[36] Needless to say, such an analysis remains comparative in some degree, if only in the sense that normative categories emerge from history and are defined through conventions which exist outside the work.

A wider frame of reference would be the genre 'fantasy'. Here the passage might be compared with the introduction to the only other fantasy of Chopin's maturity, the Polonaise-fantasy, Op. 61. There are important differences of course, but there are also connections (Ex. 38), and these would lead us to make further connections between the works as wholes, both in formal arrangement and in tonal scheme. Both works build into their reworking of sonata form a slow introduction and a 'slow movement', and in both cases the B major of the latter is embedded within a prevailing A flat major tonality. As we shall see in chapter 10, our knowledge of the genesis of Op. 61 strengthens these associations considerably.

Another frame of reference, wider still, would be the entire Chopin canon. Here the infusion of popular genres into both the introduction and the transition would lead us beyond the fantasies and encourage us to make connections with the march of the F sharp major Impromptu and the improvisatory prelude of Op. 28 No. 3 (Ex. 39). As noted earlier, these connections would lead us beyond Chopin to (respectively) the choruses of French Grand Opera and the common practice of

[35] Niecks, *Chopin as a Man and Musician*, vol. 2, p. 260; Huneker, *Chopin: the Man and his Music*, p. 134.
[36] See note 25.

Ex. 38

(a) Fantasy, Op. 49

(b) Polonaise-fantasy, Op. 61

contemporary improvisation. And it is from this base that an additional layer of meaning—one which involves some reference to extra-musical designates—might be adduced in an interpretation of the Fantasy.

It is a commonplace of criticism that 'popular' and 'significant' music became increasingly incompatible in the nineteenth century, establishing an opposition between conventional language and an avant-garde. It is less often remarked that in a substantial body of nineteenth-century music this opposition was actually embedded within the individual work, as popular genres increasingly took on a parenthetical, as distinct from a supportive or enabling, role in art music. These matters bear especially on Chopin, where the popular genre is often part of the content of the work rather than the category exemplified by the work. In such cases an ironic mode is introduced. The work is not a march, a waltz, or a mazurka but rather *refers to* a march, a waltz, or a mazurka.

227

Ex. 39
(a) Fantasy, Op. 49 and Impromptu, Op. 36

(b) Fantasy, Op. 49 and Prelude, Op. 28 No. 3

There is nothing new about such a counterpoint of genres, of course, but more than any earlier composer Chopin built it right into the substance of his musical thought. And it had a legacy. Much later, in Mahler and beyond, the tension between a controlling genre and the popular genres that invade it results in a kind of displacement and fragmentation of the traditional generic context.

The interplay of host and guest genres well demonstrates the potency of genre as an agent of communication. A genre title such as 'nocturne' sets up certain expectations of the musical content, and those expectations are subverted if, as in Op. 15 No. 3, we hear instead a mazurka followed by a chorale. In several recent writings on literature and music this communicative function has been developed into an understanding of genre as a kind of contract between author and reader, composer and listener, a contract which may of course be broken.[37] But such a contract hinges on the stability of the genre in the first place, on its conventional status. And early nineteenth-century piano music is not noted for the stability of its genres. Rather it was generically permissive, with a remarkable profusion of titles, often used casually and even interchangeably, and at times emanating from the publisher rather than the composer. A study of early nineteenth-century lexiographies is enough to confirm that for this repertory titles alone do not signify genres.

Against this background Chopin emerges as a composer deeply committed to genre as a compositional control. For all his purposeful subversion of controlling genres, it is clear that he valued genre as a force for conformity, stability, and closure, a channel through which the work might seek a fixed and final meaning. Following his rejection of conventional concert genres in the early 1830s, he embarked on a thoroughgoing generic validation of the new world of pianism he was himself in the process of developing. He did not select titles arbitrarily or use them loosely in his mature music. They had specific, though not necessarily conventional, generic meanings, established through an internal consistency in their application.

In seeking to clarify his approach to titles and their generic definitions I propose the following categories: conventional titles, conventionally defined—the sonata (the genre, not the formal archetype) and fantasy; conventional titles, conventionally defined, but with a new status—the étude; conventional titles, newly defined—the scherzo, prelude, and three principal dance pieces; conventional titles defined clearly for the first time—the nocturne and impromptu; new titles (for piano music)— the ballade. In most cases the connotative values of the titles echo familiar themes in the wider repertory of early nineteenth-century piano music, themes which are at once transcended and remembered: improvisation in the prelude, impromptu, and fantasy; vocal transcription and imitation in the nocturne; literary inspiration in the ballade.

Chopin's project and achievement was to give generic authority to the free-ranging devices of an emergent, early nineteenth-century piano repertory, crystallizing the meanings of some existing titles, transforming the meanings of others and devising new titles to meet new generic requirements. In each case there is a measure of consistency in the semiotic relation of the title to the formal and stylistic features of the piece. As we know, the 'sign' is bipartite, and both parts are essential. The title is integral to the piece and partly conditions our response to its stylistic and formal content, but it does not create a genre. Equally a taxonomy of formal and stylistic devices will not of itself establish a consistent

[37] See the chapter 'The Function of Genre' in Heather Dubrow, *Genre* (London, 1982). Jeffrey Kallberg has developed this idea in several papers, including 'Understanding Genre: A Reinterpretation of the Early Piano Nocturne', *Atti del XIV° Congresso della Società Internazionale di Musicologia* (Bologna, 1987), pp. 775–9.

basis for generic differentiation. It is enough to consider the substantial overlaps between Chopin's genres in this respect. It is the interaction of title and content which is important.

I have already remarked that the content may subvert the expectations created by the title. It can only do so, however, where a sufficient correspondence of title and content has already been established. Indeed the subversion of expectations actually helps to strengthen a generic definition, clarifying its terms through their temporary falsification. Paradoxically a genre title will be all the more integral to a work where its role is to promote ambiguity. This 'complex of meaning' will be fully active where a generic norm is conventional, validated by consensus. But it may operate within the work of a single composer, provided that there is some measure of stability in signification. It is relatively easy to establish that this stability exists in those Chopin genres where the sample is large, as with the nocturne, waltz, polonaise, and mazurka. In all these cases it is clear that Chopin substantially redefines existing generic meanings, while remaining alive to their associations; the more intriguing questions here concern his attitude to multipartite opuses.[38] But it is perhaps more challenging and interesting to consider the stability of the three genres comprising four pieces each, the impromptu, scherzo, and ballade.

When Chopin wrote his first Impromptu, the C sharp minor, in 1834, the term carried very little generic meaning, as a study of contemporary dictionaries indicates.[39] It has now been established that neither Voříšek nor Schubert had any very clear view of the impromptu as a genre.[40] Chopin drew the basic compositional technique of the C sharp minor Impromptu from his recently completed Op. 10 Études and he modelled some details of its phraseology and texture on at least one and possibly two specific impromptus by other composers.[41] But when he returned to the same title three years later he demonstrated that he had a rather specific private definition of the genre. In his second Impromptu in A flat major, Op. 29, he rebuilt to the specifications of Op. 66; we might almost say that he *derived* the second from the first. There are precise parallels of formal design, proportion, detailed phrase structure, texture, and contour. And the links are strengthened by motivic parallels. This may be demonstrated informally by presenting for inspection the openings of the two figurations and the two melodies (Ex. 40).

In the fourth Impromptu in G flat major, Op. 51, composed in 1842, generic constraints act as a force for inertia and stability at a time of

[38] See chapter 4, note 17.

[39] For a discussion, see Jim Samson, 'Chopin's F sharp Impromptu: Notes on Genre, Style and Structure', in *Chopin Studies 3* (Warsaw, 1990), pp. 297–304.

[40] See Kenneth Gordon Delong, *The Solo Piano Music of J. Voříšek* (Diss., U. of Stanford, 1982), p. 142.

[41] They are the Schubert E flat Impromptu, Op. 90 No. 2 and the Moscheles E flat Impromptu, Op. 80.

Ex. 40
Fantasy-impromptu, Op. 66 and Impromptu, Op. 29

stylistic change in Chopin's music. In formal type, texture, and phraseology there is a clear association with the first two Impromptus. Indeed
it seems likely that Chopin modelled Op. 51 on Op. 29. The construction of the outer figuration seems to have been derived from the earlier
piece, as Ex. 41 indicates. And the parallels extend beyond contour,
rhythm, and phrasing into the precise relationship between the two
hands, including the placing of dissonant notes. In the third Impromptu
in F sharp major, on the other hand, generic stability is undermined by
stylistic change. I have already argued that this piece was the single most
important harbinger of Chopin's later style, and in many ways it departs
significantly from the generic norm established in the first two
Impromptus and confirmed by the fourth.

Yet at the same time Chopin was at pains to demonstrate that he
thought of the F sharp Impromptu as belonging to the same world as

Ex. 41
(a) Impromptu, Op. 29

(b) Impromptu, Op. 51

the others, so that its unique formal and stylistic features might indeed be perceived as deviations from a norm. Again there is an obvious derivation chain. As Ex. 42 suggests, the main theme derives from the central melodies of the first and second Impromptus. Formally, too, the Impromptu follows the others, though its ternary structure builds into the reprise a variation sequence such that the figuration is not present at the outset but arrives as part of the variation process. The figuration when it *does* come, however, exhibits close associations with the other Impromptus, as Ex. 43 demonstrates. We may now present a summary of the derivations and interrelationships among all four Impromptus in diagrammatic form (Fig. 1).

Fig. 1 Cyclic links between the impromptus

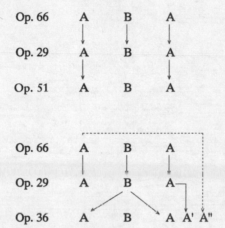

Ex. 42

(a) Fantasy-impromptu, Op. 66

(b) Impromptu, Op. 29

(c) Impromptu, Op. 36

Ex. 43

(a) Impromptu, Op. 29

(b) Impromptu, Op. 51

(c) Impromptu, Op. 36

For Chopin, then, the impromptu was a genre, such that the individual piece exemplifies as well as making its own statement. The genre is stable enough, moreover, to accommodate and contain significant deviation. On one level normative elements—embracing dimensions, formal design, phraseology, texture and gestural repertory—interlock across all four pieces in a manner which strongly suggests a derivation chain. On another level norms are established by three of the four pieces, while the fourth deviates from these norms within certain limits. The four impromptus offer, in short, a small-scale model of the larger workings of a conventional genre.

Before Chopin used it the term 'scherzo' referred to one movement of a multi-movement work, and he himself used it in this sense (and in a manner more closely resembling the Beethoven model) in his mature sonatas. By adopting the title for a single-movement work, Chopin immediately transformed its meaning, though he preserved the basic formal design, the metre, and some more specific features, such as sharply differentiated articulations (especially sforzato markings) and alternating ascending and descending melodic patterns. His transformation of the genre was indeed so radical that his four Scherzos confused not only his contemporaries, but also late nineteenth- and early twentieth-century critics.

Zofia Chechlińska has well demonstrated that the self-consistency and stability of generic meaning in the scherzos penetrates beneath obvious surface features.[42] Her essential insight is that in all four pieces Chopin reinterpreted the element of contrast at the heart of the conventional genre, building the central formal contrast into its detailed substance. This is clearest in the opening paragraphs of all four works, where fragmentary motives are presented with calculated discontinuity. In the B minor there are contrasts of texture, register, and dynamics, and the gesture is repeated at several points in the work. In the D flat major the initial contrast is part of the main theme of the work, such that the dramatic tension it generates provides a key to the character of the work as a whole. In the C sharp minor the contrast is less extreme, but the gesture is identical to that of the second Scherzo (Ex. 44). The E major, meanwhile, opens with a succession of fragments contrasted in texture and harmony.

Since it is far from common for Chopin to begin a work with discontinuous gestures in this way, the internal contrasts found at the opening of all four scherzos is striking. It seems, then, that he regarded the independent scherzo as a genre in its own right, clearly differentiated from the scherzos in his Sonatas, and marked by its own kind of musical material. Contrast, and especially contrast of texture, sonority, and

---

[42] 'Scherzo as a Genre—Selected Problems', *Chopin Studies* 5 (Warsaw, 1995), pp. 165–73.

Ex. 44

(a) Scherzo No. 2, Op. 31

(b) Scherzo No. 3, Op. 39

gesture, lies at the heart of the Chopin genre, determining its larger formal process, as well as its more detailed working. Its essential character is epitomized in the gestural contrasts embodied in short, separated ideas presented at the outset of each of the four works.

With his four Ballades Chopin established a new title for piano music, and for this reason their generic stability is of special interest. Cyclic links of a motivic kind have often been proposed for the Ballades.[43] But it is in the basic character, rather than the motivic substance, of their thematic materials that the ballades are most obviously part of a single genre. All four works have a similar metrical structure, and this in turn is related to the generic character of their themes. Ex. 45 illustrates a derivation chain based on barcarolle/siciliano material, while Fig. 2 presents further generic links diagrammatically.

Formally, too, there are strong arguments for a generic association between the four works. The first Ballade establishes a formal model, of which selected aspects are then elaborated by the later ballades. The second, for instance, again employs two generic themes—siciliano and étude—which are closer in style to a post-classical repertory than to the normative classical or early-romantic sonata. Again the relationship between its two themes is unconventional, with the major-mode theme once more a major third below the minor-mode theme. Again the devel-

[43] For a discussion see the section 'cycles' in Jim Samson, *Chopin: The Four Ballades*, pp. 72–6.

Ex. 45   Generic themes in the Ballades

Fig. 2   Generic links in the Ballades

	Recit	Slow waltz	Figuration	Barcarolle/siciliano	Quick waltz
Op. 23	intro	theme 1	middle/closing sections	theme 2	theme 3
Op. 38			Theme 2/closing section	theme 1	
Op. 47			middle section	theme 1/2	theme 3
Op. 52	intro/cadenza	theme 1	middle/closing sections	theme 2	

opment functions in part as a thematic synthesis, and again the reprise begins with the second theme in its original key, inaugurating a mirror reprise which is not in the end completed either tonally or thematically. And again there is a bravura closing section with a contrasted rhythmic character.

In the third Ballade the generic character of the two themes relates more obviously to No. 2 than to No. 1, though in motivic substance it is closer to No. 1. Once more the tonal relationship is unorthodox and third-related, here a reversal of the normal classical practice for a *minor*-mode sonata-allegro. The parallel with No. 1 extends, moreover, to the pivotal 'quick waltz' episode, lighter in tone than a surrounding material, and the formal symmetry is emphasized again by a mirror reprise. As in No. 1, the reprise is in the character of an apotheosis. The fourth Ballade returns to the tonally inductive introduction of No. 1, and the

237

generic characters of its themes are also similar, a 'slow waltz' and 'barcarolle' respectively. As in the first and third ballades, the middle section has a (relatively) lightweight character involving figuration. This is the only ballade without a mirror reprise, but like Nos. 1 and 3 it has an apotheotic reprise of both themes, and like No. 1 a bravura closing section.

All four ballades conspicuously rethink the tonal practice of the classical sonata, avoiding the double reprise—tonal and thematic—of the classical sonata-allegro, and the conventional tonal schemata of the classical exposition. Indeed the rejection of V as a means of articulating formal units is profoundly significant and it touches on the most significant of all the cyclic links between the ballades—a common approach to large-scale tonal organization. In all four works the overall progression is towards a structural V which follows rather than precedes the restatement of the main themes. The one qualified exception is No. 3 where there is no closing section and the structural V comes at the beginning of the reprise of the first theme. Moreover the approach to the structural V is in each case by way of its upper neighbour VI,[44] as Schenkerian harmonic reductions illustrate (Ex. 46).

Each ballade, in other words, transforms the sonata-form archetype in such a way that the resolution of tonal tension is delayed until the latest possible moment, usually after the thematic reprise. And each finds its way to that resolution by a strikingly similar harmonic route. The bravura closing sections function, then, as a catharsis, releasing in a torrent of virtuosity all the tension which has been steadily mounting through the piece. This in turn helps to condition the larger 'plots' of these works, which may well have been inspired by the tradition of the literary ballad. Apart from the second Ballade, they tend to be endweighted. The earlier stages are kept at a low temperature and tension is built gradually but inexorably towards the final moments when the tonic is cathartically reaffirmed. The second Ballade, on the other hand, is concerned with the integration of an initial explosive contrast, and it is in this respect above all that—like the F sharp Impromptu—it might be regarded as the (confirming) deviation from a generic norm. But there are other ways in which it stands a little way outside the territory marked out by the other three ballades, notably in its two-key scheme, its figurative second theme, and its formal 'intercutting' of contrasted materials rather than (or as well as) cumulative variation and transformation of related materials.

I have considered elsewhere the value of introducing the tempting concept of a 'narrative' in any description of the ballade as a genre.[45] The issue of music and narrative has been much discussed in the so-called

---

[44] This is noted in David Witten, 'The Chopin "Ballades": An Analytical Study' (Diss., U. of Boston, 1974).

[45] The section 'Narratives' in *Chopin: The Four Ballades*, pp. 81–7.

Fig. 46 Structural harmonies in the ballades

'new musicology', and the arguments may be presented succinctly here, as they affect the ballades. It is clear that the genre title encourages us to locate an unfolding story. The ballades take on a story-character by invoking and then modifying conventional plots (especially from sonata form), and by focusing the events through a distinctive (generic) characterization of themes, the 'personae' of the drama.[46] None of this, however, would constitute a narrative without the discursive distance of a 'narrating voice', situated outside the action, so to speak, and recalling the events in the past tense.[47]

My attempts in an earlier study to equate such a narrating voice with the compound duple metre of all four works hinged on a link with the poetic ballad, which stands in reality somewhere between narrative and drama. A more recent exhaustive study of Chopin and the 'ballad tradition' by James Parakilas strengthens such attempts and adds further grist to the mill.[48] The argument rests (for Chopin at least) on a kind of double representation—the plane of 'narrating' and the plane of 'the story narrated'. This amounts to a distinction between 'narrating themes' and 'characterizing themes', which are mediated to reflect what Parakilas describes as the 'underlying plot mechanisms of ballads', which culminate in a 'whirlwind of musical reckoning'. We may be persuaded of this in general terms without going on to accept the author's later 'tradition of the instrumental ballade' centred on the identification of sung-narrative (as distinct from the more familiar motive-signifying) approaches to representation in nineteenth-century music. The 'ballade' may not be a genre. The 'Chopin ballade' most certainly is.

[46] The 'personification' of themes in this way owes much to Edward T. Cone, *The Composer's Voice* (Berkeley, Los Angeles, and London, 1974).

[47] This problem is discussed in Carolyn Abbate, *Unsung Voices: Opera and Musical Narrative in the Nineteenth Century* (Princeton, 1991) and Jean-Jacques Nattiez, 'Can One Speak of Narrativity in Music?', in *Journal of the Royal Musical Association* (1990), vol. 115, no. 2, pp. 240–57.

[48] See chapter 6, note 55.

9

Twilight

Biography is a presumption. To describe and interpret our own feelings is hard enough. To analyse the feelings of others—and to do so when our victim is long dead—is foolhardy, even when irresistible. The retrospective fallacy rides high in all this. And speculation should be recognized for what it is. Widely different interpretations of George Sand's attitude to Chopin in 1845–6 have been confidently proposed, and all based on the same sources.[1] Was she in effect trying to extricate herself from the relationship at all costs? Or was she still committed to Chopin, for all her growing reservations about their life together? It is distinctly possible that the feeling between them was irreparably soured in the early months of 1845, but there was little outward sign of it when they set off for Nohant as usual in June. Quite the reverse. Undaunted by the vagaries of their Majorcan adventure more than five years earlier, Sand was actually proposing another winter sojourn either in Italy or in the south of France, convinced that an extended period of sunshine would put Chopin's health to rights again.

If not committed to life with the composer, she appeared at least to have been resigned to it. Chopin, on the other hand, had no doubts about the matter. George Sand was a part of his future as of his past and present. He was of course painfully aware of the inadequacies of their relationship but, much more than Sand, he was anxious to overlook them. All the same, it is perhaps revealing that in those early weeks at Nohant he sent long, chatty missives to his family in Warsaw. They are usually and rightly described as long-winded and directionless, offering colourful titbits of Parisian and Berry gossip as though to fill the time during a more than usually indolent period. But they suggest none the less that his family, deprived of news for months on end in happier days, were emerging again to the forefront of his thoughts, as other joys receded. The pendulum was swinging once again towards Poland.

If we must find a *casus belli*, we should look beyond the couple themselves to the family as a whole. Maurice and Solange were no longer

[1] Consider, for example, the very different interpretations offered by Ruth Jordan (*Nocturne: A Life of Chopin*) and Ewa Kossak, 'The Correspondence of George Sand', *Chopin Studies 1* (Warsaw, 1985).

children in 1845. Over the years their attitude towards Chopin had changed perceptibly, and the changes became more blatant as they travelled through adolescence and beyond. It seems that Maurice, already twenty-two in 1845 and transparently his mother's favourite, began to feel himself very much the man of the house and increasingly to resent Chopin's place in Sand's affections. He had never had a warm relationship with the composer, but it had at least been one of conventional friendship. During the summer of 1845 it was barely that. Solange, meanwhile, spent more and more time in Chopin's company. Now a fickle, not to say rebellious, teenager, she happily described him to her mother as 'an old grump', but none the less turned to him repeatedly for a sympathetic ear.[2] He had always tended to spoil her, perhaps even thinking of her as a surrogate daughter, and as her relations with Sand deteriorated she knew well that she could always rely on Chopin. Nor, if we are to believe Arago, was she above using the youthful charms of a seventeen-year-old to try to turn his head.[3]

Family tensions came to a head that year largely due to an external influence—in effect an addition to the household. For some time George Sand had taken a maternal interest in Augustine Brault, the daughter of an impoverished and rather uncouth cousin on her mother's side. When she learned that her relative was about to pass this pretty and intelligent girl over to a wealthy protector, with all the unpleasant implications that carried, she decided to adopt her, or at least, since this was not possible legally, to take her into her home. To all intents and purposes Augustine was treated by Sand as a second daughter, and in later life she even set aside a dowry for her. It was entirely typical of her generous, impulsive nature, and no less typical of her failure to think things through.

The decision to adopt Augustine served only to increase existing tensions and ended by polarizing the family completely. Maurice had already demonstrated his awareness of the opposite sex by making advances to Pauline Viardot, who had been at Nohant for the first few weeks of the summer, and he was quick to press his attentions on the lively and attractive Augustine. Solange was of course jealous of the girl, treated her as a social inferior (as did Chopin, incidentally) and was quick to spread rumours about her liaison with Maurice. Chopin, who had a tendency to regard himself as the voice of sanity in an often tempestuous household, supported Solange and believed, probably with good cause since 'evidence' was spoken of, that Maurice had indeed seduced the girl. He was quickly told to mind his own business by Maurice, and in effect by Sand herself, presumably in order to protect her son. Chopin was in further trouble, moreover, because of his old Polish servant Jan, who proved unacceptable to everyone except the composer himself and in the end had to be dismissed.

[2] George Sand in a letter to Mme Marliani, 9 May 1846. See GSC, vol. 7, p. 344.
[3] Ibid., vol. 8, p. 49 note.

Augustine visited Nohant for the first time in early September, accompanied by Maurice, who had returned to Paris at the beginning of the month to deliver Sand's latest manuscript to the publisher. Chopin, meanwhile, left for a brief visit to Paris a week or so later, and it is clear from Sand's letter to him that by then at least a temporary peace had broken out. On his return to Nohant for the months of October and November he tried very hard to settle down to composition, but it had become a laborious and painfully slow process. By then Chopin had become intensely self-critical as a composer. Amidst the chitchat to Ludwika in one of those letters written in the early summer there is a sentence which expresses his frustration very clearly: 'I cannot explain why, but I am simply unable to produce anything worthwhile, and it's not down to laziness; I am not spending my time wandering about as I did when you were here, but stay in my room for whole days and evenings. It is essential that I finish some manuscripts before I leave, since the winter is impossible for composition.'[4]

He had managed to complete one set of mazurkas (Op. 59) shortly after arriving at Nohant in the early summer, but that was all. The 'manuscripts' referred to in this letter were almost certainly the Barcarolle, Op. 60, the Polonaise-fantasy, Op. 61 and perhaps the Two Nocturnes, Op. 62. In December, back in Paris and with most of the family ill and out of sorts, he wrote to Warsaw again, referring to the recent German publication of Op. 59 and indicating that Opp. 60 and 61 ('a piece which I haven't yet found a title for')[5] were still not complete. He also remarked that he was trying to finish his Cello Sonata, in due course published as Op. 65. Much of the Cello Sonata must have already been in place, since in the same letter he mentioned playing it through with Franchomme. Yet more than half a year later, in July 1846, he wrote to Franchomme from Nohant that his 'poor manuscripts' were still not finished. All but the Cello Sonata were finally completed that summer and taken back to Paris in late August by Delacroix, returning from his last visit to Nohant. The sonata, however, caused him endless problems. As late as October he wrote to his family: 'Sometimes I am happy with it, sometimes not. I throw it in the corner and then pick it up again.'[6]

This creative anguish was in the sharpest possible contrast to the facility of Sand herself. During the twelve-month period from July 1845 to July 1846 she produced four novels, and in May 1846 she signed a contract with *Le courrier français* for another, to be called *Lucrezia Floriani*. Several of the novels written during her life with Chopin refer directly to the changing phases of their relationship,[7] but none is so explicitly

---

[4] Letter to his family, 1–5 August 1845. *KFC*, vol. 2, p. 146.
[5] Ibid., vol. 2, p. 155.   [6] Ibid., vol. 2, p. 175.
[7] For an intriguing discussion of the resonances surrounding the short story *Gabriel*, see Jeffrey Kallberg, 'Small Fairy Voices: Sex, History and Meaning in Chopin', in *Chopin Studies 2* (Cambridge, 1994), pp. 50–71.

autobiographical as *Lucrezia*. (There is even room for Maria Wodzińska as Prince Karol's fiancée.) The central character is an actress who abandoned fame in favour of a reclusive existence with the four children of her three earlier love affairs. When the sickly Prince Karol comes her way (with a travelling companion closely modelled on Grzymała), he initially disapproves of her casual morals, but changes his view as he witnesses her selfless devotion to her children. As she nurses him back to health, the pair fall in love. One theme, topical enough, is the tug-of-war between Lucrezia's love for her children and her love for Prince Karol. Another is the Prince's 'secret malady' which destroys their love, an insidious, creeping jealousy which taints and pollutes his view of everything and everyone, and which especially prejudices him against the children. In the end the heroine is driven to death by the prince's behaviour, worn down by the constant sacrifices she made to appease him.

This was blatantly based on the Chopin–Sand relationship, and was recognized as such by the whole of literary Paris; each new instalment was eagerly awaited, and several mutual friends of the couple, including Liszt and Heine, professed themselves shocked by Sand's blatant anatomy of her affair with the composer. It is hard to believe that Chopin could have remained innocent of the inspiration for the book, and of the tellingly personal descriptions of himself in at least some of its pages. This is the sort of thing:

> As he was predominantly polite and reserved, no one could really know what he felt. The more infuriated he was, the colder he would become, and the extent of his anger could be measured only by his ice-cold politeness. On such occasions he could be truly unbearable, as he would spoil for an argument and would subject real life, which he did not understand, to so-called principles, which he could not define. He would then use his wit, his false and ironic wit, to torture those he loved. He would be supercilious, haughty, precious and distant. He would seem to nibble lightly enough, but would wound deeply, penetrating right to the soul. Or, if he lacked the courage to argue and mock, he would withdraw in lofty silence, sulking in a pathetic manner.[8]

This was not the whole story. At other moments he could be 'happy and reveal his angelic side. Oh, what a cherub, what an angel he could have been if he had always been like that. At such times, and they could last for hours or even days, he was kind, charitable, sympathetic and approachable.'

No doubt the portrait is exaggerated, coloured not only by the licence of fiction but by the bias of current events. But some of it has the ring of truth, and it tallies with other descriptions, including that of Zofia Rosengardt. The obsessive jealousies described in *Lucrezia Floriani* put flesh of a kind on remarks to that effect in Sand's correspondence, references to an 'exclusive and jealous passion' in a famous letter to

---

[8] George Sand, *Lucrezia Floriani* (Paris, 1853), p. 249.

Frédéric François, for instance. 'At the age of forty I make myself ridiculous by having a sort of jealous lover at my side.'[9] To be fair, it was in the nature of Sand's creativity to dramatize her current predicaments and attitudes, arguing out the case, so to speak, in her fiction. Her novels reprocessed her own experience as universal truth, a modus, incidentally, which rendered them distinctly palatable for popular consumption. Grossly insensitive *Lucrezia* may have been, but it was not vindictive, and Chopin gave no outward sign of offence, offering nothing but praise for the novel. In a later letter to his family he discussed its reception in terms which suggest that, incredible though it seems, he may actually have been unaware of its autobiographical resonance. He even remarked that Ludwika 'will like [Piccinino] better than Lucrezia'.[10] Surely Ludwika, at least, cannot have been blind to its significance. With hindsight it is difficult not to read the novel as a kind of post-mortem of their relationship, but it was more probably an analysis, albeit a valedictory one, an attempt by Sand to make sense of her changing feelings. It was also, of course, a depiction of those family tensions which were reaching their high water mark just as she was working on *Lucrezia*.

Although Chopin's periods in Nohant grew longer as the years passed, he still hankered after the capital. The summer of 1846 was particularly trying due to the heat and the insects, and even Delacroix's presence in August failed to cheer him up significantly. It was with some relief, then, that he returned in November to his familiar world of teaching and socializing in Paris, where he spent more and more time in the company of fellow Poles, including Grzymała, Delfina Potocka, the composer Nowakowski ('a good fellow, but rather a clot')[11] and of, course, the circle at the Hôtel Lambert, with the 'angelic' Princess Czartoryska. Sand, in contrast, tired increasingly of Paris. Her intention was to settle more or less permanently at Nohant, and Chopin was still part of this plan. Her investigation of a central heating system, which would make the manor house tolerable in the winter months, was undertaken with him very much in mind. When Chopin returned to Paris in mid November, she decided to stay on at Nohant and to spend the winter months there. There were financial reasons for this, since Nohant was in need of renovation, but there were other factors too. She later claimed that she hoped to cure Chopin once and for all of his jealousies by just such a prolonged separation. And—most important—she had preparations to make for the forthcoming wedding of Solange to a young neighbouring landowner.

Back in June, Chopin, Solange, and Augustine had spent four days in the Brenne region, close by Nohant, and it was here that Solange had first met Fernand de Préaulx. They must have been in touch through much of the summer, for in October Chopin wrote to his family

[9] *GSC*, vol. 6, p. 915. [10] March–April 1847. *KFC*, vol. 2, p. 195.
[11] Ibid., vol. 2, p. 192.

predicting that there would soon be a wedding. Shortly after that Solange did indeed announce her intention to marry Préaulx, not it seems out of any great love, and the choice was approved by both Sand and Chopin. It may well be that Solange's marriage plans fitted well with Sand's optimistic vision of a family reconciliation, the more so in that the growing intimacy of Maurice and Augustine also promised to lead to marriage around this time. At any rate there is no real evidence to suggest that when Chopin returned to Paris she was plotting a final separation, as has been argued. Even when things were very much worse, the following May, she could write that she would not lack the courage or perseverance to stay with him.[12] But by then a labyrinthine sequence of events had begun to unfold, leading to a most unhappy conclusion.

In March 1846 the young sculptor Auguste Clésinger made his first contact with George Sand, inviting her by letter to visit him and dedicating one of his works to her. The following February, shortly after her return to Paris with the family and Fernand de Préaulx, Sand met Clésinger at the Marlianis and arranged to visit him at his studio. Things happened quickly after that. She and Solange sat for Clésinger on several occasions, and on 26 February Solange announced to the unfortunate Préaulx that their engagement was cancelled. Sand began to hear bad reports of Clésinger, not least from M. d'Arpentigny, the man who had introduced them, but she was initially placated by him when she demanded explanations of his conduct in the past. Chopin, on the other hand, quickly decided, as he saw more of him, that Clésinger was an unscrupulous character. And Delacroix, who spent much of his time with the family that spring, took a dim view of both the man and his talent. Delacroix, incidentally, was later to revise his opinion of Clésinger's work, at least with respect to his monument to Chopin at the Père-Lachaise cemetery. He remarked in his diary that he would probably have done it in just the same way.

Sand decided that the only sensible course of action was to remove Solange from the scene and on 6 April whisked her off to Nohant for a dose of sobering country air. Shortly after that Chopin wrote to his family (part of a long letter put together over three weeks), and amidst the news of Parisian music, his own playing (a performance of the Cello Sonata with Franchomme at an informal gathering) and plans to meet up with Izabella and her husband, he referred to Clésinger. 'A genuine new talent', was his rather surprising comment, and he went on to add, 'Make a note of the sculptor's name. I shall have further occasion to mention him, as he has been introduced to Mme Sand.'[13] In the same letter he announced his intention to spend the summer in Nohant as usual. Matters had still not come to a head.

Towards the end of the letter, on 19 April, Chopin referred to a note

---

[12] *GSC*, vol. 7, p. 702.   [13] *KFC*, vol. 2, p. 193.

from Sand announcing her intention to return to Paris at the end of the month. 'No doubt it concerns Solange's marriage (but not to the young man I told you about).' At this stage Chopin was probably unaware that Clésinger had followed the party to Nohant. It was there that he had pressed his suit successfully; and he had even visited Solange's father at Guillery to ask his permission to marry the girl. There was in effect a state of some panic at Nohant, with Solange, fearing pregnancy, at one point plunging herself into an icy stream. In the end the marriage was more or less forced on Sand, Maurice was called for urgently, by both Sand and Clésinger, and preparations were hastily made. Chopin, however, was not informed of any of this. Sand knew that he would disapprove, and she seemed anxious to get the whole thing over and done with as quickly as possible. She argued that Chopin had no grasp of reality and could not see the situation clearly (though in this instance he saw it all too clearly), and also that he should not be encouraged to view himself as 'the head of the family and its counsellor'. She was concerned, too, about his health. She had heard from Delacroix, Grzymała, and Marie de Rozières that he had had a very bad week in early May, and was genuinely distressed that she was unable to come to Paris. Chopin, it should be noted, took great pains to keep the news from her.

It was then (12 May) that Sand wrote a lengthy letter to Grzymała describing her life with Chopin.[14] One of the secrets of her resilience was her capacity to reorder and revise the past in accord with her present perspective. This was less dishonesty than self-deception, and it is the reason why her letters are in general more valuable than her autobiography. The letter to Grzymała was *de facto* autobiography, however, and in it she depicts herself as something of a martyr ('I have been a miracle of patience'), bending reality on numerous counts, not least her claim that she had lived as a virgin for the last seven years. There are, however, recurring themes about Chopin which do ring true—further reference to the disease (jealousy) eating away at his body and soul, and explicit comment on their physical relations. 'He complains that I destroy him by withholding my consent, while I am quite sure that I would destroy him by giving it.' She remarked that 'in the midst of all my efforts and sacrifices this man whom I love with a chaste maternal love is dying of the insane love he has for me'.

A few days later, on 18 May, the marriage contract was signed at Nohant, with Casimir Dudevant present, and the following day the pair were married at the local church and in the family home. Sand had informed Chopin by letter just before the event, and he replied sending his best wishes to Solange. After a few days at Ville d'Avraye with the Saxon consul Thomas Albrecht, whose friendship and support were invaluable to Chopin in these later years, he returned to Paris to find the

---

[14] *GSC*, vol. 7, pp. 700–1.

young couple there and called on them briefly. On 1 June Sand herself arrived with Augustine who was to be married to the landscape painter Théodore Rousseau, probably (at least according to Chopin) to the immense relief of both Maurice and Sand.[15] In fact a few days after their arrival the engagement was broken off, largely, it would seem, owing to the machinations of Solange and Clésinger, who were not slow to tell Rousseau about Maurice. Sand and Augustine then returned to Nohant (17 June) and awaited the arrival of Chopin, who was due to travel down in the company of Delacroix. He gave an account of the earlier stages of this sequence in a letter to his family dated 8 June. It is interesting that in this and other letters to his family at the time he discussed intimate details of the lives and personalities of Sand and her children. He had always avoided such subjects in the past, and it provides further evidence of a shift in the centre of gravity of Chopin's emotional world. His thoughts were increasingly of Poland and of Warsaw in these later years, and his family emerged more and more into the forefront of his affections. Ludwika in particular became a sort of confidante.

In the letter of 8 June Chopin wrote openly, and it has to be said accurately, about the whole affair of Solange's marriage. Sand had remarked to Grzymała on just the same subject that Chopin's 'advice on the real issues of life is worthless. He has never faced reality, never understood human nature in the slightest.'[16] This sits nicely with Chopin's observation to his family: 'The mother is a dear, but she is quite without common sense.'[17] With respect to Solange and Clésinger at least, his proved the more accurate judgement. Chopin went on to give a telling analysis of the behaviour of all parties, showing considerable insight in every case, even with Solange ('She is happy to be a married woman. She has her cashmere shawls and goes riding'), though he seems to have remained blind to the more cruel, vindictive side of the girl's personality. He also commented at length on Sand, remarking that although she always behaved in extraordinary ways, things had a habit of working out to her advantage, and listing some examples. 'There is just one thing', he went on. 'She does not always speak the truth.' But here the example he gave—her evasive ways of hinting to him about Witwicki's recent death—can easily be interpreted to her advantage.

Chopin was undoubtedly upset and offended by the whole saga of Solange's wedding, and in the same letter he told his parents that he might well not go to Nohant that summer. 'I should have to get used to all the new faces.' In the meantime Nohant was about to become the venue for truly extraordinary scenes. The Clésingers arrived there around the end of the month bent on causing difficulties. Clésinger was in essence making entirely unreasonable demands as to Solange's dowry, angry that Sand had had the good sense to give her the Paris property

[15] Letter to his family, 8 June 1847. *KFC*, vol. 2, p. 203.
[16] *GSC*, vol. 7, p. 700–1.   [17] *KFC*, vol. 2, p. 202.

in entailment, knowing only too well that everything would quickly be squandered. It was becoming all too clear that Clésinger was a fortune hunter. He had amassed considerable debts, and was certainly hopeful that the marriage to Sand's daughter would alleviate his difficulties, no doubt convinced (mistakenly) that the eminent novelist was a very wealthy woman. In the end they all came to blows. Clésinger threatened Maurice with a hammer, Sand interposed herself and was hit in the chest by her son-in-law. Maurice then fetched a gun. This was high drama, and Sand, not unreasonably, resolved it by expelling the couple and forbidding them to return.

From the nearby town of Le Châtre, the Clésingers proceeded to slander George Sand and to weave a web of intrigue against her. Chopin failed to see this campaign for what it was, and was quickly caught in the web. Solange even managed to feed his jealousy with stories (possibly not without some foundation, given subsequent events) of the young journalist Victor Borie, then a frequent visitor to Nohant. From Sand's perspective, Chopin appeared to side with Solange, with 'the enemy'.[18] And it was this betrayal, as she certainly saw it, that finally put paid to the relationship. It was never intended as a betrayal by Chopin. He genuinely believed that Sand would come to her senses, that the whole thing would in due course blow over and that sanity would be restored. But he had touched a deep nerve in Sand. This crisis with her difficult and perfidious daughter was a moment *in extremis*, a time when she felt entitled to nothing but support from her long-standing partner, whatever the rights and wrongs of the situation. 'Even if I had been in the wrong, even committed crimes, Chopin was not obliged to believe them, or even to *see* them . . .'[19] She felt that his disloyalty made a mockery of their many years of friendship.

His first act of disloyalty, as Sand regarded it, was to lend Solange his carriage, after she (Sand) had refused permission; and she could hardly have done other. The crucial correspondence between them at this time is unfortunately not extant, but much can be deduced. Words, apparently, were not minced. Following Chopin's 'disloyalty', Sand wrote an angry letter, presumably putting him in his place and in particular telling him to have no contact with Solange when she arrived in Paris. She also insisted that there was to be no mention of her daughter at Nohant; it should be noted that she was still expecting the arrival of Chopin and Delacroix at any time. Chopin showed this letter to Delacroix, who noted in his diary that the tone of the letter was indeed cruel, remarking that at times the novelist appeared to have taken over from the woman.[20] Chopin delayed replying for ten days, after which (24 July, 1847) he wrote a cool note, using the formal *vous*. This was his last

[18] George Sand to Chopin, 28 July 1847. *GSC*, vol. 8, pp. 54–5.
[19] Letter to Pauline Viardot, 1 December 1847. Ibid., vol. 8, p. 173.
[20] *The Journal of Eugène Delacroix*, p. 322.

letter to Sand, and in it he reminded her that Solange was about to be a mother and might reasonably expect some sign of interest, not to say support, from her own mother. But he ended the letter. 'Time will have its effect. I shall be waiting, *the same as ever*.'[21]

For Sand, this was a further disloyalty. She had no need to be reminded of her maternal obligations by Chopin, and the measured tone of his letter only succeeded in infuriating her. The letter arrived just as she was writing a long, agonized letter (some seventy-one pages) to Emanuel Arago, in which she describes the events of that spring and summer and articulates her sense of betrayal, characteristically revising the past in the light of present realities. Arago's reply had the effect of confirming her suspicion that, far from dying of love for her, Chopin had actually been under Solange's spell for some time. There is no doubt from the tone of Sand's letter to Arago that she was in a state of acute depression at the time, and no doubt she came to think better of that particular judgement. Chopin may have been blind to Solange's cruelty. He may even have been susceptible to her flirtatious manner. But the picture painted by Sand and Arago is transparently a fantasy. Sand certainly knew it was so, even at the time. The reality of her feeling is better conveyed in a letter to Marie de Rozières, dated 25 July and sent just before she received Chopin's last letter to her. 'Sometimes to comfort myself I think Chopin loves her far more than he does me, is sulky with me and takes her part. I prefer this a hundred times more than to know that he is ill. Please tell me frankly how he is doing.'[22]

When she replied to that last letter, just three days after the note to Marie de Rozières, it was with a cold, reproachful message. She told him that she had been ready to make a trip to Paris for a day just to see him, thinking him ill, that she now saw that he had been 'reflecting calmly', that his letter was 'very composed'. She thanks God for this strange conclusion to nine years of exclusive friendship. and ends: 'There is no point in ever discussing the rest.'[23] This was her last letter to him. Yet it is not certain that she really sought this finality. Chopin most definitely did not. He was at this time hearing only the accounts given by Solange, and he genuinely felt that there was wrong on Sand's side as well as her daughter's. He refused to 'give up' Solange, as demanded by Sand, and felt sure that time would do its work and some sense of normality would be restored. However, Sand's letter was read by him as a cruel dismissal, and he was much too proud to make any moves towards reconciliation.

He spent the next half-year teaching and composing (completing the Op. 64 Waltzes), but above all anxiously hoping to hear from her. Sand, too, may have hoped for a communication. In a letter to Mme Marliani later in the year she wrote, 'I have not heard from him for a full three months'.[24] She still had the same maternal concern for Chopin, but at

[21] *KFC*, vol. 2, pp. 417–18.   [22] *GSC*, vol. 8, pp. 17–18.
[23] Ibid., vol. 8, pp. 54–5.   [24] Ibid., vol. 8, pp. 112–13.

the same time she was relieved to have the burden of his love—the 'pin-pricks' (her word) of his jealousy—eased. By December her life had moved on. She had given up her rooms at the Square d'Orléans and embarked on another love affair, with the journalist Victor Borie. Six months after the breakdown of their relationship, Chopin referred to Sand in a letter to Ludwika. 'We have not seen each other for a long time. There were no scenes or arguments. But I could not visit Nohant on her condition—that I should not even mention her daughter.'[25] By then he may have finally come to recognize the finality of the break. He had spend a difficult, lonely winter, waiting for news, communicating regularly with Solange and working quietly for some reconciliation between mother and daughter. Chopin was broken emotionally by the separation from Sand. He had nothing like her powers of recovery. Indeed he never recovered.

His teaching round continued, of course, and it included some new names, notably the splendidly colourful Countess Maria Kalergis. It was also at this time that another pupil, Jane Stirling, a wealthy Scottish woman who had never married, began to play an increasingly promi-nent role in his life. She was the youngest of the thirteen children of John Stirling, Laird of Kippendavie, who had made his money through trade with India. A recently discovered diary suggests that during the months following his break-up with Sand, Chopin saw a good deal of Stirling and her widowed sister and constant companion, Katharine Erskine, and also of the Schwabes, a wealthy German–Jewish family who would later play host to him in Manchester. Fanny Erskine, a distant relative of Jane Stirling, details four meetings with Chopin during the period between 6 December 1847 and 13 January 1848.[26] She had come to Paris to audi-tion for singing lessons with Manuel García, and met Chopin several times at Jane Stirling's.

Her views are well worth recording. They confirm the impression fre-quently conveyed by Chopin as someone quite out of the ordinary, and as one who suffered. After their first meeting Fanny wrote:

> He is such an interesting looking man but Oh! so suffering . . . I felt for him for they say he is so lonely & obliged even to go out for his Breakfast & suf-fering dreadfully from asthma.

And on the second meeting Chopin

> did not come till late & looking Oh! so suffering but so kind[.] Much inter-ested in *Garcia*. He spoke so pleasantly all dinner & seems so *simply true*, with a keen sense of the good & beautiful & full of imagination . . . I was so sorry to come away & shall always be interested in him, there is something so uncommon in him altogether & so oppressedly suffering yet patient & uncom-plaining.

[25] 10 February, 1848. *KFC*, vol. 2, p. 229.
[26] Jeremy Barlow, 'Encounters with Chopin: Fanny Erksine's Paris Diary, 1847–8', in *Chopin Studies 2* (Cambridge, 1994), pp. 245–8.

Yet one of the values of this diary is its demonstration that even at this low ebb in his life, Chopin retained his sense of fun. On the first meeting:

> He asked me about the Beethoven Fest. & was so happy to see Aunt Mary again, he grew quite *playful* & seemed to forget his suffering . . .

And on the final meeting:

> Chopin played for a long time so splendidly & was quite frisky after[,] making rabbits on the wall & showing off his various accomplishments[.]

As to Chopin's playing, Fanny Erskine was as captivated as everyone else.

> and how can I describe his playing—Anything so pure and *heavenly* & delicate I never heard—& *so* mournful; his music is so like himself—& so original in its sadness . . . His preludes & his nocturnes composed at the moment were so delicious I could have jumped up with joy! & he played us a Mazurka after. He is a Pole & seems very fond of his country. I was quite sorry to come away but had his exquisite harmonies in my heart for long.

And again

> When Mr. & Mrs. S- [Schwabe] came he talked more generally & pretty late played—Oh! so exquisitely[.] Such bursts of feeling & passion.

Such performances were of course part of Chopin's virtually daily social routine, but as the year turned he was persuaded to give another concert at Pleyel's, a public concert, but one arranged very much on his own terms. There was no prior advertising, the hall was smothered with flowers, he was surrounded by friends and he played on his own piano. In other words it was as close to a salon performance as a public concert might come. Among other things he presented the last three movements of the Cello Sonata with Franchomme, and the E major Piano Trio by Mozart with Franchomme and Jean-Delfin Alard, an intimation this of the later Franchomme-Alard chamber series. It was Chopin's last concert in Paris, and it was a rousing success. At the very least this was a distraction from the current malaise. But it was also, of course, an important source of income, at a time when he was once more answerable only to himself in such matters. Its success encouraged him to plan a sequel, provisionally booked for March. But before it could take place politics intervened.

The February revolution changed the face and tone of Paris. It has been termed the 'revolution of the intellectuals', and it is true that many leading writers and artists, having identified closely with the liberal cause and the reform movement, played their part in preparing the climate for radical change. 'La bataille romantique' in France involved a search for political and social relevance in art and took its stand on the belief that the poet, no less than the politician, could change history.

Through oratory, pamphleteering and direct political action, artists involved themselves closely in the events of 1848 and their immediate aftermath, not least in the Provisional Government. Disillusionment would come, but not immediately, and one of those who embraced the changes most whole-heartedly was Sand.

It should be noted that those very events which attracted George Sand back to Paris in a fever of excitement utterly repelled Chopin. It is not certain that his livelihood would have been drastically affected by the revolution, though Charles Hallé later pointed out that most of that wealthy stratum of society on which musicians such as Chopin depended for a living fled the capital in the aftermath of the revolution.[27] But he had in any case nothing but distaste for the coarseness of the events themselves. He continued to entertain hopes (as well as fears) for Poland, of course, and events were indeed quickly triggered there as elsewhere in Europe. He wrote of this at some length to Fontana in America. But the reality of revolution and its aftermath on his own doorstep was another matter altogether—something to be avoided at all costs.

The means to do so were provided by Jane Stirling. She and her sister were devotees of the cultural and intellectual life of the French capital, and divided their time between Paris, where they had a house at St Germaine-en-Laye, and their numerous friends and family in Britain. They were obliged to return to Britain following the revolution, and invited Chopin to follow them. Stirling was six years older than Chopin, clearly devoted to him and certainly hopeful that she might very soon step into the role recently vacated by George Sand. Unhappily the feeling was anything but reciprocal. None the less, the attractions of London were considerable, and Chopin was not the only musician to find his way there in the wake of 1848, hoping to make a living from teaching and playing. Indeed the town was buzzing with exiles from political and artistic fraternities, and that included musicians. In the end Chopin took the plunge, and arranged to let out his Paris apartment. But before setting out himself he encountered George Sand on one final occasion.

They met by accident on 4 March in the passageway outside Mme Marliani's apartment. Chopin described the incident in some detail in a letter to Solange. He apparently informed Sand that she was a grandmother, and then proceeded down the stairs to the street. He then asked his companion to go back upstairs in order to convey to Sand the news that Solange was well. Her response was to come down in person to ask Chopin for further details of her daughter's health, and also to ask after his own. There is real poignancy in Chopin's account of this meeting (which differs somewhat from Sand's in her autobiography), a sense of

27 C. E and M. Hallé, *The Life and Letters of Charles Hallé* (London, 1896).

much that was left unsaid, of deeper feelings on both sides stiffened into formality. Ironically, Chopin learnt, just a few days later, that Solange had lost her baby, and in his letter of condolence he again intimated that some reconciliation with her mother might be possible. The loss of the child did in fact lead to some small improvement in the relations between mother and daughter. Chopin, however, remained on the sidelines. Throughout this period and beyond he continued to correspond with Solange, but communication with Sand was finished for good.

On 21 April he found himself in London. Jane Stirling had reserved an apartment at 10 Bentinck Street, but he found better rooms at Dover Street on the recommendation of Karol Szulczewski, secretary of the Society for the Friends of Poland. Szulczewski, along with Stanisław Koźmian, who had been Chopin's factotum during his first visit to London, helped look after him during his seven months in Britain. While waiting to move, he paid a short visit to Kingston, where several of Louis-Philippe's entourage had gathered within reach of Claremont (in Esher), where the exiled King was staying. The talk, not surprisingly, was all of politics, not least the 'Polish question' and especially the Poznań uprising. There was much support for Poland in England, with some figures in public life, the parliamentarian Lord Dudley Stuart prominent among them, actively proselytizing for the Polish cause. No doubt that support helped Chopin establish himself in his new surroundings.

When he did move to the spacious, but expensive, Dover Street apartment, he found it ideally suited to his teaching and playing needs. Not only was there the piano he had asked Pleyel to deliver, but an Erard and a Broadwood, again supplied by their makers. Chopin had met James Broadwood during his first visit to London, and Broadwood's son Henry (now running the famous firm) was anxious to oblige Chopin, and took great pains to make him comfortable in London. Chopin developed a love for Broadwoods at this late stage of his life and often used them in his performances in England. He was especially sympathetic to Broadwood's technical adviser, Alfred Hipkins.

Those performances were not as frequent as he had hoped. Initially he caused some offence by turning down an invitation to play at the prestigious Philharmonic concerts (he was distinctly unimpressed by the orchestra, and even more by the exiguous rehearsal time), but thanks to his many contacts from Paris and Polish circles, there were several private invitations. They included a matinée at Lady Gainsborough's in late April, a performance at the home of the Marquis of Douglas in early May, and an engagement at Stafford House, home of the Duchess of Sutherland (a Polish sympathizer) in mid May, with Prince Albert and the Queen in attendance. However, it was public concerts that paid the rent, and of these Chopin managed to arrange only two semi-formal occasions, one at 99 Eaton Place (home of the well-known singer Mrs Adelaide Sartoris) and the other at 2 St James's Square, thanks mainly to the assistance of Henry Broadwood, who had become a good friend. The critical response to these concerts was broadly favourable, but he quickly tired of the English attitude to music and complained bitterly of it in letters to Paris and Warsaw. His remarks to Grzymała in particular rehearse themes familiar enough from the memoirs and essays of many continental musicians visiting England. A decade or so later, one of Chopin's most persuasive advocates, Joanna Kinkel, expressed it well: 'The English like to hear music all the time. But by "hear" I do not mean listen, let alone concentrate. Music is for them something added on, like perfume.'[28]

Chopin was soon disenchanted with these conditions, though as usual he was now slow to find his way into the highest strata of society. His reputation spread, and in a short time he was able to earn a small supplementary income from teaching some of the wealthy socialites of the capital, few of whom had any real interest in music. He found the social round increasingly tiring, especially as 'the good Scottish ladies' insisted on showing him off to everyone. 'They want me to go and see all their friends, whereas it is as much as I can do to keep body and soul together.'[29] The truth is that Chopin was happiest when he could retreat to the company of fellow musicians, such as his former pupils Thomas Tellefsen (who was fast making a name for himself in London) and Lindsay Sloper, his old friend Pauline Viardot, who performed some of her own vocal arrangements of Chopin mazurkas at several venues in London, including Covent Garden, and his new friend Jenny Lind, just then appearing in *La Sonnambula* and *Lucia di Lammermoor*. And in his letters of the period, his thoughts drift constantly back to mutual friends in Paris, including Sand. At the end of the season he was shattered physically and had very little to show financially. 'What are my plans for the future?', he wrote to Paris. 'I wish I knew.'[30]

Against this background, Jane Stirling's invitation to Scotland seemed as good an idea as any. At least there seemed nothing to lose, and on 5 August he set off from Euston on the newly opened railway route to Edinburgh. Henry Broadwood, solicitous as ever, had booked three first-class seats, one for Chopin, one for his new Irish servant, Daniel, and one for Chopin's feet, but even then the journey was arduous and exhausting. He was met by the Calder House family doctor, a Pole called Adam Lyszczyński and spent the following day sight-seeing in Edinburgh before setting off for Calder House in Midlothian, where

[28] Johanna Kinkel, *Musikalisches aus London. Auch eine Seite des Londoner Lebens. Betrachtungen einer deutschen Musikantin* (Universitätsbibliothek Bonn. Nachlass Johanna Kinkel S2391).
[29] Letter to Grzymała, 2 June 1848. *KFC*, vol. 2, pp. 248–9.
[30] Letter to Grzymała, end of July 1848: ibid., vol. 2, p. 255.

Jane Stirling and Mrs Erskine were staying with their brother-in-law, Lord Torpichen. This was a restful period, with visits from Tellesfsen and Lyszczyński, but it was interrupted by a visit to Manchester in late August to perform at one of the Gentlemen's Concerts, an engagement he had previously arranged in London. He stayed at Crumpsall House with the Schwabes, whom he had known in Paris. Salis Schwabe was one of a colony of German–Jewish immigrants who settled in the city in the early nineteenth century. Along with Auguste Léo's brother, also resident in Manchester, Schwabe worked hard at promoting music in the city, and attracted some of the very best artists to perform there. Indeed it was Herman Léo who brought Hallé to Manchester.

Chopin's recital paid well, and seems to have pleased him. But the reception was lukewarm. In the first place it is clear from reviews that Mancunians were not entirely familiar with Chopin's reputation as one of the legendary figures of contemporary pianism. And secondly, his tone was inevitably too small, and his performance too dependent on nuance, to make any real impact in such a large hall, with twelve hundred people in attendance. He was of course aware of this, and before the recital he warned his fellow pianist, George Osborne, whom he knew well from Paris days: 'My playing will be lost in such a large hall, and my compositions won't come over effectively.'[31]

After Manchester it was back to Scotland, this time to stay with another of Jane Stirling's sisters, Anne Houston, at Johnstone Castle near Glasgow. Chopin was growing impatient of life in the grand houses of the Scottish aristocracy. He was out of his element, starved of the kind of conversation he loved and increasingly ground down by the endless socializing. Much of the time he just sat in the corner lost in his own thoughts, since he had little or no grasp of the language. 'They bore me with their exaggerated attentions. I can neither rest nor work. I feel alone, alone, although I am surrounded by people.'[32] Moreover his health was deteriorating. When he gave a concert at the Merchants' Hall in Glasgow on 27 September, one member of the audience was struck by his death-like appearance, ashen-faced, stooped and seemingly destined for an early grave. Back in London he had written to Grzymała: 'often in the mornings I think I will cough myself to death. I am miserable at heart, but I try to deaden my feelings . . .'[33] In a letter to Fontana, just then visiting London from America, his thoughts wandered morosely to absent friends. 'I don't know why, but I keep thinking of our late friends Jan, Antoni, Witwicki, and Sobański; all those with whom I felt in the closest harmony . . .'[34] The one thing which lifted his

[31] George A. Osborne, 'Reminiscences of Frederick Chopin', in *Proceedings of the Royal Musical Association* (1879), p. 101.
[32] Letter to Grzymała, 9 September 1848. *KFC*, vol. 2, p. 274.
[33] 8–17 July 1848. Ibid., vol. 2, p. 253.
[34] 18 August 1848. Ibid., vol. 2, pp. 259–60.

spirits was the arrival in Scotland of Princess Marcelina Czartoryska and her husband, who had been temporarily obliged to come to London following the events of 1848 (she was expelled from Vienna as a Russian subject). The Czartoryskis attended his successful Glasgow concert and returned to dinner at Johnstone Castle. But that was a brief respite from the gloomy Scottish autumn.

Still he reflected on Sand. In a letter to Warsaw he recounted the most recent downturn in her fortunes. The peasants at Nohant had turned against her, resentful of her political activities in Paris, and her problems were compounded by highly publicised accusations from Augustine's father to the effect that Sand had turned his daughter into Maurice's mistress only to reject her and hand her over to a nobody. Chopin relayed these and other stories in long letters to his family. He also enjoyed telling them of the peculiarities of the British, once again castigating their attitude to art. 'They consider everything in terms of money; they love art because it is a *luxury*.' And he continued in bemused fashion, 'They are good, kind souls, but so eccentric that I think I would be turned to stone or become a machine if I stayed here.'[35] A little later he commented to Grzymała: 'By "art" they mean here painting, sculpture, and architecture. Music is not an art, and is not called by that name. Music is a *profession*, not an art, and no one ever calls any musician an artist or uses the term in that sense in print.'[36]

The final weeks in Scotland were trying. There was a stay at Keir House with another of Stirling's many relatives, William Stirling, followed by a further concert on 4 October, in the Hopetoun Rooms in Edinburgh, where he stayed with Adam Lyszczyński, who treated him with homeopathic medicines. And this was followed by another tiring bout of travel, including a stay at Lady Bellhaven's at Wishaw, Calder House once again and a few days at Hamilton Palace, where he took pleasure in the lively company of the exiled Prince and Princess of Parma. When he took ill there he retreated to his compatriot Dr Lyszczyński, not least because he was beginning to discover something of Jane Stirling's larger plan. Having introduced him to just about all her relatives, she clearly hoped that marriage would be the next step. But anything less amenable to Chopin would have been hard to find. The critical point is that whereas Sand had facilitated his creative work, Stirling suffocated it. And for Chopin this was the worst of all worlds. 'I cannot compose anything', he wrote to Grzymała. Again, 'What has become of my art?'. And, in the same letter, hoping to quieten gossip once and for all, 'I am closer to a coffin than a marriage bed'.[37]

When Chopin finally returned to London on 31 October he weighed less than seven stones. His tuberculosis was now at an advanced stage,

[35] 10–19 August 1848. Ibid., vol. 2, p. 268.
[36] 21 October 1848. Ibid., vol. 2, p. 282.
[37] 30 October 1848. Ibid., vol. 2, p. 284.

and it took all the efforts of the Stirling's homeopathic doctor to restore him to some semblance of normality. He stayed first with Henry Broadwood before an apartment was found for him at 4 St James's Square, close by Lord Dudley Stuart who had already arranged for Chopin to play at a charity concert on 16 November for the Polish Literary Association of the Friends of Poland, with the proceeds to go to the relief of Polish refugees. It was an annual event held at the Guildhall, in which a concert would be followed by a fancy-dress ball. It was Chopin's last public appearance. By then the doctors were aware that he was in the terminal stages of his illness and recommended a return to Paris as soon as possible.

He left London on 23 November, relieved to have escaped the clutches of his Scottish ladies, the elder of whom had occupied his final days on British soil in a fruitless attempt to convert him to the Presbyterian faith! Chopin's reactions to this need scarcely be spelt out. But he was too polite and too ill to protest. 'My face is puffed up with neuralgia', he wrote to Solange. 'I cannot rest and I cannot sleep. I have not left my bedroom since 1 November (apart from the 16th, when I played for an hour at a charity concert for Poles). Since then I have had a relapse. I am simply unable to rest here . . .'[38] As before, Henry Broadwood took care of the travel arrangements, and Chopin set out with Leonard Niedzwiedzki (one of the Czartoryski circle) and Daniel. Princess Marcelina Czartoryska, who had been a great comfort during the previous few weeks in London, saw him off at the station, *en route* Folkstone and Boulogne, and the following day he was in Paris.

Chopin was greeted at the Square d'Orléans by Franchomme, Grzymała, and Marie de Rozières, who, after a shaky start, had come to be counted among his closer friends. The Square d'Orléans must have seemed a less congenial place, now that all the old circle, including the Marlianis, had left. Only Alkan remained. But friends rallied round, taking care of him and keeping him company. Grzymała was no longer based in Paris, but he kept in touch as much as possible. Franchomme was a solid support, and looked after his affairs. Marie de Rozières helped take care of his domestic needs, and there were regular visits from Maria Kalergis and Delfina Potocka. He also saw Thomas Albrecht and Adolf Gutmann and, in the new year, Marcelina Czartoryska, when she came over from London. It was also at this time that Delacroix became a regular visitor to Chopin, noting fragments of their conversations in his journal entries between January and June of 1849, and thus providing us with our few reliably documented recorded observations by Chopin on the essential nature of his art.[39] The two also discussed George Sand, and Delacroix noted in his journal some perceptive observations from Chopin, triggered by the news that she was

[38] 22 November 1848. Ibid., vol. 2, p. 290.   [39] See chapter 2, note 46.

writing her autobiography. 'She has forgotten the past. She has power-ful emotions, but forgets quickly . . . She never feels guilty about things others accuse her of.'[40]

On his good days he would go for a drive with Daniel in his carriage, occasionally accompanied by Delacroix. And as the warmer weather of spring came, he organized some musical evenings at his home and even spent an evening at the opera to see Meyerbeer's newest offering, *Le prophète*. His disillusionment with this music is an intriguing measure of the distance travelled since his early days in Paris, back in the early 1830s. Then he had enthused endlessly about *Robert le diable*. Now he found nothing of substance in what is in truth the more substantial of the two operas. Summer approached, and Chopin was moved by his friends to an elegant residence in Chaillot, then almost in the country, partly because cholera was again raging in Paris. He was even provided with a night nurse, Katarzyna Matuszewska, by Princess Czartoryska. Although he was unaware of it, the rent for this apartment was partially paid by his friends. Money was becoming a problem in these closing months of Chopin's life. He had exhausted his savings from England, and he was no longer able to teach. Perhaps inferring that this would be the case, his elderly mother sent him some money from Poland, and instructed him to ask Izabella about the means of obtaining more.

But the real saviour was Jane Stirling. Hearing from Franchomme that Chopin was in financial difficulties, she pointed out that she had sent a sum of 25,000 francs in March, an enormous sum at that time. The concierge failed to deliver the envelope, perhaps with an eye to the future, but the money was eventually produced, and Chopin reluctantly accepted half of it as a loan. The Scottish ladies made their way to Chaillot and joined the procession of people, including Jenny Lind and Angelica Catalani (the singer who had presented him with a watch all those years ago in Warsaw), who called on the failing composer in the knowledge that his time was now limited. The Polish poet Cyprian Norwid, who later wrote several works inspired by Chopin, also visited him in these last months.

In June he had two particularly bad attacks, and wrote to his sister Ludwika, expressing his wish to see her again. Arrangements were made, and on 9 August Ludwika arrived with her husband and daugh-ter. She quickly provided just the kind of family environment that Chopin craved and desperately needed. His spirits were lifted by her arrival and he even began to think again about the future. He had little faith in the group of doctors then attending him (Dr Molin had since died), but he did follow their advice in moving to alternative, south-facing accommodation in Paris. Spacious rooms were found near Thomas Albrecht's office in the Place Vendôme and the move took place

[40] *The Journal of Eugène Delacroix*, p. 86.

on 9 September. There were five rooms on the first floor and a kitchen with servants' quarters on the ground floor.

Throughout September Chopin was visited constantly by friends and acquaintances, for the word quickly spread that he was dying.[41] Pauline Viardot remarked cynically that 'all the grand Parisian ladies considered it *de rigueur* to faint in his room.'[42] Solange was rarely absent, Marcelina Czartoryska likewise. Thomas Albrecht, Gutmann, and Franchomme were also regulars, along with the Scottish ladies. In these late stages George Sand made some indirect attempts to extract reliable news of him, including a clumsily worded letter to Ludwika, to which there was no reply. But right to the end, she seemed not to believe in the seriousness of the situation. 'I have so often seen him at death's door that I never despair of him.' There was also music. Delfina Potocka arrived from Nice on 15 October and sang to him, while Franchomme and Marcelina Czartoryska played cello and piano. Another friend, Teofil Kwiatkowski, was an almost constant presence, making numerous sketches which would later form the basis of famous oils and water colours of the death-bed scene.

Then, on 12 October, Alexander Jelowicki, an old acquaintance from Warsaw days, who had since taken orders, persuaded Chopin to partake of the last sacrament, though he was initially reluctant to do so. His death came in the early hours of 17 October, at around two o'clock. Solange was with him, holding his hand, when he had a kind of seizure. Solange later described how she called for Gutmann, who took Chopin in his arms. 'He passed away with his gaze fixed on me', she went on. 'He was hideous, I could see the tarnishing eyes in the darkness. Oh, the soul had died too.'[43]

---

[41] The view that tuberculosis caused Chopin's death is contested by J. A. Kuzemko in 'Chopin's Illnesses', *Journal of the Royal Society of Medicine*, vol. 87, December 1994, pp. 769–72. Kuzemko suggests that the symptoms of both Chopin and his sister Emilia are more compatible with α1 antitrypsin deficiency than with tuberculosis. I am grateful to Kenneth van Barthold for drawing my attention to this source.

[42] Letter to George Sand. Quoted in *KFC*, vol. 2, p. 464.

[43] Bibliothèque Nationale, George Sand, *Visages de Romantisme* (1977), no. 349, p. 83.

10

'Simplicity itself'

Chopin described simplicity as the 'highest goal', achievable 'when you have overcome all difficulties'.[1] A hard-won 'Periclean simplicity', marked by a severe exclusion of the extraneous and the merely ornamental, is indeed a feature of much of the music of his final years. Here Chopin reached a new plateau of creative achievement, almost as though the agony of composition, the resistance it set up, wrested from him only music of an exceptional, transcendent quality. Even in song, where Chopin seldom gave of his best, he mustered a refinement of technique and a depth of feeling which transcended the limitations of the salon romance. At least two of the late songs would not have disgraced the finest of the Lieder composers, evidence again that he was less and less capable of producing hack work in these final years.

'Nie ma czego trzeba' (There is no need), Op. 74 No. 13, was composed in 1845 to a text by Chopin's friend Józef Zeleski. It is a measured, dignified elegy, strophic in design, but easily sustaining our interest through its four unvaried stanzas. The simplicity of the vocal line here is of a different order altogether from that of the early songs. From an emaciated background of folksong, a beautifully shaped, powerfully expressive melody unfolds, the more refined and eloquent for its delicate, restrained cadential melisma and for the gentle modal archaisms of its accompaniment. It is difficult to dissociate this deeply expressive melody from an inescapable autobiographical resonance. 'To love, Oh, to love! and there is no one to love! To sing, oh, to sing! and there is no one to listen!' And even more telling: 'Here in a foreign desert, I dream just as I did at home.'

In the last and finest of the songs, 'Melodia' (Melody), Op. 74 No. 9, composed in 1847 to a text by Zygmunt Krasiński, Chopin gave expression to a more mystical, less directly personal sadness than that of 'Nie ma czego trzeba'. Yet this, too, may have caught and crystallized something of his own mood at the very moment of his most crushing sorrow, as though the anguish of personal loss could be sustained only by invoking the more universal grief suggested by Krasiński's characteristically

[1] 'Madame Streicher's recollections of Chopin . . .', quoted in Frederick Niecks, *Chopin as a Man and Musician*, vol. 2, p. 342.

Messianic text. Certainly none of the other extant songs attempts anything like the expressive range and the harmonic richness found in 'Melodia'. The vocal idiom is declamatory, a through-composed dramatic arioso which stabilizes only briefly into a suggestion of aria to evoke the march of the pilgrims. The (three times) repeated 'zapomnieni' ('forgotten') of the final line is a moment of exquisite poignancy, as Chopin allows the vocal line to draw briefly upon the melodic shapes of the piano prelude before easing the pain with a final consolatory phrase. 'Melodia' tantalizes us with what might have been. It stands apart from any attempt to trace a developmental line from the early to the later songs. Here, perhaps for the first time, Chopin engaged fully with the aesthetic of the art song, evidence of a much more general rethinking in the final years of his life.

A new-found simplicity is also discernible in the mazurkas composed during these final years, the three of Op. 63 (the last published during his lifetime), the second and fourth of the posthumously published Op. 67, and the sketched mazurka which was reconstructed and published as Op. 68 No. 4. Before composing these last mazurkas, however, Chopin wrote his Op. 59 set. This was the first completed opus of the summer of 1845, and stylistically it belongs with Opp. 50 and 56 rather than with Opp. 63 and 67. Like their immediate predecessors, the Op. 59 pieces are dance poems on the largest scale, displaying (or rather concealing) a wealth of harmonic and contrapuntal subtlety. The first expands the basic model of the dance piece by transforming its opening period (a characteristic sequential alternation of minor and relative major) into a twelve- rather than an eight-bar unit, and allowing this to become the normative unit for the first paragraph—four twelve-bar phrases in all. The middle section in the tonic major is a remarkable fantasy, whose intricacies of harmony and voice leading are signalled by the reharmonization of its opening two-bar motive, and whose hidden repetitions and discreet variations are among the most sophisticated to be found anywhere in the mazurkas. Tonally, too, the sequence is unusual. The second half of this middle section (bar 57) begins to veer in directions which make the unorthodox setting of the reprise (G sharp minor rather than A minor) as inevitable as the later tonal adjustment (bars 92–3) is imperceptible. (Compare the identical, but much less successful, tonal sequence in the F sharp major Impromptu.)

The generous lyricism which opens the A flat major Mazurka promises a less demanding experience, but in its very different way this second piece is just as adventurous as the first. The insistent repetitions and lucid diatonicisms of the opening section are offset by a brief middle section of highly unorthodox part movement (note the long delayed and oblique resolutions of the major second pedal point), by a reprise which dissolves into one of the most tonally elusive of Chopin's chains of sliding chromatic harmonies, and by an extended multi-sectional coda.[2] The F sharp minor Mazurka, in contrast, is a lively *oberek*, with characteristic lydian modality in its opening theme, a second section in the major and a bourdon-style refrain. And here, too, the simplicity is deceptive. The canonic bridge to an abbreviated reprise hints at subtleties to follow, as the closing phrase of the principal theme flowers into a passage of astonishing chromatic and contrapuntal resource (bars 122–34), leading to one of the freshest and most imaginative of Chopin's codas.

Chopin's last complete set of mazurkas, the three of Op. 63, was composed in 1846. Here he returned to the simpler outlines and more modest dimensions of his early mazurkas, as indeed he did again in the G minor and A minor Mazurkas composed a year or two later and published as Op. 67 Nos. 2 and 4 (the latter exists in several versions), and in the F minor, Op. 68 No. 4. It is now accepted that this F minor Mazurka, whose only extant source is a rather chaotic sketch, was not Chopin's last work. Indeed Jeffrey Kallberg's hypothesis that it was originally intended as the second of the Op. 63 set and subsequently abandoned in favour of the present piece, with which it shares not only the F minor tonality but several tonal and thematic features, carries much conviction.[3]

Along with their simpler outlines, these later mazurkas bring the folk model back a little closer to centre stage. Not that it had ever receded totally, but in Opp. 50, 56, and 59 it is often absorbed by more sophisticated harmonic and contrapuntal structures. Indeed there is a kind of dialectic in some of these larger pieces between the folkloristic presence and more complex materials which threaten (but only threaten) to obscure that presence. In the later mazurkas the folk presence is seldom in doubt. The bourdon fifths in the opening section of Op. 63 No. 1 are typical, as are the third-beat accents of the second section. So, too, is the 'exotic' modality in the middle sections of Op. 63 No. 3 and Op. 67 No. 2, and the alternation of perfect and lydian fourths in Op. 67 No. 4. There is an attractive symbolism in this return to Polish roots, as also in the fact that the last completed composition was indeed almost certainly a mazurka, albeit not the one wrongly so described by Fontana and a host of later commentators, myself included.[4]

It is now widely agreed, on both stylistic and paper evidence, that the C minor Nocturne (KK 1233–5) is a late work, probably dating from 1847. It remained unpublished until 1938. With its restrained ornamental melody and ostinato-like accompaniment, it recovers (and if anything understates) techniques familiar from the earlier nocturnes rather than

[2] See the discussion in Kallberg, 'The Chopin Sources', pp. 189–247.
[3] 'Chopin's Last Style', *Journal of the American Musicological Society* 38/2 (1985), pp. 264–315.
[4] See the discussion in Jean-Jacques Eigeldinger, 'Placing Chopin: Reflections on a Compositional Aesthetic', in *Chopin Studies 2* (Cambridge, 1994), p. 104.

breaking new ground. In this it contrasts strikingly with the Two Nocturnes, Op. 62. These pieces, composed in 1846, represent the pinnacle of Chopin's achievement in the genre. The mood is detached and controlled, a rarefied, almost Olympian calm. The opening section of the B major once more achieves an inspired simplicity of utterance, a melody of exquisite restraint which is at the same time immensely subtle in its inner working. That subtlety is partly a matter of phrase structure and partly of counterpoint. Chopin promotes a sense of endless flow, a kind of musical prose, through the metrical relocation of melodic repetitions, inviting us incidentally to think again about the very opening of the piece. The contrapuntal interest lies mainly in the multivalent richness of the accompaniment, where motivic fragments interact delicately with the principal melodic layer, gradually transforming the initial texture of accompanied melody into one approaching genuinely independently part movement.

Formally, the B major nocturne permits interruptions and discontinuities of a kind found elsewhere in the works of this final period, most noticeably in the great Polonaise-fantasy. The even flow of the opening paragraph gives way, for instance, to an abrupt change of texture at bar 21. Here the independent part movement is replaced by quite new material, with a syncopated accompaniment which hints briefly at the sostenuto middle section, and a semiquaver motive which looks ahead to the extended coda. This new material has something of the character of an interruption, and it culminates in a dramatic ornamental flourish, before the main theme is allowed to resume its course. As we shall see, there are similar formal interruptions in the reprise.

Throughout this opening section and the middle section Chopin exercises the greatest possible restraint in the ornamentation of his basic material. It is all the more magical, then, when the reprise of the main theme is presented entirely in trilled notes and allowed to open out, albeit briefly, into ecstatic, yet carefully controlled *fioriture*. Precisely because of the earlier simplicity of presentation, this reprise emerges as one of the supreme achievements of Chopin's ornamental melody. And characteristically it is halted in its tracks, interrupted by new sequential material, clearly derived from the opening section (the later stages), but essentially different from it and itself supplanted by a restatement of the semiquaver motive, now elaborated into the extended, curiously disembodied tracery which forms a coda to the nocturne. The overall shape of the piece transparently derives from a large-scale ternary design, but the detailed sequence of events—incorporating what we might describe as Chopin's strategies of formal concealment—is entirely unpredictable.

An examination of both the opening melody and the sostenuto middle section of this B major Nocturne reveals something rather akin to Chopin's own version of *endliche Melodie*. This is taken even further in the E major Nocturne. I have demonstrated elsewhere the skilful balance between repetition and variation in the long thirty-two bar melodic paragraph which forms the opening section of this Nocturne, essentially a theme and three 'variations'.[5] Exact repetition is kept to a minimum in this opening section, and the abbreviated reprise of the melody (bars 58–70) reinforces this by offering yet another variation of the theme. The B section (which also forms an extended coda) employs a form of differentiated counterpoint commonly found in the later music, where tension–release patterns arise as much from dissonance–consonance relationships within a contrapuntal texture as from underlying harmonic progressions. It is striking that in these very late works Chopin arrived— within the constraints of his own, highly individual stylistic world—at some of the major technical preoccupations of late-nineteenth-century music. In the Op. 62 Nocturnes he approached in his own way both the so-called 'developing variation' of Brahms and Schoenberg and the 'dissonant counterpoint' of Mahler.

The late waltzes follow the pattern of the nocturnes in that there is again a single independent piece of relatively traditional cast (the A minor, KK 1238–8, whose date of composition is uncertain, but which was first published as late as 1955) and a complete set, Op. 64, composed in 1847. The three pieces of Op. 64 represent Chopin's art at its most polished and urbane, drawing the familiar gestures of the earlier waltzes into a miniature compendium of all those most delicate sentiments we associate with the Chopin waltz. The key word is charm, since this overrides more individual moods, the airy, breezy quality of the D flat major (the so-called 'minute waltz'), the alternating melancholy and abandon of the C sharp minor, the grace and elegance of the A flat major. Familiarity cannot dull these pieces, which somehow retain their freshness and spontaneity through repeated performances. Every nuance is exquisitely shaped and honed to perfection; every detail is skilfully crafted and carefully placed.

Italian traits, mediated or not, are often identified in Chopin's melodic style, especially in the nocturnes, where the term 'bel canto' seems inescapable. But Italian vernacular traditions—Sicilian and Venetian respectively—are also evoked generically on two occasions, in the rather light-weight Tarantella, Op. 43 and in the magnificent Barcarolle, Op. 60, one of the three great extended works of the final years. Admittedly generic features associated with the barcarolle appear in several earlier works, including all four ballades and more particularly the G major Nocturne, Op. 37 No. 2. This latter piece explicitly draws upon the popular genre, not only through the familiar rocking accompaniment but through the 'sweet' parallel thirds of its gondolier's song. But the Barcarolle, Op. 60, composed in 1845–6, remains in the end a solitary and majestic work, accepting the untroubled disposition of the genre,

[5] *The Music of Chopin*, pp. 94–5.

but carrying its gentle, swaying lyricism through to powerfully climactic perorations in the final stages. It has a mixture of luminosity and strength quite unlike anything else in Chopin's music, but shares with the other very late works a transparency and clarity of expression which points to a plane well beyond technique.

The three-bar introduction, characteristically elaborating dominant harmony, immediately suggests a world yet to come, the liquid textures and harmonic opacity of Fauré, and even more of Debussy and Ravel, none of whom was a stranger to the barcarolle. *En bateau* seems just on the horizon, rather than half a century in the future. Then, as in the Berceuse, composed two years earlier, Chopin defines his genre with a two-bar accompanimental frame before giving the melody its head. As in the Berceuse, moreover, he allows the popular genre to dictate a relatively static left-hand layer, approaching at times the ostinato quality found in some of his late works. Over this accompaniment the melody (A1) unfolds in an extended arc, incorporating its own subsidiary section (A2) before returning in richly varied form. Variation is indeed the life blood of this music, as of many of the late pieces, and it ranges from the ornamental elaboration of minor details to the transformation and 'enlargement' of extended paragraphs.

The second theme (B1) in A major is approached by way of a figure which draws on the introductory bars and is itself absorbed by the right-hand accompaniment pattern, the middle 'voice' of the texture. The left hand again establishes an ostinato-like platform, not unlike that found in the late polonaises, while the principal melody just about maintains its precarious distance from the middle voice. It is with the repetition of this extended paragraph (bar 51) that Chopin first builds the music towards the kind of apotheosis which we associate with the final stages of the ballades, giving way in due course to a secondary theme (B2). It is odd how pre-echoes of early-twentieth-century music strike us in this piece. French composers of the *fin de siècle* have been cited. But the elaboration of this secondary theme (bar 66 ff.) looks to another successor. It is achieved by methods which would in due course become part and parcel of the musical language of Rachmaninov.

The exposition of these two thematic groups is interrupted by independent material whose structural function is more that of a 'buffer' than a 'transition' or a 'development'. The separation of the two structural halves of the fourth Ballade by independent (non-developmental) material is not dissimilar, and it is perhaps worth pointing out the similarity between the *meno mosso* material at the start of this 'buffer' and the second, barcarolle-influenced theme of the Ballade. This gently pulsing, chromatically evasive *meno mosso* gives way to an improvisatory 'dolce sfogato' whose nocturne-like melody (related to the subsidiary theme of the 'second subject') introduces a new, if short-lived, texture to the Barcarolle. It leads directly to the triumphant, fore-shortened reprise of the first theme, and of the two components of the second theme (in reverse order, but transposed to the tonic major in conformance with a sonata-form tonal dialectic). But the masterstroke has yet to come—in the unexpected drama and beauty of the coda.[6]

Chopin's correspondence makes it clear that for some time he was undecided about a title for the Polonaise-fantasy, Op. 61, which occupied him for some eighteen months during 1845–6.[7] Only the first presentation of the principal theme and its brief subsidiary theme (bars 66–91) have close links with the familiar polonaise rhythm. From that point the dance elements recede, and it becomes much more helpful to consider the work in relation to the genre title 'Fantasy'. Links with the Op. 49 Fantasy are especially pertinent here. The two introductions are explicitly linked motivically (see Ex. 38), and there are associations, too, between the formal and tonal schemes in that both works have a 'slow movement' in B major embedded within their prevailing A flat major tonality. Indeed this combination of a slow, improvisatory introduction and a lengthy 'slow movement' at the heart of the work is one which seems to link both works to the tradition of the early nineteenth-century fantasy.

Yet the differences are also striking. Whereas Op. 49 takes its starting point in a sonata form, stretching its conventions in the spirit of improvisation, Op. 61 begins rather from the outline of a large-scale ternary design, adapting this in various ways, enriching it, and in the best sense obscuring it. The work offers us the single most inspired example of Chopin's capacity to maintain vitality and interest over the span of a greatly extended ABA design. The first flank of this design (following the tonally inductive introduction) is the 'polonaise' theme, together with its subsidiary theme and a series of transformations. The theme itself is another of those expansive melodic paragraphs based on 'developing variation' which are typical of Chopin's later works, their conquest of symmetry setting them apart stylistically from earlier works with which they still have a clear affinity. Already in its first presentation it is allowed to reach a point of considerable expressive intensity, before giving way to a contrasted subsidiary theme, and a powerful series of sequential transformations (bars 92–115).

The central part of the ternary design is the B major slow movement, which has its own introduction (bars 148–52) and its own nocturne-like subsidiary theme in G sharp minor (bars 182–205). The principal slow movement theme then resumes briefly at bar 206. More important than this sequence, however, is the formal discontinuity with which it unfolds. Something of this has been noted in relation to the Op. 62

[6] For a detailed reading of the work, to which several observations here are indebted, see John Rink, 'The Barcarolle: Auskomponierung and apotheosis', in Chopin Studies (Cambridge, 1988), pp. 195–219.

[7] KFC, vol. 2, p. 155.

Nocturnes, and it is of paramount importance to the Polonaise-fantasy. The course of the slow movement is quite literally interrupted by the G sharp minor 'nocturne', and the flow of this is in turn halted by the remarkable series of trills (single, double, triple, and quadruple) which leads to the resumption of the principal slow movement material.

Such formal discontinuity is a feature of the work as a whole, and is one means by which Chopin achieves necessary obfuscation while projecting a simple ternary design over such an extended time scale. If we return to the first flank of the design, we will note that the transformations of the polonaise theme do not lead directly and straightforwardly into the central 'slow movement'. Instead they resolve on to a stable nocturne-like melody in B flat major (bar 116), whose ornamental melody and (relatively) closed phrases would scarcely be perceived as transitional by the innocent ear. When the true tonal and thematic goal—the slow movement—is reached (bar 148) this B flat major 'nocturne' needs to be reinterpreted retrospectively as *en passant* in relation to the larger outlines of the structure. In other words, Chopin has deliberately obscured the first of the two formal divisions of his large-scale ternary design.

He does much the same with the second formal division, between the slow movement and the reprise.[8] The resumption of the slow movement material at bar 206 is hardly allowed to establish itself before Chopin unexpectedly brings back the introduction. Nor is this allowed to continue beyond a few bars, before the second theme of the slow movement returns, no less unexpectedly, in F minor. These two interpolations are entirely unpredictable and obscure the approach to the apotheotic reprise of both the polonaise theme (bar 242) and the main slow movement theme (bar 254). Again, as in the Barcarolle, the two main themes are now brought into the fold of the tonic, an element of synthesis which owes much to the sonata principle. And the A flat major of the slow movement reprise is the more powerful for the exhilarating tonal parenthesis to B major which immediately precedes it (bars 249–52). This minor third relation between A flat and B, present right from the first two chords of the work, is a major integrating element of the work, present on many levels of its structure.[9]

These two works, his last extended compositions for solo piano, demonstrate clearly that in the final years of his life Chopin was approaching his art in a spirit of renovation and renewal astonishing for one in such a mental and physical state. It is true that following his departure for Britain he was unable to compose much. But in a sense this merely confirms that there was a change of compositional aesthetic, no sudden change, but one which became qualitative in these years.

[8] See the discussion in Kallberg, 'Chopin's Last Style'.

[9] I have demonstrated this in 'The Composition-draft of the Polonaise-fantasy: The Issue of Tonality', in *Chopin Studies* (Cambridge, 1988), pp. 41–58.

Chopin was intensely, painfully self-critical as a composer at this time. Each piece had become a struggle, and he delayed as long as he dared sending his music to the publisher, since this in a sense sealed its fate, defining it as 'complete'. Moreover he set himself new and ever more challenging problems in these later years, tackling new generic problems (the Barcarolle), new formal problems (the Polonaise-fantasy) and—most surprising and challenging of all—the problems associated with a new medium.

Strictly speaking, the cello-piano medium was not new to Chopin. He had already composed the Op. 3 Polonaise in Warsaw and its introduction in Vienna, and he collaborated with Franchomme on the *Duo concertant* on a theme of Meyerbeer during his early years in Paris. But these were occasional pieces, in which he did not even attempt to grasp the nettle of combining the two very different instruments on something like equal terms. It was, at any rate, a nettle for Chopin, whose entire compositional output to 1845–6 had been centred on the gradual, painstaking refinement and perfection of a single medium. In the late Cello Sonata, Op. 65, on the other hand, he set out to write a full-blown duo sonata for the first time in his life. He had to tackle a special set of problems here, and it is hardly surprising that the attempt caused him more anguish than he had endured with any other single composition.

One consequence of working with a new medium is that the Cello Sonata inhabits a significantly different stylistic world from the other late compositions. To put it over simply, this work moves somewhat in the direction of German models, Schumann and Mendelssohn in particular. This is apparent even in the general layout of its piano writing, which is at times oddly un-Chopinesque. If anything, the Sonata looks back stylistically towards the terrain occupied by some of the early Warsaw-period works, such as the Trio, Op. 8 and the two Piano Concertos. This connection is reinforced, moreover, by an unmistakable reversion to some of the motivic and rhythmic gestures characteristic of those earlier works. It is hard to know if this was a conscious gesture of reprise on Chopin's part, or simply an inevitable by-product of the chamber medium; probably the latter. The certainty is that any retrospective element remains a matter of style rather than substance. This is a work of full maturity—meditative, introspective, and profoundly original.

One of the easiest, and least fruitful, of analytical quests is for the unifying 'basic shape' underlying a musical work. I have already suggested, however, that there are works in which Chopin legitimized such a quest through explicit compositional strategies. The first notes assigned to the cello in this Sonata are a case in point. Preceding the cello statement of the piano's opening theme, they stand apart, an opening before the opening. By dislocating their three-note motive from its original setting and isolating it from the thematic repetition, they mark it out for our attention.[10] That motive plays a role in the work somewhat analogous to that of the three-note motive in Brahms's Second Symphony (of which, incidentally, it is an inversion). It appears unchanged as a device of formal articulation later in the movement, especially at the beginning and end of the development section, where it is associated with the piano figuration which precedes its first appearance. It recurs in the mazurka-like Scherzo, making up the opening notes of the first theme, and later in that movement, too (bar 81 ff.), it is strategically isolated and attention-seeking. Even the lyrical, elegaic, yet contrapuntally rich slow movement (marked by its subtle use of invertible counterpoint) is launched by the same three-note motive, and so, too, is the final Allegro, a sonata-rondo without development. The integrative role of the motive is enhanced, moreover, by its privileged harmonic setting on all these occasions, since it appears consistently on adjacent members of the cycle of fifths relative to the overall tonic.

The concern for organicism evidenced by this cyclic use of the motive is further evidenced by its developing variation throughout the first movement, and the first subject group in particular. This is achieved partly through intervallic change (the second interval is expanded to a minor third, major third, and perfect fourth) and partly through its varied placing within unfolding melodic paragraphs. The effect is of a constantly changing, 'continuous' melodic line woven from a small repertory of basic shapes, and against this background the clear periodicity and sequential repetition of the second subject is especially beautiful. The close-knit thematicism of this first movement underpins a relatively clear formal design, which includes a repeated exposition, but (as in the two mature piano sonatas) omits the first subject group in the recapitulation. The leaning towards German models is apparent here, too. But far from signalling a slavish imitation, it represents a significant expansion of Chopin's compositional resources. His renovative attitude to his art is nowhere plainer than in his decision to tackle a string sonata, leaving the security of his own instrument to engage with the classical canon. There is some reason to think that Chopin's future direction as a composer (no longer a pianist-composer) would have continued along this path. Among the sketches for the Cello Sonata, there are drafts of a work for violin and piano. They could plausibly have been intended as the scherzo movement (in D minor) of a violin sonata.

Compositional process: sketches, fair copies, editions

Like many pianist-composers, Chopin allowed his first thoughts about a piece to take shape at the piano. 'Invention came to his piano, sudden,

---

[10] A more far-reaching interpretation of motivic unity is offered by Anatole Leikin in 'The Sonatas', in *The Cambridge Companion to Chopin*, pp. 160–88.

complete, sublime', was George Sand's description.[11] It was a process not so far removed from improvisation, and it would seem that for Chopin much of the agony of composition concerned his attempts to recapture on paper nuances which had already been perfectly realized at the keyboard. We can know very little about these earliest stages of the creative process, about the ways in which a composer first begins to restructure existing ideas to create new ones. Janáček described such moments as 'the most interesting ones in the history of composition—and yet the darkest ones',[12] What we can say is that the compositional process involved at this stage operates largely at a pre-conscious level and usually involves 'thinking in sounds' rather than 'thinking in concepts'.[13] The end result, in any case, is that Chopin would draft complete pieces or large stretches of pieces at the piano, retaining them *in intellectu* before he picked up his pen.

When he did so it might be to sketch some of the basic ideas as a preliminary to making a fair copy. Extant Chopin sketches are not copious. More often than not he would proceed straight to a fair copy. What few sketches there are tend to be for the later music, which, as we have noted, caused him much greater difficulty than earlier pieces. Characteristically he would sketch on twelve- or fourteen-stave loose bifolia, spread out so that the second recto page might be used to draft extended paragraphs (continuity-drafts), while the first verso might serve for working out details, often attempts to negotiate the trickier corners—the joins or links—of the structure. The sketches are of course private documents and contain various mnemonic and abbreviation signs. They are also in general rather messy, with copious scratches and ink blots where Chopin removed excess ink from his pen.

Some brief notes on three of the later sketches will indicate the extent to which they may throw light on the compositional process. In some cases, for all their intrinsic interest, they function largely as mnemonics. A case in point is the highly unusual sketch for the Berceuse where the separate *variantes* are presented in columns made up of four-bar segments.[14] This tabular formulation, ordered by numbers, as shown in Plates 16 and 17, then enabled Chopin to identify the role and placing of each 'variant' within the form as a whole. In other words, the sketch offered Chopin a mnemonic for the notation of the entire piece in a remarkably economic way. Such a presentation is far from typical for

[11] George Sand, *Historie de ma vie. Œuvres autobiographiques*, ed. Georges Lubin, 2 vols. (Paris, 1978), vol. 2, p. 446.

[12] 'How Ideas Came About', in *Janáček's Uncollected Essays on Music*, ed. and tr. Mirka Zemanová (London and New York, 1989), pp. 69–78.

[13] I elaborate this in 'The Composition-draft of the Polonaise-fantasy: The Issue of Tonality' (see note 9).

[14] This sketch is discussed at length in Wojciech Nowik, 'Fryderyk Chopin's op. 57—from *Variantes* to *Berceuse*', in *Chopin Studies* (Cambridge, 1988), pp. 25–40.

the Chopin sketches, however, and is largely a function of the special formal conception of the Berceuse.

A quite different sketching procedure was adopted for the Poloniase-fantasy. Here the three main sections of the large-scale ternary design were sketched as continuity-drafts, presumably on the 2r. folia, while linking materials were worked and reworked on what were probably the 1v. folia. The sketching process, in other words, confirms the interpretation of the piece as a 'problematized' ternary structure. This is one of the most interesting of all Chopin manuscript sources, and it reveals some surprising things about compositional process. It is clear, for example, that Chopin only decided to give the first theme a polonaise accompaniment at a very late stage of the creative process, probably after most of the piece had been composed as a 'fantasy'.[15] The polonaise rhythm was added in a different ink, and preparatory bars of accompaniment were inserted at the same time to establish the generic point (rather as in the Berceuse and Barcarolle). A glance at the score reminds us that it is indeed only this first statement of the principal theme, and the immediately subsequent episode, which carries the characteristic polonaise rhythm, and the episode is also sketched without the rhythm.

The sketch further reveals that Chopin arrived at the complex formal design of the work in two distinct stages. There are, in short, two layers of sketching. The first layer consists of three continuity drafts, comprising the principal theme, with its subsidiary episode and transformations, the slow section (without its subsidiary theme) and the reprise. The second layer complicates this basic ternary design by inserting the two nocturne-like melodies, and it was probably also at this stage that Chopin decided to bring back the introduction and second nocturne-like melody after the slow section. It was while drafting the 'second nocturne' that Chopin made the most radical of all the changes to his first conception of the piece, a change to its tonal structure. As I have demonstrated elsewhere,[16] the 'slow movement', including its subsidiary theme, was originally sketched a semitone higher (C major/A minor rather than B major/G sharp minor), and so too was the preceding 'first nocturne' (B major rather than B flat major). It was in the course of sketching several approaches to be trilled 'cadenza' (the relevant folio is Plate 18) that Chopin decided to lift the slow movement down a semitone, thus altering fundamentally the tonal relations of the piece as a whole.

The initial impulse here was probably related to the manual difficulty of the trills themselves. An attempt to play them in C major will quickly make the point. But the ramifications of the decision, practical and structural, were enormous. Chopin immediately faced the difficulty of

[15] See the analysis in Kallberg, 'Chopin's Last Style'.   [16] See note 9.

redrafting the later stages of the transformations of the 'polonaise' theme in order to change the tonal setting of the 'nocturne'. And it was probably at this late stage that he returned to the very opening of the work, rethinking the harmonic setting of the opening bars in the light of his revised tonal structure. He had initially begun with a C minor harmony, and the sketch records his attempts to rethink this, replacing it first with an F minor harmony and then with the A flat minor harmony of the final version. The effect of all these changes was to create a powerfully integrative minor third relation at several levels of structure, from the opening chords of the piece to its larger tonal scheme. Even the link to the reprise could exploit this relation (F minor–A flat major) once the material following the trills—the resumption of the slow movement—had been dropped from C major to B major.

The majority of Chopin's work sheets belong to the Cello Sonata.[17] They range from the intractable materials relating to the first movement, containing extraneous materials, innumerable 'non-sequiturs' and many reworkings of detail, to the apparently straightforward continuity-draft of the rondo finale. Yet, as Nancy S. Morgan has shown, there are hidden complexities in even the finale sketches.[18] Morgan derived several alternative models for the genesis of the rondo from a close analysis of the available evidence, and she went on to demonstrate that—just as in Op. 61—these amount to two quite distinct 'layers' of sketching practice. The first layer consists of relatively closed thematic statements, fluently written and largely unedited, while the second is concerned with larger formal problems, with transitional sections, altered thematic returns and a coda. Again as in the Polonaise-fantasy, formal problems were addressed at a later stage, after the main thematic elements were in place.

For Chopin it was more usual in any case to bypass the sketch stage and proceed to an engraver's manuscript (*Stichvorlage*). However, these are very often 'dirty', with changes made either at the time of writing or later (sometimes in a different pen), involving heavy tesselations and revisions on the third staff above or below the main text. In many cases Chopin abandoned the manuscript to begin again, and such 'rejected public manuscripts' are valuable documents. Again the late works are especially rich in these sources, and there are valuable accounts by Jeffrey Kallberg of rejected manuscripts for the second and third of the Op. 59 Mazurkas in particular.[19] We might add the incomplete autograph for the fourth Ballade, with a 6/4 rather than 6/8 time-signature

---

[17] They have been transcribed, though in a far from ideal arrangement, by Ferdinand Gajewski in *The Worksheets to Chopin's Violoncello Sonata* (New York, 1988).

[18] Nancy S. Morgan, 'Formal Redefinition and the Genesis of the Finale to the Sonata for Violoncello and Piano, Opus 65, by Frédéric Chopin' (Diss., U. of Pennsylvania, 1983).

[19] Kallberg, 'The Chopin Sources'.

Fig. 47 Rejected autograph of Ballade No. 4, Op. 52: transcribed extracts

and with numerous variants to the final version, not least a major change in the shape of the principal theme (Ex. 47).[20]

It may be worth focusing a little on two lesser-known rejected engraver's manuscripts. I have described elsewhere the history and provenance of the rejected engraver's manuscript of the C minor Polonaise, Op. 40 No. 2.[21] The essential difference between this first version and the one we know today is a much simpler middle section for the trio, affecting bars 71–82. Ex. 48 reproduces the passage in full (a), together with the beginning of the final version (b). Both versions fulfil the same harmonic function, deflecting the A flat major trio towards its relative minor and both use the same two-note motive as the basis of their repetition structure. Yet within these shared frames the later version is infinitely the richer in harmonic and textural details. By drawing the appoggiatura motive into the substance of the melodic line and combining it with an entirely new left-hand semiquaver tracery, Chopin both enriched and concealed the underlying harmonic movement, generating in the process lively points of dissonance between the two hands. He also corrected by this means the most serious weakness of the first version, the absence of any real harmonic progression to the cadential pattern at bar 8 of Ex. 48(a). By extending the repetition unit from two to four bars and ensuring that the sequential pattern escapes any premature reference to C major harmony, Chopin invests the arrival of the

[20] See my discussion in *Chopin: The Four Ballades* (Cambridge, 1992), pp. 24–5.
[21] 'An Unknown Chopin Autograph', *The Musical Times*, July, 1986, pp. 376–8.

Fig. 48 Polonaise, Op. 40 No. 2
(a) Rejected manuscript: transcription

(b) Final version

dominant chord at bar 79 with a structural weight which eluded it in the first version.

The rejected manuscript of the F sharp major Impromptu, Op. 36 comprises only the material from bar 70 to the end.[22] Bars 70–96 are on both recto and verso of a single folio, held in the Chopin Society, while bars 97 to the end, together with a separate draft of the codetta (bars 30–8), are at the end of the *Rondo à la krakowiak* autograph in the Czartoryski library of the National Museum at Cracow. At the beginning of the final variation (bar c) there is clear evidence of three stages in the creative process, all of them presenting compositional difficulties (see Plate 12). First the variation was written in semiquavers, flowing naturally from the triplet variation but resulting in eccentric formal proportions. Then Chopin composed a quite new line in triplet semiquavers (the third-staff variant), solving the problem of proportions but creating a gapped rather than conjunct line with some consequent loss of elegance. Finally he simply halved the note values of the original (a third stem was added and the bar lines cancelled), solving that problem but creating a new one, the break in continuity between the triplet quaver variation and what was now a demisemiquaver variation.

With the final version now much more compact, Chopin may well have felt that the original, prelude-like ending (see Plate 13) was inadequate and he composed a short coda, with connections of character to the central march. He then added a version of this to the end of the first section as a codetta (the 'x' in the manuscript establishes that this codetta was a later insertion). None of the three versions is ideal. The difficulties registered in the rejected manuscript reflect a basic problem of form which Chopin never really solved.

Even those engraver's manuscripts which were sent to the publisher often contain evidence of several distinct stages of the compositional process. In this respect Saint-Saëns's discussion of the autograph of the second Ballade remains something of a classic study, revealing different layers of decision-making behind the final version.[23] Among other things he showed that there were an additional two notes at the opening (depriving the beginning of the theme of its metrical subtlety), that the melody note at bar 7 was F rather than A, that at one stage an extra two bars were inserted at bar 83, and that the caesura in the main theme at bar 88 was originally a bar later and lasted a complete bar. He also demonstrated several stages in the genesis of the figuration at bar 47 and of the bass passages at bar 189. Not one of these observations is trivial. Each is revealing of the gradual stages of refinement and polish which were deemed necessary by Chopin before he felt able to release a work to the public. And even then the 'finality' was largely expedient.

[22] See Jim Samson, 'Chopin's F sharp Impromptu: Notes on Genre, Style and Structure', in *Chopin Studies 3* (Warsaw, 1990), pp. 297–304.
[23] See chapter 6, note 16.

Since for copyright reasons his music was published more or less simultaneously by publishers in three different countries, Chopin in many cases needed three different engraver's manuscripts (another option was to use the proofs of one edition for the preparation of another). These were not all autographs, of course, but for some works there is more than one autograph *Stichvorlage*, and for shorter pieces there may be additional presentation autographs, some of them written several years after the piece had been composed. This amounts to a manuscript tradition of some complexity, with endless variants raising difficult questions about any so-called definitive text. And the complexity is increased when we add to the mix the work of the copyists. Julian Fontana was Chopin's principal copyist, but there were numerous others, including pupils such as Adolf Gutmann, and these were used more frequently in the years following Fontana's departure for America. Two brief examples of the information carried by such copies will suffice.

In addition to the sketch of the Berceuse, there are two manuscript sources, an autograph and a copy with autograph glosses. As Wojciech Nowik has pointed out,[24] the two autograph glosses on this copy significantly change the character of the work. The final bar in Chopin's autograph closed on a dotted minim, and this was faithfully reproduced by the copyist. Chopin then altered the copy by changing the final bar to crotchet followed by minim rest, an apparently trivial change which in fact makes a significant difference to the effect of the work's ending. At the same time, and more crucially, he changed the opening of the work. The autograph begins at bar 3 of the final version, launching immediately into the melody without any preliminaries. Again the copyist faithfully reproduced this. By subsequently adding the two-bar introduction, Chopin radically changed our perception of the piece, underlining its generic character before introducing the melody, and it is surely no coincidence that this change was accompanied by a change of title—from 'Variantes' to Berceuse.

Along with the autograph of the second Ballade (the manuscript analysed by Saint-Saëns) there is a copy by Adolf Gutmann, again with autograph glosses. Stemmatic analysis of these sources in turn explains some of the discrepancies between the first editions of the work. The final bars will serve as an example. In the first French edition (Troupenas), the penultimate chord has the bass note E' while in the first German edition (Breitkopf & Härtel), it is an octave lower, E''. An examination of the autograph reveals that Chopin originally opted for E'', and subsequently revised it to E'. Since the autograph served as the *Stichvorlage* for Troupenas, the French edition duly reproduced the E'. Gutmann also followed Chopin's revision in his copy. But Chopin then

---

[24] See note 14.

added a gloss to the Gutmann copy and restored his original thought of E". And since the copy served as *Stichvorlage* for the Breitkopf & Härtel edition, the German edition reproduced E". Strictly speaking, this was Chopin's 'final intention', and that fact should be duly noted by the modern editor. At the same time, for reasons already intimated in this study, the so-called 'law of final intentions' has limited usefulness in Chopin editing.

The truth is that Chopin was an inveterate reviser, and never really felt that any piece was finished. That fact is evidenced by the discrepancies between the three first editions, reflecting, of course, discrepancies in their manuscript sources. It is evidenced even more tellingly by the autograph glosses on first (mainly French) editions belonging to family and pupils. There are several collections containing such glosses, including Ludwika Jędrzejewicz's three-volume collection, Camille O'Meara-Dubois's three-volume collection and—most importantly—Jane Stirling's seven-volume collection. The status of these glosses, which post-date publication, is naturally deeply problematical; in many cases the annotations were no doubt made for pedagogical reasons peculiar to the pupil in question. But the Stirling scores arguably have special significance as complete corpus of music and one almost certainly compiled and corrected under Chopin's direct supervision. It is likely that he intended these scores to form the basis of a collected edition which might supersede the first French editions, but their status in relation to an authentic edition will no doubt remain controversial.[25]

Enough has been said to give some indication of the confusion of manuscript and early printed sources and of the consequent difficulties facing Chopin editors. But a brief postlude on the editions may well be useful. Following the posthumous publications of 1855 and 1859 (Meissonier, Paris and A. M. Schlesinger, Berlin), the earliest collected editions were French, the Schonenberger, edited by Fétis, and the Richault, edited by Tellefsen, both of 1860. Two opposed philosophies are already apparent in these editions, the first marked by editorial licence—an implicit belief that the editor knows best—and the second by an attempt to recover Chopin's performing and teaching methods, even where this involves departures from manuscript and printed sources. Both, in other words, are permissive with sources, but for entirely different reasons.

These very different editorial philosophies continued to inform later nineteenth- and early twentieth-century editions. Tending towards the first approach were two heavily edited Russian editions, one (Stellowsky) of 1861 and the other (Jurgenson) of 1873–6. This latter, edited (heavily, and with liberal additions to Chopin's expression and tempo markings) by the Liszt pupil Karl Klindworth, was well travelled

---

[25] See Jean-Jaques Eigeldinger, *Chopin: Pianist and Teacher*, pp. 200–11.

and much used. It was later reprinted by Bote & Bock (Berlin, 1880–5) and is best known today as the 'Augener' edition (London, 1879), with further revisions by Xaver Scharwenka in a reissue of 1910. Also in this category are the Köhler edition for Litolff (Brunswick, 1880–5), the Biehl edition for Bosworth (Leipzig, 1892–7), and the Bowerman edition (London, 1892). In all, the changes to dynamics, pedalling, phrasing, expression marks, and even fingerings found in manuscript and early printed sources proceed from the assumption that the original texts can be improved upon—'perfectionnés', as Saint-Saëns remarked caustically.[26] As a result, these editions are a valuable source for students of late-nineteenth-century performance practice.

Among the editions which tried to maintain a living link with Chopin were Gebethner & Wolff of Warsaw (1863), authorized by the composer's family and based largely on German first editions, and Heugel of Paris (1867), edited by Marmontel and based on first French editions. Of special significance was the Kistner edition (Leipzig, 1879), produced by the Chopin pupil Karl Mikuli, based on annotated French and German first editions supplemented by copious notes which he made at his own lessons and those of other pupils, and supplied with helpful introductions. This edition was later reprinted by Bessel (Moscow, 1889) and Schirmer (New York, 1949). Mikuli's reliance on Chopin's glosses on first editions is also found in the Peters edition (Leipzig, 1879), compiled by Hermann Scholtz using autographs and the annotated printed editions belonging to the Chopin pupils Mlle R. de Könneritz and George Mathias. And the whole approach is spelt out clearly in the subtitle of an edition prepared by Jan Kleczyński for Gebethner & Wolff (Warsaw, 1882). Kleczyński refers specifically to 'variants supplied both by the author himself and as passed on by his most celebrated pupils'.

Arguably this approach reached its culminating point in the celebrated edition by Edouard Ganche, known as the Oxford Original Edition (London, 1932), and based almost entirely on the seven-volume annotated collection of Jane Stirling. For reasons indicated earlier, an edition which was faithful to the Stirling scores would have considerable merit, but since the Stirling originals have become widely available it is now clear that Ganche did them very much less than full justice. Other early twentieth-century editions include Pugno for Universal Edition (Vienna, 1901), Friedman for Breitkopf & Härtel (Leipzig, 1913), Sauer for Schott (Mainz, 1917–20), Brugnoli for Ricordi (Milan, 1923–37), and Cortot for Salabert (Paris, 1941–7), the last including detailed commentaries, instructions and exercises. There is also a broadly faithful edition by Debussy for Durand (Paris, 1915–16).

Unlike many nineteenth-century editions, most of these (Pugno, Brugnoli, Cortot, Debussy) include no variants in the main text,

[26] 'A Chopin M.S.: the F Major Ballade in the Making'.

working from the assumption that the edition should be based exclusively on the composer's final version, as far as this can be identified. The same is true of a much more ambitious scholarly edition which appeared in Poland following World War II (Warsaw, 1949–61). Ostensibly based on the editorial work of Paderewski, Bronarski, and Turczyński, it was produced in the main by Bronarski (Paderewski died before the project was properly under way). The Polish Complete Edition was in many ways a pioneering venture, referring to the widest possible range of manuscript and printed sources in an attempt to produce a 'definitive' text, but its realization was deeply flawed. Among other things, Bronarski's practice was to select freely from different sources, arriving at a 'new' version which permissively conflates material from autographs, copies (many of which were mistaken for autographs), and all three first editions. In many cases orthography and phrasing are based not on any legitimate source but on unidentified recent editions and even on personal judgements made in the light of particular harmonic theories.

Of the other so-called 'source' editions which have been produced in recent years (Henle Verlag, Wiener Urtext, and Polish National), the only one as yet nearing completion is the Henle, edited mainly by Ewald Zimmerman (Duisburg, 1956–) and accompanied by a detailed commentary. Again this is flawed, despite its declared intention to work from a uniform basis of sources, to select a 'best' source and to adhere to it. As Zofia Chechlińska points out, there are in practice numerous importations from other versions and also many inaccuracies.[27] After many years of gestation, the Polish National Edition (Warsaw, 1967–), under Jan Ekier, seems at last to be making some headway, albeit only by sacrificing (or delaying) for subsequent volumes the remarkably detailed commentary which accompanied the first volume, the ballades. The edition has its shortcomings, but it may be recommended to performers on two important counts. First, it is an edition based largely on a single ('best') source which is clearly identified, rather than a conflation of several sources. And secondly, it indicates, in an admirably detailed separate commentary (at least for the ballades; and presumably for the rest in the fullness of time) the most important existing variants, enabling the performer (rather than the editor) to make a conflation where appropriate.

The last word has not been said on Chopin editions. The imperative now is to challenge some of the assumptions underlying the so-called Urtext edition. The Polish National, probably the best all-round edition available today, claims to give 'the most thorough presentation of the authentic, unadulterated musical text of Chopin's works as the composer intended it'. It is doubtful that such a claim can be validated.

[27] See her review of the Polish National Edition in *Chopin Studies* 2 (Warsaw, 1987), pp. 7–20.

Indeed we may question whether it is a desirable, let alone an achieveable, aim. It goes without saying that the editor should seek a 'best' text, drawing upon a uniform basis of sources which is clearly identified, but it is scarcely appropriate, given what we know of the social status of manuscripts within nineteenth-century concert and salon music, to seek a 'final' or 'definitive' text. The edition of the future will abandon spurious scientism in favour of a pragmatic approach. The best resources of scholarship will be harnessed. But they will be channelled very directly to serve the intelligent performer, drawing on historical and analytical, as well as textual, evidence to facilitate interpretation.

Such evidence will include manuscript and printed sources (including sketches and working autographs, where these throw light on interpretative issues); accounts by Chopin's pupils of his views on particular pieces and particular techniques (there is copious information here); notes on performance practice (pedalling, phrasing, expression, and tempo rubato, for example) drawn from contemporary methods, including his own and his pupil Tellefsen's; comparative readings drawn from late nineteenth-century editions; comparative readings from the recorded heritage (highlighting distinct pedagogical traditions and national schools); performance-related critical and analytical insights presented in non-technical language. For obvious practical reasons this pool of knowledge will be tapped sparingly, but the editors will be in a position to access it easily, and through it to supply the performer with any kind of textual and contextual information which has the capacity to illuminate the music.

11

Images of Chopin

Chopin's funeral at the Madeleine, paid for by Jane Stirling, was delayed until 30 October, while special permission was sought for women to sing in Mozart's Requiem, in accordance with Chopin's last wishes. After it the body was taken to the Père Lachaise cemetery, with Prince Czartoryski as Chief Mourner. But well before the funeral the Chopin cult had begun. The day following his death Kwiatkowski made several sketches of Chopin's face, the sources for innumerable later replicas. Clésinger also made a death mask and worked several plaster casts from two negatives, one of them commissioned by Jane Stirling. He was further charged by a committee chaired by Delacroix with the task of sculpting the monument that would be unveiled at a special ceremony at Père Lachaise a year later. Thomas Albrecht dealt with all the more immediate concerns, such as renting the flat and dealing with legal questions, while Jane Stirling bought up all the contents of the apartment. Some of the relics she distributed to friends and pupils, and the Pleyel, along with countless momentos (manuscripts, letters, portraits, and engravings), she shipped to Ludwika in Warsaw. But most of the furniture was despatched to Calder House, where it formed the basis of a small collection which she called the Chopin Museum.

Ludwika, meanwhile, carefully sorted through her brother's private papers. She kept the correspondence from Sand, and when she set off for Warsaw it was with her, along with the composer's heart. The unhappy fate of those letters has been described in chapter 7. As to the unpublished manuscripts, Chopin had left strict instructions that, with the exception of the incomplete *Méthode*, they should all be burned (the *Méthode* was left to Alkan, though Tellefsen was charged with completing it). Happily Ludwika did not respect this wish. She bequeathed many of the manuscripts (including the journal) to his friends, and above all to Kwiatkowski and Franchomme, and the subsequent history of these and other collections makes for a long and complicated story, involving widespread dispersal to family descendants and private collectors. Many of these items were sold at public auctions, and in some cases anonymity was preserved. As a result there are still important autographs whose present whereabouts is unknown.

On Stirling's death in 1859, much of her collection was sent to Warsaw to be divided between Chopin's mother and Izabella (Ludwika had died four years earlier), while the remainder was left to Stirling's niece Anne D. Houston and in due course became the property of Edouard Ganche in Lyon. The Ganche collection was subsequently donated to the Bibliothèque Nationale in Paris and to the Jagiellonian Library in Cracow. The fate of the Polish collections, on the other hand, was less fortunate. Much was stored in Izabella Barcińska's flat in the Zamoyski palace, which was destroyed during the 1863 uprising. Some of the family collection, however, remained with Ludwika's daughter, Ludwika Ciechomska, who lived in Sucha on her husband's estate. This material, including the Pleyel, was preserved into the present century. It passed through to Ludwika Ciechomska's daughters, first Maria and then Laura, but much of it subsequently perished in World War II. Most of Kwiatkowski's collection was also destroyed during the war, along with other private collections by Aleksander Poliński and Ludwik Binental and public collections in the Krasiński library and the Warsaw Music Society. The loss was enormous. Yet so great had been the dispersal that a good deal survived intact, including Princess Marcellina Czartoryska's collection (incorporating some sketch material) donated to the Czartoryski Library in Cracow.

The autographs and sketches given by Ludwika to Franchomme were of special importance, and happily many of them have now found their way to the Archive of the Chopin Society in Warsaw. Others are currently in public and private collections in America. Franchomme did at one point consider preparing a posthumous edition, but in the end the task of editing and publishing those works which had remained unpublished during Chopin's lifetime fell to Julian Fontana, who performed it conscientiously but indifferently. One can only speculate about Chopin's own intentions regarding the subsequent publication of his music. But the list of incipits prepared by Ludwika at Jane Stirling's instigation, together with the autograph glosses on the Stirling scores, might well have pointed to a revised collected edition to be prepared with Chopin's blessing.

Another tantalizing might-have-been is the biography proposed at one stage by Grzymała, who knew more than most of Chopin's inner life. In the end he stood aside and left the task to Liszt, who 'reacted' to Chopin's death on several levels, as composer, performer, and critic (it is tempting to draw a comparison with Stravinsky's response to Schoenberg's death). Liszt began his study by preparing a questionnaire which he sent, somewhat insensitively, to Ludwika. She in turn sent it to Jane Stirling, who replied in a rather cursory way. This formed the skeletal basis of the biography, which was then poeticized to the level of (at times) pure fiction, though it rises at other times to the highest criticism. It is impossible to determine just how much of the book was the work of Liszt's mistress, the Princess von Sayn-Wittgenstein, who 'collaborated' in many of his literary ventures.[1] But there can be no doubt that the Liszt book set the tone for the idealized Chopin biography prevalent in the late nineteenth century. Few composers have been quite so susceptible to apocrypha as Chopin, effectively transforming a figure of classical orientation into the archetype of a romantic artist. And this idealized biography in turn created the climate for particular readings of the music, embracing a manner of performance, listening, and even editing.

Liszt's biography was published in Paris, and it was in Paris above all that the image of Chopin as an archetypal romantic composer was promoted in the second half of the nineteenth century.[2] His reputation had been largely created there, and it was preserved and enhanced by French journals after his death. Yet from the start a very particular view of Chopin was presented by French critics, one which highlighted the notion of expression. Not only do we have the rather novel idea that a musical work might be fragment of autobiography. We further learn that it might act as a channel between the inner emotional world of the creator and that of the listener—a form of communication. As one critic put it, '[the listener] will weep, believing that he really suffers with one who can weep so well'.[3] A cluster of images gathered around this central preoccupation with expression. There is the poet of the piano: 'To listen to Chopin is to read a strophe of Lamartine';[4] there is the talent of the sickroom: 'Through music he discloses his suffering';[5] there is the feminine topos: 'Music for a woman's sensitiveness of finger'.[6] Above all there is the assumption that value may reside in a personal identity, a personal style, or, as one French critic said of Chopin, 'a mysterious language known only to himself'.[7]

In assessing this portrayal of Chopin, we need to look behind the scenes, to examine contexts and motivations. I have already suggested in chapter 3 that there were sub-texts underlying the promotion of some composers at the expense of others in the French press. Undoubtedly the most influential of the journals was the *Revue et Gazette musicale*, and its promotion of Chopin contributed greatly to his high standing in France. There was some partisanship in this. It helps to know that the founder-editor of the journal was Chopin's publisher Maurice

[1] For a discussion of the problem, see Alan Walker, *Franz Liszt: The Virtuoso Years 1811–1847* (London, 1983), pp. 19–23.

[2] Much of the subsequent discussion is drawn from my chapter, 'Chopin Reception, Theory, History, Analysis', in *Chopin Studies 2* (Cambridge, 1994), pp. 1–17.

[3] Hippolyte Barbedette, *Chopin. Essai de critique musicale*, p. 65.

[4] *Le Ménestrel: Journal de musique*, 2 May 1841. Quoted in Olgierd Pisarenko, 'Chopin and his Contemporaries: Paris 1832–1860', in *Studies in Chopin*, ed. Dariusz Żebrowski, tr. Halina Oszczygiel (Warsaw, 1973), p. 35.

[5] Barbedette, *Chopin*, p. 65.   [6] *Revue et Gazette musicale*, 2 January 1842.

[7] *Revue et Gazette musicale*, 2 March 1843.

Schlesinger. But that aside, the construction of a particular image of Chopin by the *Gazette* was in part a polemic directed against the shallow virtuosity of public pianism, and against the support of such pianism elsewhere in Paris, notably by *La France Musicale*. It should be noted that for some of the *Gazette*'s critics, the charge of 'shallow virtuosity' did not exempt Liszt.

Arguably more than any other single factor, it was the long-term success of the *Gazette* that established the prevailing view of Chopin in late-nineteenth-century France, translating his preference for intimate performance contexts, for an art of nuance, sophistication, and refinement, into a kind of survival kit for French music. Through the *Gazette* Chopin came to be regarded as a necessary bulwark against encroaching German influence in the later nineteenth century, against the pretension of a 'music of the future' on the one hand and the populism of a so-called *Trivialmusik* on the other. The concealed social energies in French Chopin criticism worked, then, to preserve a peculiarly French form of patronal culture, associated with the salon at its best. And increasingly this was bolstered by style-historical interpretations. By that I mean that Chopin came to be viewed in France as a kind of vital missing link connecting the *clavécinistes* to the great pianist-composers of the *fin de siècle*, Fauré, Debussy, and Ravel. Something of that perception persists today. One of the greatest of all French pianists of our own century remarked that 'French thought and feeling have never been expressed with such a wealth of understanding' as they were in Chopin.[8]

Publishers, no less than critics, played their part in determining the prevalent images of Chopin. Precisely because he avoided the public concert with its associated promotional apparatus, Chopin depended on the publisher more than most pianist-composers. And it was German publishers in particular who were responsible for the world-wide dissemination of his music in the late nineteenth century. I will focus on just one part of this story, the publication of the Breitkopf & Härtel collected edition in 1878–80. Breitkopf was not the only publishing house to produce a collected edition following Chopin's death. Several appeared in France, Russia, and Poland in the 1860s and 70s, prepared in the main by his pupils. But whereas these editions had limited circulation and impact—at least in the short term—the Breitkopf edition represented a major landmark in Chopin reception. Leipzig was the centre of music publishing; and Breitkopf was the leading publisher, with outlets all over the world.

The significance of the Breitkopf edition extended beyond this. To understand it fully we need to be aware of the background. From 1850 onwards, Breitkopf embarked on a whole series of collected editions of major composers, completed only some forty years later. This series,

[8] Alfred Cortot, *In Search of Chopin*, tr. Cyril and Rena Clarke (London and New York, 1951), p. 75.

described by one recent commentator as 'the first serious and systematic attempt to establish the works of musical authors in a canonic way',[9] was launched by editions of Bach and Handel, clearly viewed as the foundation stones of German music, and it went on to include Mozart, Beethoven, Schubert, Mendelssohn, and Schumann. This of course touches a larger issue. The formation of a musical canon and the development of the associated category 'classical music', with all its atemporal resonance, was very largely a product of the nineteenth century, though it was already well under way in the eighteenth. It can be traced most clearly in concert life, of course, as the early nineteenth-century salon and benefit concert gave way to the late nineteenth-century recital and subscription concert, complete with a repertory centred on the Viennese classics. But it can also be traced through music criticism, and through publishing history. The Breitkopf editions were part and parcel of a development famously described by one historian as 'the invention of tradition'.

Canon formation was not of course unique to Germany (indeed it began in England and France rather earlier),[10] but it was above all in Germany that the canon became associated with a dominant national culture, perceived as specifically German yet at the same time representative of universal values, a paradox well in tune with German classical art and the new philology. The Viennese classics became literally that, with all the Hellenistic connotations. The practical and ideological force of the German canon is of course well known. Practically it allowed the significant to push into obscurity the only marginally less significant (the Brahms symphony obscures the Bruch symphony). Ideologically it manipulated an innocent repertory—changed its meaning—in the interests of status confirmation.

For present purposes it is unnecessary and inappropriate to probe in any detail the issue of canon formation. But it is worth pointing out that of the long list of composers embraced by Breitkopf from Bach onwards, Chopin and Palestrina were the only non-Germans. This was tantamount to a kind of adoption, and it represented an almost symbolic moment of resolution in German Chopin reception, following a lengthy polemic which had begun in his lifetime with Schumann, Rellstab, Kahlert, and many others, and continued through into the later nineteenth century. In a culture no longer willing to make an easy equation between the significant and the well-composed, Chopin's associations with the salon had proved a major obstacle to his public success in Germany, in sharp contrast to France. The Breitkopf edition helped to change that, conferring dignity on Chopin in the German world. And

[9] Philip Brett, 'Text, Context, and the Early Music Editor', in *Authenticity and Early Music*, ed. Nicholas Kenyon (Oxford, 1988), p. 86.
[10] See William Weber, *The Rise of Musical Classics in Eighteenth-Century England: A Study in Canon, Ritual and Ideology* (Oxford, 1992).

other indicators quickly followed. Among the most telling was the reclassification of several of Chopin's works in the later editions of certain popular German music guides, where they were quite literally removed from their former category of salon pieces.[11] Chopin, in short, was admitted to the canon by Breitkopf. He became a classical composer.

And once this status had been achieved, it was secured by other means as the century turned. A German translation of selected letters was published by Breitkopf, together with serious biographies by Adolf Weissmann and Bernard Scharlitt, clearly designed to dispel lingering associations with the ephemeral and the lightweight.[12] And a major analytical study by Hugo Leichtentritt followed shortly after, subjecting virtually every work of the published music to detailed analytical scrutiny.[13] This huge study by Leichtentritt was an astonishing venture for its time. Very few composers were granted such treatment. It really was a monument to the recently established and increasingly specialized discipline of *Musikwissenschaft*. In keeping with its philological inspiration, the new science of music in Germany effectively distanced the unworthy art of the present from the perfection of a classical canon and at the same time it reduced that classical canon to the rigid categories of the new science. Historicism and scientism met in this endeavour, and Leichtentritt's study, confirming Chopin's place in the classical canon, was a characteristic product.

Yet powerful voices were raised in protest. Some time after Nietzsche railed against the narrowness of academic philology, Heinrich Schenker turned his back on the institutions and the developing orthodoxies of academic musicology, and in very much the same spirit; they even turned to the same major sources of renewal.[14] It is telling paradox, then, that Schenker's canon, cultivated with no less chauvinism than that of academic musicology, should also have adopted Chopin as an honorary member of the great tradition. Schenker spelt it out in these extraordinary terms. 'If I elevate the name of Frederic Chopin for inclusion in the roll of great German masters, it is because . . . I wish the works of Chopin, too, to be accessible as a source of the highest operations of genius, and in this most exalted sense to place them newly at the service of German youth.' And even better: 'For the profundity with which

[11] See Andreas Ballstaedt, 'Chopin as "Salon Composer" in Nineteenth-Century German Criticism', in *Chopin Studies* 2 (Cambridge, 1994), especially pp. 29–32.

[12] Adolf Weissman, *Chopin* (Berlin, 1912); and Bernard Scharlitt, *Chopin* (Leipzig, 1919).

[13] Hugo Leichtentritt, *Analyse der Chopin'schen Klavierwerke*, 2 vols. (Berlin, 1921–2).

[14] Friedrich Nietzsche, *Untimely Meditations* (see especially the second of these, 'On the Uses and Disadvantages of History for Life'), in *Basic Writings of Nietzsche*, tr. Walter Kaufmann (New York, 1968).

Chopin

nature has endowed him, Chopin belongs more to Germany than to Poland.'[15]

Conflicting images of Chopin were also registered through compositional influence in the late nineteenth century. This is an especially revealing dimension of reception, since any musical influence beyond surface imitation involves an act of misreading. I have already referred in chapters 1 and 4 to Chopin's influence on Balakirev and his circle. Balakirev's particular misreading was to view Chopin as a Slavonic composer first and foremost, and he could do this only at the expense of other, no less vital, aspects of the music. For Balakirev, Chopin represented a fusion of nationalism and modernism, and it was just such a fusion that he himself tried to promote at his Free School of Music in St Petersburg. Not surprisingly, then, Chopin's stylistic influence on progressive tendencies in Russian music was a decisive one.[16] But Russian composers selected carefully from the fused whole of Chopin's musical style. In the harmonic sphere they focused on modalities and chromatic symmetries. Melodically they favoured elements which prioritize ornamentation and variation rather than dissection and development. And structurally they picked up on a subtle and prophetic change in the relative weighting of components in Chopin, and especially a promotion of texture and figuration to a quite new status. All are features which provided Russian composers with alternatives to the forms and methods of an already established Austro–German tradition, and that fact was to prove of enormous significance for the later development of twentieth-century musical styles.

It is intriguing to compare this with Chopin's influence in England. In his study of domestic music-making in eighteenth-century England, Richard Leppert well illustrates the role of music as social regulation, a role which was strengthened through the early nineteenth century and the Victorian age.[17] This is not the place to debate how religious and social values promoted and fostered music-making in the middle-class English home. Nor to analyse those Victorian attitudes which ensured that women were the main consumers and practitioners of an art firmly centred on the piano—the 'household orchestra'. It is enough to highlight the outcome of all this: a flood of music suitable for performance by the Victorian woman, including short, manageable piano pieces—simple transcriptions, dance pieces, 'character' pieces. Stylistically this repertory was modelled on the European art music of half a century earlier. One writer refers to a 'stylistic time-lock'; to 'lacklustre reflections

[15] These extracts from *Der Tonville* and *Das Meisterwerk in der Musik* are translated by Ian Bent in 'Heinrich Schenker, Chopin and Domenico Scarlatti', *Music Analysis*, 5/2–3 (1986), pp. 131–49.
[16] See Anne Swartz, 'Chopin as Modernist in Nineteenth-Century Russia', in *Chopin Studies 2* (Cambridge, 1994), pp. 35–49.
[17] Richard Leppert, *Music and Image: Domesticity, Ideology and Socio-cultural Formation in Eighteenth-Century England* (Cambridge, 1988).

of the living, breathing art of early-Romantic progenitors'.[18] Now among the most prominent of those progenitors was of course Chopin, and the external features of his nocturnes and mazurkas proved especially vulnerable to imitation by Victorian composers. Technically this amounted to a reduction of Chopin's closely-woven textures and delicately shaped phrases to a handful of easy gestures. The contrast with Chopin's influence on Russian composers could scarcely be more marked.

And in due course his own music was lumped together with this progeny. We find the nocturnes published in collections called 'drawing-room trifles'; we encounter the preludes described as 'pearls' and the études as 'tuneful gems'. We meet publications of simplified and short-ened versions of some of the tougher, more technically demanding works, including the G minor Ballade. Compare that with the Breitkopf enterprise in Germany. Charles Hallé put it in a nutshell with his remark that Chopin had become 'the property of every schoolgirl'.[19] And *The Musical Gazette* claimed that 'the grand-daughters of the young ladies who trundled through *The Battle of Prague* now trundle through Chopin'.[20] Chopin, in short, was domesticated in England, as he was deified in Russia. His unique features, well noted in early nineteenth-century English criticism, were smoothed out by association with sur-rounding lowlands of mediocrity. They became indistinguishable from their environment in a manner all too familiar in today's culture indus-try.

It is worth reflecting for a moment on this dispersal of meanings in late nineteenth-century Chopin reception. It forms one part of a larger story, the story of Chopin's 'afterlife', or rather the afterlife of his com-positions. In their afterlife musical works thread their way through many different social and cultural formations, attaching themselves to their surroundings in different ways, and adapting their own appearance in the process. The works remain at least notionally the same objects— at any rate they are usually the product of singular creative acts—but their manner of occupying the social landscape changes constantly. In locating and describing these changes, a reception study can light up the ideology concealed in the corners of music history. And it can expose in the process some of the vested interests at work in the promotion, dis-semination, influence, and evaluation of musical works.

The picture I have painted is over-compartmentalized without a doubt. Yet it is clear that Chopin's music was prey to appropriation in

[18] Derek Carew, 'Victorian Attitudes to Chopin', in *The Cambridge Companion to Chopin*, pp. 226–7.

[19] *The Autobiography of Charles Hallé*, ed. Michael Kennedy (London, 1972; original ed. 1896), p. 54.

[20] *The Musical Gazette*, 4 December 1900. *The Battle of Prague* was a popular genre piece by Kotzwara, composed in the late eighteenth century.

the late nineteenth century. It was an intimate communication; it was an icon; it was an agent of cultural and even political propaganda; it was a commodity. It is rather as though Chopin held a mirror to the conflicting ideologies attending a critical period in music history, right on the cusp between classical and modernist notions of art. French critics sought to preserve him as a sophisticated 'Ariel of the piano', an ideal romantic composer, a poet. English music lovers tried to domesticate him, absorbing him easily into a musical culture which affirmed, with no significant critical element, the middle-class ascendancy. Russian composers turned him into a modernist, drawn into the orbit of a pioneering music responsive neither to the professional establishment nor to public taste. It is especially intriguing to see this polarity of response in England and Russia, two countries on the edge of Europe, an advanced industrialized nation and a backward feudal one. In these opposed perspectives we view separately, and with particular clarity, the two strands which were held in a sort of forcefield in Germany, resolved only when Chopin was elevated to the canon, and thus absorbed by history—a classical composer.

Following this dispersal there was something of a closure of meaning in twentieth-century Chopin reception. However, this new determinacy stands out in the sharpest possible contrast to the perceptions of Chopin's own era, and that contrast is well worth exploring. It is immediately apparent when we consider the relationship between performance and text. I have already noted that Chopin was shaped by the world of post-classical concert music, the so-called 'brilliant style', and that within that world the musical text and the musical performance were inextricably tied together. To his contemporaries Chopin remained a pianist-composer, writing 'pianists' music' rather than 'pianoforte music', as one highly influential critic put it. The performance moment, and the act of communication involved, took precedence over any authority wielded by the text *qua* text.

In later reception, on the other hand, performance and text were prised apart. The drama of separation was enacted on several fronts. Editors played their part. On one hand we have the attempt by Chopin's pupils and grandpupils to preserve a living Chopin tradition (one which gave precedence to his own practice as a performer), recreating in print memories of versions played by Chopin and his pupils, even where these depart from manuscript and printed sources. On the other hand we have the concern of historically minded editors to investigate a manuscript tradition of great complexity in a paper chase for the definitive text, a text supposedly validated by final intentions—as though it might be so simple.

Pianists also played their part in separating performance and text, as that modern institution, the piano recital, developed its two opposing cultures. It was above all the great Russian pianist Anton Rubenstein who acclimatized Chopin's music to the public concert in the late nine-teenth century, forcing it into a new kind of performance arena, bend-ing it to his will. As Hallé remarked, 'It is clever, but it is not Chopin'. This was no longer the pianist-composer playing to the gallery, proudly displaying his own wares. Rather it was the public recitalist exerting control over someone else's music—a form of ownership, as Edward Said has suggested—where the text is not just dominated, but may even be reshaped.[21] Leschetizky and his many pupils played their part, and at the end of the road were the remarkable arrangements and transcrip-tions of pianist-composers such as Leopold Godowsky.

Again, this subjugation of the text gave way to a growing respect for its authority in other quarters. The historically aware performance, aim-ing to recover the composer's intentions through a careful examination of primary sources and performance conventions, was already very much a reality in the late nineteenth century. And I might add in pass-ing that women pianists found in this approach one of their few routes to the concert platform. In due course historically aware performances were absorbed by a growing so-called authenticity movement which now offers us performances and recordings of Chopin on early nine-teenth-century fortepianos in a studied and notoriously problematic attempt to let the music speak as once it did. This, ironically enough, is almost as far from the spirit of Chopin as the Godowsky transcriptions.

The contrast between Chopin's time and ours is of course made explicit in music criticism. It was common practice for Chopin's con-temporaries to relate his music to real or imagined contexts. The work was understood to mediate larger realities, and of several kinds: it expressed an emotion; it told a story; it exemplified a genre; it articu-lated a style; it confirmed an institution. And its meaning was therefore contingent. These assumptions leap from the pages of innumerable early nineteenth-century accounts of his music. As we read these accounts we are made aware of just how far removed from Chopin's world our own critical and musicological writing has drifted. To put it simply, the work was habitually described in sequential terms by early nineteenth-century critics. It was less a structure than a narrative.

In contrast, our own century's criticism sought to de-contextualize the work. It became a world in and to itself, claiming an ideal relationship of part to whole. From early beginnings in theorists such as Adolf Bernhard Marx, the idea of a structural sense of form gained unstop-pable momentum, sweeping music theory before it, and in the end build-ing on its premise the entire edifice of a newly independent discipline, music analysis, essentially a discipline of our age. Unity and wholeness, whatever these may mean in a temporal art, were assumed a priori, and the analytical act was their demonstration. The work became a

[21] Edward W. Said, *Musical Elaborations* (London, 1991). See the chapter 'Performance as an Extreme Occasion', pp. 1–34.

structure, and in that lay its value. And just as the critic had replaced the patron, so the analyst replaced the critic as the ultimate arbiter of quality. The experience of listeners is another matter, no doubt influenced at some level by these lofty organicist meditations, yet at the same time separate from them. I doubt very much if listeners habitually experience musical works as closed and unified, excluding the world outside the work. Indeed the divergence of rhetoric and reality here has been seen by at least one commentator as culturally defining for our century.[22]

Let us, then, contrast Chopin's world and ours through an exercise in imaginative recreation. In the reprise of the fourth Ballade we may hear a triumphant synthesis of two very different surface styles—strict canon and ornamental bel canto, Bach and Italian opera. As noted in an earlier chapter, Chopin's world might have related this sequence to a conventional succession of contemporary improvisation, described in those very terms in the method books, and it might even have heard in the bravura coda a distant echo of the familiar applause-seeking perorations of popular concert pieces. In the second Ballade we may hear a dramatic confrontation of sharply contrasted materials, heightened by a two-key scheme which points daringly to Wagner and Mahler. Chopin's world might have related this to the classic formal ingredients of the brilliant style—bravura figuration squared off against popular melody, étude against siciliano. As for the two-key scheme, it would have remembered enough of these from the post-classical repertory not to worry unduly. In the introduction to the F minor Fantasy we may hear a multi-sectional upbeat to the first tonal and thematic cycle. Chopin's world might rather have heard the stylization of an operatic scena, slow march, recitative, grand chorus.

One could continue along these lines. We signally fail to notice generic features which would have struck Chopin's contemporaries—those gestures in the A minor Prelude which signal a funeral march; those features of the G minor Ballade which identify it as a lament; above all, the waltzes and barcarolles which infuse extended works such as the scherzos and ballades. And where we do notice this play of genres, we interpret it as an early fissure in the integrated world of a notionally unified period style, foreshadowing Mahler rather than echoing the gestures of post-classical traditions. The point here is that the analytical mode of our century has not just elevated the concept of structure, and with it the myth of the musical work; it has also reduced the rich diversities of stylistic history to its own canon of competing and successive period styles. Not only is the work a unity in itself; it must belong to one of two unified style paradigms, 'classical' or 'romantic'. Its true origins are lost.

There are clear signs today that the analytical mode of our century is

[22] Nicholas Cook, *Music, Imagination, and Culture* (Oxford, 1990).

meeting once again with history; indeed in some quarters it is suggested that analysis as a separate discipline (though not as an activity) will lose its identity in a mesh of wider critical perspectives. Whatever the outcome of this relocation of analysis, it seems likely that the austerities and exclusions of formalism (themselves closely linked to the era of cultural Modernism) can find only a limited space in our so-called 'postmodern' world. There is a renewed interest in context, in the social cause of the work, in the social production of its meanings (the concern of a reception history), and even (though this is more elusive) in the social 'trace' left on its musical materials. In attempting to recover something of Chopin's world in this chapter, and at the same time to mediate between that world and our own through the multiple images of late nineteenth-century reception, I am responding in some measure to this recent evolution of our discipline. But it goes without saying that Chopin's music will not be confined by the vagaries and fashions of scholarship. It will always remain larger than any of our attempts to describe it. That will not stop us trying. The need for criticism is as fundamental as the need for art.

Appendix A

Calendar

Year	Age	Life	Contemporary musicians and events
1810		Chopin born, 1 March, in Żelazowa Wola, son of Mikołaj Chopin and Justyna Krzyżanowska. The family moves to Warsaw in October.	Schumann born, 8 June. Auber aged 28; Beethoven 40; Bellini 9; Berlioz 7; Boieldieu 35; Cherubini 50; Clementi 58; Cramer 31; Czerny 19; Donizetti 13; Dussek 50; Field 28; Grétry 69; Halévy 11; Hérold 19; Herz 7; Hummel 32; Kalkbrenner 25; Mendelssohn 1; Meyerbeer 19; Moscheles 16; Paer 39; Paganini 28; Reicha 40; Ries 26; Rossini 18; Salieri 60; Schubert 13; Spohr 26; Weber 24. Beethoven: music of *Egmont*.
1811	1		Liszt born, 22 Oct.; Hiller born, 24 Oct. Beethoven's Fifth Piano Concerto performed, Leipzig. Weber's *Abu Hassan* given, Munich.
1812	2		Thalberg born, 8 Jan. Field's first nocturnes published, Moscow.
1813	3		Wagner born, 22 May; Verdi born, 10 Oct. Rossini's *L'italiana in Algeri* given, Venice. The Philharmonic Society formed, London.
1814	4		Final version of Beethoven's *Fidelio* given, Vienna.
1815	5		Schubert: *Erlkönig*. Maelzel invents the metronome.

Year	Age	Life	Contemporary musicians and events
1815	5		Napoleon defeated at Waterloo. Kingdom of Poland established.
1816	6	Begins to take piano lessons from Adalbert Żywny.	Schubert: Fifth Symphony. Rossini's *Il barbiere di Siviglia* given, Rome.
1817	7	Polonaise in G minor published.	Weber appointed Kapellmeister, Dresden. Part I of Clementi's *Gradus ad Parnassum* published.
1818	8	Plays at a charity in Warsaw, followed by numerous invitations to aristocratic homes.	Beethoven: 'Hammerklavier' Sonata.
1819	9		Offenbach born, 20 June. Schubert: 'Trout' Quintet.
1820	10	Hears the singer Angelica Catalani, who gives him a gold watch. Plays for the Grand Duke Constantin.	Moniuszko born, 5 May. Metal piano frames first used.
1821	11	Dedicates his A♭ Polonise to Żywny.	Weber's *Der Freischütz* given, Berlin. Beethoven: Piano Sonatas Opp. 110–11. Death of Napoleon I.
1822	12	Has composition lessons from Józef Elsner. Composes the G♯ minor Polonaise.	Franck born, 10 Dec. Schubert 'Unfinished' Symphony. Royal Academy of Music founded, London.
1823	13		Beethoven begins the composition of his late string quartets. Spohr's *Jessonda* given, Kassel.
1824	14	Enrols at the Warsaw Lyceum, where his father teaches.	Bruckner born, 4 Sept. Beethoven's 'Choral' Symphony performed in Vienna, and his *Missa Solemnis* in St Petersburg. Schubert: *Die Schöne Müllerin*. Rossini director of the Théâtre-Italien, Paris. Death of Louis XVIII; succeeded by the reactionary Charles X.
1825	15	Edits the holiday diary *Szafarnia Courier*. Plays to Czar Alexander I. Rondo, Op. 1 published.	Smetana born, 2 Mar.; Johann Strauss the younger born, 25 Oct. Schubert: 'Great' C major Symphony. Johann Strauss the elder forms his own orchestra, Vienna.

Year	Age	Life	Contemporary musicians and events
			Death of Tsar Alexander I; succeeded by younger son Nicholas I. Decembrist rising crushed in Russia.
1826	16	Enters Warsaw Conservatory. Polonaise in B♭ minor. Gives several concerts in Warsaw.	Weber's *Oberon* given, London. He dies there, 5 June. Mendelssohn: Overture to *A Midsummer Night's Dream*.
1827	17	His youngest sister, Emilia, dies. Sonata, Op. 4, Variations Op. 2. Visits Prince Radziwiłł at Antonin.	Beethoven dies, 26 Mar. Schubert: *Die Winterreise* and two piano trios. Liszt settles Paris.
1828	18	Visits Berlin. *Fantasy on Polish Airs*, Op. 13, *Rondo à la krakowiak*, Op. 14.	Schubert: String Quintet in C and last three piano sonatas. He dies, Vienna, 19 Nov. Auber's *La Muette de Portici* given, Paris.
1829	19	Meets Hummel and hears Paganini in Warsaw. Finishes at the Conservatory and gives two successful concerts in Vienna. Second visit to Antonin, where he writes the Polonaise, Op. 3 for cello and piano. Infatuation for Konstancja Gładkowska.	Rossini's *Guillaume Tell* given, Paris. Mendelssohn conducts Bach's St Matthew Passion.
1830	20	Plays the two concertos at public concerts in Vienna. Leaves for Vienna with Tytus Wojciechowski.	Berlioz: *Symphonie fantastique*. Mendelssohn: 'Reformation' Symphony. July revolution in France. Louis Philippe elected King. Uprising in Poland.
1831	21	Unsuccessful months in Vienna. Friendship with Dr Malfatti. Leaves for Munich, where he gives a concert, then Stuttgart, where he learns of the failure of the Polish uprising. The 'Stuttgart Diary'. Arrives in Paris early October. Meets Kalkbrenner, Hiller, and Liszt.	Bellini's *La sonnambula* and *Norma* given, Milan. Meyerbeer's *Robert le diable* given, Paris. Schumann writes his early piano music.
1832	22	First concert in Paris. Friendships with Mendelssohn and Berlioz. First publications in Paris and London. Begins a highly successful and lucrative teaching career.	Donizetti's *L'elisir d'amore* given, Milan.

Year	Age	Life	Contemporary musicians and events
1833	23	Plays with Liszt at a benefit for Harriet Smithson. Friendship with Bellini. Opp. 8–12 published.	Brahms born, 7 May. Mendelssohn: 'Italian' Symphony.
1834	24	Visits (with Hiller) the Rhenish Music Festival, where he renews his acquaintance with Mendelssohn. Plays at one of the prestigious Conservatory Concerts in Paris. Opp. 13–19 published. The Fantasy-Impromptu composed.	Borodin born, 12 Nov. Liszt: *Harmonies poétiques et religieuses*. Berlioz: 'Harold in Italy' Symphony. First issue of *Neue Zeitschrift für Musik* published, Leipzig.
1835	25	Travels to Karlsbad to meet his parents. Visits Dresden and begins his friendship with Maria Wodzińska. Visits Leipzig, where he meets Mendelssohn, Schumann, and Clara Wieck. Seriously ill at Heidelberg. Opp. 20 and 24 published.	Bellini dies, 23 Sept.; Saint-Saëns born, 9 Oct. Donizetti's *Lucia di Lammermoor* given, Naples. Schumann: *Carnaval*. Mendelssohn appointed conductor of the Leipzig Gewandhaus Orchestra.
1836	26	Visits Marienbad to meet the Wodziński family. Proposes to Maria, but is pledged to secrecy by her mother. Opp. 21–3, 26 and 27 published. First meeting with George Sand.	Glinka's *A Life for the Tsar* given, St Petersburg. Meyerbeer's *Les Huguenots* given, Paris.
1837	27	The Wodzińska engagement is severed by her family. Visits London (with Pleyel) in July. Growing friendship with Sand. Opp. 25 and 29–32 published.	Balakirev born, 2 Jan. Field dies, 23 Jan.; Hummel dies, 17 Oct. Berlioz: *Grande messe des morts*. Liszt: *12 grandes études*.
1838	28	Plays for Louis Philippe and at a concert by Alkan. Goes to Majorca with Sand. Completes the Preludes Op. 28 and the Second Ballade at Valldemosa. Opp. 33–4 published.	Bruch born, 6 Jan.; Bizet born, 25 Oct. Schumann: *Kinderszenen* and *Kreisleriana*. Donizetti settles in Paris.
1839	29	Ill in Valldemosa. Returns to Marseilles in spring and spends summer at Sand's home, Nohant. Completes the B♭ minor Sonata. On return to Paris meets Moscheles, with whom he plays at Saint-Cloud. Op. 28 published.	Musorgsky born, 21 Mar. Berlioz: *Roméo et Juliette* Symphony.

Year	Age	Life	Contemporary musicians and events
1840	30	Quiet year spent composing in Paris. Opp. 35–42 published.	Paganini dies, 27 May. Schumann marries Clara Wieck and composes over a hundred songs.
1841	31	Concert in Paris in April. Summer at Nohant including music-making with Pauline Viardot. On return to Paris joins Sand at Rue Pigalle. Opp. 43–9 published.	Chabrier born, 18 Jan.; Dvořák born, 8 Sept. Schumann's 'symphonic year'.
1842	32	Concert with Viardot and the cellist Franchomme in February. Summer at Nohant, where Delacroix is among the guests. Death of his close friend Jan Matuszyński. Moves to Square d'Orléans. Op. 50 published.	First performances of Wagner's *Rienzi*, Dresden; Verdi's *Nabucco*, Milan; and Glinka's *Ruslan and Lyudmila*, St Petersburg. Schumann: Piano Quintet and other chamber works. Meyerbeer appointed Court Musical Director, Berlin.
1843	33	Summer at Nohant. Opp. 51–4 published.	Grieg born, 15 June. First performances of Wagner's *Der fliegende Holländer*, Dresden, and Donizetti's *Don Pasquale*, Paris. Berlioz's treatise on orchestration published. Leipzig conservatory opens.
1844	34	Death of Mikołaj Chopin. Fryderyk's sister Ludwika visits him in Nohant. Opp. 55–6 published.	Rimsky-Korsakov born, 18 Mar. Mendelssohn: Violin Concerto. Liszt's connection with Weimar begins.
1845	35	Health deteriorates. The beginning of a major rift in his relationship with Sand. Opp. 57–8 published.	Fauré born, 12 May. Wagner's *Tannhäuser* given, Dresden. Schumann: Piano Concerto.
1846	36	Quarrels with Sand exacerbated by family difficulties. Publication of Sand's novel *Lucrezia Floriani*, a 'portrait' of her relationship with Chopin. Opp. 59–61 published.	Mendelssohn's *Elijah* performed, Birmingham. Berlioz's *La damnation de Faust* performed, Paris.
1847	37	Marriage of Sand's daughter, Solange, to the sculptor Clésinger. Labyrinthine family quarrels resulting in Chopin's break with Sand. Opp. 63–5 published.	Mendelssohn dies, 4 Nov. Verdi's *Macbeth* given, Florence.

Year	Age	Life	Contemporary musicians and events
1848	38	Last concert in Paris. Visits England and Scotland under the protection of his pupil Stirling. Plays at many Jane functions and gives public concerts in Manchester and Glasgow. Returns to London, very ill, in November and plays at the Guildhall. Returns to Paris.	Glinka: *Kamarinskaya*. Donizetti dies, 8 Apr. Year of revolutions, including the uprisings in Paris, Vienna, and Dresden. Abdication of Ferdinand I of Austria: succeeded by Franz Josef. Abdication of Louis-Philippe and proclamation of the Second Republic, with Louis-Napoleon elected President. Wagner flees to Weimar to escape arrest following the uprising in Dresden.
1849	39	Unable to teach or give concerts. Assisted financially by Stirling. His sister arrives in Paris to nurse him at his final home in Place Vendôme. He dies there on 17 October.	Meyerbeer: *Le prophète*.

Appendix B

List of works

The chronology of Chopin's music is anything but well established. The present list is based largely on Chomiński and Turło, *Katalog Dzieł Fryderyka Chopina* (Cracow, 1990), which differs in numerous ways from Jan Ekier's *Wstęp do wydania narodowego*. Several changes from the Chomiński/Turło chronology have been made, based either on my own research or on Jeffrey Kallberg's dating of autograph manuscripts as reported in John Rink, 'The Evolution of Chopin's "Structural Style" and its Relation to Improvisation', Ph.D dissertation (Cambridge, 1989).

1 ORIGINAL OPUS NUMBERS

Opus	Title	Date of composition	Date of publication
1	Rondo, c; pf	1825	1825
2	Variations on 'Là ci darem la mano', Bb; pf, orch.	1827	1830
3	*Introduction and Polonaise brillante*, C; vc, pf	1829–30	1831
4	Sonata, c; pf	1827–8	1851
5	*Rondo à la mazur*, F; pf	1826	1828
6	Four Mazurkas, f#, c#, E, Eb; pf	1830–2	1832
7	Five Mazurkas, Bb, A, F, Ab, C; pf (1st version of No. 4, 1825)	1830–2	1832
8	Piano Trio, g	1828–9	1832
9	Three Nocturnes, bb, Eb, B; pf	1830–2	1832
10	Twelve Études, pf	1830–2	1833
11	Concerto No. 1, e; pf. orch.	1830	1833
12	*Variations brillantes*, Bb; pf	1833	1833
13	*Fantasy on Polish Airs*, A; pf, orch.	1828	1834
14	*Rondo à la krakowiak*, F; pf, orch.	1828	1834
15	Three Nocturnes, F, F#, g; pf	1830–2	1833
16	*Introduction and Rondo*, c, Eb; pf	1832–3	1834
17	Four Mazurkas, Bb, c, Ab, a; pf	1833	1834
18	Waltz, Eb; pf	1831–2	1834
19	Bolero, C/A; pf	*c.*1833	1834
20	Scherzo, b; pf	*c.*1835	1835
21	Concerto No. 2, f; pf, orch.	1829	1836
22	*Andante spianato and Grande Polonaise brillante*, G; pf, and Eb; pf, orch.	1830–5	1836

Opus	Title	Date of composition	Date of publication
23	Ballade, g; pf	c.1835	1836
24	Four Mazurkas, g, C, A♭, b♭; pf	1833	1836
25	Twelve Études, pf	1835–7	1837
26	Two Polonaises, c♯, e♭; pf	1835	1836
27	Two Nocturnes, c♯, D♭; pf	1835	1836
28	Twenty-four Preludes, pf	1838–9	1839
29	Impromptu, A♭; pf	c.1837	1837
30	Four Mazurkas, c, b, D♭, c♯; pf	1837	1838
31	Scherzo, D♭; pf	1837	1837
32	Two Nocturnes, B, A♭; pf	1837	1837
33	Four Mazurkas, g♯, D, C, b; pf	1838	1838
34	Three Waltzes		1838
	A♭	1835	
	a	c.1834	
	F	1838	
35	Sonata, b♭; pf (slow movement 1837)	1839	1840
36	Impromptu, F♯; pf	1839	1840
37	Two Nocturnes, g, G; pf	1838–9	1840
38	Ballade, F/a; pf	1839	1840
39	Scherzo, c♯; pf	1839	1840
40	Two Polonaises, A, C; pf	1838–9	1840
41	Four Mazurkas, e, B, A♭, c♯; pf	1838–9	1840
42	Waltz, A♭; pf	1840	1840
43	Tarantella, A♭; pf	1841	1841
44	Polonaise, f♯; pf	1841	1841
45	Prelude, c♯; pf	1841	1841
46	Allegro de concert, pf	c.1834–41	1841
47	Ballade, A♭; pf	1841	1841
48	Two Nocturnes, c, f♯; pf	1841	1841
49	Fantasy, f/A♭; pf	1841	1841
50	Three Mazurkas, G, A♭, c♯; pf	1842	1842
51	Impromptu, G♭; pf	1842	1843
52	Ballade, f; pf	1842–3	1843
53	Polonaise, A♭; pf	1842–3	1843
54	Scherzo, E; pf	1842–3	1843
55	Two Nocturnes, f, E♭; pf	1842–4	1844
56	Three Mazurkas, B, C, c; pf	1843–4	1844
57	Berceuse, D♭; pf	1844	1845
58	Sonata, b; pf	1844	1845
59	Three Mazurkas, a, A♭, f♯; pf	1845	1845
60	Barcarolle, F♯; pf	1845–6	1846
61	Polonaise-fantasy, A♭; pf	1846	1846
62	Two Nocturnes, B, E; pf	1846	1846
63	Three Mazurkas, B, f, c♯; pf	1846	1847
64	Three Waltzes, D♭, c♯, A♭; pf	1847	1847
65	Sonata, g; vc, pf	1845–6	1847

2 PUBLISHED POSTHUMOUSLY WITH OPUS NUMBERS BY FONTANA

Opus	Title	Date of composition	Date of publication
66	Fantasy-impromptu, c♯; pf	c.1834	1855
67	Four Mazurkas, pf		1855
	G	c.1835	
	g	1848–9	
	C	1835	
	a	1846	
68	Four Mazurkas, pf		1855
	C	c.1830	
	a	c.1827	
	F	c.1830	
	f	c.1846	
69	Two Waltzes, pf		1855
	A♭	1835	
	b	1829	
70	Three Waltzes, pf		1855
	G♭	1832	
	f	1842	
	D♭	1829	
71	Three Polonaises, pf		1855
	d	1827–8	
	B♭	1828	
	f	1828	
72	Three Écossaises, D, g, D♭; pf	c.1829	1855
73	Rondo, C; 2 pfs (originally solo pf)	1828	1855
74	17 Songs		1859
	1 'Życzenie' (Witwicki)	c.1829	
	2 'Wiosna' (Witwicki)	1838	
	3 'Smutna rzeka' (Witwicki)	1831	
	4 'Hulanka' (Witwicki)	1830	
	5 'Gdzie lubi' (Witwicki)	c.1829	
	6 'Precz z moich oczu' (Mickiewicz)	1827	
	7 'Poseł' (Witwicki)	1831	
	8 'Śliczny chłopiec' (Zaleski)	1841	
	9 'Melodia' (Krasiński)	1847	
	10 'Wojak' (Witwicki)	1831	
	11 'Dwojaki koniec' (Zaleski)	1845	
	12 'Moja pieszczotka' (Mickiewicz)	1837	
	13 'Nie ma czego trzeba' (Zaleski)	1845	
	14 'Pierścień' (Witwicki)	1836	
	15 'Narzeczony' (Witwicki)	1831	
	16 'Piosnka litewska' (Witwicki)	1831	
	17 'Leci liście z drzewa' (Pol)	1836	

Chopin

3 WORKS WITHOUT OPUS NUMBER (KK = Kobylanska, *Katalog*)

Title	Date of composition	Date of publication
Polonaise, B♭; pf (KK 1182–3)	1817	1834
Polonaise, g; pf (KK 889)	1817	1817
Polonaise, A♭; pf (KK 1184)	1821	1908
Introduction and Variations on a German air ('Der Schweizerbub'), E; pf (KK 925–7)	1824	1851
Polonaise, g♯; pf (KK 1185–7)	1824	1850–60?
Mazurka, B♭; pf (KK 891–5)	1825–6	1826
Mazurka, G; pf (KK 896–900)	1825–6	1826
Variations on a theme of Moore, D; pf 4 hands (KK 1190–2)	1826	1865
Funeral March, c; pf (KK 1059–68) [Op. 72 no. 2]	*c.*1826	1855
Polonaise, b♭; pf (KK 1188–9)	1826	1881
Nocturne, e; pf (KK 1055–8) [Op. 72 no. 1]	*c.*1829?	1855
Souvenir de Paganini, A; pf (KK 1203)	1829	1881
Mazurka, G; pf (KK 1201–2)	1829	1879
Waltz, E; pf (KK 1207–8)	*c.*1829	1867
Waltz, E♭; pf (KK 1212)	1830	1902
Mazurka, G; voice (KK 1201–2)	1829	1879
Waltz, A♭; pf (KK 1209–11)	1830	1902
Waltz, e; pf (KK 1213–14	1830	1850–60
Czary, voice, pf (KK 1204–6)	1830	1910
Polonaise, G♭; pf (KK 1197–1200)	1829	1850–60
Lento con gran expressione, c♯; pf (KK 1215–22)	1830	1875
Grand Duo concertant on themes from Meyerbeer's *Robert le diable*, E; vc, pf (KK 901–2)	1831	1833
Mazurka, B♭; pf. (KK 1223)	1832	1909
Mazurka, D; pf (KK 1224, 1st version KK 1193–6)	1832	1880
Mazurka, C; pf (KK 1225–6)	1833	1870
Cantabile, B♭; pf (KK 1230)	1834	1931
Mazurka, A♭; pf (KK 1277–8)	1834	1930
Presto con leggerezza, A♭; pf (KK 1231–2)	1834	1918
Variation No. 6 in *Hexameron*, E; pf (KK 903–4)	1837	1839
Trois Nouvelles Études, pf (KK 905–17)	1839–40	1840
Canon, f; pf (KK 1241)	*c.*1839	
Mazurka 'Notre Temps', a; pf (KK 919–24)	*c.*1839	1842
Sostenuto (Waltz), E♭; pf (KK 1237)	1840	1955
'Dumka', voice, pf (KK 1236)	1840	1910
Fugue, a; pf (KK 1242)	*c.*1841	1898
Moderato, E; pf (KK 1240	1843	1910
Two Bourrées, g, A; pf (KK 1403–4)	1846	1968
Largo, E♭; pf (KK 1229)	1847	1938
Nocturne, c; pf (KK 1233–5)	1847	1938
Waltz, a; pf (KK 1238–9)	1847	1955

Appendix C

Personalia

Agoult, Marie, Comtesse d' (1805–76), wife of Charles d'Agoult and mistress of Franz Liszt between 1833 and 1843. Published under the name Daniel Stern. Her friendship with George Sand brought her into contact with Chopin.

Albrecht, Thomas (1803?–?), wine merchant and the Saxon Consul in Paris; a keen music-lover, who was part of Chopin's close circle of friends during his later years in Paris.

Alkan, Charles Henri Valentin (1813–88), French pianist and composer of strikingly original virtuoso works for the piano. He was Chopin's neighbour in the Square d'Orléans.

Arago, Emmanuel (1812–96), politically active lawyer and writer; friend and confidant of George Sand. In later years he was French ambassador to Switzerland.

Balzac, Honoré de (1799–1850), celebrated novelist and friend of George Sand. Occasional visitor to Nohant.

Bocage, Pierre François Touzé (1799–1862), actor, friend, and one-time lover of George Sand; between 1849–50 the Director of the Paris theatre 'Odéon'.

Broadwood, Henry Fowler (?–1893), son of James Broadwood and member of the famous firm of piano manufacturers; he befriended Chopin during his second visit to England.

Brzowski, Józef (1805–88), Polish composer, pianist and cellist, teacher at the Warsaw Conservatory. Following his studies in Poland he spent the years 1836–7 in Germany and Paris, where he was befriended by Chopin.

Catalani, Angelica (1780–1849), Italian soprano, who presented the young Chopin with a gold watch during her Warsaw recitals of 1819. She was manager of the Italian Opera in Paris from 1814 to 1817.

Cauvière, François (1780–1858), medical doctor and relative of George Sand's friends the Marlianis. He tended Chopin during his convalescence in Marseilles following the visit to Majorca.

Châtiron, Hippolyte (1799–1848), half-brother to George Sand. After mismanaging his own property, he lived for a time at Nohant, before moving to his wife's nearby estate of Montgivray.

Cherubini, Maria Luigi (1760–1842), influential composer and (from 1822) Director of the Paris Conservatoire. His treatise on counterpoint, a standard text at the Conservatoire, was studied by Chopin.

Clésinger, Gabrielle Solange (1828–99), daughter of George Sand and officially of her husband, Baron Dudevant, though it is widely believed that her real father was Stéphane Ajasson of Grandsagne. She played a large part in the eventual break-up of the Chopin–Sand relationship, and remained close to Chopin subsequently. Married to Auguste Clésinger.

Clésinger, Jean Baptiste Auguste (1814–83), French sculptor, who studied in Besançon and Florence. His stormy affair with Solange Dudevant-Sand began while he was making a bust of George Sand in 1847, and they were married on 19 May of that year. Later, immediately following Chopin's death, Clésinger made about seventeen sculptures devoted to him, including the monument on his grave in the Père-Lachaise cemetery.

Custine, Astolphe, Marquis de (1790–1857), French writer, especially of travel books, including *La Russie en 1839* (*Lettres de Russie*). Following a homosexual scandal he was banished (temporarily) from the best society in Paris, and devoted himself to literary and artistic pursuits. He was famous as a host at his villa at St Gratien.

Czartoryska, Anna, Princess (1799–1864), wife of Prince Adam; she founded the Benevolent Association of Polish Ladies in Paris in 1834, and later held court (and worked ceaselessly for the Polish cause) at the Hôtel Lambert, centre of Poland in exile.

Czartoryska, Marcellina, Princess (1817–94), born Princess Radziwiłł, she married Prince Aleksander Czartoryski, nephew of Prince Adam. Based in Vienna, she was one of Chopin's most talented pupils, and gave occasional recitals, even in her years of retirement in Cracow.

Czartoryski, Adam Jerzy, Prince (1770–1861), Polish statesman, a key figure in Polish society and politics, first as an ally of Alexander I in the 'Kingdom of Poland', and later (in Paris after 1830) as the most influential figure in the conservative camp working for Polish independence.

Davison, James William (1813–85), English writer on music, critic of *The Times* (1846–79), editor of *The Musical World*.

Delacroix, Eugène (1798–1863), French painter of great fame and distinction. He was a friend of both Chopin and George Sand, and made a famous painting of them during the early stages of their relationship. He visited them in Nohant and socialized with them in Paris, and his *Journal* is an important source of information about Chopin's views on art and music.

Dessauer, Josef (1798–1876), Czech cellist and composer of songs, piano music, and chamber music; a friend of Chopin and George Sand, he was the dedicatee of Chopin's Polonaises, Op. 26 and the model for Sand's play *Maître Favilla*.

Dubois, Camille O'Meara- (1830–1907), French pianist of Irish extraction, student of Kalkbrenner and Chopin (1843–8). As a teacher, she did much to perpetuate a living tradition of Chopin playing.

Dudevant, Casimir (1795–1871). Son of Baron François Dudevant of Guillery and husband of George Sand. They were separated formally in 1836.

Dudevant-Sand, Jean François Maurice (1823–89), son of George Sand and Casimir Dudevant; painter and writer, pupil of Delacroix. He married Lina Calamatta in 1862 and collaborated extensively with his mother on literary and artistic projects.

Dumas, Alexandre fils (1824–95), French author and friend of George Sand. It was Dumas who discovered the Chopin–Sand correspondence left at the Polish border by Ludwika Jędrzejewiczowa following Chopin's death.

Elsner, Józef Xavier (1769–1854), composer and teacher of Silesian origins; Director of the Warsaw Conservatory and later of the High School of Music. He was Chopin's principal teacher.

Fétis, François Joseph (1784–1871), Belgian writer on music, appointed professor at the Paris Conservatoire in 1821 and librarian in 1827. His influential reviews (notably for *La Revue musicale*) included several critiques of Chopin as pianist and composer.

Fontana, Julian (1810–1869), Polish pianist and composer; fellow student of Chopin at the Warsaw Lyceum and at the Conservatory, he moved to Paris in 1832. He acted as copyist and general factotum to Chopin until his departure for America in the early 1840s, and later (at the request of Chopin's family) prepared a posthumous edition of the unpublished music. He died at his own hand, following a debilitating illness.

Franchomme, Auguste (1808–84), French cellist, professor at the Paris Conservatoire and close friend of Chopin. He collaborated with Chopin on the *Grand Duo concertant* and was later the dedicatee of the Cello Sonata, Op. 65. Many of Chopin's manuscripts were given to Franchomme by Ludwika Jędrze-jewiczowa following the composer's death.

Gładkowska, Konstancja (1810–89), a student of singing at the Warsaw Conservatory, she was Chopin's adolescent love. She later married a well-to-do gentleman and (in her old age) professed to be quite unaware of Chopin's feelings for her.

Grzymała, Wojciech (1793–1870), Polish man of letters and patriot, who was a critic in Warsaw before the uprising and later settled in Paris where he made a living through financial speculation. He was a close friend (almost a father figure) of Chopin, and also of George Sand.

Gutmann, Adolphe (1819–82), German pianist and composer, he was Chopin's favourite pupil, and one of his first, having arrived in Paris from Heidelberg in 1834. He was the dedicatee of the Scherzo, Op. 39.

Habeneck, François Antoine (1781–1849), French violinist and conductor; pupil of Baillot and professor at the Paris Conservatoire. He founded the immensely influential and prestigious *concerts du conservatoire* at which Chopin made a single appearance.

Hiller, Ferdinand (1811–85), German pianist and composer; pupil of Hummel. He moved to Paris in 1828 and was a close friend of Chopin's until his return to Germany in 1835.

Jędrzejewiczowa, Ludwika (1807–55), the eldest of Chopin's three sisters and the one to whom he was closest. His letters to Ludwika reveal much about him-self, and she visited him twice in France, on the second occasion to be with him during his final weeks.

Kalkbrenner, Friedrich Wilhelm Michael (1788–1849), German pianist and com-poser who settled in Paris and was one of the city's most influential teachers. Chopin considered having lessons with him on his arrival in Paris.

Klengel, Auguste Alexander (1783–1852), German organist and composer, pupil of Clementi and court organist at Dresden. Chopin visited him twice as a young man and heard him play his Canons and Fugues in all the Keys.

Kurpiński, Karol Kasimir (1785–1857), the leading Polish composer of opera before Moniuszko. He conducted the early concerts in Warsaw at which Chopin performed his two piano concertos.

Kwiatkowski, Teofil (1809–91), Polish painter who made many sketches of Chopin during his final weeks.

Lablache, Louis (1794–1858), Italian bass singer of repute, much admired by Chopin.

Lamennais, Félicité, Abbé de (1782–1854), French philosopher and mystic; one-time Catholic priest, who edited *Le Monde* and whose ideas had a powerful influence on the social philosophy of George Sand.

Legouvé, Ernest (1807–1903), French playwright and journalist; friend of George Sand and Chopin. Author of *Soixante ans de souvenirs*.

Léo, Auguste (?–?), banker, music-lover; relative of Moscheles and friend of Hiller and Chopin. Chopin frequented his salon and dedicated to him his Polonaise, Op. 53.

Leroux, Pierre (1797–1871), socialist philosopher, who collaborated with George Sand on several ventures, including *La Revue indépendante* and *L'éclair de l'Indre*. Author of *De l'humanité* (1845) and *De l'égalité* (1848).

Liszt, Franz (1811–86), celebrated pianist and composer of Hungarian origin. He was close to Chopin in the 1830s, but drifted away from him (while still admiring and performing his music) in the 1840s. Author of the first biography of Chopin (1852).

Malléfille, Félicien (1813–68), French writer; secretary to George Sand, tutor to her son and (for a time) her lover. He wrote an appreciation of Chopin for the *Revue et Gazette musicale*, just before the composer replaced him in Sand's affections.

Marliani, Charlotte, Countess (1790–1850), wife of the Spanish consul in Paris and friend of George Sand. Her salon was a regular meeting-place for Sand and Chopin, and she later lived alongside them in the Square d'Orléans.

Mathias, Georges-Amédée-Saint-Clair (1826–1910), composer, pianist, and teacher of German–Polish descent; a pupil of Chopin from around 1838–9, he later taught at the Paris Conservatoire and did much to promote the Chopin tradition in French musical circles.

Matuszyński, Jan (1809–42), medical doctor who had been a pupil with Chopin at the Warsaw Lyceum. He shared an apartment with Chopin in Paris between 1834 and 1836, when he married Thérèse Charlotte Clotilde Boquet. Chopin was especially close to Matuszyński and was devastated by his early death from consumption.

Mickiewicz, Adam (1798–1855), celebrated Polish poet of 'messianic' orientation. A key player in the Polish Literary Society in Paris, with which Chopin had tangential links. Both Chopin and George Sand attended his lectures on Slavonic literature at the Collège de France.

Mikuli, Karl (1819–97), pianist, composer, and teacher of Armenian–Romanian descent; a Chopin pupil and disciple, who did much to promote the composer's music and performance traditions as teacher, editor, and performer. He eventually settled in Lwów in 1858, where he became Director of the Conservatory.

Molin, Jean Jacques (1797–1848), medical doctor who used homeopathic remedies. He treated Chopin during the composer's later years (1843–8).

Moscheles, Ignaz (1794–1870), Bohemian pianist and composer, who studied in Prague and Vienna and later lived in London and Paris. He met Chopin through his cousin the banker Auguste Léo, and the two men gave several concerts together.

Nourrit, Adolphe (1802–39), French tenor, attached to the Paris Opera for many years before moving to Naples, where he committed suicide. Chopin, who greatly admired him, played the organ at a memorial service in Marseilles.

Osborne, George Alexandre (1806–93), pianist and composer of Irish extraction; pupil of Pixis and Kalkbrenner in Paris; settled in London in 1843.

Paër, Ferdinando (1771–1839), Italian opera composer, *maestro di cappella* in Venice, and later settled in Vienna, Dresden, and Paris, where he was professor of composition at the Conservatoire.

Papet, Gustave (1812–92), medical doctor who lived near Nohant; a friend of George Sand, who dedicated her novel *Mauprat* to him. Sand consulted him about Chopin's health during the latter's visits to Nohant.

Plater, Ludwik, Count (1774–1846), wealthy Polish diplomat exiled to Paris in the early 1830s. He and his family played host to Chopin on several occasions, and he taught their daughter Paulina.

Pleyel, Camille (1792–1855), pianist, publisher, and piano manufacturer in Paris. Chopin loved his pianos above all others and his Paris concerts were usually at Pleyel's *salle*. The two men were friends and visited England together just as the Wodzińska affair was drawing to a close.

Potocka, Delfina, Countess (1807–77), wife of Mieczysław Potocki, but lived separately from him; famous as a hostess, for her *amours*, and for her fine singing voice. Chopin certainly admired and may even have been infatuated with her, but there is no reliable evidence to support the theory that they were lovers.

Radziwiłł, Antoni, Prince (1775–1833), Governor of the Duchy of Poznań, and a gifted amateur composer. He greatly admired the young Chopin and invited him to his estate on two occasions.

Rozières, Marie Élizabeth de (1805–65), pianist and teacher; for a time the governess and piano teacher to Solange Dudevant-Sand, her relations with Chopin were at times strained (she had an affair with Maria Wodzińska's brother Antoni), but in later years she did much to support him.

Schlesinger, Moritz Adolf (1797–1871), son of the Berlin music publisher Adolf Martin Schlesinger, he founded the Paris publishing firm and the journal *Gazette musicale*, later *Revue et Gazette musicale de Paris*. He was Chopin's principal French publisher.

Skarbek, Fryderyk Florian, Count (1792–1866), university professor; a noted economist and historian, he was Chopin's godfather, and his memoirs are a valuable source of information about the context of Chopin's early life in Warsaw.

Stirling, Jane Wilhelmina (1804–59), wealthy Scottish spinster who spent much of her time in Paris and was Chopin's pupil. Following the break with George Sand, she was his hostess in England and Scotland.

Stockhausen, Nathaniel, Baron (?–?), Hanoverian Ambassador in Paris, music-lover and friend of Chopin; the dedicatee of the Ballade, Op. 23.

Streicher, Friederike Müller- (1816–95), pianist, one of Chopin's most advanced pupils, having moved to Paris from Vienna expressly to study with him; she gave up her professional career on her marriage to J. B. Streicher.

Tellefsen, Thomas Dyke Ackland (1823–74), Norwegian pupil of Chopin, who entrusted him with the completion of his Pianoforte Method. He later prepared a collected edition of Chopin for the publisher Richault.

Viardot, Pauline García (1821–1910), French (contralto) singer of Spanish origins, daughter of Manuel García and sister of the famous and short-lived soprano Maria Malibran. She was a close friend of George Sand (who based the novel *Consuelo* on her) and of Chopin.

Witwicki, Stefan (1802–47), Polish poet and patriot, whose poems were set by Chopin in some of the songs posthumously gathered as Op. 74. The two men were acquaintances in Warsaw and later in Paris. Witwicki was one of those who urged Chopin to write a Polish national opera.

Wodzińska, Maria (1819–96), one of the Wodziński family, whose sons boarded with the Chopins in Warsaw. Chopin proposed to her, but was in the end rejected by the family. She later married one of the Skarbeks, but divorced him shortly afterwards.

Wodziński, Antoni (1812–47), brother of Maria Wodzińska, he boarded with the Chopins while attending the Warsaw Lyceum. He arrived in Paris in 1836 and was helped (including financially) by Chopin, before he left to fight in Spain.

Woyciechowski, Tytus (1808–79), one of Chopin's closest friends at the Lyceum, he was a confidant during the final year in Warsaw and accompanied Chopin to Vienna a week before the outbreak of the insurrection.

Żywny, Adalbert [Wojciech] (1756–1842), Bohemian violinist resident in Warsaw, he was Chopin's first teacher.

Appendix D

Select bibliography

BACKGROUND

Amster, I., *Das Virtuosen-konzert in der ersten Hälfte des 19. Jahrhunderts* (Berlin, 1931).

Bie, O., *A History of the Pianoforte and Pianoforte Players*, tr. E. E. Kellett and E. W. Naylor (New York, 1966).

Carew, D., 'The Composer/Performer Relationship in the Piano Works of J. N. Hummel' (Diss., U. of Leicester, 1981).

Castil-Blaze, F. -H. -J., *Dictionnaire de musique moderne*, 2 vols. (Paris, 1825).

Chechlińska, Z. (ed.), *Szkice o kulturze muzycznej XIXw*, 4 vols. (Warsaw, 1973–80).

Czerny, C., *Complete Theoretical and Practical Pianoforte School*, tr. J. A. Hamilton (London, 1938–9).

Delacroix, E., *The Journal of Eugène Delacroix*, ed. H. Wellington, tr. L. Norton (New York, 1948).

Ehrlich, C., *The Piano: A History* (London, 1976; rev. Oxford, 1990).

Fétis, F.-J., and Moscheles, I., *Méthode des Méthodes de Piano* (Paris, 1840).

Fraczyk, T., *Warszawa młodości Chopina* (Cracow, 1961).

Gate, Curtis, *George Sand: A Biography* (Boston, 1975).

Gerig, R. R., *Famous Pianists and their Technique* (Washington and New York, 1974).

Hallé, C. E. and M., *Life and Letters of Charles Hallé* (London, 1896).

Jenkins, G., 'The Legato Touch and the "Ordinary" Manner of Keyboard Playing from 1750–1850' (Diss., U. of Cambridge, 1976).

Lenz, W. von, *The Great Piano Virtuosos of our Time*, ed. P. Reder (London, 1983; original Ger. edn., 1872).

Loesser, A., *Men, Women and Pianos* (London, 1955).

Marmontel, J. F., *Les pianistes célèbres* (Paris, 1878).

Moscheles, C., *The Life of Moscheles with Selections from his Diaries and Correspondence*, tr. A. D. Coleridge, 2 vols. (London, 1873).

Ott, B., *Liszt et la pédagogie du piano* (Issy-les-Moulineaux, 1978).

Poniatowska, I., *Muzyka fortepianowa i pianistyka w wieku XIX: Aspekty artystyczne i społeczne* (Warsaw, 1991).

Sand, George, *Histoire de ma vie. Œuvres autobiographiques*, ed. G. Lubin, 12 vols. (Paris, 1978).

Spohr, L., *Louis Spohr's Autobiography* (London, 1965).

Chopin

CATALOGUES, BIBLIOGRAPHIES, ALBUMS, LETTERS

Binental, L., *Chopin. W 120-ta rocznice urodzin. Dokumenty i pamiątki* (Warsaw, 1930).

Brown, M. J. E., *Chopin: An Index of his Works in Chronological Order* (London, 1960, rev. London and New York, 1972).

Burger, H., *Frédéric Chopin. Eine Lebenschronik in Bildern und Documenten* (Monachium, 1990).

Chomiński, J. and Turło, D., *Katalog dzieł Fryderyka Chopina* (Cracow, 1990).

Duleba, W., *Chopin* (Cracow, 1980).

Hedley, A. (tr. and ed.), *Selected Correspondence of Fryderyk Chopin* (London, 1962).

Karłowicz, M., *Nie wydane dotychczas pamiątki po Chopinie* (Warsaw, 1904).

Kobylańska, K., *Chopin in his Own Land*, tr. C. Grece-Dąbrowska and M. Filippi (Warsaw, 1955).

—— (ed.), *Korespondencja Chopina z rodzina* (Warsaw, 1972).

—— (ed.), *Rękopisy utworów Chopina: Katalog*, 2 vols. (Cracow, 1977).

—— (ed.), *Frédéric Chopin: Thematisch-bibliographisches Werkverzeichnis*, ed. E. Herttrich, tr. H. Stolze (Munich, 1979).

—— (ed.), *Korespondencja Chopina z George Sand i z jej dziećmi* (Warsaw, 1981).

Lubin, G. (ed.), *George Sand Correspondence*, 12 vols. (Paris, 1964–76).

Michałowski, K., *Bibliografia Chopinowska (1849–1869)* (Cracow, 1970). Updated in issues of *Rocznik Chopinowski*, ed. H. Wróblewska-Straus.

Mirska, M. and Hordyński, W., *Chopin na obczyznie. Dokumenty i pamiątki* (Cracow, 1965).

Opienski, H., *Chopin's Letters* (New York, 1931; rev. 1971).

Smoter, J. M. (ed.), *Album Chopina 1829–1831* (Cracow, 1975).

Sydow, B. E. *Portret Chopina* (Cracow, 1952).

——, Chainaye, D. and Chainaye, S. (eds. and trs.), *Correspondance de Frédéric Chopin*, 3 vols. (Paris, 1953).

—— (ed.), *Korespondencja Fryderyka Chopina*, 2 vols. (Warsaw, 1955).

Tomaszewski, M. and Weber, B., *Chopin: A Diary in Images*, tr. R. Hunt (Warsaw, 1990).

MONOGRAPHS

Belotti, G., *Chopin l'uomo*, 3 vols. (Milan and Rome, 1974).

—— *Chopin* (Turin, 1984).

Belza, I., *Fryderyk F. Chopin* (Moscow, 1960).

Barbedette, H., *Chopin. Essai de critique musicale* (Paris, 1869).

Bidou, H., *Chopin* (Paris, 1925).

Binental, L., *Chopin* (Paris, 1934).

Bourniquel, C., *Chopin* (Paris, 1957; Eng. tr. 1960).

Chomiński, J., *Chopin* (Cracow, 1979).

Czartkowski, A., and Jeżewska, Z., *Fryderyk Chopin* (Warsaw, 1958).

Clavier, A., *Dans l'entourage de Chopin* (Lens, 1984).

Ganche, E., *Frédéric Chopin: sa vie et ses oeuvres* (Paris, 1909).

Gavoty, B., *Frédéric Chopin* (Paris, 1974).

Hadden, J. D., *Chopin* (London, 1903).

Hedley, A., *Chopin* (London, 1947).
Hoesick, F., *Chopin: życie i twórczość*, 3 vols. (Warsaw, 1910–11).
Huneker, J. G., *Chopin: The Man and his Music* (New York, 1900; repr. 1966).
Iwaszkiewicz, J., *Fryderyk Chopin* (Cracow, 1955).
Jachimecki, Z., *Chopin. Rys życia i twórczości* (Warsaw, 1911).
Jordan, R., *Nocturne: A Life of Chopin* (London, 1978).
Karasowski, M., *Fryderyk Chopin. Życie, Listy, Dziela* (Warsaw, 1882).
Liszt, F., *F. Chopin* (Paris, 1852).
Marek, G. and Gordon-Smith, M., *Chopin: A Biography* (New York, 1978).
Murdoch, W. D., *Chopin: His Life* (London, 1934).
Niecks, F., *Chopin as a Man and Musician*, 2 vols. (London, 1988; repr. New York, 1973).
Opienski, H., *Chopin* (Lwów, 1909).
Orga, A., *Chopin: His Life and Times* (Tunbridge Wells, 1976; rev. 1978).
Pourtalès, G. de, *Chopin ou le poète* (Paris, 1927).
Samson, J., *The Music of Chopin* (London, 1985; repr. Oxford, 1994).
Scharlitt, B., *Chopin* (Leipzig, 1919).
Siepmann, J., *Chopin. The Reluctant Romantic* (London, 1995).
Szulc, M. A., *Fryderyk Chopin i utwory jego muzyczne* (Poznań, 1873).
Szymanowski, K., *Chopin* (Warsaw, 1925).
Valetta, I., *Chopin. La vita, le opere* (Turin, 1910).
Weinstock, H., *Chopin: The Man and his Music* (New York, 1949).
Weissmann, A., *Chopin* (Berlin, 1912).
Wierzyński, K., *The Life and Death of Chopin* (New York, 1949).
Willeby, C., *Frédéric François Chopin: A biography* (London, 1892).
Zamoyski, A., *Chopin: A Biography* (London, 1979).
Zieliński, T., *Chopin: życie i droga twórcza* (Cracow, 1993).

OTHER STUDIES

Abraham, G., *Chopin's Musical Style* (London, 1939).
Barbag, S., *Studium o piesniach Chopina* (Lwów, 1927).
Belotti, G., *Saggi sull'arte e sull'opera di F. Chopin* (Bologna, 1977).
Branson, D., *John Field and Chopin* (London, 1972).
Bronarski, L., *Harmonika Chopina* (Warsaw, 1935).
Chechlińska, Z., *Wariacje i technika wariacyjna w twórczości Chopina* (Cracow, 1995).
Chomiński, J. M., *Preludia Chopina* (Cracow, 1950).
—— *Sonaty Chopina* (Cracow, 1960).
Cortot, A., *Aspects de Chopin* (Paris, 1949).
Davison, J. W., *Essay on the Works of Frederick Chopin* (London, 1843).
Dunn, J. P., *Ornamentation in the Works of Frederick Chopin* (London, 1921).
Eigeldinger, J. -J., *Chopin: Pianist and Teacher*, tr. N. Shohet with K. Osostowicz and R. Howat, ed. R. Howat (Cambridge, 1986; original French edn., 1979).
—— (ed.), *F. Chopin: Esquisses pour une méthode de piano* (Mayenne, 1993).
Ekier, J., *Wstęp do wydania narodowego* (Warsaw, 1974).
Gajewski, J., *The Worksheets to Chopin's Violoncello Sonata* (New York, 1988).
Golab, M., *Chromatyka i tonalność w muzyce Chopina* (Cracow, 1991).

Higgins, T., 'Chopin Interpretation: A Study of Performance Directions in Selected Autographs and Other Sources' (Diss., U. of Iowa, 1966).

Hipkins, E. J., *How Chopin Played* (London, 1937).

Jonson, G. C. A., *A Handbook to Chopin's Works* (London, 1905).

Kallberg, J., 'The Chopin Sources: Variants and Versions in Later Manuscripts' (Diss., U. of Chicago, 1982).

Kreliew, J., *Friderik Chopin* (Moscow, 1960).

Kubień-Uszokowa, M. (ed.), *Chopin a muzyka europejska* (Katowice, 1977).

Landowski, W. L., *Frédéric Chopin et Gabriel Fauré* (Paris, 1946).

Leichtentritt, H., *Analyse der Chopin'schen Klavierwerke*, 2 vols. (Berlin, 1921–2).

Lissa, Z., *Studia nad twórczościa Fryderyka Chopina* (Cracow, 1970).

—— (ed.), *F. F. Chopin* (Warsaw, 1960).

—— (ed.), *The Book of the First International Musicological Congress devoted to the Works of Frederick Chopin* (Warsaw, 1963).

Mazel, L., *Studia Chopinowskie* (Cracow, 1965).

Methuen-Campbell, J., *Chopin Playing* (London, 1981).

Miketta, J., *Mazurki Chopina* (Cracow, 1949).

Mirska, M., *Szlakiem Chopina* (Warsaw, 1949).

Nowik, W., 'Process twórczy Fryderyka Chopina w świetle jego autografów muzycznych' (Diss., U. of Warsaw, 1978).

Ottich, M., *Die Bedeutung des Ornaments im Schaffen Friedrich Chopins* (Berlin, 1937).

Paschalow, W., *Chopin a polska muzyka ludowa* (Cracow, 1951).

Pistone, D., (ed.), *Sur les traces de Frédéric Chopin* (Paris, 1984).

Pożniak, B., *Chopin: prakische Anweisungen für das Studium der Chopin-Werke* (Halle, 1949).

Rink, J., 'The Evolution of Chopin's "Structural Style" and its Relation to Improvisation' (Diss., U. of Cambridge, 1989).

—— and Samson, J. (eds.), *Chopin Studies 2* (Cambridge, 1994).

Samson, J. *Chopin: The Four Ballades* (Cambridge, 1992).

—— (ed.), *Chopin Studies* (Cambridge, 1988).

—— (ed.), *The Cambridge Companion to Chopin* (Cambridge, 1992).

Walker, A. (ed.), *Frédéric Chopin: Profiles of the Man and the Musician* (London, 1966).

Windakiewiczowa, H., *Wzory ludowej muzyki polskiej w mazurkach Fryderyka Chopina* (Cracow, 1926).

Wójcik-Keuprulian, B., *Melodyka Chopina* (Lwów, 1930).

Żebrowski, D. (ed.), *Studies in Chopin* (Warsaw, 1973).

Index

Index

Index